Travel
Photography

A Complete Guide to
How to Shoot and Sell

Susan McCartney

ALLWORTH PRESS, NEW YORK

Published by **Allworth Press**, an imprint of
Allworth Communications, Inc., 10 East 23rd Street, New York, NY 10010.

Book and cover design by Douglas Design Associates, New York\

ISBN: 1-880559-00-5

Cover Photographs by Susan McCartney © 1992
Interior photographs and illustrations © 1992 by Susan McCartney

Hyper Card Stack Options in Professional Lighting Equipment
© 1991 by Scott Geffert, used by permission.

The interior photographs have been transposed to black-and-white from color, except those on pages 6, 158 and 192, which are black-and-white originals.

Table of Contents

*This book is dedicated to my darling daughter Caroline,
and to the memory of my mother.*

Acknowledgments

I owe thanks to many people. First and especially, to Phillip Leonian for reading the manuscript and making valuable suggestions based on his inexhaustible knowledge of everything photographic, most particularly small flash.

On the subject of lighting, thanks to Scott Geffert for kind permission to reproduce part of his HyperCard stack on lighting equipment, to A. J. Nye for checking my facts on electronics in general and strobes and transformers in particular, and to Jon Falk for information on power inverters.

Tad Crawford took the plunge of publishing this book in a time of recession, and has been most constructive about forms and legalities in particular.

My colleague and good friend Michal Heron gave me courage by writing her own book; she read mine and put me right on a few points. Photographers Patricia and Wayne Fisher made useful comments (and translated some of my words into good American too). Edith Leonian gave me the insights of a rep and Les Fincher those of a professional location scout. Jean Anderson and Regina Weinrich taught me whatever I know about writing.

Two lifelong friends helped enormously; Joanna Harris very generously gave me much time and her professional editing skills and Patricia Collyns contributed the viewpoint of a dedicated amateur travel photographer.

To the many others—clients, colleagues, students and friends in photography, publishing and the travel business who have all helped directly and indirectly with this book, also my most sincere thanks. Any errors that have crept in despite my best efforts are not theirs.

I have not received any financial or other considerations for listing anything. There are a few major places not mentioned in the "Travel Highlights" chapters, either because I know nothing whatever about them, or prefer not to recommend them.

Susan McCartney
New York City

Introduction

True travelers are probably born, not made; and if you're anything like me, travel is a necessity, not a luxury. The howl of jet engines, the gassy smells of a busy interstate entrance or the crush at a railroad terminal or pier are not trials to be endured but the magic preludes to new adventures. Hotels don't have to be luxurious, the food gourmet or the weather perfect (although those things are all very enjoyable) because the discovering and rediscovering of new places and people and experiences and making the best photographs you can of them are what count.

This book is not (alas!) a guide to instant fame and riches. I have tried to make it a useful resource for established photographers on how to obtain, plan and approach travel, tourism and location assignments. The book is also a guide for photography students, semi-professionals and those amateur photographers who travel a lot, who love taking pictures, and who want to record their travel experiences on film in the way that their inner eye sees them.

Travel costs money, and sometimes lots of it, so the book is intended for people like me who need to earn a living while financing their travel and photography habits. It offers concrete suggestions and sources for getting travel assignments, shooting and marketing travel stock, and suggests places to go that are under photographed and not on every traveling photographer's itinerary. Some possible places to "sell" as assignment destinations to magazines and other clients are suggested.

The tourism industry around the world uses many, many still pictures, and I cover this branch of travel photography, and its staples—people, landscape and architectural photography, and location still lifes—in some detail.

Location photography for business and industry is challenging and creative and a good source of income for people with the skills of the travel photographer, so I include information about it in a travel book without apology.

I believe in searching out past and present masters of travel-related subjects, both photographers and painters, for enlarging photographic vision and giving yourself stars to shoot for, so my favorites are recommended.

How To Use This Book

Each chapter of the book is self-contained, and can be read as questions arise, or skipped if the subject doesn't interest you at the moment. I intend this book to be a tool that will be useful, and enhance your skills in photography and travel. I hope that it will also contribute to your enjoyment, business success and personal fulfilment.

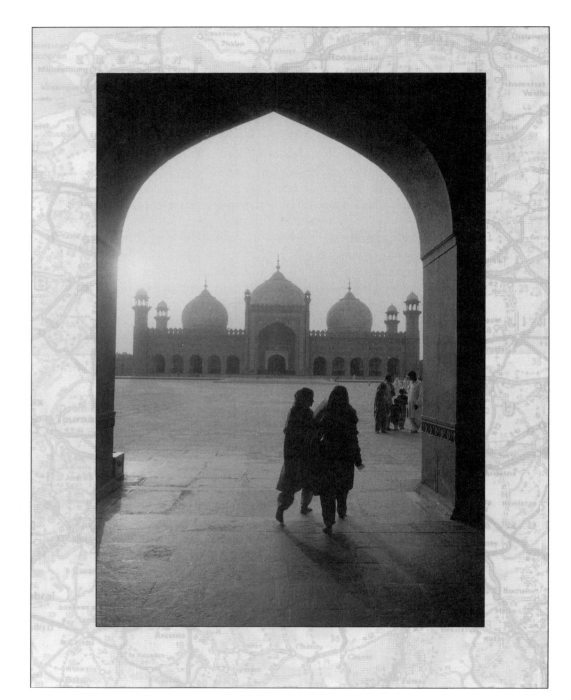

Chapter 1

The Pleasures, History and Business of Travel Photography

People who haven't traveled very much think that if only they could go to some historic, exotic, scenic or remote places like Rome, Bali, Arizona or Patagonia, they would immediately start taking wonderful pictures and getting wonderful assignments. Alas, this is not usually true, as photographers who have been to those places will tell you. It is just as easy to take boring pictures in Bangkok as it is in Brooklyn (which, in fact, is both very photogenic and exotic in its own fashion). Patagonia sounds very romantic—and it is in some ways—(read Bruce Chatwin's book *In Patagonia* for the legends and history). The part of the region I have seen though, is flat and rather bleak, with gray stones, gray thorn bushes and gray skies; and hard to do much with visually.

Today, because so many people travel, and because there are so many stock (already existing) travel pictures easily available, unless you're very well-known indeed, the mere fact that you're going somewhere is rarely enough to land you an assignment. You have to present potential clients with a fresh style or a good story idea, or another good reason to use you.

If you can take wonderful pictures in the drier, emptier parts of Texas in winter, or in the Chicago loop in a July rush hour, you can certainly also take good photographs around Trelew, Patagonia or in Canton, China—the photographic advantage of being in very unfamiliar places is mainly that you don't take anything for granted.

Marcel Proust wrote "the real voyage of discovery is not in seeing a new landscape, but in seeing with new eyes." I think that is a pretty fair statement of what it takes to be a good travel photographer.

To take good travel pictures anywhere you need a sensitivity to people and different cultures, an appreciation of light, and of landscape in all its forms; a sense of what makes a place unique, and of what makes it universally appealing.

What Is Professional Travel Photography?

Professional travel photography is creative, often glamorous, varied, exciting and artistically rewarding, and almost always interesting. I've climbed the Great Wall and Hadrian's Wall, and waited at the Kremlin Wall to photograph Soviet pilgrims paying their respects at Lenin's tomb. I've whizzed on the bullet train to Mount Fuji and the TGV to Nice. I've photographed the Taj Mahal by moonlight and the sound and light shows at the Pyramids and the Parthenon. I've been alone at the temples of Angkor Wat and I once set up a special performance of the Monkey Dance in a Balinese village temple, directing a cast of hundreds. I went to Africa when I was pregnant and photographed fighting elephants, herds of giraffe at sunset, and the great migration of zebra and wildebeeste in Kenya, between bouts of morning sickness. I've been moved by the piety of faithful Jews at the Western Wall and devout Muslims at the Dome of the Rock, both in Jerusalem; and I have floated in a barge down the holy River Ganges photographing thousands of pilgrims making their ablutions from the steps lining the western bank.

I've dined at the three-Michelin-starred Auberge de l'Ill in Alsace, the star-studded Savoy Grill in London, eaten salt cod stew in a fisherman's house in Newfoundland and forced-down a few bites of grilled intestines at a barbecue in Argentina (it would have been impolite to refuse). I've seen and photographed great actors at Stratford-upon-Avon and the Noh theater in Tokyo (as well as quite a few good and bad actors in off, and off-off, Broadway theaters who shall remain nameless). I've made portraits of hairy old-timers in copper mining towns in Arizona, business executives in Ohio, blond surfing gods and goddesses on the beach at La Jolla and charming Indian kids in New Mexico. I've had tea with eccentric nobles in England, drunk too much ouzou with fisherman at an impromptu street party in a tiny village on Santorini (and had my legs rubbed raw laboring up the cliffs there on a balky donkey).

I've been seasick on cruise ships, catamarans and coracles; slept in beds where Royalty preceded me, and in public bath houses, airports and train stations when connections or reservations were glitched. I've had food poisoning after eating a delicious couscous in one of the best restaurants in Tetuan, Morocco; also after Beluga caviar, ice cream and champagne in a top Moscow night spot; and of course I've endured innumerable cheap highway and motorway rest-stop meals.

Glamorous or not, 99% of all that travel has been paid for by clients. I'm not rich, but I make a fair living. I'd have to be a millionaire to have done all of these things without my cameras. So of course it's worth the occasional headache.

To work professionally in any field is very different from doing it when you feel like it. Professional travel photography is almost always done to describe and "sell" a place, sometimes it's a hard sell and sometimes a soft, but it's nonetheless "commercial" photography. You are not working just to please yourself, but also to please the person or organization who sent you there. This client has definite feelings about what you should bring back or specific photographic needs that have to be filled. To do professional travel assignments, you must be master of your equipment, well organized and usually have a specific advance plan of what has to be photographed. You must be able to summarize, select, distill and interpret your impressions, and guide your ultimate audience. Ideally, they visit the country, region or resort vicariously through your pictures. You must convey to the viewer positive emotions that make them feel how nice, or interesting, or luxurious it is to be in Sanibel or San Sebastian or San Francisco and, most especially, make them want to go there too.

To accept assignments—a big responsibility—you will have to hone your photographic skills so that they become second nature, in order to leave yourself free to concentrate on the important things, which are aesthetics and logistics. Pianists don't get to be concert pianists without long and continual hours of practice, and the same is true for photographers who want to do the best possible professional work. I'm not of course talking about just selling the odd picture occasionally, which almost anyone can do with luck, but about making a decent living in travel, tourism and location photography.

How Does a Professional Travel Photographer Get Started?

Unless you have an art director uncle who loves your work, it's almost a given that you will have to travel before seeking paid travel assignments. You won't be credible unless you have done so. You must have a portfolio of travel-related pictures. If you haven't yet traveled very far afield, refine your seeing and approach to travel, and work out any bugs in your equipment by traveling and photographing in the next town or county (which, of course, may very well be a travel destination for someone from far away). Without involving yourself in any great expense, you can photograph the travel basics, which are landscapes and beauty spots in different light and weather, architecture outside and in, people in their environment, special events and whatever makes a place unique.

Start by trying to see even very familiar places with fresh eyes. No matter where you live, nearby there are unspoiled landscapes, historic or important new buildings, and good-looking, characterful and accomplished people. Tourist attractions of greater or lesser magnitude exist everywhere, as do outdoor markets and farms, local celebrations, pockets and regions where people of different cultures live and work. There are also museums, churches, temples, mosques, historical societies, restaurants, stores and hotels where you can refine your photography and lighting of interiors if necessary, and practice still lifes and set up scenes for the commercial side of travel photography.

It may help you to pretend to be an Icelandic photographer, or an Indonesian or Irish one, who has never been to the place before. When you photograph your own region with the eyes of a foreigner, you will find a surprising number of interesting subjects.

A good travel photographer should never take anything for granted, but seek out the back roads as well as showing the best-known scenic and historic places. I believe that people bring any travel subject to life. Farmers, fishermen, shopkeepers, local notables, craftspeople, elders, entertainers, anyone in a colorful costume or uniforms are all excellent "travel" subjects. But when photographing people, don't just focus on the quaint or exotic, ordinary people are wonderful subjects too. Tight telephoto shots of faces are okay, and can be powerful, but it's often more revealing to use a wide-angle lens and show the surroundings in a travel portrait. Include the mountain behind the ski instructor, the historic inn as well as the innkeepers, the freckled kid with the blue ribbon and her prize cow at the county fair, the honeymooners and the lake or beach. Move in closer for shots of craftspeople; show faces plus hands painting or weaving or hammering. That way, your viewers will get an intimate portrait plus a good look at what is being made.

Communicating well with people of all kinds is one of the most important skills a travel photographer can possess. You may be personally rather shy, as I am, but you will find that your camera in some way uninhibits you—it's rather like wearing a mask at a masked ball—and with its protection you can approach and talk to and photograph most people quite easily. Approach strangers slowly, it's a bit like photographing small frightened animals (which most of us are, deep inside), or moving in on someone you fancy at a cocktail party. If you move too quickly you will scare them off. Read facial and bodily reactions to see how close you can approach someone. After a while it's not too hard to do.

I'm probably best known for my people pictures. I take most of the best ones with a 28mm lens, from about three feet away. I want a real feeling of intimacy. It usually takes at least half an hour of talking to and slowly photographing someone (whether you speak their language or not!) to get that close.

Speaking of languages, they are obviously a great advantage to any travel photographer, but not essential—you can also communicate well with smiles, hands, gestures, and through friends, guides and interpreters!

What Makes a Good Travel Photograph?

John Lewis Stage, a great travel and people photographer, once said to me, "What clients ultimately pay for is one's taste." Taste is a loaded word, yet not to address the subject is to avoid an extremely important issue. Good taste for everyone is what they like; bad taste, what they don't. But there are acknowledged masters in photography as well as all the arts, and if your aim is to do the best possible professional work, you need and can acquire standards for taste— an artistic frame of reference if you will, as well as technical and seeing skills.

All truly ambitious photographers should see and study as much great original photography as possible by visiting museums and galleries, by joining and attending meetings of professional photographers' associations and by talking to people who are working in their field of interest. Fine-art photography books, top travel magazines and avant garde magazines, promotional directories and some of the best stock catalogs will give you many points of view, styles and tastes. You will have to decide what you truly like, and where your own taste lies.

Technical Requirements of Professional Travel Photographs

Good travel photographs are technically excellent, well composed (the picture frame is filled elegantly or interestingly), exposed the way the photographer wants it (this usually means rich color, or a full range of black to white tones) and not unintentionally blurred (to avoid blurring use a tripod).

If you still have to struggle with some points of photographic mechanics, don't despair or be embarrassed. Some people have more mechanical facility than others, but if you persist you will get the hang of it all eventually. I am one photographer who had to work hard to understand the mysteries of f/stops and reciprocity and flash synchronization, and after exposing many thousands of rolls of film I still need to shoot all the time to keep in peak practice. (I strongly recommend that people who still need to improve basic technical skills take photography courses with good instructors—such courses are offered now in high schools, community colleges and art schools almost everywhere—and practice till you've got technique licked.)

Aesthetic Requirements of Good Travel Photographs

Good travel photographs are fresh and reveal something about the photographer as well as about the subject. That is why it is extremely important to take the time to photograph what personally interests you, not just what an assignment dictates or stock agent or class calls for. I like artists for instance, and always try to seek them out when I travel anywhere. I ask for introductions to local artists, especially "folk" or "primitive" artists. I find out about and attend current exhibits wherever I travel, try to go anywhere else artists are in evidence and make a point of including artists and their work in my coverage of a place wherever possible. (One day perhaps someone will make use of all these photographs of artists. If not, talking to many painters and seeing their work has enriched my life as a different kind of artist.)

If you are still a bit unsure about how to approach a serious travel subject, you might consider taking a travel photography workshop. Some are given by fine photographers—even contemporary masters—in lovely locations, and are a good way to sharpen your seeing, assess your interests and strengths, develop your point of view and (kindly I hope) compare your work with that of others. Some individual travel photographers give workshops, and a number of photography schools give travel-related courses from time to time. (Books that list photography courses are noted at the end of this chapter.)

A Very Brief History of Travel Photography

Try to get a chance to look at some original early travel photographs. There are superb photography collections in the Metropolitan Museum and the Museum of Modern Art in New York, and the National Gallery of Art in Washington D.C. The Amos Amon Carter Museum in Fort Worth, Texas, the George Eastman House in Rochester, New York, and the Victoria and Albert Museum in London are also outstanding. Many other museums around the country and around the world have very good photography collections, where you can see the best contemporary work also. If you can't get to see originals in museums and galleries, or libraries and historical societies, check out some photo books.

One book I own and love is *Masters of Early Travel Photography* by Rainer Fabian and Hans Christian Adam. It's out of print, but you may be able to find a copy at a good secondhand bookstore. Another book worth owning, and still in print, is *A World History of Photography,* by Naomi Rosenblum. It includes many travel pictures.

All old pictures are fascinating as historic records; some are awe-inspiring when you consider both what the photographers had to do first to get there and then make them. Many historic travel pictures that survive are master-pieces—beautiful, evocative and powerful on any terms.

Serious travel photography began a very few years after the invention of photography itself, in 1839. Following other French photographers, Maxime Du Camp set out from Paris in 1849 with immense amounts of equipment, and a neurotic friend, the novelist Gustave Flaubert, to make a calotype (paper negative) record of the antiquities of Egypt. Du Camp's pictures of the Pyramids and Sphinx, the ruins of Abu Simbel and assorted hieroglyphics were individually printed and bound and issued in Paris. This was probably the first travel photo book, and was very successful. Du Camp was quickly followed by the Briton Francis Frith, who traveled up Egypt till he reached the Fifth Cataract of the Nile. He used the collodion process, and wrote about the difficulties of working with damp glass plates in blowing sand and 125° heat!

In the 1860's another Englishman, John Thompson, went to China, and spent four exhaustive years traveling and photographing the people, customs, costumes, landscape and architecture of that still enigmatic land. Italian-born Felice Béato made some of the earliest and most beautiful landscapes and portraits of Japan (then still closed to the world) in the 1870's and '80's. With the opening of the American West, William Henry Jackson, Edweard Muybridge (who was British born), Timothy O'Sullivan and Carleton Watkins were only the most famous of many American photographers who first recorded on film the glories of some of the most magnificent scenery in the world.

We who instantly see great events from all over the world, even know other planets by satellite, are entertained by movies and sitcoms made in spectacular locales everywhere, and need only money to get almost anywhere around the globe in a dozen or so hours by jet, cannot possibly appreciate the sensation those early travel photographs created. In the nineteenth century, despite railroads, a trip of hundred miles from home was a major undertaking to most people. Steriopticon "views" (of famous sights photographed with a horizontal twin-lens camera and mounted together) were all the rage in middle-and-upper class households in Europe and America, bringing the distant world into people's homes.

We can still admire many old travel photographs as enduring classics of composition, light, mood, interest in and respect and feeling for other cultures. These things are still what make great travel photographs.

Modern Masters

In the 20th century Ansel Adams (look at the way he uses backlighting on landscapes); Henri Cartier Bresson (best known for freezing the decisive moment); Bill Brandt who photographed Britain (also see his late nudes and portraits); Brassai (unbelievable how he got so close to underworld Paris) and Ernst Haas (a superb colorist) are my personal favorites. Two contemporary masters who take wonderful travel (and other) photographs in different styles are Arnold Newman (who invented the environmental portrait) and John Lewis Stage (who has a relaxed easy way with people and landscape). The work of both of them for *Holiday* Magazine in the early 1960's when I was starting to "see" was an inspiration to me. I also think that William Albert Allard, Peter B. Kaplan, Jay Maisel, Mary Ellen Mark, Joel Meyrowitz, Harvey Lloyd, Jake Rajs and Galen Rowell are all wonderful travel photographers in very different ways. Try to see and study their work. (See the Bibliography for suggestions on beautiful photography books by and about these and other contemporary masters.)

Personal Travel Photography for Fine Art and Fun

Some of my friends are accomplished semi-professional or serious amateur photographers. They early established other careers and have no wish, or no need, to make a living as photographers. Some exhibit their work, a few sell some stock pictures to help defray expenses. Stock pictures are well-organized collections of existing photographs, sold through specialist stock photo agencies, or directly (and discussed more fully in Chapter Thirteen). Some people find that to travel with a camera gives them the motive to go places and the opportunity to meet people they otherwise would not.

Other friends are strictly amateur photographers who just enjoy recording their travels as best they can. My close friend Pat Collyns' father was a professional photographer and she is a very good amateur. Her husband is an oil company executive and consultant. They have lived in Europe, Africa, North and South America. They have five sons who live now in England, America and Australia. She has made about thirty albums of wonderful color prints that document the family's life, friends and experiences all over the world. The albums are future heirlooms.

I know a doctor and a lawyer, both very busy, who travel with their cameras as often as they can for relaxation from stressful careers. Both perfectionists (I'd trust my life or my fortunes to them), they have worked hard to also become very good photographers. So far, they have confined their exhibits to big prints for the office. Another friend is a great traveler, a photographer part-time; she teaches languages when the budget gets tight. She sells many stock pictures, has received grants for her photography, and exhibits in New York and Europe. A former student is a financial writer. He branched out into travel writing for relaxation, and has now illustrated a number of his own pieces. All of these people are successful travel photographers in their own way.

Fine-Art Photography

Of course, in the long run, we do not know which photographs will last as art. Julia Margaret Cameron was a wealthy housewife in nineteenth-century London. Her photography started as a hobby to relieve her loneliness when her children left home. She passionately photographed her family, friends and servants, but was not taken very seriously by the professionals of her day. Now her esteemed prints are in all the great collections of photography throughout the world.

Many serious fine-art photographers today get an MFA degree and teach in colleges, some sell black and white and color prints and publish postcards, calendars, posters and books. Grants to support important projects and exhibits are available to the persistent and dedicated. And fine-art photography is sometimes used in some of the very best magazines.

A good and thorough book on this whole subject is *Photography for the Art Market* by Kathryn Marx.

Who Buys Travel Photography?

Magazine and book publishers are big users of still photographs. A good magazine store half a block from my studio carries about 3,000 different titles; over 2,000 are magazines published in the United States! About 60 consumer-oriented travel magazines alone are listed in *Bacon's Publicity Checker*, a trade guide to magazines (see Chapter Ten). Other magazines that assign travel photography and use travel stock include national and regional magazines, city magazines, and controlled circulation leisure-time magazines aimed at professionals like doctors. Airlines, resort and cruise operators publish "in house" travel publications that are given away free to clients; travel business and tourism trade publications also use travel pictures from many sources. Many photo books include individual travel shots, and trade books, guidebooks, textbooks and even some cookbooks all use travel pictures at times. Travel picture books are now big sellers. A new trend is to visit the locales of popular television series! Some photographers produce their own books; some are on travel, or travel-related subjects. Self-publication is of course very expensive, and demands entrepreneurial skills, but can be creatively and financially rewarding if successful.

Travel advertising is a very big business for international and national clients like airlines; campaigns are almost always photographed by big name photographers, but big travel advertisers buy a lot of stock as well, and pay top prices for pictures. Pictures used for advertising must always be "model released," which means that people or private property owners must give legal permission for the use of their, or their property's, image. (See Chapter Twenty for English and foreign-language model release forms). Regional and local travel advertising is for smaller airlines, states, resort areas, theme parks, hotels and more. Audio/visual slide shows continue to be used in promotions for the travel industry. (A/V's made from still photographs are usually, but not always, low-budget jobs, therefore open to new talent.) Still photographs are sometimes used in combination with video or film for travel commercials or programs. Advertisers of many products like glamorous backgrounds, and use quite a few landscape stock shots.

The Enormous Tourism Business

Tourism photography is the "commercial" side of travel photography. (I define commercial travel photographs as those that sponsor or advertise something, like television commercials do, not as in cheap, hack photography.)

Commercial travel photographs are shot for print advertising, promotional brochures or catalogs, leaflets, public relations handouts and audio/visuals. Still photographs are used by airlines, bus tour companies, cruise operators, hotel and motel chains, resorts, theme parks, restaurants, clubs and festivals, national, regional, state/provincial and local tourist authorities and national, regional or even historic railroads. In fact, you photograph for tourism anywhere that people go in fairly large numbers or in organized groups when they are away from home. Also do not forget that what is routine to you may be a tourist attraction to someone else, even rural America is increasingly being discovered as a foreign tourist destination.

The word "tourist" has always carried something of a stigma, implying that tourists are somehow less worthy than other travelers. There is a 1930's Noel Coward song called *"Why do the Wrong People Travel, When the Right People Stay at Home?"* I don't know that this is so. The great majority of tourists I have met are curious, intelligent people of all social classes who are interested in other places and people and who want to enjoy themselves. For reasons of time, money, comfort and convenience and sometimes for reasons of inexperience, age, health or fears about safety, they prefer to go to places where they will probably be with some others like themselves.

Tourists often, but not always, travel in escorted groups. Or they go on a well-earned vacation to relax and enjoy the ocean, sun, snow, lakes or mountains. Some tourists are history or culture or music buffs, others are interested in shopping bargains. Some travel to study or to meet people. Since at least some of the above descriptions fit almost everyone who has done more than take a taxi across town, and everyone is a tourist at some time or another, I don't know what there is to be snobbish about. I have always had the greatest respect for tourists' judgement, because major tourist attractions are always outstanding attractions, period. Obviously, there are some problems concerning tourism, most especially over-building and crowding in some very popular spots, as well as the dilution of certain cultures. (But tourism also preserves many things that would be lost if they did not attract visitors—and their money.)

These are problems of the highly-populated, mobile modern world, not just of tourism. I feel very fortunate to have been paid for photographing many things that others spend a lot of money to see and experience. It is something I am proud of, not condescending about.

The first true tourists, who traveled with specific sightseeing in view, were British aristocrats. At the end of the eighteenth century they finished their education after university with a Grand Tour of Italy, then as now considered the greatest place to study art and antiquity in the world. Another Briton, Thomas Cook, organized the first group tour, a moderately priced train trip from the industrial English Midlands to continental Europe, in the 1850's. Well-to-do Germans, French and Americans began going abroad in large numbers to view antiquities at about the same time, and all these countries still produce huge numbers of tourists. Mass tourism overseas for the North American middle class took off in the 1960's with the introduction of passenger jet planes.

It is an amazing thought that today millions of "ordinary" people have been to more places than even the greatest explorers had seen a hundred years ago. The newest tourist movement is from East to West, as anyone who has seen the Japanese-language signs in tourist shops everywhere (or been to the Grand Canyon lately) will testify. Visitors from Singapore, Taiwan, Hong Kong, Korea and India as well as Japan are coming to America, Canada and Europe in increasing numbers. Worldwide, tourism is the second largest business, after oil. In many countries, including my native Britain, it is the single largest earner of foreign currency. The point of all this for the photographer is that tourism is heavily promoted. A great deal of that promotion is in printed advertisements, brochures, leaflets, flyers, posters and public relations pictures. Tourism is therefore a very, very good market for travel assignments and stock sales.

Location Photography

Hollywood coined the term "going on location," which means shooting away from the controlled lighting available in studios. Still photographers also shoot on location, primarily for business, industrial and corporate clients. Since the skills required for travel photography and for location photography are substantially the same, many travel photographers do some of this kind of work. I personally find it interesting and challenging to make beautiful pictures of industrial scenes; much of this kind of work is assigned by graphic design firms who are exacting but appreciative people to work with. Location photography at the top level of corporate annual reports is very well paid (and highly competitive because of this). Lower-budget location work includes audio/visuals and public relations photography, special event and even party photography, which are all good ways for up-and-coming photographers to gain experience. It is how I started.

Travel Photography Courses and Workshops

The major schools listed below operate workshops in travel photography and many other subjects for serious photography students and professionals, and are well-established and regarded. Famous photographers participate from time to time. Call for specifics, the names and biographies of instructors, references, dates, and of course, prices.

- **The Art Kane Photographic Workshops** are held in summer in the restored Victorian seaside resort of Egg Harbor, NJ. Phone (609) 884-7117.

- **The International Center for Photography** (ICP) in New York City offers many courses on all levels year-round. Phone (212) 860-1777.

- **The Maine Photographic Workshops** offer courses most of the year in the pretty Maine seacoast village of Rockport. Phone (207) 236-8581.

- **The Nikon/Nikonos School of Underwater Photography** courses are given year-round off the coast of Florida and in the Caribbean. Phone (800) 272-9122.

- **The Santa Fe Photographic Workshops** are held in summer in New Mexico's beautiful capital. Phone (505) 983-1400.

- **The Steamboat Conference and Workshop** is held for one week each July in scenic Steamboat Springs, Colorado. A professional-level portfolio is required for admission, places are limited. Faculty members are on the staff of the National Geographic. Phone (303) 879-6111.

- And, you may care to know, my own **Travel/Location Photography** class is one among many courses given year-round by the School of Visual Arts in New York City, one of the world's great travel destinations! For information on all SVA offers, phone (212) 679-7350 or (800) 366-7820.

I shall be leading my first photo tour this summer, it will be a safari to East Africa operated by R M Expeditions LTD., a Washington, D.C.-based company that specializes in highly personalized tours to Africa, Asia and the Pacific. Later photo tours will be to India, Nepal and Pakistan, and to Australia and New Zealand. Some will feature game parks not on the usual itineraries. If you would like more information, please contact R M Expeditions direct, at (202) 337-3368; fax (202) 337-3530.

Some very well-known travel photographers give workshops. One is a friend, Lisl Dennis. I'm told by a former student who also took Lisl's course in Santa Fe that it is very worthwhile.

Additionally, see *The Guide to Photography Workshops and Schools,* and *The Photography and Travel Workshop Directory.* These useful annuals also list photo tours, and residencies and retreats open to fine-art photographers. (See Directories, in Chapter Twenty.)

If you would like to formally study photography overseas, contact The Institute for International Education, 809 United Nations Plaza, New York, NY 10017. Phone (212) 883-8200. They have detailed information.

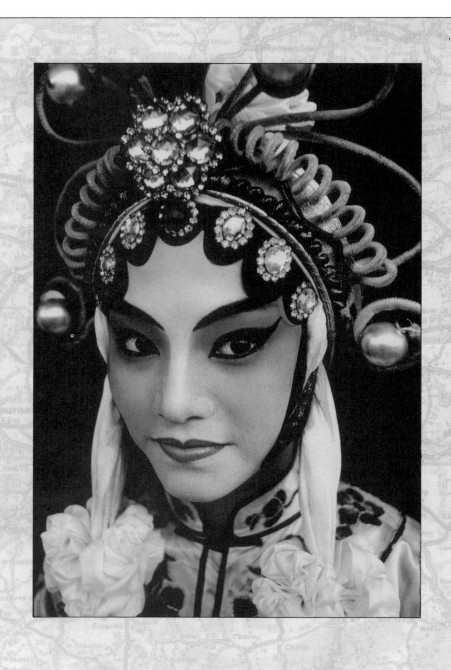

Chapter 2

Travel Photography Skills

Fluency in photography comes, as it does with everything else, with much practice. Sometimes you will hit plateaus and seem to make no progress, but if you persist you will sooner or later find your own "look".

Developing a Style and a Personal Way of Looking at the World

Photographically literate people can usually recognize the work of famous photographers, because their work has a distinctive style. If your pictures have a "look," it will greatly contribute to your personal and professional success. How do you acquire such style, a signature as it were? Photographic style is a combination of technique, taste and point of view. These things come from childhood and family, and from where you grew up, and from whatever other important influences you have been exposed to. Innate talent and education are also factors.

Your visual point of view and "eye" for a picture can almost certainly be improved with training, especially if you gave up early on art studies. Because it's fairly easy to record family, friends and impressions, photographic beginners are encouraged to go further. This makes photography widely appealing. Creating anything well is one of the truly satisfying pleasures that life offers and the camera makes this relatively accessible. Just how much desire you have to carry your photography to its limits will determine how far you will ultimately go. But once you get good, even on a non-professional level, once you've sampled that creative joy for a while, you will never want to give it up.

Study Art for Better Photographs

Looking at great paintings as well as photographs is another way of refining your seeing. I don't mean that you should photograph in a highly pictorial style, or actually try to copy paintings. Look at art just to develop your visual knowledge and sense of what and why something is beautiful. Consider Breughel's harvest scenes, Vermeer's interiors and any 17th century Dutch landscapes. To learn more about lighting portraits look at Rembrandt and Leonardo da Vinci. For light and landscape, there are golden studies of Italy by Turner; and just about any Impressionist painting (but especially Monet's series of the cathedral at Rouen and of haystacks). To think about weather, and people in a landscape, as well as color at different times of day and in different seasons, enjoy Hokusai and Hiroshige's woodblocks of their travels in 19th-century Japan and see how relevant they are to travel photography today.

When I travel, my relaxation is to go to as many art museums as possible and see originals, but of course you can also look at art books. And today, more and more artworks and collections are available for viewing and study on video. *The Traveler's Guide to Museum Exhibitions* (see Chapter One) is an annual which covers major permanent collections and traveling shows of art and photography in the United States and Canada. Guidebooks of course list major museums in other countries. (See also Chapter Twenty.)

Refining Your Photographic Style

In any type of art, including photography, there is a big difference between being inspired by a master or someone you admire, and working in that spirit (which everybody starting out does to some degree) or copying someone else's work exactly. A few rather desperate photographers (beginners and others) try to copy successful photographers because they think this makes their work more saleable. This is a horrible pitfall. At best such work is boringly derivative, at worst it's plagiarism and can lead you into problems—even lawsuits—over copyright infringement.

Current travel stock landscapes that rely on the heavy use of color filters for instance, are almost all only a very poor imitation of the work of the renowned photographer, Pete Turner, who originated the concept in his traveling days and has long since stopped using it. If you want to make a real mark you must be original. Of course if you can find truly new ways of using color filters or gels (like the flash pictures of the talented and currently "hot" young photographer Chip Simons) then of course do it.

Try all kinds of new and even crazy things. Some will fail, others seem promising. Shoot and re-shoot the promising things until something succeeds. Don't forget to play, to break the rules, to risk the improbable or impossible, and recognize and seize the occasional marvelous lucky accident when it happens. And if you do come up with something new, don't despair if you are ahead of your time. It took Simons several years of shooting in his special style to catch on and get offered a lot of work.

It is very helpful to your development to study your images carefully every few weeks. Pin 40 or 50 work prints (or mini-lab prints) to a wall or lay them out on the floor, and leave them there for a while. Projecting the same number of slides enlarged onto a white wall every few days has the same effect. Sort the slides or prints you are studying into groups, sets, or categories, as you might a deck of cards. Can you see any affinities? Perhaps a leaning toward people? Humor? Moody landscapes? Complex arrangements of shapes? A preference for black and white or monochromatic color? If you see a trend emerging (you will after you have been photographing for a while) trust your instincts and follow that lead. The best and most important thing you can do for your photography is to nurture your unique viewpoint.

To be a practitioner or artist of any kind you must both know about and be sensitive to the past. You must be aware of what present masters are doing, yet at the same time insulate yourself from those things. You should be like a race-horse wearing blinkers so that it can only see to the front and doesn't get distracted or scared by what's happening to the sides.

Some people worry that every photograph, especially every travel photograph, has already been taken. It is unhelpful to think that way, because although pretty well everything has been photographed (or written about, or painted or composed), there are always new ways of doing the same thing. We all have unique sensibilities, training and values. New technology affects the way things are recorded. If you gave Polaroid cameras to 200 photographers, who then all aimed at that great travel cliché, the Eiffel Tower, no two snaps would be taken from exactly the same angle or distance or show precisely the same thing. Some photographers would include people, some go for design, others wait for beautiful light, others photograph tourists photographing the tower, others still notice the clouds between the iron work or the mechanics of the elevators. And some people would scribble on the print, peel and transfer it onto paper, melt it, or invent something that hasn't been done yet.

Technical Skills

A mastery of photographic tools is obviously and always a requirement for a highly developed personal photographic style, which takes a lot of work and practice. Shoot every day if you can. It is the only way you can acquire real fluency. If your film budget is very tight, you can practice seeing photographs in your head, but actually shoot them as often as you possibly can. It's also good to keep up with trends. Polaroids, color copiers, hand coloring, still video cameras, and of course computers are all affecting the "look" of still photography today. The newest thing in advertising and editorial travel photography is a return to black and white, which is now beautifully reproduced in top magazines and books by the four color process method used for color pictures. Ultimately, creative and honest seeing—starting your own trend—will get you the most work and recognition.

When working to acquire style, don't constantly compare your work and your achievements to other people's; this can inhibit you seriously and even dry you up if you do it often. Measure your present photographs against those from years or months ago, and let your feelings tell you if you are making progress.

On the other hand, be realistic with yourself in deciding when you are "ready" to compete in the travel assignment marketplace, to market your travel pictures as stock, to exhibit your photographs. If you do technically good, original work and respect it, it is very likely that others will admire and use it. Don't expect instant gratification or success. Photography is a crowded field, and even if your work is truly excellent, it still takes time to get your pictures and name around and to carve a niche for yourself. If you want to succeed commercially you will need a lot of drive and the ability to accept rejection at first. If you do get stuck in a blank period, or if work isn't coming in and you are depressed, shoot your way out of it. Pictures that you force yourself to take will not be your best, but may lead you in a new direction, and will contribute to your development. Dry periods almost always pass, unlikely as it may seem at the time. Believing in what you are doing is also important. Remember the law of the self-fulfilling prophecy!

Composition, or Filling the Picture Frame

Can good composition be learned? Up to a point, absolutely. Some compositional sense is probably intuitive. To start seeing photographically always compose your picture when actually looking through the lens. This sounds elementary, but you probably will have to school yourself to do this at first. What you see with the naked eye (and what you feel) when you stand on a mountain top is most likely not what the film will record even if you have a panoramic camera. You have to choose the part of the view, and time of day, to best express your feelings, not only about the physical look of the mountains but about the space, the light, the height and the effort it took to get there.

Varying Composition for Creative Pictures

To photograph a mountain panorama, for instance, don't just stand and aim the camera straight in front of you from eye-level. You may want to get down low and have foreground rocks loom large in front of distant peaks to give depth, or prefer to show just a thin rim of mountain at the bottom of the frame, and have nine tenths of your picture clouds and sky. Or, shoot down onto jagged peaks or rolling receding domes and show no sky at all. Perhaps you can include distant climbers or hikers or skiers in some of the mountain views which would give scale. If you are very lucky or patient or in the right area you can include a wild animal. Maybe there is a cairn or marker at the summit of your climb to put in the foreground of your composition. Silhouette someone against the low lit mountains—sunrises and sunsets are usually the best times to get any dramatic landscape pictures, but the movement of clouds obscuring and revealing the sun any time of day is important too. Of course, if you can allow enough time, you can try all of the above approaches to the mountain scene; that would be my way of getting the best out of it.

Negative Space in Your Photographs

It is sometimes helpful to think about what you're not going to include in your picture.

Negative space—blank sky, concrete, water, grass, etc.—or where the main subject isn't—can be used as a design element. How much of it you use, compared to your main subject can make the background either very important or insignificant. Usually, keep backgrounds uncluttered. Think about the shapes between shapes, behind shapes, or in front of other shapes. Shapes, composition and positive/negative space relationships can be altered by moving your angle of view, and by using different focal length lenses. Wide-angle lenses make the foreground large in relation to the background, giving an appearance of great depth and space. Telephoto lenses have the opposite effect, often causing a flattened, posterish look, and making the background appear to be closer to the foreground than it actually is.

To help you to think about the negative space, or backgrounds of scenes, which have a great effect on your final picture, make a habit of using the "stop-down" or depth of field preview button which manually reduces the f/stop (lens aperture) to the opening which you have chosen for the picture so that you can see the actual depth-of-field (zone of sharp focus) This is important, at least until you are accustomed to thinking about backgrounds, because modern lenses focus at the widest, brightest aperture, for easy viewing and sharp focusing, stopping down automatically only when the shutter is fired.

That soft golden blur you ignored when viewing red tulips at f/2 may actually be a rather ugly broken fence. It will show up all too clearly in your elegant flowerbed composition on film exposed at f/11, which has great depth of field.

The inexperienced photographer tends to see or mentally focus on only the most important thing in any picture at first. The camera records everything dispassionately, so consider backgrounds carefully, use aperture and depth of field creatively, and check the edges and corners of your picture frame as well your main subject. Think about what you may want to leave out of a picture, by changing your angle, moving your subject, blocking or masking something ugly, and by putting something between your lens and the offending object. If you do all these things your photographs will rapidly improve.

What Makes Good Composition?

Composition is the arrangement of everything in the "frame" or picture space, and there are no hard and fast rules or guidelines. Anything pleasing is okay. But to be more specific, you usually want to keep horizontal and vertical lines as straight as possible, or lean them so they look decisive, not accidental or tentative. It usually isn't interesting to divide a land or seascape exactly in half; try a picture with more cloudy sky and less green field, or more stormy sea and less rocky shore. If you center a person in the picture frame, which most beginners tend to, the subject can look a bit like a target; try moving yourself (or them) so that they are to the right or left of the frame's center, or mostly in the top or bottom half of the photograph. Looking through the lens while changing your angle to the subject, trying different focal length lenses for different perspectives, and not being afraid to ask your subject to move will all help you get interestingly arranged elements.

Of course, experienced photographers can and frequently do ignore these informal composition guidelines. Having someone exactly in the middle of a shot, glaring straight at you, may convey their personality exactly. A tilted horizon might say everything you want to about sailing, skiing or the view from a cathedral, looking down from its spire. Disembodied arms and legs emerging from the sides of a Manhattan streetscape could capture the nervous energy of a great city to perfection. Once you know the rules, dare to break them!

How to Fill the Frame Elegantly

Elegance is almost always very simple. Think about very expensive clothes, made of beautiful material, well crafted, perfectly fitting. Or the unfussy lines of beautiful cars. The best designers in all fields say "form follows function" and leave out a lot. Try and keep your compositions clean and spare, with beautifully arranged subject matter and light. Less is better than more for me, but I would be presumptuous to try to teach you elegance; study the masters and develop your own.

Solving Visual Problems

To mask a small unwanted element in a scene, such as an immovable trash can (when you can't lose it by shifting it or you) block it by shooting at a low angle through flowers or foliage out of focus in the foreground. If there aren't any flowers or leaves right there, pick some elsewhere, and hold them very close to the lens placed to hide the ugliness. They will dissolve the unwanted object into a blur of color. In cities, wait till a person or vehicle masks the offending sight.

Dusk is very kind to cities that have less than marvellous maintenance.

You can often angle a shot to mask ugly telephone poles, or break up the line of a TV antenna with well positioned trees.

Careful arrangement helps people problems too. Have a very large person sit down behind a table with their arms on the table. Make older people smile or laugh, and semi-backlight them, or shoot them through soft flowers or foliage. All these techniques soften hard lines.

Professional Compositional Skills

When composing for assignments remember the needs of the art director, who will need both verticals and horizontals. Covers are almost always vertical, with clear uncluttered space where the magazine logo (title) goes. If you know that a given publication's style is to run most pictures on the left hand side of a two page spread make sure you have plenty of shots that face right, into the spread.

As a general rule, don't put faces or other important picture elements into the exact center of the frame. An art director won't usually use such a shot as a double-page spread because part of the faces will get lost in the "gutter" (space lost in binding).

Try using unusual lenses for any subject. I have made interesting portraits and still lifes using a 500mm lens, for instance. The flattened effect is somewhat like a Japanese print.

Things Travel Art Directors Don't Ever Want To See

Garbage—even little bits can ruin a beautiful picture—pick it up if you have to); litter containers; graffiti; ugly or too many street signs; public toilets; junk cars; overhead wires, utility poles and antennas; anyone you don't want to be there. Back views and rear ends of almost everything and everyone are awful. Never photograph lots of footprints, crowds or brown seaweed on a beach; discarded towels, wet chairs and empty drinks at poolside; cigarettes in general (except if your client is a tobacco company!) Don't photograph full ashtrays, the remains of a meal, dirty plates or cluttered dining tables, ever. Brand names and advertising signs should be avoided wherever possible.

Avoid people wearing casts or bandages; people carrying plastic bags (just count how many there are on any street!). And avoid Elvis or any inappropriate tee shirts in places where colorful local costumes still predominate. Especially avoid those tee shirts with revolting slogans or dominating designs (ask non-professional models to put them on backwards if desperate). Tight shorts do nothing for most people.

Dirt and clutter of any kind is always out as far as commercial travel photography is concerned, as is scaffolding on major monuments if possible. I say if possible because about five years ago Big Ben, the Eiffel Tower, the Colosseum and the Acropolis were all in heavy scaffolding at the same time that I was shooting a European tourism brochure for a new client. Luckily I had plenty of pictures of these "must" tourist icons in my stock files.

Demolition and messy construction sites should be avoided. I always remove, or ask people to remove, all those horrible little notices, cards and other visual clutter that people unthinkingly tack onto walls in hotel lobbies, restaurants, classrooms and offices, not to mention all the junk they keep on their desks, computers and workbenches.

Poverty, overcrowding, disease and unhappy people are always out, even if they exist at your destination. If you want to photograph those things, be a photojournalist, not a travel photographer. Of course, if you photograph for your own fine-art pictures, or as personal mementoes of your trip, you can be as all-encompassing as you like. However, the poorest and saddest people everywhere usually hate being photographed, and may let you know that in no uncertain terms. Local and national authorities in many regions do not like any depiction of their country that is deemed unflattering, and you may be asked, told, or even made to leave if you persist in making such pictures.

Photographing Ordinary Things Beautifully

One of the most-needed skills of professional photographers is to be able to make things look as good as possible, sometimes better than reality. Using appropriate lenses is one of the best ways of doing this.

To give a couple of specific examples; car interiors are often photographed with a 28mm lens on a 35mm camera, it makes the interior look a little more spacious, without distorting reality too much. If you photograph a swimming pool with a 20mm lens from a low viewpoint and hang over the water to eliminate the near edge of the pool, it makes the pool look bigger than it actually is. Light is important too; backlighting especially is flattering to food, landscapes and most people. See also the chapters on equipment, light and lighting.

Consider the Egg

To practice making the most of whatever you must photograph, try this self-assignment in imagination and composition. Take six plain white eggs, cook them, and take them for a walk with a wide-angle or telephoto lens. I have given this exercise to students with some very creative results. I've seen eggs waiting to be killed on a busy highway; huge eggs in wide-angle closeup gathered in a nest near an airport runway with small 747's taking off behind them, and eggs being used as golf balls on a seaside putting green, among other creative solutions.

How to Nail Down the Great Shot

For the best possible pictures, as well as to perfect your technique, you must not be afraid of shooting enough film. Although expensive, the cost of film is not as high as the costs of a trip. It may take two or three rolls to get just the picture you want of a shepherd and his flock,—the first few from a distance showing him small in the surrounding hills, then closer, moving along with him the sheep and the dogs, and finally a portrait shot. When he's used to you, perhaps you can ask (with words or gestures) to have him hold a lamb in one hand and his crook in the other. Never take your eyes away from the viewfinder and keep shooting. When everything comes together, you will know it, and you will have your definitive shepherd picture. Perhaps it was the moment when the lamb wriggled and he grabbed it, or the dog barked for attention and he laughed and patted it, or whatever. (More subtleties of people photography are discussed in detail in Chapter Eight.)

You'll also need many exposures to get excellent shots of moving people and lights in a disco. It usually takes a whole series of pictures to get the peak moments of a sunset, because you cannot predict when the maximum effect will be, and sometimes because the afterglow is even better than the sunset itself.

To me, the physical act of taking several pictures, rather than one, especially of people, warms me up as well as the subject and usually results in my seeing things and juxtapositions that I didn't notice at first.

Travel Skills

Professional and serious personal travel photography is demanding. It challenges your social and organizational skills and your physical endurance.

What specifically do you need to know besides photography to bring home fine images? You have to be able to think on your feet and improvise and be flexible and work fast. You should be able to wait patiently and be philosophical and resilient when something doesn't work out as planned. You must be comfortable talking to the great, the humble, and good plain people everywhere. You should be able to enjoy an occasional stay at the Ritz or tolerate a hard night's semi-sleep on the floor of a none-too-clean peasant's hut, not to mention making the best of innumerable nights in innumerable boring motels.

Keeping pictorial goals in mind while coping with the minor problems that happen on almost every trip is a routine skill every traveling photographer needs.

A professional travel or location job requires meticulous advance planning, constant checking of details, good management (and a bit of luck) to avoid expensive mistakes or photographic disasters on a difficult trip. Finally, professional photography is a business and you must be able to handle finances, both cash and credit. Keep immaculate records for yourself, your clients and Uncle Sam or the Canadian tax man.

Traveling Alone

Because it is usually difficult to photograph professionally while traveling with anyone other than an assistant who is being paid to do exactly what you want (and sometimes even with them!), I usually prefer (or the budget dictates) that I go by myself. I keep maximum sensitivity to my surroundings, have freedom to make last minute changes to the itinerary, and keep a low profile to be as unthreatening to the local people as possible. I'm not usually lonely if the shoot is going well, and if I have a good book for company. When needed, I get local assistance—from people who speak the language, know the area, have good contacts and access and especially knowledge of local driving conditions. Sometimes, a "local" becomes a good friend. You are much more likely to make such friends when you travel alone.

Traveling With an Assistant, Loved Someone, Friend or Client

The best travel is done with an assistant who is trained to anticipate your every need, is quiet, pleasant, and unflappable, doesn't ever complain about the food, the climate, the job or the boss, and who always gets up at dawn without complaint. Obviously such paragons are rare. To have a spouse as an assistant is not easy, but there are some successful travel photographers who habitually work with a spouse or friend as partner or assistant. I think they too are rare. Perhaps it is the clash of egos. Some location specialists travel with a crew. (They then have a lot of logistical problems to contend with.)

If you do travel with someone else it helps to discuss what has to be covered very thoroughly before you leave, but this does not always guarantee that you and they will work together well on the road. A good traveling companion or assistant is a joy on any trip and enhances it and makes it much easier in most ways, but they are hard to find. An incompatible assistant or traveling companion is sheer misery, which is why (I think) many travel photographers are essentially loners.

I personally prefer not to travel with a writer—not that I don't like these usually very nice people—but their agenda is often not related to photography. The same thing applies to clients. Art directors are fine, as long as they don't want to shoot all the pictures themselves (it has been known to happen). If you must travel with someone else, agree in advance with any of the above that you cannot spend all your time with them en route.

If you are a dedicated amateur photographer who travels with your spouse, consider the solution of a former student of mine. He bought his wife a very nice Sony Palmcorder (a tiny, advanced, 8mm video camcorder) and now she is almost as enthusiastic about her kind of photographic recording of their travels as he is about his!

Traveling in a Group

Group travel is often convenient and comfortable, and may offer big savings over individual trips; sometimes tours are the only way you can visit a country or region (as it was when I went to China from Hong Kong in 1977, before the United States and China had resumed diplomatic relations). Group travel, however, is never ideal for serious photography, because most tours adhere to a timetable. Some have extremely tight schedules. If you are in a group and photographing for yourself, your main problem will be finding ways to separate yourself from everyone else. Even if you get up very early every day and go out shooting before breakfast, you will probably have to skip some or most planned activities or sightseeing visits to have sufficient photography time. Choose a tour that doesn't have a lot of one-night stop-overs for better picture-taking opportunities.

I have photographed professionally while travelling with a group; the biggest no-no is keeping the paying passengers waiting. Even if you are a passenger yourself, keeping a number of people waiting more than very occasionally will make you highly unpopular with the tour manager and with the other tourists on whose goodwill you depend!

If you are photographing a group for a tourism client, the best arrangement is to have your own car available, so that you can be with the group when you need to be, but are free to wait longer somewhere for that special shot, catching up with the tourists later, or at the planned evening stop.

Small group tours specifically planned for photographers are increasingly popular (see Chapter One).

Researching a Photo Trip or Assignment

To make the most of your time and maximize your photography opportunities, to get the best value for your and your client's money, and to be considered polite by the locals, find out ahead of time as much as you can about your destination, and what you will be photographing.

Through research, you'll learn, for instance, that you won't want to go on safari in Kenya in May (it's the rainy season) or travel by train in France the first or last days of August (the French government subsidizes vacation travel for its citizens and trains are packed solid). People present cards everywhere in formal Japan, and it's courteous to hand them back—you can get yours printed in English and Japanese overnight at good hotels. Take your turn buying a round in a British pub, or you will be considered stingy. When you go on a shoot for business clients, read the previous year's annual report (as well as any relevant guidebooks) to find out as much as your can about the company and the location in advance.

Business Skills

Business know-how is essential if you are to make it in professional photography, including stock photography. This is not realized by everyone when they start out! Those photographers soon learn, if they survive, the very hard way. Foreign travel makes business and record keeping and communicating more complicated because you have to deal with different languages, currency, social mores and even varying electrical systems. If it's a professional trip, you will probably have to make a bid, and submit a cost estimate to get the job. Sample bid and estimate forms are published in a monograph—Forms—by the American Society of Magazine Photographers (ASMP); the Advertising Photographers of America (APA) also has bid/estimate forms. *Business and Legal Forms for Photographers* by Tad Crawford also includes such forms. (See also Chapters Eleven, Fifteen, Sixteen and Twenty.)

Business courses for photographers are offered by photo schools, and ASMP and APA as well as other photographers' associations have frequent seminars on such business subjects as taxation, insurance and "paper trails"—necessary business paperwork. You can usually attend these even if you are not a member. Community colleges and schools and other places have small business management courses. My own publisher, Allworth Press, puts out a number of useful books on various aspects of business and legalities for established and aspiring arts professionals, including photographers. Check the inside back page of this book for titles.

Negotiating Skills, and Getting it Down on Paper

When you travel on assignment, you will need to negotiate the terms of the agreement with the client. You must understand the financial terms and the photographic requirements of the assignment very clearly, and have them in writing, before you go. (For specifics, see Chapter Fifteen.)

Social Skills

Professional photographers today work in a very competitive business, and in a way, it's related to show business. It is a given after a certain point that you are highly competent at what you do, can deliver a job that meets the client's

The Computer and Managing Your Business

The computer is almost essential today for the small business owner of any kind. Now that I have one I don't know how I ever lived without it. I like the Macintosh, because it is very easy to learn and has many programs that are fun and terrific for photographers and visual people. I now design, typeset and print my own stationery and model releases and stock forms; design my own promotion pieces, and keep track of clients, invoices and stock submissions.

I keep my bank account (more or less) balanced, write checks and pay bills —all on my Macintosh SE. Last year I art directed and laid out a brochure for a travel client on my Mac (using the QuarkXPress program), which was very satisfying because I could choose the pictures I wanted to use, and size and place them to their best advantage—not always true when other people lay your work out! (I am currently using the Adobe Photoshop program for manipulating and retouching black-and-white and color photographs, (and photographing the results off the screen with a macro lens). It's a lot of fun. I don't yet know if I will work with it seriously or not. Formerly quite expensive, Macs have come down in price a lot recently.

Whether for the IBM or the Mac, there are many generic and specific programs to help you run your business. Accounts and billing, payroll and taxes and more are covered. Specialized photo business software programs and stock labelling programs, are advertised in the *Photo District News* (PDN). This is a monthly publication for professional photographers, see later in the chapter. There seem to be more photographers' programs for the IBM than the Mac. I don't have any because they are expensive and I haven't yet found a Mac program that does just what I want so I use generic business programs.

General business programs are written up and advertised in such personal computing magazines as *MacWorld* and *MacUser*, *P.C.*, *Byte*, etc.

If you aren't yet computer literate, take heart from this not particularly mechanically adept middle-aged lady who didn't know a mouse from a megabyte two years ago (but I did go to art school for graphic design). I still can't type properly (this book and my invoices are written with two fingers on the Microsoft Word program); but I can now retouch pictures, using a (rented) Mac CX computer, and Microtek or Tamron or Nikon scanners and the Adobe Photoshop program. I can set type and lay out pages (using QuarkXPress) and draw pictures and diagrams like the ones in this book (using the Super Paint, Aldus Freehand and HyperCard programs). I use Intuit's Quicken program for finances, but I have to admit defeat on doing my own taxes, because the schedules for a self-employed person are quite complicated. It is my sincere belief that a CPA's skills are still worth paying for!

I recommend saving yourself agony and taking a computer course (available just about everywhere) to get you started. I took one in basic desktop publishing, and then spent about three months struggling and practicing in my every spare minute. Then, I bought my own computer. Two years later, I'm an advanced intermediate user. I will never be without a computer again.

requirements, and add a certain unique vision to the project that marks the work as your own. In the current marketplace that is not usually enough to get you a lot of work. Clients of all kinds like to work with photographers whom they like. Nice guys and gals don't finish last in this business, they finish first if they also have talent. You don't have to be handsome or beautiful to be a successful photographer (but it never hurt anyone in any occupation!) but you should strive to be as physically attractive and well-groomed as you can be.

You must also be able to talk fluently on the phone, know how to research a subject, write a reasonably literate business letter, and be able to "sell" your ideas and yourself on a face-to-face basis.

Most travel editors are reasonably well-educated people. Quite a few are cultured. And when you travel you will meet people of all social classes. I still remember a lunch on my first big job, an audio/visual shoot for a Latin American airline. I traveled with a writer and a director. We ate with about twenty house guests seated around a long table in the formal dining room of a beautiful "estancia" (estate or ranch) in the pampas south of Buenos Aires. The conversation was in Spanish, English, French and German. A handsome silver-haired dowager opposite said to me, "Oh, you've come from America. Do you know Winthrop Rockefeller?" Needless to say I didn't, but managed to ask a reasonably intelligent question about Argentine gauchos; horse-related subjects are usually a safe bet for conversation with the super-rich!

You should be able to handle different social situations gracefully; good conversational skills will help you get assignments, and will always help you get better pictures, because you often have to talk people into helping you when you are shooting.

Of course there must be some mean, or unattractive, or unkempt or very boring photographers who are very successful. I personally don't know any.

The Photo District News

This is a monthly publication for professional photographers, edited in New York. It has correspondents nationwide and overseas, and Eastern, Mid-West and Western editions. Each month has a theme, with annual Travel, Stock, Lighting and Self-Promotion issues among others. Ads are for equipment and services, with a strong classified ad section. Buy PDN at photodealers and good magazine stores, or subscribe. Address is P.O. Box 1983, Marion, OH 43305. Phone (800) 669-1002.

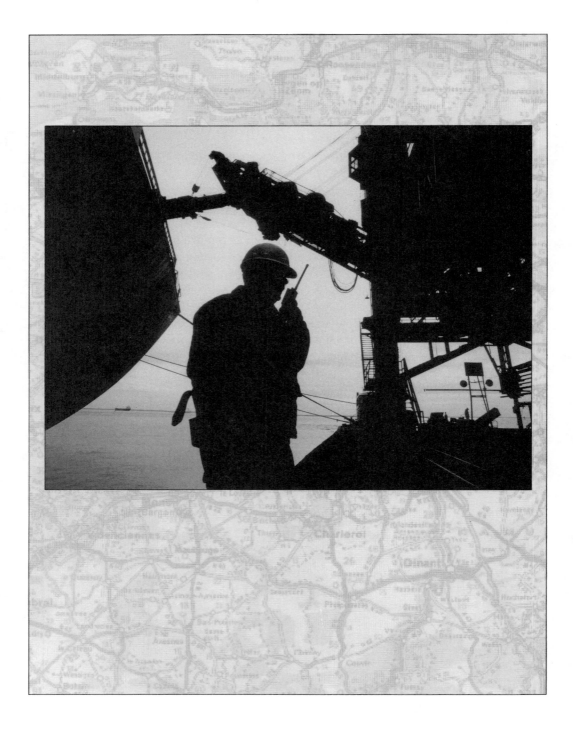

Chapter 3

Equipment: Cameras, Lenses and Accessories

My mother was an enthusiastic photographer. She often snapped away (mostly at my sister and me growing up) with a very large black box Brownie she had originally bought to photograph the great adventure of her life, two years of touring South America with an English theater company in the late 1920's. I loved poring over her albums of slightly faded black and white prints of Pernambuco and Valparaiso, Montevideo and Buenos Aires, and listening to the stories attached to each picture, but I could never get the pictures that I took with her camera to come out. I usually cut people's heads off.

Equipment Today and Yesterday

In my childhood, cameras were still a far cry from today's wonderful "point and shoots" that everyone takes for granted. When I was twelve, my movie actress aunt in Hollywood sent me a plastic Ansco twin lens reflex camera for my birthday. It arrived in a shiny red and blue box, with six rolls of (I believe) 127 film. I'm sorry that I don't think I ever thanked her properly. That little camera allowed me to actually see what I wanted to photograph, and I fell in love with it, and photography. Mother was generous about paying for developing at Boots Chemists (and for more film later) so I continually photographed variations on the themes of my guinea pigs, my cat, our dogs, my mother and my sister, in that order. I still have those little black-and-white pictures, as well as the ones I took with the same camera when I was sixteen, in the fifties, traveling around England as an assistant stage manager in a very third-rate touring theater company. When I was eighteen I used it to record my shipmates and willing and unwilling crew members during a stormy February Atlantic crossing on the old Queen Elizabeth. My shots of the skyline of New York are still quite good, considering the equipment I worked with. (I have copied some of those old pictures onto slides. Perhaps one day I'll include them in a slide show for any future grandchildren. You can do the same with your old prints. They can even be copied onto video tape or retouched on the computer.)

Today's neophyte travel photographers have a lot more equipment options than Mother or I did. There are bewildering arrays of camera formats, systems, lenses and accessories to choose from. Camera manufacturers imply that to select their product will instantly transform you into a terrific photographer. Sad to say, that's not true (you knew it anyway, deep down). Good photography is only a little easier now than it was in the 19th century, because it's the photographer's taste and point of view that counts, not the equipment or the film.

The "Point and Shoot" Camera

"Point and shoot" cameras are a lot of fun and you can get very nice snaps with them, even if you're an absolute beginner. They are almost (but not quite) foolproof. If your Aunt Minnie is going on the trip of her life, and asks you as the family photographer for advice on what camera to take with her, tell her to buy one of the many 35mm "point and shoots" made by good manufacturers (see later in the chapter for some recommendations). She'll come back with pictures, memories, and no hassles because the camera was not too complicated for her to use. (Aunt Minnie or someone a bit more advanced might also find Kodak's *Pocket Guide to Travel Photography* helpful.)

However, if you are very serious about travel photography and going on your first great trip, and you want to bring back more than good snaps, you'll have to know more than just how to "point and shoot". You will need to understand the basics of composing or "framing" pictures; exposure and metering techniques (yes, you need to know even with clever cameras) and why you need filters to get the best results in some situations. When do you need fast film, and when is medium speed or slow film better? How can you photograph that minaret without cutting the top off or leaning it back? And more.

This book will tell you about travel photography and suggested equipment from the intermediate level and up. You can also learn more from photography columns in travel magazines. Two general "how to" books I thoroughly recommend are by famous British photographer John Hedgecoe, now a professor of photography at the Royal College of Art in London. One is called *The Art of Color Photography*, the other *The Book of Photography*.

Good Basic Equipment

If you are an intermediate photographer, just starting to get serious, here is the equipment I suggest, to begin and to build on. (If you are a professional, but want to know more about travel and tourism and location photography equipment specifics, skip the next few paragraphs.)

Aunt Minnie should stick to the "point and shoots". Serious amateurs and students should probably aim to own two 35mm single lens reflex (SLR) cam-

Why Serious Beginners Should Take Photography Courses

If you want more than good snaps, advanced equipment alone is not the answer. I can and I will recommend equipment (see later in the chapter), based on my experience as a travel photographer, and as someone who has taught photography majors, professionals and enthusiastic amateurs. But if your vision outruns your skills, this book cannot teach you basic photography. You will save yourself much time and frustration by taking a class if you don't know what an f/stop, depth of field, or sync speed is. (These things are all important for creative control.) The only way to learn photography is to take pictures, but having someone close at hand to guide those first shaky steps is very helpful. Basic photography courses are offered at high schools, colleges, art schools, community colleges and adult education centers. Take a course or two!

era bodies. (One good 35mm single lens reflex and one good 35mm "point and shoot" camera with a 35mm lens will do in an absolute pinch.) Ideally, both camera bodies should be identical, and take the same interchangeable lenses. That way, fingers won't fumble for unfamiliar controls, which can cause missed shots. When I drive a car, I don't have to think where the brakes are, or the turn indicator, I use them by instinct and by reflex. I'm sure you can do the same. Of course, it took training and a good bit of driving to reach that point. The same thing is true of the controls of advanced cameras. You have to learn how to use them, and practice the skills often, before mastery of the camera functions become second nature.

If you carry two camera bodies when traveling it will prevent total disaster if one malfunctions or is dropped on the trip. It also allows you to work with two different focal length lenses at the same time. A friend who is a professional writer/photographer went on a walking tour in England recently and came back crying. She had short-sightedly taken only one of her Leicas to cut down on weight. (It had just been reconditioned so she felt quite safe.) But it jammed after four rolls, and she was reduced to using the guide's "point and shoot" for the rest of the trip, and lost some good photographic opportunities as a result.

Besides being safer, and letting you work with two lenses simultaneously, carrying two camera bodies also permits the use of color slide and color print film, or color and black and white film at the same time, which clients sometimes need. (I always stick to the same speed films, (100 or 400 ISO) when I have to do that, to avoid potentially disastrous mix-ups under pressure.) Professionals primarily use several bodies at the same time so they can quickly shoot with different focal length lenses, but also so they can rotate the cameras and lenses to minimize chances of loss if one camera fails/malfunctions.

A Basic Travel Photography Kit

If you are not going too far from home, the following should suffice:

❑ One 35mm SLR (single lens reflex) camera body (of the system you like and want to grow with).

❑ One 35mm "point and shoot" camera with built in flash and a "normal" lens. (This may save your vacation pictures if something happens to your other camera. If you get a water-resistant model, you can use it at the beach and in bad weather too. All the big SLR camera manufacturers also make "point and shoot" models.)

❑ A wide angle lens and a zoom telephoto lens for your SLR. (See later in the chapter for suggestions.)

❑ A tripod or a "table top" tripod. (Or a camera clamp, for attaching to fences, chairs, car windows, etc.)

❑ A well made but inconspicuous padded camera bag, or a military-style canvas shoulder bag or back pack which you have padded with foam inside. (I recommend backpacks for keeping a low profile, and leaving both hands free, one for you camera and one to hold onto a fence, ladder or whatever. There are also camera backpacks built purposely to carry cameras.)

The more serious photographer will add:

❑ Another SLR camera body, the same or closely similar to the first. (It can be instead of, or in addition to, the "point and shoot" as you wish.

❑ Several more lenses (see later in chapter for suggestions).

❑ A hand held light meter (see later in chapter).

❑ A small automatic or TTL (through the lens) bounce flash unit and a cord permitting its use off camera (for details see Chapter Seven, Photographic Lighting).

❑ A light but sturdy tripod that extends to your eye level (see later in chapter).

❑ A 36" round folding fabric reflector, silver and white (see Chapter Seven).

❑ A pair of folding "wheels" (a luggage cart; for recommendations, see later in the chapter).

All of these items will be used all the time by anyone who is even moderately serious about their travel pictures.

Choosing Your First Lenses

Unless you are going to photograph exclusively outdoors in bright daylight, I strongly recommend buying the fastest possible (largest f/stop or aperture) lenses made by the camera manufacturer. An extra stop or two can make all the difference between getting a picture or not getting one under poor lighting conditions. Two stops can mean the difference between shooting at 1/30 or 1/125 of a second under the same lighting conditions. Or, between 1/8 and 1/30. The slower the shutter speed, the more chance of blurred shots. So although fast lenses are heavier and more expensive than slower ones, they are well worth the difference in weight and money.

Generic or Independent Manufacturers' Lenses

These lenses are made by several companies with mounts for all the popular 35mm SLR camera systems. While some generic lenses are very good optically, they aren't all very good optically; cheaper zoom lenses, especially, are susceptible to flare and vignetting (darkening at the corners).

Generic lenses are almost all less rugged mechanically than top brand lenses, and they all have a lower trade-in or resale value than camera system lenses. But if you budget or taste dictates, consider Sigma and Tokina, who both make good lenses at good prices; many professionals use their fastest, longest telephoto lenses.

Most Useful Lenses to Take When You Travel

I recommend:

- A fast (f/2 or faster if possible) medium wide-angle or "normal" focal length lens (35, 45 or 55mm) Such ultra-fast lenses are especially useful for low-light shooting, in or out of doors.
- The fastest wide-angle lens you can afford. Wide-angle lenses have great depth-of-field (zone of sharp focus), are good to work with in crowds, and make the foreground look large in relation to the background. The 28mm is my favorite lens, a good focal length for people in a landscape, and for many interior, building and view shots.
- A 20mm is what I usually use for the most sweeping landscapes, and for architecture and interiors.
- The fastest possible medium focal-length zoom lens you can afford (not slower than f/4.5) in the range of about 80-200mm. This lens is good for precise framing of distant scenes, for bringing distant cityscapes and landscapes closer, and for unposed people shots.
- A short zoom lens (35-75mm range, not slower than f/4). It will fill the gap between your wide angle and tele lenses. Zooms are great for framing compositions precisely.
- A 2x tele-extender made for your lenses (do not get a cheap generic brand). Tele-extenders increase the focal length of telephoto and moderate and long zoom lenses. I like my 2x extender, which doubles focal lengths (200mm becomes 400mm and so on) at the cost of two stops in exposure.

Why Use Very Fast Lenses?

The faster any lens, the easier it is to use for low light pictures. You can't always use a tripod or flash, and even when you "push" fast film (increase the ISO speed rating and development time) an extra stop in exposure may make an available light, dimly lit interior or night shot possible. Wide apertures permit the use of fast shutter speeds, good for fast moving events, people and sports too. So, always buy the fastest lenses you can afford. The lenses listed above will handle many if not most of the average travel, tourism or location situations you are likely to encounter, which are landscapes, location portraits, people photography, architecture, and the odd still life against an interesting background.

> **Note:** *I do not recommend extreme range wide-angle to telephoto zoom lenses. They are strictly for casual holiday use by lazy snapshooters in my opinion. The reason I don't like them or use them are:*
>
> - These lenses are heavy, and hard to work with especially used as wide-angles.
> - They have smaller apertures than zooms with a lesser coverage, making low light or indoor photography without flash much more difficult.
> - They are prone to considerable "flare" (which causes light blips on film when shooting into, or close to the sun or other bright light source) because of the complexity of the optics.
> - Few zoom lenses are noted for their sharpness, most that are extremely sharp are in the two to one zoom ratio. Probably no zoom is as sharp as the best single focal length lenses. For further information on lenses for specific jobs, see the section following Camera Systems, later in the chapter.

Important Accessories
All Serious Travel Photographers Should Own

These are not frills, but will make picture-taking in difficult to impossible situations possible.

Hand-Held Exposure Meters

Whether or not your cameras have sophisticated built in light meters (almost all modern 35mm single lens reflex cameras do), you will probably decide one day to own a hand-held exposure meter. If you decide to do it now, you'll avoid deciding later the hard way. Built-in camera meters can fail, and probably will do so if a camera is dropped, or given a hard knock. Dust, humidity and extreme cold can also cause meter failure. And today's hand-held meters measure incident as well as reflected light, flash (and strobe) exposures and more. A hand-held meter is picture insurance. I always carry at least one. (See Chapter Four, for specifics.)

Tripods

A good, sturdy, lightweight tripod that extends at least to your eye level is a "must" piece of equipment any serious travel photographer should own. Almost all good ones tilt from from side to side as well as front to back. (I especially like ball heads which are quick to level, see later in chapter.)

Low light, dusk and night shooting, the pre-composing of location portrait backgrounds, wildlife photography, and architecture and interior pictures are all dramatically improved when you habitually use a tripod. When you work with long lenses which are difficult to hold steady, a tripod will prevent many blurred, lost pictures.

A tripod is indispensable for composing still lifes on location, which you often have to do in professional travel photography. Whether it is the famous author's possessions arranged on his desk at the front of his study, or a delicious lobster dish posed in a formal dining room with chefs and waiters hovering behind, choose the point of view you want for the whole scene with the camera on a tripod. When you've got that right, arrange the foreground by moving from camera position to the still life set-up, improving the arrangement until it all looks great through the lens. There are many occasions when you need to make long exposures at a very small aperture, for great depth of field, or to cause color shift which intensifies colors at sunset or dusk. A tripod makes these things possible. And long lenses and medium and large format cameras should always be used on a tripod to guarantee sharp pictures.

My Tripod Recommendations:

- Bogen has a good range of sturdy, medium weight tripods, (their large format camera stands are widely used in studios).

- Gitzo manufactures equipment for the French military, space and aviation industries. Their tripods are precision made, and come in all sizes from minute six inch table-toppers to humongous eight footers for view cameras. I have two Gitzos. My Tota Luxe extends to five and a half feet, I use it with Gitzo's "Number One" ball head. (Ball heads make very slight adjustments easy, get one sturdy enough for your heaviest lenses.) If I need more height or am using a long, heavy lens or a 6x7cm camera I carry a Gitzo Reporter model, with a sturdy "Number Two" ball head, the tripod extends to seven feet. I often use it to shoot down onto food, but it's heavy. (If you are going to France, pick up your Gitzo there; I saved by buying my big one at the huge Fnac discount store in Montparnasse.)

- Linhof makes very fine super-light tripods, primarily used for large format cameras.

- The Slik tripod line is well made, good for the budget conscious; and Sliks come in many different heights and weights.

- The Tiltall tripod is a classic design, quick to set up, now marketed by Uniphot. It is a seven footer which has given me no trouble in 20 years of carrying it round the world. It's relatively light for it's height, and very sturdy. It's my second Tiltall, I froze the first solid by using it to photograph models playing in the ocean off Copacabana Beach for twelve hours, and not washing the salt water off immediately. The aluminum corroded. Beware! There is now a Tiltall Junior model, which I have not used.

Why It Is Worth Carrying a Small Flash Unit

If you add a small flash that can be used off camera to your kit, you will increase your versatility considerably. Even a tiny, simple flash can help you get good pictures in low light, and "fill" ugly shadows in contrasty light. Once you've learned how to use a small flash well, you'll carry it everywhere. (See Chapter Seven, Photographic Lighting.)

What Equipment Should a Professional Travel Photographer Own?

Professional assignments call for quality equipment, carefully selected for reliability, durability and ease of use. It is always a pleasure to own beautiful things and I enjoy my cameras, which I think of as elegant tools. Good tools make doing difficult things much easier. Which top brand camera system you choose is not so important (except perhaps for prestige purposes and resale value) as sticking to the same system and building on it, buying classic lenses and not loading yourself down with unnecessary weight or gadgets.

To shoot assignments, you will need an absolute minimum of two or three camera bodies that accept the same interchangeable lenses. You will often need to work with several different focal length lenses at a time, or shoot both color and black and white film at the same time, and even the best equipment can malfunction, and accidents do happen, usually in the middle of a shoot, far from a repair service.

My Choice of Camera System

I own two different groups of camera bodies. I have four Nikon FM2's (fully mechanical except for a built in meter). This camera is light, small enough for my hands, the metering is extremely accurate, and the in-camera meter is the simplest to see and adjust that I have ever used. I now use my FM2's mostly in bad weather or when rugged conditions make me feel insecure about relying totally on electronics. I would certainly take them on any assignment where I thought electronic camera repair would be hard to find. For my personal photography I walk around New York with a couple of FM2 bodies and two lenses— a (manual) 28mm f/2 and a (manual) 43-80mm f/3.5 zoom.

When I'm shooting a job I now use, and love, Nikon N8008 electronic cameras. I take three bodies (sometimes with one mechanical FM2 as a spare). All my cameras are black models, and I put black tape over the nameplates so they are very inconspicuous, and don't say "expensive camera, steal me."

Why Several Camera Bodies are Needed

I usually work with three camera bodies at the same time, with different lenses, and I rotate the cameras (especially when shooting an assignment) to minimize losing all-important pictures in case of equipment malfunction.

Cameras are not fragile, but if you don't rotate, that will be the day a shutter starts to act up or you have an accident. (I did drop an N8008 two feet onto a dry lawn in England last year. The camera and lens mount both needed considerable work.)

Some photographers, including the marvellous travel photographer Jake Rajs, use and rotate four, five or six bodies at a time. People who shoot a lot of sports, like top photojournalist Ken Regan, work with a lot of cameras, because changing film in the middle of peak action would mean important shots lost. (And, have you ever tried to change film while riding uphill on a donkey, or with numb fingers in a snowstorm or on a hurricane ride at an amusement park?)

Features and Options for Electronic 35mm SLR Cameras, for Professional Use

You should choose:

❑ Internal TTL (through the lens) metering with a choice of full-frame averaging, or center weighted or spot metering, for very accurate exposure.

❑ Aperture priority operation, for creative control of depth of field.

❑ Shutter priority operation, for creative control of movement and for long exposures combining available light and flash "fill" (see Chapter Seven).

❑ Program operation, for very fast changing or contrasty lighting conditions, or (sometimes) outdoors at night. (Dedicated electronic cameras require a special cable release for time exposures.)

❑ Fully manual operation, for creative variations in exposure and depth of field (I use my program cameras on manual more often than not.)

❑ Auto focus, especially useful in poor light.

❑ Manual focus, which is important when subjects are moving in different directions.

❑ Double exposure provision, for creative effects.

❑ Depth of field preview button, to preview "flare" blips as well as zone of sharp focus.

❑ Hot shoe on camera for flash unit, for a slave "trigger" as well as a flash.

❑ Self timer (put self in picture; sets off long exposures without shake.)

❑ Bulb shutter speed setting for indefinitely long exposures.

❑ High shutter flash (or strobe) "sync" speed (best is 1/250 of a second with current 35mm SLR cameras). This is important for daylight flash "fill" (see Chapter Seven).

❑ Internal motor drive (or provision for one). This allows concentration on the subject; also a requirememnt for sports and other fast action photography.

❑ A "sync" or PC cord outlet for strobe shooting (see Chapter Seven). (My N8008's don't have one. They require an adaptor on the hot shoe, the only flaw in a great camera!)

❑ Cameras with all these features are at the top, or close to the top of each manufacturer's line. All the features listed above will contribute to making the best possible photographs and are not just "gimmicks" or sales features.

35mm SLR Camera Systems

35mm single lens reflex (SLR) cameras are used by the great majority of professional and amateur travel photographers and many photojournalists. Lightweight, and with an unmatched range of lenses and accessories, they have probably accounted for 90% of all professional travel pictures taken since they first came on the scene in the late 1950's.

The most popular 35mm single lens reflex camera systems used by professionals are Nikon and Canon, with (in alphabetical order) Contax, Minolta, Olympus and Pentax close behind.

Leica, of course, is famous for both rangefinder and single lens reflex cameras. The former, which are whisper quiet in operation are beloved by many news photographers and photojournalists.

I feel that the ease of viewing makes SLR's infinitely preferable to rangefinder cameras for travel/location photography, where you often want to preview depth of field and are usually working in places where somewhat noisy camera shutters are not a problem. And you can rent a "blimp" that deadens sound if noisy shutters are a problem (during performances, for instance).

All of the above systems include many camera models, a wide range of lenses, tele-extenders and close-up attachments, flash units, motors, etc. Some systems offer underwater housings, photomicroscopy attachments and more. All of these camera manufacturers have excellent or very good support services for photographers; some loan equipment to professionals in emergencies or for special needs, all provide detailed literature on their products, as well as technical advice and support. (For addresses of recommended equipment manufacturers, see Chapter Twenty.)

Investigate Different Brands Before You Commit to a System

A camera system represents a major investment, which you will have for a long time. Once you have bought a few lenses, you are generally locked in, because each system (regrettably but understandably) has different lens mounts. My strong recommendation is that you do as much research as possible before you buy. Read manufacturers' literature, talk to other photographers about what they like/don't like about their system, visit a photographic trade show, shop at a few different camera dealers, and ask questions. Rent (or if you can, borrow) camera models and lenses you are seriously considering. Find out how the cameras feel, both in terms of ease of operation, weight, size and "fit" in your hands. Some cameras are simpler to operate than others. You may love or hate digital readouts as opposed to the more traditional shutter speed dials. You may do 90% of your photography on "Program" setting, or prefer to make all the decisions about shutter speed, f/stop and focus and depth of field yourself.

If your budget is tight, you may choose to start with a lower price camera model of a system you want. Make sure though, that you will be able to use the same lenses when you add high-range cameras with more features later. Consider getting a good used second or third camera of your preferred model, if needed. (First have it thoroughly checked by a good repair shop!)

Buying Equipment

At one time, traveling photographers could save big bucks by buying cameras and lenses in Japan, Hong Kong or Singapore. This is no longer true. At the time of writing the exchange rate for the dollar is so low that the cheapest places to buy most camera equipment anywhere in the world (to the best of my knowledge) are the deep discount dealers in New York City, with professional dealers here not too much higher than discounters because of intense competition. Many good New York stores have toll-free 800 and fax numbers. The stores where I buy are listed later in the chapter.

In 25 years of travelling professionally, I have never found that buying at duty free airport shops at places like Saint Thomas, Schiphol or Shannon saved me money over New York dealers.

Choosing a Dealer

I recommend paying a few bucks more and acquiring your equipment from a professional photography dealer. Building a long-term relationship with a good dealer can be very helpful. You may get loaners, first shot at a hard to find "hot" item, a good trade in, good used stuff, or just good advice on what's available for a specific need. The U.S. warranties you get with authorized dealer purchases are valuable if you have equipment problems, although I personally have never needed to use one in my 30 years of serious photography. (Note: Discounters who sell so called "gray-market"—imported without U.S. warranties—equipment offer their own store warranties. Check warranties and be sure when buying from such stores that the merchandise is returnable.)

Top professional stores offer the chance to browse, handle and compare equipment, and many give outstanding service. I buy many items from Ken Hansen Photographic in New York. They offer special services. For instance, they often loan out equipment being considered, hold "teach-ins" on equipment, and offer leases on high-end lighting equipment. And, the used stuff they sell is in top condition. Such services are worth a reasonable price differential in my opinion.

A few deep discount stores are also good, but you must check out discounters carefully, particularly as to their returns policy. If dealing with discounters, know exactly what you want before you buy, and don't accept substitutes. Find out what warranty the store offers to replace the warranty offered by authorized dealers. I have dealt for years with B&H Photo, a deep discounter who caters to professionals in New York, and have returned items to them with no difficulty. And, much appreciated, they don't try to sell me something else when they are out of something I want. (I have never, though, dealt with them by mail.) Find professional photo dealers by looking at advertisers in photographers' association bulletins, *Photo District News* and of course classified phone books.

Let the Buyer Beware

I'm sorry to have to say I do not have the highest opinion of some camera salespeople. In certain mass-market camera stores they seem to take the short-term view of getting the highest possible commission, without thought to the advantages of building up a long term relationship with a customer. Also, some photo store salespeople are past, future or part-time photographers, and have preferences for their own equipment, which may or may not be right for your needs. Don't automatically take what any salesperson says as gospel, don't let them intimidate you with their use of a few abstruse technical terms, and don't get talked out of a system, camera or lens you really want or need.

Recently, three New York stores told my friend Pat Collyns that the small bounce flash unit recommended to her by the Pentax Customer Service department did not exist. Salesmen in two stores tried to sell her a bigger, heavier, more expensive one. One guy told her that it was impossible to take even small group pictures with a small flash! Only by continuing the search did she locate the recommended flash in the fourth store she tried. It was exactly what she wanted. The sad thing is, the other stores are otherwise honest!

If you should decide to come to New York for the Photo Expo (held in November or December each year), to buy equipment, to shoot, or to take a class or vacation, stay well clear of tourist-trap, rip-off, combined camera, electronic and luggage stores. There are quite a few here, many on Fifth Avenue between 34th and 57th Streets.

Because there may not be a good professional dealer within your easy reach, it may be a good idea to contact manufacturers' direct for the latest literature (and suggested list prices) if you can't get them locally. (See Chapter Twenty for addresses and phone numbers of major manufacturers recommended in this book.)

On Purchasing Equipment

Charge purchases on a major credit card whenever possible. This protects you in case there is any problem before you pay for the item. Some credit card companies double the warranty of the equipment, and may replace accidentally damaged, lost or stolen goods for a limited time after purchase. You can also add to your frequent flyer mileage with some credit card purchases. (Check with different credit card companies for up-to-the-minute details of what they offer.) Whenever you buy anything at any store, of course save all receipts, needed for returns, warranty repairs, for insurance purposes, and for tax deductions if you are professional. Complete and mail in warranties too.

Top 35mm Single Lens Reflex Camera Systems

These cameras are used by most professional travel photographers, and in my opinion are unequalled for travel/location work. 35mm SLR's are rugged, reasonably lightweight, and have the widest range of lenses and accessories of any camera system.

Nikon

This system is my choice. I have used Nikon cameras since I got my first model F's and lenses in 1967. I'm not being paid in any way to say this (nor are any of my other recommendations "commercials"). I use the Nikon because it is a rugged and very complete system which includes just about anything I'm ever likely to need. I treat cameras poorly, and my Nikon F's, F2's, FM2's and now 8008's have always been repairable when dropped, banged or otherwise maltreated.

Nikkor lenses in my opinion are unsurpassed for sharpness, and, important to me, Nikon has kept the same lens mount for many years. I can still use favorite older lenses (some had minor adaptations) with my newest electronic camera bodies. I expect to be able to go on doing so as new cameras appear. All Nikon SLR bodies, new or used, from basic to top of the line, take the same lens mounts, so if you start with an inexpensive model, you can move up later. I've sold or traded in older Nikon equipment when I acquired new autofocus models, and even shabby-looking Nikons have a high resale value. Nikon is also a "high prestige" camera, which may mean more to photographers starting out than it does to me now.

When I do a travel assignment, I take three or four camera bodies, which are exactly the same model, so that I do not have to think about where my fingers go when I am actually photographing. If I fumble, I miss the exact moment when a model laughs, or horse throws up its head, or the flag catches a puff of breeze, or some other fleeting thing that can make the average picture good and the very good picture great.

My current N8008 cameras are relatively small, motorized, fully automatic autofocus cameras with all the manual options I want. They are not too heavy, and I have found the TTL metering system gives good exposures in fast changing light. (I prefer to shoot on manual exposure based on experience outdoors. I "bracket" my shots slightly—see Chapter Four.)

I like the flash "fill" exposures I get with N8008's combined with its dedicated/TTL SB24 (a bounce unit) and its small SB23 (a simple flash unit). However, I still use a flashmeter and test exposures with a Polaroid camera, or both, when doing any serious lighting on assignment. (See also Chapter Seven.)

Nikon cameras continually evolve—the N8008S model now has faster autofocus, and a new spot-metering option. I will get one as soon as I need a new camera body. My only complaint about the N8008 (and N8008S) is that they do not have an outlet for a flash synchronization/PC cord for use with strobe, a silly omission I think Nikon should rectify. There is a hot shoe special adaptor needed for using Nikon's TTL flash units off camera. A different adaptor is used for strobe.

Why didn't I buy top of the line Nikon F4's? Size, weight and money, not necessarily in that exact order. Cameras are fine tools to me, no more and no less. The N8008 does everything I need, and is easier for me to hold than the F4. I usually work alone, for long days; so ounces and pounds that I don't need to carry are that much energy saved. The price difference was certainly a consideration. I don't want to travel with equipment that I feel has to be treated like jewelry.

Basic Lenses for Travel Photography

I take the following Nikkor lenses wherever I go on any job:

20mm f/2.8 autofocus

28mm f/2 (My favorite, normal, lens. It's not autofocus, but the fastest 28mm lens I can get. I've owned three of them.)

35 to 70mm f/2.8 zoom autofocus

80 to 200mm f/4 zoom telephoto (an older, non-autofocus lens, it is very sharp, and lighter and easier for me to hold than the newer auto focus model).

Additional Lenses for Specific Situations:

For available and low light, particularly in factories, etc., and sometimes for indoor portraits, I use two very fast lenses:

- ❏ 35mm f/1.4 (a nice sharp, fast lens).

- ❏ 80mm f/1.8 (bought in Japan in 1969, it is the sharpest lens I have ever owned; too sharp sometimes, it shows up every pore on a portrait).

For parties, or events where I will be shooting a lot of quick TTL flash pictures in dim light:

- ❏ 24-50mm f/3.5-4.5 zoom autofocus—this is what they call in the travel trade BA (Best Available) Nikkor lens in this zoom range.

- ❏ 28mm f/2.8 autofocus.

For landscapes and architecture:

- ❏ 15mm f/5.6 rectilinear super wide angle lens (it does not distort if carefully used; a very nice lens).

- ❏ 28mm f/4 PC (perspective correction) lens (I wish Nikon made a wider-angle one).

For closeups, nature, copying, photographing off a computer, TV, etc:

- ❏ 55mm f/3.5 macro (my oldest lens, it's very sharp; bought in 1967, it still works fine).

For animal and bird photography and sport (I am not a specialist), compressed views of cities, details of monuments and buildings, even sometimes for interesting portraits:

- ❏ 500mm f/8 mirror telephoto lens (I like this one a lot, bought in 1972, it is very light, sharp, and still works fine).

❏ 2x tele-extender, it doubles focal length of my tele-zoom lenses. (It costs two stops in exposure, I carry it almost everywhere, it's very light).

You may have noticed that I list three different 28mm lenses. This is my favorite focal length, I use it as my "normal" lens. I like it for my specialty, people in a landscape, for many interior and street shots, and because of its considerable depth of field at wide apertures.

Other photographers would certainly make other choices for their basic lenses, everyone develops their own way of working, and favorite lenses.

Nikon also makes the professional 35mm rangefinder underwater Nikonos camera. I no longer own one.

Canon

Canon is the other truly great and extremely complete single lens reflex camera system in my opinion, rivalling (some say surpassing) Nikon. Canon cameras too have very high prestige, and a high resale value. Many of my professional friends swear by the top Canon EOS 1 autofocus model, the lenses focus extremely fast. EOS cameras have new lens mounts, older Canon lenses don't fit EOS cameras, but the EOS system has bodies in all price ranges, so you can move up with those cameras. I'd kill for a couple of Canon lenses—the f/3.5 20-35mm zoom and the 24mm f/3.5 Tilt and Shift lens. I have used photographer friends' Canon T90's occasionally and think the in-between shutter speeds, and 1/3 stop lens click stops are very useful indeed. (These are available on some EOS cameras also.) I like the EOS 1's included data backs. (Data backs are optional on my N8008's.)

Other Major Camera Systems

The **Contax** SLR system is also very high prestige. Contax (now owned by Yashica) is a famous German-designed camera with superb lenses.

The **Leica SLR** has very fine workmanship and the lenses are legendary, but the price is very high.

Minolta pioneered auto focus cameras and lenses, their popular current autofocus models work very fast. You may like the "program extension cards" offered on some Minoltas, I personally don't care for them. (Minolta makes excellent meters too.)

Olympus is noted for cameras that are compact, and well crafted. Another woman photographer I know likes Olympus because she has small hands, she says they "fit" her comfortably. Olympus has some good lenses, including a 24mm PC lens which I'd like to have also.

Pentax. My first camera system was Pentax and I used three bodies and four lenses hard and beat them up for for about five years. My best friend has taken her successive Pentaxes on dozens of vacation and business trips with her husband. Her current Spotmatic is five years old, and hasn't needed repairs yet. Many photography majors start by using budget-priced, all-manual Pentaxes. They are good for learning photographic fundamentals.

Good 35mm "Point and Shoot" Cameras

For Aunt Minnie, backup, fun, and some professional uses too:

Canon, Chinon, Contax, Fuji, Konica (which has a neat water-resistant model), Nikon, Minolta (which has a dual-range water-resistant model), Olympus, Pentax, and Yashica all make nice little cameras designed to slip into your pocket or pocket book. Get a model with a built-in flash that can be used in daylight.

I have a small, non-zoom model for those rare occasions when I want to carry only a camera that slips into pocket or pocketbook. My Nikon Action Touch (no longer made but you may find a reconditioned one) has a 38mm f/2.8 lens, (it's waterproof to ten feet, all I now ever want to go down). I use it at the beach, or sometimes in heavy rain or spray.

Other Useful Cameras

Polaroid. You can use an adjustable shutter and lens Polaroid camera to preview pictures and test lighting and exposure and set ups (see medium format, below) or get an NPC Polaroid back for your 35mm SLR. These were developed by Marty Forscher, founder of Professional Camera Repair Service here in New York. It is still going, owned by two of Marty's former employees (see Chapter Twenty). I personally find 35mm Polaroid prints hard to read and prefer my old folding Polaroid 110B model, which gives 3 1/4" by 4 1/2" prints. (These and other folding Polaroids can still be found used; see medium format cameras, below. For more on using Polaroid film for testing, see Chapters Four, Five, and Seven.)

The **Widelux** (see also panoramic cameras listed later in the chapter) is a professional 35mm panoramic camera. Amateurs may like Kodak or Fuji's inexpensive throwaway panoramic cameras; they make surprisingly good prints if you want to try panoramic-style photography without a big investment.

Medium Format Cameras

These cameras make nice big negatives, which many professional advertising, corporate and stock photographers are favoring today. Medium format is used for much advertising photography. I personally find that the one "people" thing that 35mm does not do well is group portraits; and often use a 6x7cm Pentax for formal portraits and large group shots (and occasionally for landscapes too).

If you have to show a lot of small heads in group shots of people, grain shows even when using Kodachrome 25 with 35mm format, but a 6x4.5cm, 6x6cm or

6x7cm camera takes care of the problem very nicely. The 6x6cm format permits easy horizontal or vertical cropping without moving the camera, the 6x7cm is the ideal "landscape" format. Some 6x7cm's now have revolving backs.

Mamiya 6x7cm cameras are especially popular with top professionals, they make medium-format rangefinder cameras too.

Pentax makes a good budget 6x7cm; I own one, and use it for portraits and groups sometimes, the lenses are very sharp.

I hardly need to describe the legendary **Hasselblad** 6x6cm, which went to the moon and is beloved by many advertising photographers.

Bronica SLR's are well-priced and favored by many students.

Fuji makes medium format SLR and rangefinder cameras, and panoramic cameras too.

Rolleiflex makes medium format SLR's today, their classic twin-lens reflex cameras, while still available used, are now highly-priced collector's items.

In alphabetical order then, Bronica, Fuji, Hasselblad, Mamiya, Minolta, Pentax and Rolleiflex make fine medium format cameras in different price ranges with many different options.

Polaroid medium format cameras and backs include older 110A, 110B and 185 and 195 models (which have adjustable lenses and shutter speeds; take Type 42 roll film (or 3x1/4x 1/4" pack film if adapted) and can still be found used. Polaroid's current press-type 600SE model, and a very similar Minolta camera both take 3x1/4x4 1/4" filmpacks.

Caution: For shake-free results, and sharp pictures with medium format cameras, always use them on a tripod unless you are shooting at a very high shutter speed, or using flash or strobe!

Large Format

My first job in photography was as assistant to a man who didn't like doing still life, but took those jobs when they came in for obvious reasons. I spent three months on a tall ladder looking down into an 8x10" camera, arranging watches for catalog pages. I got very good at moving tiny bits of black, silver and gold paper around, and learned I could never be a still life photographer. Perhaps if that hadn't happened, I'd be keener on view cameras than I am. But I admire the people who care enough to travel with large format cameras. They are a hardy breed, many today are fine art, corporate or stock specialists. Travel photographers are most likely to use 4x5" flatbed folding field cameras because they are compact. The design hasn't changed all that much since the late 19th century. Technical cameras and monorail cameras with elaborate swings and tilts are used mainly by architectural and still life specialists.

In the spirit of Maxime du Camp and Francis Frith and their successors, I salute the dedication and strong backs of all of you who are thinking about large format, and list some well-known makes.

Calumet/Cambo are Calumet's brand name view cameras. Workhorse studio favorites for years, they now make wood and metal 4x5" and 8x10" cameras in different price ranges. People who want to try large format inexpen-

Panoramic Photography

You can have fun with Kodak or Fuji throwaway cameras, make overlapping prints, or, use a specialist panoramic camera. To use these well requires practice. Keep the horizontal and vertical lines level.

For serious panoramic photography, very popular today, Fuji, Linhof and Widelux are the best-known brands of camera. I suggest renting and trying out expensive panoramic cameras before buying.

Some people, like top corporate/stock photographer Robert Herko, use a 6x12cm roll-film back on a large format camera, for a panoramic effect plus full control of swings and tilts.

For much more on this whole subject, read and see Joseph Meehan's *Panoramic Photography*.

sively should look out for an old used wooden Calumet flatbed camera. They can be found at used equipment dealers. I own a 4x5" monorail Calumet, and three lenses for it. I use it in the studio for still lifes sometimes, portraits occasionally, but it's too heavy for me to take on location. Maybe when I have time to think more about art, I'll try it in the field.

Horseman has been making folding flat-bed metal 4x5" cameras for ever.

Linhof is famous for superbly crafted technical rangefinder cameras (used by many architectural photographers) in various formats and panoramic cameras too.

Polaroid makes 4x5" and 8x10" camera backs (for making Polaroid prints) for view cameras. (See also 35mm and medium format, earlier in the chapter; also Chapters Four, Five and Seven.)

The **Sinar Bron** is probably the most complete view camera system. 4x5" and 8x10" monorail cameras; incredible swings and tilts, film plane meters etc, etc..

Toyo makes rugged metal flatbed field cameras in the popular 4x5" and 8x10" formats, and in the (rare today) 5x7" landscape format too. Busy corporate/stock photographer (and technical whiz) Robert Herko told me he uses the Toyo 45A model for most of his assignments, (he likes various-size Mamiya rollfilm backs for it). Bob says the Toyo is the only field camera that has stood up to the demands he makes of it.

Wista makes 4x5" and 8x10" flatbed and monorail views in wood and metal, and a folding 4x5" rangefinder camera too.

Zone VI of Vermont markets beautifully-made classic wooden 4x5" and 8x10" flatbed view cameras.

Roll-film backs in many sizes are made for 4x5" and 8x10" cameras, especially by **Mamiya.**

There are too many large format lenses to discuss here, but **Schneider** optics are renowned. For more information on view cameras, backs and lenses, see your professional photo dealer, or contact camera manufacturers direct.

Gyro-Stabilizers

Gyro-stabilizers are used when low light means long exposures are needed, and a tripod and/or flash are not appropriate, most often for aviation photography (see Chapter Fourteen.) Gyro-stabilizers are also suitable for shooting from moving vehicles, boats or, if you are an expert rider, horseback. They permit sharp hand-held exposures down to about one second. They are expensive but can be rented from some professional photo dealers. When you use one, practice before you shoot that first job, they are a little tricky to get the hang of initially. Ken Labs manufactures the Kenyon gyro-stabilizer for different types of camera. Contact them at P.O. Box 128, Old Lyme, CT 06371, phone (203) 434-1619. They will send information and a list of dealers.

Taking Care of Cameras and Lenses

Cameras and lenses are precision instruments and, without being ridiculous, should be protected as much as possible when traveling. I don't use leather camera or lens cases (they are heavy, clumsy and slow to undo or unpack, and take up too much room in my kit) but I travel long distances with my autofocus lenses protected in soft chamois pouches with drawstring tops; these take up much less room when not in use than the hard lens cases supplied by manufacturers. Some people protect lenses with thick cotton socks. I keep narrow nylon straps on all my camera bodies. I use body caps and keep the camera strap wound around the body to further protect it. New "wraps"—squares made of padded material with Velcro closures—come in different sizes and are great for wrapping cameras, lenses, flash units and more before you put them together in under plane seat hard cases. Domke is one manufacturer; or, make your own wraps.

Clear filters on lenses protect delicate surfaces, I use very slightly pink Skylight 1A filters on all my lenses all the time instead of lens covers. The warming effect is pleasant with most films, if not, I remove the filter when shooting. (Some people prefer UV filters.) Use back lens caps whenever lenses are carried off camera. A scratch on a rear lens element is even worse than a scratch on the front. (I don't use lens shades, they get in my way.)

A Great Catalog

The long established Chicago based photographic equipment manufacturer and dealer Calumet has a catalog that is a treasure trove of information on just about every make, model and format of camera. It also lists lighting equipment, accessories, filters, film and more. The catalog costs $5, (refundable when you buy) sometimes it's available free at photo shows or their stores. Calumet sells their own brands and just about everybody else's too. Get the catalog by mail, from 890 Supreme Drive, Bensenville IL 60106. (Phone 1-800-225-8638) or from their Chicago, New York and Los Angeles stores.

Filters protect lenses from dust and rain as well as scratches, and protect the filter threads from being bent out of shape by sharp knocks. In fact, I've dropped lenses several times and smashed only the filter, which absorbs some of the impact. (See also camera repair and insurance, Chapter Fifteen.)

Camera Bags, Travel Cases and Luggage Carts

I use different camera bags for different purposes. When I want to look as smart as possible, or as though I'm carrying a unisex handbag (where cameras are not permitted) I use a smart black cowhide bag made by Minolta. I have bought three of them on different trips to Japan, I've never been able to find one here. When I want to work with several lenses off my shoulder, I carry them in a canvas Domke bag, mine is khaki and has a waterproof lining.

When travelling by plane I have a heavy cowhide bag that just fits under the seat. This bag looks respectable but is not too conspicuous. I bought it in Japan when I was photographing a very smart hotel and was ashamed of my luggage. I can carry three or four 35mm SLR camera bodies and about six lenses plus a hand-held meter, a few rolls of film and toiletries and a book for the journey onto the plane in this bag.

The leather bag holds my soft canvas Domke bag for working off my shoulder (if I don't pack that in my checked luggage) a sweater and and my courier-style flat document case—which is slim, about 4x6" and has a wrist strap and lots of zippered compartments for passport, tickets, travelers checks, business cards, eye glasses, a pen and currency. (I got it at the Frankfurt airport). Occasionally I still use a Halliburton aluminum under-plane-seat-sized case, but it looks like "expensive equipment" and worries me today in airports and hotel lobbies.

On the New York subway or other places where I want to look extremely inconspicuous I use a leather reinforced East-Pak backpack, to which I added a piece of foam at the bottom. (Quite a few friends use padded LowePro or Tenba backpacks designed especially for photographers.)

I ship my strobe equipment by air in a custom-made, metal-framed wooden case, that I bought used ten years ago. It will probably outlive me; I've added a lot more foam inside. (Calzone makes similar cases). I have a round fiberboard case which I use (stuffed with work clothes or foam) for shipping tripods and lightstands. I sometimes use a canvas Domke over shoulder tripod/lightstand bag.

I usually put clothes and personal things in a round canvas stuff bag. If I'm only carrying a tripod and a couple of lightstands and umbrellas, I put them in a padded Tenba tripod bag along with my personal effects bag, inside a large padlocked army-type duffel. (The airlines don't mind how big or heavy a bag is as long as there is only one, and I save excess baggage charges.)

I have had a number of wheeled luggage carts (essential if you want to avoid major back problems, because in many places, especially European train stations, porters are an endangered species). I seem to destroy or leave carts where I can't get them back quite regularly, so I buy the only cheap ones one that hold up, a PFC model rated for 225 lbs. I had a good aluminum Folda Truk once, but, sadly it was taken from a luggage compartment under a bus in Yugoslavia. (See also Chapters Seven and Fifteen).

Maintaining and Repairing Your Equipment

However tenderly you care for your cameras (I don't) travel is rough on equipment, and your camera bodies should be checked out about once every six months, and immediately after working in dust, damp, or extreme heat or cold for any length of time, or of course if you have dropped something. Also, shutters can slow down or vary, especially on mechanical cameras. Good camera repair services can give you a chart of the actual shutter speeds on each of your camera bodies, which will save a lot of bracketing exposures. It is a good idea to have each body notched on the film plane so that you can quickly identify a malfunctioning camera; your repair service can take care of this also. I use Professional Camera Repair Service and also Flash Clinic (for flash and strobes), both here in New York, (see Chapter Twenty). Other repair services advertise in *The Photo District News,* or can be recommended by your equipment manufacturer.

It has been my experience that there are many good repair shops for mechanical cameras, even in the most unexpected places overseas. Find them in emergencies through hotel concierges, camera stores, local studio and newspaper photographers, and classified phone books.

Repairing electronic cameras is more of a problem; to fix them you should in most cases use only the manufacturer's authorized repair service. Ask your camera manufacturer for their worldwide list before you travel.

Shipping Equipment Home for Repair

You can also air express carefully packed cameras home for repairs. Ship cameras to the manufacturer or your favorite repair place. Professional Camera Repair Service here in New York (see Chapter Twenty) gets in cameras from all over to be fixed. Mark packages "Broken Optical Equipment, for Repair". DHS, Federal Express and other shipping services will help you take care of paperwork details. (See also Chapter Fifteen and Chapter Sixteen.)

Use Mechanical Cameras for Ease of Repair

If you are going somewhere remote for a very long stay, consider taking along several reliable mechanical camera bodies (like my Nikon FM2's) for the likelihood of being able to find local repair shops fairly easily (and you won't have to worry about batteries, except for the camera meters).

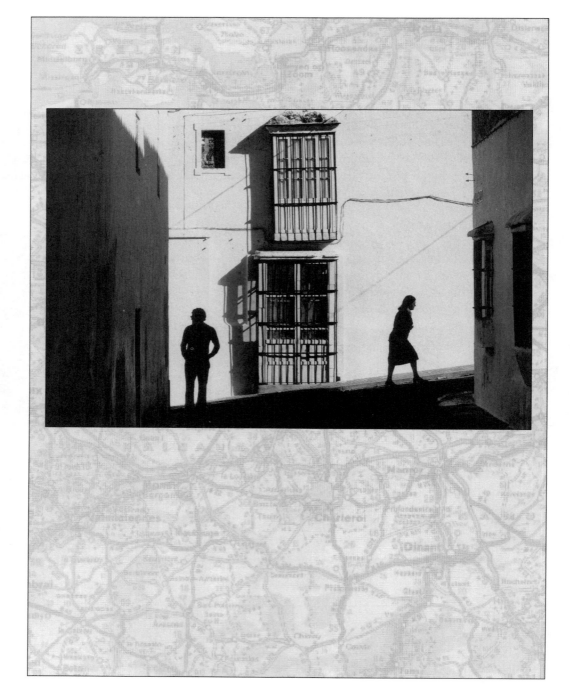

Chapter 4

Exposure and Metering

The aim of good exposure is either to reproduce a subject as accurately as possible on film; or to express a desired mood, in which case you will probably break some rules.

Black-and-White Exposure

Most photographers' ideal black-and-white prints are fine to moderate grain, with deep blacks, all tones of gray and subtle details in the almost-white highlight areas. A good negative can record seven f/stops, but a good black-and-white print can only reproduce a tonal range from light to dark of about 32 to 1, or a 5 f/stop range.

One of the greatest of photographers in terms of technique alone was Ansel Adams, whose "zone system" (for exposing and developing black-and-white film to place gray tones where he wanted them) is widely taught in photo schools. With profound respect to the achievements of Mr. Adams, some lesser practitioners have made mastery of the zone system an end in itself, which it should not be. You can make fine black-and-white negatives and prints without knowing a thing about the zone system as long as you expose and develop accurately.

I sometimes bracket black-and-white film when I want particularly subtle effects, and I sometimes "push" and "pull" black-and-white film (increase or decrease ISO speed rating and development time) about 20% in very flat or very harsh light to increase or reduce contrast; I call that the poor man's zone system.

ISO, ASA and DIN

Film speeds are rated by the International Standards Organization (ISO). This ISO rating (speed index) has replaced the old (equivalent) American Standards Association (ASA) ratings. In Europe, film speed was formerly measured by the DIN scale, which is why you see DIN scales as well as ISO scales on some film boxes and on many older cameras, exposure meters and flash units.

Color Transparency (Slide) Film Exposure

Accurate exposure is essential with all color transparency films, although some adjustment of seriously over-or-under-exposed transparencies is possible with duping and retouching, especially with today's scanners and computer programs like Adobe Photoshop. Such corrections are expensive, and clients don't want to pay for them unless the pictures are otherwise truly great or unique.

Electronic scanners used for color separation and reproduction today can add a slight amount of color to an image more easily than they can subtract it, which has changed the exposure habits of some photographers, including myself. I used to go for deeply saturated, about one half to one stop under-exposed pictures. I now go for a picture that is perfectly, "normally" exposed. Some photographers, especially fashion and beauty specialists, like a "high key" look—a one-half to one stop over-exposed effect. (Over-exposed slides look thin, pale and washed out; under-exposed transparencies look dark, greenish and dense.)

Color transparency films have the capacity to reproduce a range of highlights to dark shadows of only about five f/stops. If you are shooting pictures that contain both blacks-and-whites, you had better decide which is more important to you; highlight or shadow detail, and concentrate on that, because today's color transparency films are very contrasty. Ideally, I like to use color film in soft "bounce" sunlight, or on hazy sunny days, where the lighting ratio is no more than about three to one, when you can get very beautiful color indeed. (Reflectors and flash "fill" light can be used to reduce contrast; see Chapters Six and Seven.)

Color Negative (Print) Film Exposure

Color negative has more latitude than transparency film (like black and white a good negative can record a seven stop range, but prints will only handle about five stops). Color prints can, of course, be color corrected with filters, and "dodged" and "burned in" when custom printing. Accurate exposure is necessary for optimal quality color prints.

If you have very difficult low or contrasty lighting problems to solve, using negative film may be your best bet; some newsmagazines and newspapers are now using negative film extensively, and reproducing from prints rather than transparencies. Be sure to check with the art director first though, many publications and location clients still use only color transparencies. There are fast color negative films in the 1000 ISO range, so there is often no reason to "push" film (increase the speed index and development time). If you need to, you can push Ektapress 1600 high-speed negative film two or more stops, to about 6400 ISO.

How Exposure Meters Work

Until you know a film or films very well (as I do with Kodachrome 25 exposures made outdoors) you will almost certainly rely on a built-in camera meter, or a handheld meter to determine exposure. (If meterless for any reason, you can look inside the film box for exposure guidance, or use the old "f/16" rule outdoors in sunshine—use the closest shutter speed to the film speed, and a lens aperture of f/16.)

As I have met some not too experienced photographers who have problems understanding exactly how meters work, here is a capsule description:

All types of meters (both reflected and incident types, see below) contain a light sensitive cell, and are designed to give correct exposure with "average" photographic subjects. In fact, meters are very slightly biased on the side of underexposure, so as to not overexpose color transparencies, and because until very recently most (not all) color photographers preferred a rich, saturated (very slightly underexposed) "look".

An average photographic subject is usually defined as including some sunny sky with clouds (but not the sun itself), some grass and trees and some people. It reflects back about 18% of the light that falls on it. If this scene were faithfully painted in oils, and all the wet colors were then quickly mixed together, they would come out a middle grayish shade.

Reflected-Light Meters

Reflected-light meters measure the light that reflects off the subject back to the meter. All built-in camera meters are reflected-light meters. Reflected-light meters of all types are aimed at the subject, normally from the position you choose to frame the composition, but from very close-up when the main subject is back-lit.

Because the color or tone of the subject influences the amount of light reflected from the subject to the meter, you have to think when metering very light or very dark subjects with a reflected-light meter. For instance, you should close down your lens one to one-and-a-half stops (or use a faster shutter speed) when metering reflected light off a black or very dark subject, or you will not get a true black, but a tone close to black 18% middle gray. You will have to open up your lens one or one-and-a-half stops (or lower the shutter speed) when metering reflected light off a white or extremely light subject like snow or white sand, or the white will reproduce underexposed, also somewhere close to 18% middle gray. (Note that this rule applies also to automatic flash units; which are also designed to render average subjects middle gray, see Chapter Seven, Photographic Lighting.)

Reflected-Light Metering With an
18% Gray Card or Gray Card Substitute

If you take careful reflected light readings off a standard 18% gray card (made by Kodak and others for a few dollars and sold at all photo stores) you will get good exposure no matter what the color or tone of the subject (with this method you are in effect turning your reflected meter into an incident meter, see below). Be sure to place and angle the card in the same light as the subject. Meter off the palm of your hand as a substitute for a gray card (correlate your palm with the card by testing; skin tones vary). My palm gives one-half stop under exposure compared to a gray card. You can take reflected meter readings off any reasonably "average"-toned subject and use them to get good exposure. Use a favorite mid-toned jacket or a mid-gray rock to meter a snow scene, not the snow itself. Use the gray sidewalk, not the neon signs to meter a bright-lit city street scene.

Exposing for Backlighting

Backlight (from behind your subject; see Chapter Six) is very, very pretty but can fool inexperienced photographers. Go in very close to take reflected-light meter-readings off brightly back-lit subjects, such as people against sunsets, or sunny windows. If you meter far from the point you plan to make the picture, you run a big risk of underexposed, even silhouetted, main subjects—even with modern electronic cameras that offer multi-point metering.

Use the Memory Lock button to meter up close for backlighting with program cameras (see camera manuals).

Multi-Point Metering

The most modern electronic cameras, when used with lenses designed for them, offer sophisticated "matrix" (or similar name) metering, plus center-weighted metering or spot metering (see below) as options. But even metering which measures several areas in the picture frame and which gives excellent exposure for most subjects, is not totally foolproof. If the subject is very light or very dark, or very contrasty (such as a small light-skinned face in a large dark room), "bracketing" (increasing or decreasing exposure with lens aperture, or shutter speed) is still advised. Some high-end cameras offer automatic bracketing, either built-in or as an option.

Dedicated Flash "Fill" Exposures

The light from dedicated/TTL flash units (see Chapter Seven), when used with the cameras they were designed for (and used in "fill" mode) is taken into consideration when making "flash fill" exposures in daylight, dawn or dusk, and brightly lit night scenes.

Incident-Light Meters

Incident light meters are all hand-held and are used from the subject position, aimed at the camera position. They measure the light that falls on the subject, and are therefore not influenced by the color or tone of the subject. Incident meters can be identified by their opaque white dome (which is what you aim at the camera). This type of meter was originally designed for use in studios with controlled light sources, and is still mostly used by studio photographers.

Incident meters can be used out of doors, but care must be taken to align the dome correctly. In a landscape for instance, an incident meter should be held vertically so it receives light from the sky and the ground. Overexposure will result if the dome is aimed down, reducing light from the sky; the film will be underexposed if the dome is aimed too much up, including too much light from the sky. (Flat white discs replace the domes when incident-light meters are used for flat-copy work.)

Note: Never use an incident meter when photographing distant subjects which are in different light from the light where you are working. If you are in shadow at the bottom of a mountain, and your subject is skiers on a distant sunlight slope for instance, an incident-light meter cannot possibly give you an accurate reading.

Why You Should Carry a Hand-Held-Exposure Meter

A hand-held meter is insurance in case your in-camera meters fail, or even (horrors) all read differently—it has happened to me. (In-camera meters can easily be damaged if the camera is dropped or knocked sharply.) Hand-held meters can do some things that in-camera meters can't. Some, with or without separate adaptors, can be used in either reflected or incident mode, useful if you are photographing the light filtering through stained-glass windows one day and a white on white still life in a restaurant the next.

Although some high-end cameras have built-in meters offering a spot metering option (narrow angle measurement) hand-held spot meters are still useful for sports, theatrical and concert/show photography. This is especially true when you are not using telephoto lenses.

Flash meters (almost essential if you work seriously with flash or strobe) and color temperature meters (which help determine filtration when using difficult mixed lighting in industrial locations) are very useful to essential for professional work.

Special-Purpose Meters

These are probably best rented to try before you buy.

Spotmeters

Spotmeters are hand-held reflected light meters that measure a very narrow angle of the subject, through a telephoto viewing lens, providing very accurate exposure readings for distant subjects.

Sports and news photographers and people who photograph a lot of rock shows, theater, dance and similar events where one cannot get close to meter find spotmeters extremely useful. (Note: Some electronic cameras today offer excellent internal spotmetering capacity when used with compatible long telephoto lenses.) The Gossen Ultra-Spot meter is very easy to read; exposure can be read while looking through the eyepiece.

Avoiding Common Exposure Errors

Dead meters can't read exposures. Check meter and camera batteries before starting any important or long trip. Always carry spare batteries; many meters use hard-to-find sizes; common batteries like AA's are often expensive at tourist sites.

Remember that all built-in camera meters measure the light that reflects off the subject, that all meters are designed to reproduce average scenes, and that they can't think. Bracket (vary) exposures.

When using an incident-light meter (which measures the light falling on the subject) take care to align the white dome correctly. (See earlier in this chapter and the meter manual.)

Avoid photographing people and scenes in partial bright sun and partial deep shadow. Color transparency film especially can't handle those extremes of contrast. Move your subject or angle to full sun or open shade for better results.

If possible wait for the light to change, or use a reflector or "fill" flash to lighten close shadow areas.

Remember that meters are designed to avoid overexposing transparencies. If your camera shutter speeds are accurate, you can save film by only bracketing for a half-stop over-exposure for the most flat-lit of subjects.

Electronic camera shutters are very accurate, you can trust the marked speeds unless your exposures are obviously way off. Mechanical camera shutter speeds should be checked before you go on a big trip, or every six months or so. (They can be slow, which can give you consistent over-exposure.) A good repair shop can give you charts of your cameras' actual shutter speeds.

Meters and camera shutters are somewhat fragile. Have your camera or hand-held meter checked out immediately if you drop it or bang it hard.

Study your camera, flash or meter manual again if still in doubt.

Don't forget to set film speed correctly on meters, manual cameras and flash!

Check all film-speed (ISO) settings regularly even when shooting with electronic cameras and dedicated flashes that read film casette DX codes.(The automatic film-speed index can be accidentally altered too easily on some cameras; I have taped the DX over-ride buttons on my Nikon 8008's for that reason!)

Allow for filter/gel factors (see Chapter Five) when using hand-held meters.

Use the same film outdoors consistently; you will soon learn how to expose it correctly under normal conditions without being dependent on a meter.

If shooting slide and print film, or color and black-and white with two cameras at the same time, use identical speed films for both!

Set the camera shutter on sync speed (or any speed below sync) when exposing for flash pictures, or part of the image will be blacked-out.

Choose S (shutter priority) setting and slow shutter speeds to include some background detail in low-light flash pictures.

Use rear-curtain sync setting to minimize "ghosts" with flash "fill" at low shutter speeds. (See your camera and flash manual and also Chapter Seven).

Flash/Strobe Meters

Flash meters can be incident or reflectance meters (some are both). They measure the very short burst of light from any small flash or large strobe unit. Flash meters can be used to measure available light also. Depending on the features offered by the flash meter you choose, it can be used with or without a sync cord to measure available light, or flash/strobe light, or both combined. Some flash meters measure cumulative flashes, and available light, at all shutter speeds; and can be used for calculating combination flash and time exposures. My hand-held meter of choice is a Minolta III flashmeter (now replaced by the similar but not identical Minolta IV) that also measures available light, and flash/available light combined at all shutter speeds. I also have a Sekonic Digi-Lite F that is almost (not quite) as versatile. (See also Chapter Three).

Color Temperature Meters

Minolta makes a three-color temperature meter that is a valuable research tool It can be set for use with daylight or tungsten film, or with films of slightly different color (Kelvin) temperatures. It measure the amounts of red, green and blue light reaching the meter and advises the amount of orange or blue Light Balancing, and/or magenta or cyan Color Compensating filtration needed to balance the light source with the film type being used. (Note: This color temperature meter does not measure exposure.)

Color meters can't replace filtration tests, because films have different inherent characteristics, and color variations of film are caused by many things in addition to the film emulsion and the color temperature of the light source. For instance, lenses have very slightly different colors, labs vary, and run differently on different days. Long exposures can cause color shift, so color temperature meters cannot eliminate careful color testing.

If you use a color temperature meter without advance film emulsion, lighting, filtration and processing lab tests, you should get acceptable to good, not perfect, color. Color meters are most popular with location specialists who must almost daily deal with difficult mixed light sources in factories and industrial locations.

To use a color temperature meter, you must own a set of gelatin Light Balancing and Color Compensating Filters. (See also Chapter Five.)

"Bracketing" Exposures and "Pushing" and "Pulling" Film

Despite knowing my films and flash/strobe units well, and checking my camera shutter speeds periodically, and metering carefully, I "bracket" (vary) color slide exposures whenever possible. I don't feel there is any other way to get the most beautiful possible pictures. Some color subjects may look best saturated and rich, others need a very slightly overexposed or "high-key" effect.

I sometimes bracket black-and-white by full f/stops (see above) because over or under exposed black-and-white pictures are very hard to print, and the loss in grain quality is considerable. By over exposing and under developing black-and-white by 20% you can reduce contrast in very bright light; by decreasing exposure and increasing development by 20% in flat light you can increase contrast.

Bracketing costs film and money certainly but not as much as lost pictures. Especially with color film the difference between perfect and almost perfect exposure can make a great difference to a photograph.

I use "normal" exposures, plus one-half stop over and under exposure brackets in average light conditions when shooting color, because I like rich, saturated color. In very contrasty light I add a half stop over exposure bracket.

I bracket an additional half-stop in each direction with very dark subjects, and very light subjects. Most of all these pictures are good, and are perfectly usable. (In many shots I'm the only one that cares about the subtlest differences in exposure.) When shooting in very contrasty light (with Fujichrome or Ektachrome films, which can easily be pushed or pulled) I sometimes overexpose by one-half or even, in desperation, one stop, and have the film "pulled" (first developer time decreased) to reduce contrast a little. Basically though "pulling" color film in development does not reduce contrast much before the color goes very blue. (Try "pulling" if you wish, using a 1/2 stop or a full stop over-exposure, and telling you lab to "pull" or reduce time in the first developer—they will know how much—when they process the film.)

It is easy to increase contrast in E-6 transparency films (but they are all, without exception, inherently too contrasty for my taste) by increasing the speed rating, and having the film "pushed" in development by a professional later. This can be useful on very flat overcast days. (See later in the chapter.)

Please, Kodak and Fuji, make a lower contrast film for when we must shoot in bright sunlight!

Using "Clip Tests"

"Clip tests" are used to get desired exposure, either when the film has been "pushed" or "pulled", or to get optimum exposure when the subject is fast moving and bracketing exposures would cause missing important shots. When you deliberately (or accidentally) expose a roll rated other than at the marked ISO speed, mark "Clip" and the speed used on the roll with a label or Magic Marker. The clip tests are then done by professional labs (they cut off and develop two or three frames from designated rolls) and then you or they judge the clips to determine developing time for the best exposure for balance of the roll. Clips can be done in 1/4, 1/3, 1/2 and one stop increments. I always have clips made when pushing or pulling film a lot or when I don't feel sure I have good exposures. Clip tests are expensive, they cost the same as processing a whole roll of film, but are obviously worth it when you need them!

Note: Any Process E-6 film (film developed by the E-6 process)can easily be pushed a full stop, or pulled a half stop; the fast films (400 ISO and higher) and the Push 800-1600 ISO transparency films can be pushed three, four or more stops, with some increase in grain, contrast and color shift. Fuji Velvia (50 ISO) is better exposed at 40 ISO I think. It takes a very nice 1-1/3 stop "push" to 100 ISO, with no real color shift, and only minimal increase in grain.

Kodachrome requires the Process K-14, and was not designed to be pushed. Kodachrome 25 and 64 films look poor, very contrasty indeed when pushed in my opinion, but Kodachrome 200 takes quite a nice 1-1/2 stop push to 500

ISO. (This is best used at night, because there is a perceptible shift to magenta.)

The only color negative film I know of that can be pushed is Kodak Ektapress Gold 1600 Professional. This film can be pushed to 6400 ISO or even higher, at some cost in grain and contrast.

Talk to your professional lab if you are interested in learning more about color clips and pushing and pulling film. (See also Chapter Five.)

Using Polaroid Films for Measuring Exposure

The Polaroid or Minolta cameras you use for professional Polaroid tests must have adjustable lens and shutter speeds, and provision for a "sync" (flash synchronization) cord to connect it to your flash or strobe. (Spectra and Minolta non-adjustable, simple Polaroid cameras will not do.) Polaroid's current fully adjustable camera model is the 600SE.

Polaroid backs for most 35mm and many medium-format cameras are made by NPC. Polaroid makes backs for 4x5" and 8x10" view cameras.

You can measure exposure, refine lighting set-ups and preview your compositions by making color or black-and-white Polaroids prints. (If you want to test color, you can do so only approximately; and you should first make comparison tests between the Polaroid color film and the color transparency film you use.

To test in color or black-and-white, you must compensate for any difference in the speed of the Polaroid film you are using with the speed of your transparency or negative film, either mathematically or with neutral density (ND) filters (which reduce the amount of light reaching the lens in 1/3 stop increments).

Polaroid tests are used by a great many professionals to measure strobe exposures and fine-tune lighting and composition. For most accurate exposure with either color or black-and-white Polaroids, include a large Kodak gray scale (which runs from black to white in 19 steps) in the picture. If all the shades are separated in the Polaroid print, exposure is perfect; if the light end of the scale runs together the film is over-exposed, if the dark squares start to blend, the film is underexposed. Color Polaroids will not be exactly the same as color transparencies.

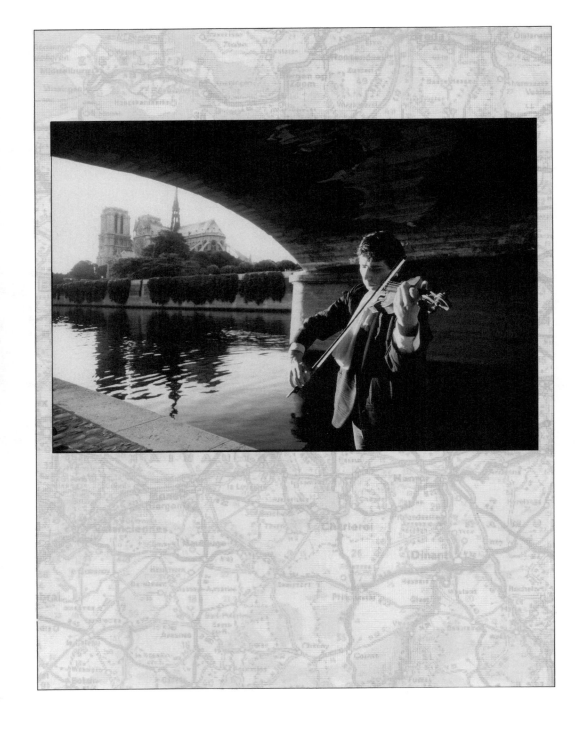

Chapter 5

Films,
Filters
and Gels

Both Maxime Du Camp and my mother had very limited film choices available to them when they went on their great trips. Maxime, when he went to Egypt in 1849, had to sensitize and develop his paper calotype negatives on the spot, exposures were very long. My mother took some rather large rolls of slow Kodak black and white film to South America in 1928; the speed was probably about 25 ISO by our standards. (She had film processed by local druggists, who did a lot of photography work at the time.)

Today's traveling photographers have the option of a vast range of films—with speeds between 25 and 3200 ISO—and must also decide between color reversal film for slides or color negative film for prints; brand K or brand F (or other makes), they must weigh the advantages of professional vs. amateur emulsions for long hot trips, and choose whether to take slow fine-grain film or fast film, or "push" film for that voyage up the Amazon or down the Colorado. They must decide whether it's worth carrying any black-and-white film or instant film to Borneo, and whether they can replenish their supplies in Bora Bora or Belize, or dare risk processing color in an unknown lab in Buenos Aires.

I will attempt to deal with these problems in some detail in this chapter, because choosing the right film, and using it well are a critical part of bringing back good travel photographs.

Whether you are photographing for an assignment, a stock shoot or personal pleasure or for fine art, take the best possible film on your travels.

My advice based on much experience is to take along all the film you will need for the trip. Film is very expensive in most places overseas (and also at tourist sites in the United States and Canada) and the kind you prefer may not be readily available. Also, even the good brands of film you can buy in supermarkets, drugstores, etc., may not have been properly stored and can therefore be off-color. Avoid unknown brands, bargain and repackaged and so-called free films everywhere; you get what you pay for. Bad color is what you usually get with such films.

Film for Personal and Fine Art Travel Photography

Most amateurs and fine-art photographers want color prints, and should therefore shoot negative color film. Such films almost always have the word "color" in the title. Fujicolor, Kodacolor, Vericolor etc. (Kodak Ektar and Ektapress professional color negative films are an exception.)

With quality 35mm negative (print) film, serious amateur travel photographers can get inexpensive small or medium-sized prints for albums, framing, mounting, portfolios and exhibition. For personal and fine-art prints you can choose between good "one-hour-photo" labs and do-it-yourself machine prints, or even color laser copy (thermal transfer) prints made from snapshot-sized prints (not directly from negatives). Laser copies can be made from transparencies also; they are used as mailers and "drop-off" pieces by some professionals.

Fine-art photographers almost always want good-sized enlargements. Many serious amateurs do too. If your primary aim is to make prints for exhibition and/or sale, I strongly recommend learning how to print. You will save a lot of money, and once you are proficient, the quality of enlargement you make yourself will be far higher than those you will get in all but the best custom labs, which are expensive. Most photo schools teach black-and-white and color printing, and labs with facilities for quick color processing are available for rental in some schools, and professional labs in major cities.

Recommended Color Negative (Print) Films

Kodacolor and Fujicolor are amateur color-print films, made in medium, fast and ultra-fast ISO speeds, that are widely available. They can be used with any lighting. If you are going to take mostly family album pictures and have them processed at a one-hour-photo store, you will be happy with any of these. With amateur color-print film you don't have to worry overmuch about filters, because most color correction can be done in printing.

Some professional labs offer to print frame numbers on the back of machine-printed Fujicolor 100 negative film. As matching names and numbers to print and reprint orders can be a huge chore, this is obviously a reason to use this film if you do much public relations work!

The color negative film I usually use for personal work (and for portraits etc. when prints are required) is Kodak Ektar 25 Professional (PHR), a daylight film which is extremely fine grain. It is available in 35mm and 120 sizes. Ektar 100 and Ektar 1000 Professional are also excellent daylight negative films, they come in 35mm size only.

Fujicolor Reala (CS; 100 ISO) is also a very good color negative film.

Kodak Ektapress Gold color negative films were developed for professional news photographers; the film does not require special storage, and comes in 100 (PPA), 400 (PPB) and 1600 (PPC) ISO speeds. Ektapress is the only color negative film I know of that can be pushed, the 1600 ISO film can readily be pushed two stops to 6400 ISO (Kodak recommends filtration for this).

I suggest taking a fine-grain, slow or medium speed color negative film for most travel uses, along with a few rolls of ultra-fast film for when you must shoot in low light without a tripod.

Watch for Kodak digitized negative film, announced to be available in 1992.

Large Format Color Negative Films

To shoot 4x5" or 8x10" film on your travels, Kodak and Fuji offer options. Professional negative films must be used with the light source intended for best color.

Kodak Vericolor III Professional, Type S (VPS; 160 ISO) is used with daylight and flash/strobe exposures of 1/10 of a second or shorter. Vericolor II Professional, Type L (VPL) is for long tungsten-light exposures. (This film is exposed at 100 ISO under 3,200K tungsten lights and can be used with an 85B filter in daylight at 64 ISO.) Both films come in 120, 4x5" and 8x10" sizes; VPS comes in 220 size also.

Fujicolor Reala (CS) is a 100 ISO daylight negative film that can also be exposed in 3,200K light with an 80A Kodak filter at an exposure index of 25 ISO. It comes in 35mm and 120 sizes, and gives beautiful color prints. Fujicolor 160 Professional S (NSP) is Fuji's standard professional negative sheet film for short exposures. It comes in 120, 4x5" and 8x10" sizes. Fujicolor 160 Professional L (NLP) film is designed for long exposures under tungsten lights. (NLP is available in the same formats as NSP.)

Black-and-White Films

For the dedicated black-and-white photographer I unreservedly recommend Kodak T-Max Professional films, which come in speeds of 100, 400 and a push film, P3200, which can be exposed at 800, 1600, 3200 or even higher ISO. T-Max has a fine, very sharp grain and a long tonal range. I use T-Max 400 for my black and white work. It can easily be "pushed" (the exposure index increased) up to three stops with T-Max developer. T-Max 100 and 400 ISO films come in all formats from 35mm to 8x10"; the P3200 in 35mm and 120 size only.

Note: Kodak still makes Tri-X (400 ISO) and Plus-X (125 ISO) which have been professional favorites for years.

Black-and-White Slides

If you shoot Kodak's T-Max 100 film, you can process it normally as negatives, or have the option of slides. Use Kodak's special T-Max 100 Reversal Developing Oufit (catalog number 1954155) to get beautiful, rich-toned black-and-white slides instead of negatives (there is an extra chemical reversing agent involved). I like the look of these slides a lot, and am using them increasingly. (T-Max reversal developing service is now offered by a few professional labs.) T-Max slides can be scanned for reproduction by the same machines that scan color slides.

Other fine black-and-white films are Fuji's Neopan, Ilford's HP and Agfa's Pan, all of which come in ISO speeds that compete with the Kodak films, and which you can choose with confidence.

Get free data sheets from manufacturers to learn the specific characteristics of any professional color or black-and-white film. They contain filtration recommendations for different types of use too.

Black-and-White Prints

Once again, you should learn to print yourself if you want to make the best possible black-and white enlargements at a reasonable price.

Note: For optimum quality prints, it is just as important to expose black-and-white film accurately, as it is for color film.

What Film Should I Shoot for Saleable Travel Pictures?

About 95% of travel pictures that are assigned or sold as stock today are shot on fine or medium-grain color transparency film (they include the word "chrome" in the title). The letters after the names are manufacturers' codes.

Kodachrome 25 Professional (PKM), Kodachrome 64 Professional (PKR), Ektachrome 64 Professional (EPR), Ektachrome 100 Professional (EPN), Ektachrome 64X Professional (EPX), Ektachrome 100X Professional (EPZ), Ektachrome 400X Professional (EPL), Ektachrome 100 Plus Professional (EPP), Fujichrome 50 Professional (RFP), Fujichrome 100 Professional (RDP), and Fujichrome Velvia Professional (RVP) are just some current choices for 35mm users.

Fast transparency films and films designed to be "pushed" one or two stops, and tungsten light-balanced transparency films are also widely used. I will discuss each in detail later in this chapter.

Note: Black-and-white travel stories are being assigned today by a few trendy publications, but even they still use black-and-white only occasionally.

Color prints of travel-related subjects are made by some primarily fine-art photographers. Their work is occasionally reproduced in top travel magazines.

What is Good Color in Photography?

Good color is pleasing to the eye, and most often looks on film the way our eyes see it. The color should not be too light or washed out; rich and fully saturated but not so dark that important details are lost. Color transparencies tend to darken slightly in reproduction, so many photographers "bracket" (vary) all their exposures very slightly in order to get optimum color density (see also Chapter Four). Color filters are used to correct slight color problems in daylight, and to balance color with film as far as possible when different light sources are used. The aim, usually, is that the picture appear "normal" to the eye. Color filter effects in travel photography should be subtle, in my opinion.

Good color prints, like good transparencies, have no color bias; flesh tones and grays look neutral, and detail is reproduced in both shadow and highlight areas.

The Films I Take on My Travels

Kodachrome 25 Professional (25 ISO) has superfine grain and unrivalled sharpness. I use it mostly for for people pictures and portraits (I like the flesh tones) and for landscapes and interiors where extremely fine detail must be recorded.

Fujichrome Velvia Professional (nominally 50 ISO; I rate it at 40) has very fine grain and beautiful saturated color; this film can easily be pushed 1 1/3 stop to 100 ISO without noticeable color change) and I rely on it for most landscapes. It is especially good where green is important. The film is too warm for my taste for "people pictures" where natural flesh tones are important, but it's fine if stylized warm colors are OK.

Ektachrome 100 Plus (EPP; 100 ISO) is a "bright" film which I like to use at dusk, for its lovely natural blues at long exposure times. It is also useful on grey days.

Ektachrome 400 (EL) not made in a professional emulsion but excellent nontheless. This is the film I always use for low available light. I generally rate it at normal speed but also routinely push it one or two or more stops when needed. (I occasionally push it up to five stops when desperate, or when a very grainy effect is wanted.)

Kodak Ektar 25 and 100 are the fine-grain color-negative films I use if I need to shoot color prints.

Kodak T-Max 100 and 400 are my favorite black-and-white films.

What is Good Black-and-White?

Good black-and-white prints should reproduce a full, rich, range of tones from black to white, with details readable throughout the tonal range. Grain should usually not be obtrusive. Black-and-white prints for reproduction are usually made slightly less contrasty, and slightly lighter than prints for exhibition, to compensate for darkness and contrast added as an inherent part of most printing processes. Black-and-white slides are becoming more popular; they too should reproduce a full tonal scale.

Selecting and Getting to Know Films

Make comparison tests of two or three similar ISO speed films on similar subjects, with similar light conditions, and have the film processed at the same good lab. Then, look at the film projected or on a light box to compare pictures and see which film "look" you prefer. When you have selected a slow or medium speed film, and a fast film that you like, work with them until you get to know them. Write down what you do. Soon, you won't be totally dependent on a meter, for outdoor exposures anyway. When you get to know a film very well by shooting with it often, and by testing it under different contrast and weather and lighting conditions, you will know if you prefer exposing the film at the manufacturer's ISO speed rating, or at slightly higher or lower exposure indexes.

By using a film consistently, you will learn about its renditions of different colors and how it behaves at very long exposures, and when it is advisable to choose a different film for a specific purpose or effect.

If you use the same film consistently, you will become aware that not all photolabs do equally good work. Saving a few pennies on processing is usually a false economy which could result in off-color pictures. Having a good relationship with a professional lab is a big help almost always. It can be a lifesaver if you have exposure problems.

How to Select Films

You will need to become familiar with at least a slow and a fast transparency film. Here is how to "test" to find the films you want to use,

Arrange a still life outdoors on a neutral gray or beige background on a clear day with blue sky, sun and clouds about. Place the still life in soft, even light (not direct sunlight; and away from trees and colored walls). Test between 10 a.m. and 3 p.m. Include bright red, yellow, green and blue objects in your set-up, as well as a black-and-white photograph (or a Kodak gray scale) some pastel colored objects, and a person (or your own hand) for critical skin tones. Use two or three different brands of slow or medium-speed daylight film, to photograph this setup. Record you exposures. Compare the results to find film whose color and grain characteristics please you most, and the film-speed you find comfortable to work with.

Then, choose a couple of different high-speed films (400 ISO and up) and compare them under low light, out and indoors to see which you prefer for color, grain structure and contrast. You can also compare ultra-fast films "pushed" one or more stops if you wish.

Testing Film Emulsions

Make tests to check variations in film emulsions (batches) before you buy any large quantities of film for a long trip or important assignment. (Film emulsion numbers are printed in computer type on film boxes.)

Tests for emulsion variations need subtle subject matter. Make a set-up that includes a Kodak gray scale, a few bright colors (or a Kodak or Macbeth color scale) some shades of white (try eggs or china), tones of grey and beige and soft pastel colors (use toilet paper rolls or Kleenex) and especially people with light and dark skin. Test two or three different emulsions of each of your favorite film or films. Use the same lens for all the tests (lenses can vary very slightly in color). Note the exposures you use (you can write them on a card and photograph them into the shot), and use the same, good processing lab.

Project your test photographs or look at them on a good light box. Check especially how each emulsion records subtle skin tones, which are very important to all serious photographers. You will find after testing bright colors and subtle skin tones, in sun and shade, with flash, available light and time-exposure that no one film does everything well, but that two or three will take care of most travel subjects.

Choosing and Testing Film for Long Trips

Be sure and test different film emulsions (batches) to avoid any problems before buying film in quantity for a long trip, emulsion numbers are printed on the side of each film box. (Avoid any emulsion with a slight magenta or green bias, which can occur occasionally even with the best films.)

I recommend using only your favorite films in professional emulsions (the best; some use a different film base from amateur films) unless you are going on a very extended assignment/trip where you cannot keep film cool or send it home promptly for processing. (I store film in hotel and motel room mini-bars where available; if there's no mini-bar, I ask if my film can be kept in the hotel refrigerator.) For optimum color, professional films must be refrigerated before and after exposure (frozen if kept for longer than a few months) and processed as soon as possible, or the color may shift towards magenta as the film ages. (Allow film to warm up or thaw before use.)

If you are taking a trip of a month or so to a cool climate I wouldn't worry much about color shift with professional film, but for a year-long trip to a hot climate I suggest testing to find the best available amateur emulsions of Fujichrome 50 or 100, or Kodachrome 25, or Ektachrome 64 or 100 ISO, and Ektachrome 400, and then keep the film as cool as possible in an insulated bag or wrapped in newspaper while you are traveling.

When you are on a very long trip, and must buy film overseas, of course make tests and choose a newer, slightly greenish rather than an older, slightly magenta biased emulsion if those are the only choices. The green film should age slowly towards neutral color; you can correct slight bias with CC (color compensating) filters. (See later in this chapter.)

Some professional negative films, like Kodak Ektapress Gold, are designed to be very stable without refrigeration. If you want, or can use, color prints (professionals on assignment should check with art directors) this is a big reason to choose these films.

Processing Film

I am not crazy about foreign processing, and I've occasionally had lab problems even in large North American cities (including New York it must be said). When you have a lab you like, have them process all your work if possible.

If this not possible, ask Kodak and Fuji for their recommended lab lists; see the ads from professional labs in the *Photo District News* (see Chapter Two) and ask other photographers' advice. In desperation, locate labs in classified phone books.

On a very long trip if you know the labs where you are going are not up to scratch, it's probably best to ship film home periodically for processing, either direct to your lab, or to the person taking care of business at home. Mark the film package "Exposed Film for Immediate Processing" and "Keep Cool and Dry and Away from X-Rays". Of course, label each roll and include instructions to your lab about clip tests, etc., in the package.

DHL Worldwide Express, an air-shipping agency, is experienced in shipping film, and will handle the customs formalities for you. (Some paperwork is required). As an example of cost, current rate for a five pound package from London to New York is about $65; insurance is extra, the service takes two days. They ship from almost anywhere in the world to almost anywhere in the United States and Canada.

Members of Kodak's Pro Passport professional network get a discount on DHL, (which I have used). Call DHL at (800) 225-5345. Check also with Federal Express and other shipping services to get best possible services and rates. It's a good idea to check before you leave home with the Consulate(s) of the country(ies) you will be visiting, and the closest United States or Canadian Customs Office, about any possible problems, such as censorship and duty. Duty is not normally charged on exposed film returned to the United States. (See also Chapter Sixteen).

Processing Film Overseas
I never recommend Third World or even much Second World, (i.e., non big American or major foreign city professional lab) color film processing except in dire emergency. I like my own lab, and with one you don't know, even a good one, results may not be quite what you are used to. Avoid small and non-professional labs just about everywhere, you are too likely to get bad color. But, if you must process overseas, I say again ask Kodak and Fuji for their list of recommended labs in that country or region, or ask local professional photographers for suggestions. Then, try one or two non-important rolls first. If you like what the lab does, proceed with the rest of your film a few rolls at a time to minimize chances of loss or damage. But remember I said I don't recommend it! (Professionals can get film and re-shoot insurance that will cover processing loss; see Insurance, Chapter Fifteen.)

"Bracketing" Exposures
For the best possible color, "bracket" (vary) your exposures. Use a half-stop and a full stop over and under "normal" exposure for your chosen film until you find out if you like "saturated" rich dark color, or prefer "normal" color or "high key" very slightly pale color. When you know your film and equipment well, you can bracket much less. Bracketing will often save a picture when light conditions are difficult, especially in contrasty light. In very low light, bracket by giving longer shutter speeds.

The newest automatic bracketing backs, which come included or as an option with top-of-the-line electronic cameras permit precise brackets of as little as 1/3 of a stop; this is especially useful for subtle variations in skin tones. (See also Chapter Four).

The "Look" of Color Transparency (Slide) Films
When I teach, I look at many students' work projected on a screen in a darkened room, and I can usually tell which film was used. Each color-transparency film has in fact quite definite characteristics, a "look" of its own. Different Kodachrome, Kodak Ektachrome (universally called Ektachrome) and

The Airport X-Ray Problem

X-ray damage to film is a constant worry for all professional traveling photographers. Perhaps it it overstated. I have been traveling for 25 years and have never had a problem with film damaged by X-rays. I recently attended a meeting where about 40 Kodak scientists were present. Only two had ever seen X-ray damage, which apparently shows up as shadows from nearby objects on the film, or sometimes as faint wavy lines.

However, to minimize the possibility of problems I do the following:

I hand-carry my film at United States airports, in a clear plastic bag. I arrive very early and very politely request a hand-examination of the film. (The security agent must agree, it's actually required by Federal law.) I have never been refused. Some foreign countries (like Germany and Switzerland) absolutely insist on X-raying all film, and you must either go along or take a car or train across those borders. Israel has stringent security (and censorship) regulations; best check with an Israeli consulate before you go. Some British airports (and those of some Commonwealth members) use some high powered X-ray machines and the security people will usually hand examine film if formally requested to do so.

I put all my film in Sima lead-foil bags then into my checked luggage when travelling between overseas airports and just carry a few rolls onto the plane in case my luggage is delayed. (Sima bags come in two sizes, the large size holds about 60 rolls of 35mm film and costs about $20. They are sold at professional photo dealers) As I said, I have never even met a photographer who has had X-ray problems, but to be on the safe side, use the lead bags.

Fujichrome films, all in professional emulsions, are most pros' transparency films of choice. (Agfachrome, made in Germany, is also a good transparency film, but is not very widely used in this country. If you are overseas, have run out of film, and it is the only choice available, you can buy it with confidence.)

Knowing which film does what best will help you make better travel photographs. On the next pages, you will find my analyses.

Kodak Color Transparency Films

Eastman Kodak has been the premier photographic company in the world since the 1880's, when George Eastman in Rochester, New York, invented and sold the first dry film plates and then mass-marketed Brownie roll-film cameras. The photographic world would be much poorer without Kodak, which still sponsors a lot of valuable original research and puts out a large number of useful publications to help photographers at all levels.

Kodachrome

Kodachrome film, Kodak's greatest triumph, was invented by two brilliant musician/scientists, Leopold Mannes and Leopold Godowsky, who were spon-

---

The Kelvin Scale, the Color of Light, and Color Film

The color of light is measured by the Kelvin scale. Lord Kelvin, a 19th-century British physicist, heated a "black body" (iron) in a furnace. As the iron heated, it glowed first red, then orange, then yellow, until it was white-hot. Ultimately it emitted a bluish gas. This is why we refer to "color temperature" in photography, and why the Kelvin temperature rises when light gets bluer.

Daylight film (also used with flash and strobe) is rated at 5,500 degrees Kelvin (written 5,500°K, or 5,500K).

The indoor film usually used today is rated at 3,200°K (the film is designated Tungsten (marked with a T on the box after the film name). There is also a Type A film, rated at 3,400°K, for Type A Kodachrome (a film used in studios). See later in this chapter for more.

---

sored by Kodak in the 1930's. It ushered in the modern age of color photography. Kodachrome has always been a slow film, considered somewhat difficult to use, partly because, unlike other color transparency films, until recently it was almost never pushed or pulled to compensate for slight over or under-exposure, so you either exposed perfectly or you had big problems.

The very precise Process K-14 is difficult too; it requires expensive and precise controls, and Kodak lost its monopoly on Kodachrome processing in the United States several years ago. Kodak now has only a partial interest in Kodalux (formerly Kodak) labs and they, plus only a few independent labs, process Kodachrome. The rumor is that it is hard for Kodachrome processing to be profitable. (Note: In Canada, Kodachrome is still processed directly by Kodak; the K-14 lab is in Toronto.)

Until a few years ago I, and most other professional users of 35mm color transparency film, used almost nothing but Kodachrome. Then, for various reasons including, so I've been told, pollution, Kodak altered the film formulation. They made Kodachrome higher in contrast and reduced the silver content. At about the same time they had some manufacturing problems that caused a lot of slightly magenta or green Kodachrome emulsions to reach the market. Some of the howls of anguish from the photographic community (ASMP even formed a Kodachrome Committee) were heard by the Great Yellow Father in Rochester, and Kodachrome 25 and 64 Professional (designated PKM and PKR; the selected best, optimally aged emulsions) came into being. This solved most of the magenta and green problems, but not the high contrast problem, which remains.

Kodachrome's color does not seem to me to be quite as beautiful today as it used to be. I no longer use Kodachrome in poor weather, because the colors look lifeless and dreary when skies are overcast. It wasn't always so.

There is still no film as fine-grain as Kodachrome 25, and used under ideal conditions (soft, low or bounce sunlight) it is still beautiful. Kodachrome is noted for its reproduction of yellows and blues. (It used to be excellent for reds too; it is now just good.) It is still unrivalled for nice, neutral skin tones.

I like it for portraits. I use Kodachrome 25 Professional when I want maximum detail, as in group and especially crowd shots, where any grain interferes with "reading" the picture. But the film is now so contrasty that in bright sunlight I can't use it without "fill" light (see Chapters Six and Seven). For these reasons, I no longer rely on Kodachrome 25 as my only daylight film as I once did.

I am told that Kodachrome 64 (PKR) is now much more popular than PKM. I personally don't care about the extra speed and dislike the fact that PKR is even more contrasty that PKM.

Kodachrome 200 (PKL) is a very good moderately fine-grain film that was introduced in the last few years for use in low light; it can easily be "pushed" 1 1/2 stops (to 500 ISO) by labs that process Kodachrome. The film does have a very slight magenta bias, but that is easily corrected with filtration. Quite a few travel photographers like this film. (I use it only occasionally, because I prefer the "look" of Ektachrome 400 in low light.)

Kodachrome Type A (PKA) is a 40 ISO film designed for use with 3,400K tungsten studio lighting.

Kodachrome emulsions are extremely stable, and resistant to color fading with aging. All the Professional Kodachromes are available only in 35mm, except Kodachrome 64, which comes also in 120 size.

Kodak Ektachrome

There are now a lot of films called Ektachrome around, so I will try and sort them out. (Kodak is, I am told, currently working on explaining and identifying the differences between various types of Ektachrome more clearly.)

Ektachrome, a much easier film to work with than Kodachrome, was invented in the 1940's. I used to think of it as a dependable but not very exciting film, but Kodak has been working very hard on Ektachrome recently and new versions that seem very promising have been introduced just lately. The current E-6 films and processing are extremely stable, and I have Ektachromes over twenty years old that have not shifted in color at all. (My oldest Ektachromes, taken in student days when the E-3 process was used, are purplish today).

Ektachrome films can readily be "pushed"—the exposure index increased (with increased development time) one, two, or in some versions three or more stops. It can also be "pulled" (the exposure index and development time decreased) for up to one stop, which reduces contrast somewhat.

Ektachrome 400 (EL) is an amateur emulsion and is a favorite of mine. It is the only fast film I take on location. It is even better lately than it used to be, with a nice sharp grain structure, somewhat reduced contrast from former days, and pleasant neutral to cool color under all kinds of available light situations. It holds a good black when "pushed" (speed index and development time increased) unlike some other fast films, and the warm effect of the film used unfiltered under tungsten lights is often pleasant. I recently compared Ektachrome 400 and Fujichrome 400 films under contrasty light at several tungsten-lit summer festival performances. Because of low light, I rated both films at 800 ISO and pushed them one stop. I liked the Ektachrome better; the film held a good black with less shift to yellow/brown and had slightly finer grain.) I like EL film in very low daylight if I can't use a tripod or flash. Ektachrome 400 comes in 35mm and 120 sizes.

Ektachrome P800-1600 Professional (EES) a "push" film, is a neutral to very slightly blue 400 ISO film, designed to be pushed one or two stops without appreciable color shift. It can be pushed even more to 3,200 or even 6,400 but shifts towards brown at those speed indices. 35mm size only. (I don't use this film only because Ektachrome 400 works fine for me.)

Ektachrome 100 Plus Professional (EPP) seems to be Kodak's current favorite, and their answer to bright Fuji colors; it seems to me superior to Fuji 50 and 100, because the color is a touch more neutral for skin tones. I like it very much for long exposures at dusk. Ektachrome 100 Plus blues stay true, and it gives a very good black at night. EPP is available in all formats.

The traditional studio workhorse Ektachrome 64 (EPR) and the newer Ektachrome 100 (EPN) are known as slightly bluish, cool films. Ektachrome 64X (EPX), 100X (EPZ) and 400X (EPL) are new professional offerings from Kodak. According to Kodak, they are designed to fall between the cool EPR/EPN and the saturated EPP. I like EPX, it has nice skin tones. However, there are are only so many different films one wants to carry on a trip, so I stick to EPP for my medium-speed E-6 film.

Ektachrome 160T Professional (EPT) is the film I use under 3,200K tungsten "hot lights," it gives pretty good skin tones. I normally push it one stop to 320 ISO without noticeable color shift, because I need a relatively high shutter speed to stop movement. The speed can go higher (with slight color shift to yellow). It comes in 35mm and 120 sizes. All of the above E-6 films take a one-stop push, (double the speed rating) quite nicely. Ektachrome 320T (EPJ) has just been announced, and will be in stores shortly.

I just don't like the color of Ektachrome 200 film (EPD) it always seems a bit dead, yellowish, to me. I never use it, it's my least favorite film.

Fuji Color Transparency Films

If you must buy film when traveling, an advantage in buying Fuji films is that (to the best of my knowledge) Fuji films are all made in Japan and are usually very consistent. (Of course, storage and age can affect this.)

Fujichrome

I do not know when Fujichrome film (which also uses the Process E-6) was first made, but it was introduced into the United States market from Japan in 1970. To start with the upstarts in green boxes were almost laughed at by the photographic community, but Fuji puts out excellent products, and have marketed them very aggressively, especially to professional photographers. The bright "look" of Fuji films appeals to people accustomed to the hues of color television, and Fuji today has a healthy slice of the professional film market.

Fuji 50 and 100 films are moderately fine-grain, and immediately recognizable for their excellent, somewhat intense renditions of blues and especially greens. Both Fuji 50 and 100 perform well in poor weather, or dull light, and can cheer up a scene to a surprising degree even on a bad day. Both these Fujichromes render skin tones too warm, in my opinion, and when there is plenty of red and yellow around Fujichrome 50 and 100 colors are a trifle exaggerated. All the slower Fuji films run somewhat purple when used for long exposures at dusk, and are somewhat green used for time exposures at night. Both Fujichrome 50 and 100 films have very moderate grain. When shooting in contrasty light, and when you cannot use a fill light of some kind, it is worth shooting Fuji 100 at 50, and having the lab pull the film to reduce the contrast somewhat. (I advise clip tests—development of the first few frames for inspection—when doing this, see below.) You can push Fuji 100 one or even two stops, with an increase in contrast but not much increase in grain. Fuji 50 and 100 come in all formats except 5x7".

Fujichrome Velvia
The film I have fallen in love with recently is Fujichrome Velvia Professional (RVP). A fine-grain film rated by the manufacturer at 50 ISO, I usually shoot it at a rating of 40 ISO on the recommendation of my lab (Lalli and Inder Color, here in New York). Velvia can also be rated at 100 ISO, and pushed one and a third stops without noticeable color shift. I do this at dusk sometimes. In either case, Velvia's colors are beautiful, rich and just right for everything except skin tones, which photograph a touch warm, very slightly reddish, even when the film is used without my normal Skylight 1A filter. (I am now testing to see which if any cooling filter gives a more pleasing result with Velvia for skin tones.) Velvia color runs purplish for long dusk exposures; like other Fuji films it looks green for long night exposures (which Fuji doesn't recommend).

Today I use Velvia for a lot of my travel work; I have used it in green and gray England for the last two years with great success; a recent trip to Arizona where the colors and light are warm convinced me that Velvia is excellent for just about all landscapes. I compared Kodachrome 25 Professional and Velvia Professional at sunset at the Grand Canyon and Monument Valley. The Velvia red and yellow rock colors were richer and more saturated than Kodachromes; the spring ground cover greens were excellent with Velvia also. I preferred the softer Kodachrome blues of the sky; the Kodachrome greens were very muted. (To be fair, when I showed these comparisons to Kodak, they replaced my Kodachrome with a better emulsion.)

Velvia, although fine grain, cannot be compared for grain with Kodachrome 25 (the finest-grained film made); I still use Kodachrome whenever really fine detail must be recorded. Velvia is no better than Kodachrome under bright sunlight conditions and can look awful in really harsh light. (If only a film manufacturer would make a low contrast color film specifically for use in bright sunshine!) Velvia must also be "filled" when the light is harsh, or shadows block up or highlights overexpose (or both). Velvia comes in all film formats.

Fujichrome Fast and Tungsten Films
Fuji offers a 400 ISO professional film (RHP) and a 1600 ISO "push" film, (RSPII) which like Ektachrome 800-1600 is a basically 400 ISO film designed for pushing one or two stops.

Fujichrome 64T Professional (RTP) is a reversal film balanced for 3,200K tungsten lights. Since one always needs as much speed as possible when shooting under "hot" lights I prefer Ektachrome's 160 ISO offering.

The main problem with all Fuji films is that if you need to use filters (with fluorescent or sodium vapor lighting for instance) a lot of correction is needed,

---

Free Data on Professional Color Films

Kodak and Fuji put out handy, diary-sized booklets giving detailed information on all their professional films; both include filtration recommendations for different light sources, suggestions on compensating for reciprocity failure for long and short exposures and other helpful information.

The *Reference Data Book for Kodak Professional Photographic Products* and the *Professional Fujchrome/Fujicolor/Neopan Data Guide* can be obtained from the Professional Relations Departments of these companies direct, or, sometimes, from professional labs and photo dealers.

Free, comprehensive Data Sheets on individual professional films are also put out by Kodak and Fuji (and other film manufacturers); get these from film dealers and labs or direct from the manufacturers.

Kodak's toll-free professional customer service number is (800) 242-2424.

The Fuji toll-free number is (800) 526-9030.

---

considerably more than with most Ektachrome or Kodachrome emulsions.

All Fujichrome films use the E-6 process, and are considered very stable for long-term storage in a dark, cool, dry place.

Other Color Transparency Films

Agfa films are made in Germany and widely sold in Europe. I know a couple of photographers that use and like them here in the United States. I have tested a few rolls of Agfachrome and liked it quite well, however, I see no reason to switch from my Kodak and Fuji choices. If you are stuck without film somewhere in Europe where Agfa is the only choice, you can certainly use it with confidence.

Scotch 640T film, made by the 3M company, is the fastest tungsten film on the market. Its black is noticeably bluish, and it is very grainy. Balanced for 3,200K lights, it can be used in stadiums and other places where added light is not allowed or possible. Scotch 1000 ISO daylight-balanced film is also very grainy. Both come in 35mm rolls only.

Note: Some people "push" Scotch films several stops when they want a graphic effect with grain like small rocks—this can be very interesting!

All color film colors shift somewhat to brownish when "pushed" more than a stop or two; this is especially true at night.

Polaroid Films

Polaroid instant film was invented by the great Dr. Edwin Land in the 1940's for his daughter, who wanted to see pictures at once. Polaroid print films are used by just about every professional photographer for testing exposure and lighting set-ups, and for previewing compositions, for studio advertising illustration, and portraits, and for fashion and location work. Polaroid slide films are popular for instant slide shows, and fine art. Prints require the use of Polaroid cameras or backs. (Note:Polaroid Spectra film is used in Polaroid Spectra or Minolta instant cameras. Spectra prints are great for photo "gifts" when travelling, for fine art and just for fun, but they aren't used for professional tests, because the lenses and shutters on Spectra and Minolta instant cameras cannot be manually adjusted.)

Polaroid Transparency Films

All Polaroid transparency films are interesting graphically (more of a reason to use them, in my opinion, than the not-quite-instant development time). Developing takes about five minutes and requires great care to avoid scratches, as well as a dust-free environment, and a hand-wound film processor that costs about $60, discount. (The fully electric-powered processor cost around $120.) You have to be very careful when handling Polaroid slides. To avoid bad scratches on the fragile emulsion it is best to hang the film up to harden for 30 minutes or so before cutting and mounting it.

When you look at Polaroid continuous-tone slides projected (they look strange to the naked eye) you are carried back in time to the early days of photography. I love both the next two, for graphic effects.

Polapan (a 125 ISO black and white film) has soft, warm, almost sepia tones.

Polachrome is a 40 ISO color transparency film that reminds me of the historic Autochrome process, with soft bluish/purplish colors.

Other Polaroid transparency films are: Polagraph, a 400 ISO high-contrast black-and-white film and PolaBlue, a blue and white graphic arts film. Both can be used for fine-art effects.

All come packaged with a separate developer pod, and all are fun to play with. 35mm size only. (I sometimes have Polaroid slides duped onto conventional film; to protect delicate originals which are fragile and scratch easily.) For more on this whole subject read *The Polaroid 35mm Instant Slide System, A User's Manual,* by Lester Lefkowitz.

Polaroid Print Films—
Used for Testing, Previewing, Fine-Art and Photographic Gifts

Polaroid Type 42 is a 200 ISO roll film used in Polaroid 3 1/4x4 1/4" folding cameras like my compact old 110B model. (You still can find these and the folding 110A model used, quite cheaply; see also Chapter Three).

Inexpensive Type 42 is a black-and-white general-purpose film (easily correlated to 25, 50 100, 400 and 800 ISO color films for test purposes) I find it is all I need for testing lighting and exposure on location shoots.

Polaroid 600 series films are made for Polaroid 3 1/4x4 1/4" cameras, like the current 600 SE, and the old model 180 and 195 folding cameras, which can still be found used. NPC camera backs for many 35mm and medium format cameras are all designed for, or modified for, type 600 film packs. (For more on Polaroid cameras and backs see Chapter Three).

Type 664 is a black-and-white 100 ISO film. Type 665 P/N gives a black-and-white print and a negative for subsequent enlargements. A lot of fine-art photographers like this film.

Type 669 is Polaroid's color print film, same size, 80 ISO, is widely used for color testing in studios, and also by fine-art photographers. (This is the film that is being widely used for the currently fashionable Polaroid transfer process, where the image is transferred to damp watercolor paper, and rolled down a few seconds after development. For more about this process see Polaroid's *Test* magazine.)

Polaroid also makes large-format sheet and pack black-and-white positive film, black-and-white positive-negative film and color print film in packs and sheets; the 500 series films fit 4x5", and the 800 series films fit 8x10" Polaroid film holders.

Spectra film color prints (made for the Spectra and a similar Minolta instant

---

What Films do Art Directors and Picture Editors Want to See?

Glenn Nakahara, the art director of *Diversion* magazine, recently told me that he didn't care which film anyone uses, the pictures are what matter. A well-known travel magazine that I work for supplies film to assignment photographers. It is currently handing out mostly Fujichrome Velvia Professional.

Terry Cordaschi, chief picture editor of my stock agency, Photo Researchers, tells me that if all else is equal, she wants to see pictures shot on the finest-grain, therefore the slowest possible film. She says she recommends Fuji Velvia and Fuji 50 to people going to cool green places like Washington State, or Scotland or Japan, where there is a high likelihood of grey skies, and Kodachrome 25 or 64 to people going to hot places like Mexico or Australia, because she feels Fujichrome films "heat up" colors too much in warm places.

---

camera), are great for giving out as "thank you's" to people who pose for you.

4x5" and 8x10" Polaroid color films can be used for fine-art image transfers onto watercolor papers.

Polaroid puts out free information on all its professional films, including how to transfer images. Their toll-free number is (800) 225-1618.

Filters and "Gels"

Because film does not record light the way our eye sees it, or sometimes because we want special effects, colored glass, plastic or gelatin filters (or sheets of colored gel) are used in front of lenses and/or in front of light sources to correct or change the way colors reproduce on film. Different films have slightly different color characteristics, and may vary from these very slightly from one emulsion (batch) to the next. The age, storage, processing, time of day, weather conditions and type of light used are all factors in the way color records on film, and can cause variations of color. Filter correction may be needed or wanted even when film is used with the light it is balanced for, and if the lighting or time of day and weather conditions are theoretically perfect.

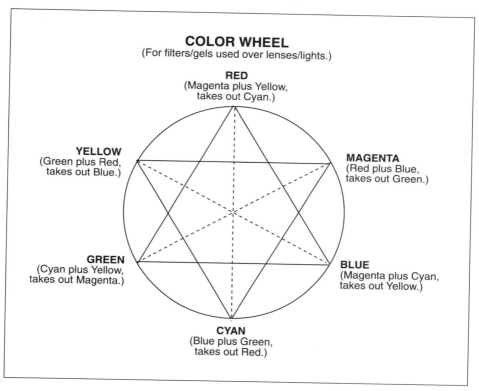

COLOR WHEEL
(For filters/gels used over lenses/lights.)

RED
(Magenta plus Yellow,
takes out Cyan.)

YELLOW
(Green plus Red,
takes out Blue.)

MAGENTA
(Red plus Blue,
takes out Green.)

GREEN
(Cyan plus Yellow,
takes out Magenta.)

BLUE
(Magenta plus Cyan,
takes out Yellow.)

CYAN
(Blue plus Green,
takes out Red.)

Photographic Filters

There are only a few kinds of filters. Get the ones that are important to you in the form of round screw-in filters in glass, they fit unobtrusively in front of lenses. Be sure to get filters large enough for your widest-angle lenses; the corners of pictures taken with too-small filters will "vignette" (go dark) especially at small apertures. (3" square plastic or gelatin filters are cheaper but a lot less convenient than glass for the filters you use a lot; they require the use of special filter holders and sometimes a lens adaptor ring.)

Color compensating (CC) filters alter or add color to a greater or lesser degree (they can correct minor color bias in film emulsions).

Light-balancing filters (called LB on color meters) change the color-temperature or color of the light source to balance with the film being used, or to balance several different types of lighting in the same scene; so that they all can be rendered on the film as our eye sees them.

Neutral density and Polarizing filters reduce light and glare/reflections respectively but do not change the color of what is being photographed.

Diffusion filters soften, special effects filters can produce starbursts, multiple images etc., and may or may not alter color.

Gels

Gels (or gelatins) come in sheets or rolls, and were originally used in the theater, and then movie and TV lighting. They are used by many still photographers in front of strobe and flash and tungsten lights, to bring light and film into balance for best possible correct color rendition. They can also be used to alter colors, slightly or considerably, for creative effects, "mood" and fun. Small pieces of gel can substitute for filters in front of lenses in many cases (where optium color is not required). Because gels are cheap compared to photographic filters, and because a large number of colors are available, they are increasingly popular with still photographers.

Filter and Gel Factors

All but the very palest filters (and gels) reduce the amount of light transmitted (reaching the film). The amount of reduction is called the filter factor. A filter or gel in front of a lens, or a gel in front of a light may reduce the amount of light reaching the film plane by 10, 20 or 50%, or even more for certain filters/gels. Manufacturers supply information on filter factors with their products. In practical terms, do not worry about the factors when using in-camera meters. The factor for filters on lenses must be taken into account when using hand-held exposure meters, including flash meters and spot meters, or you will get varying degrees of underexposure.

A Basic Color Filter Kit

• Skylight 1A (or UV). Both these can protect lenses, have a very slight warming effect, and somewhat reduce the bluish color of haze (but very minimally in my experience). I use one or other on all my lenses instead of covers all the time.

• 30M (or, an FLD filter). Both compensate for the green effect you get when photographing with daylight film under cool-white fluorescent lights, the cheapest, and most commonly-used fluorescents. (Both these filters can also be used to liven-up dull sunsets.)

• 80A. This filter converts daylight film to balance with 3,200K photolamps. (This is deep-blue and can also be used for blue "mood" or "moonlight" effects.)

• 85B. (Optional; not especially recommended except in an emergency, but those emergencies do arise) this orange filter converts Tungsten, 3,200K color film for use in 5,500K daylight. It can also be used with black-and-white film to darken blue skies and show up clouds.

• Polarizing filter (or Polarizer). This rotating gray filter eliminates some light waves and reduces the amount of light reaching the film by up to two full f/stops. It cuts glare on water and other shiny surfaces. It darkens blue sky to varying degrees when used with the sun behind it. (Use this filter with caution, some people over-use the Polarizer, which to me often looks unnatural). The Polarizer can also double as a two-stop neutral density filter, when a larger f/stop is wanted for shallow depth of field but this also gives a Polarized effect.

Get all the above filters in glass, large enough for all your lenses, you will use them frequently. I recommend the Tiffen and Hoya brands.

Note: All the filter designations given here and below are the photographic standard Kodak and Polaroid designations, which are also used by the Tiffen and Hoya brands among others. Some other filter manufacturers (like Nikon and Cokin) use different designations.

Why Filters Are Used

Our eyes are amazingly efficient, and can see detail in the deepest shadows and the brightest highlights at the same time. Our eyes also very quickly "correct" color. Skin tones appear natural under the bluish-white light of a sunny beach or ski slope, the warm red glow of a sunset, or the yellow or greenish cast of street lighting.

Indoors, our eyes adjust to make the light of fluorescent and household lamps, and even the orange or red flickers of candles or firelight seem "normal" or naturally colored to us. Color film can make no such adjustments. It uncompromisingly records the light that is actually there, which is why faces photographed with daylight film in a lamplit room look orange on daylight film.

Faces exposed under the fluorescent lights common in offices, schools, stores and factories look sickly green on daylight film. In daylight, scenes taken on very overcast days, or at high noon on the beach or sunny ski slopes, often look too blue, or sometimes too warm for our taste very early or late, because variations in time of day, weather, season and latitude affect the true color of daylight. And, as I described above, different brands of film have different color qualities, which are usually recognizable by anyone who knows color photography. Each film batch (called the emulsion) varies by a tiny amount from those that precede and follow it, just as paint, yarn and fabric dyes vary from batch to batch. Even professional film emulsions, carefully chosen and stored at optimum temperatures, can vary very slightly from normal color.

Some inexpensive small, and older large, electronic flash units emit a light slightly higher in color temperature than the 5,500K daylight film is balanced for. Processing lab colors vary slightly too.

Filters (and gels) can compensate for all the above, and be used to change mood too, so it is important for serious photographers to become familiar with at least the basic filters. Professionals need to know much more.

Filters for Black-and-White Photography

Black-and-white films are filtered for different reasons than color films. All black-and-white films, of course, convert colors and shades into tones of grey, but even today's panchromatic films that are sensitive to all colors are not equally sensitive to all colors. Some colors look darker, some lighter than they actually are when translated into black-and-white prints. Filters for black-and-white correct this, and alter tonal relationships for a normal or exaggerated range of tones, for faithful translations from color, or artistic variations of normal tones.

Basic Filters for Black-and-White Photography

All filters for black-and-white darken opposite colors and lighten similar colors in the print.

- A #12 or #15 (deep-yellow) filter is considered indispensable for darkening blue skies (blue does not record as deep as other colors on black-and-white film.
- A #25 (red) filter makes blue skies look black; paler red or orange filters lighten lips.
- A #87 (red) filter is used with black-and-white infra-red film for scientific and artistic purposes.
- A #21 (orange) filter makes blue skies look very dark.
- A #11 (yellow/green) filter lightens foliage, and can darken blue skies.

Note: To save carrying an extra filter, I use an 85B (orange) light-balancing filter with black and white film to darken blue skies. It works fine. Black-and-white filters can also be used for extremely strong effects with color film, if you like that sort of look.

Types of Filters

Filters can be round or square; glass, plastic or gelatin. Get them large enough, especially for wide-angle lenses, or you will get vignetting (a darkening at the corners of your pictures).

Kodak Professional Filters

Kodak (formerly called Wratten) filters have been the standard in photography for over 100 years. Kodak gelatin Light Balancing and Color Compensating filters are used for balancing light source and film; and for very slight changes of color. Kodak filters are still the standard of professional photography.

Other Filters

Tiffen Industries makes all its filters to Kodak color specifications, they make custom CC and LB filters in glass, and many special effect and black and white filters in glass, plastic and gelatin.

Hoya is a top Japanese filter maker with a very complete line.

Singh-Ray makes filters formulated for use with different film brands and types of fluorescent and industrial lighting, and also graduated, underwater and special effects filters.

Cokin filters, made in France, are especially popular with people who like a lot of added filter effects; Cokin uses a different numbering system for standard filters than the Kodak system.

Nikon and Hasselblad are among camera manufacturers who market filters under their own brand names. These tend to be expensive and have other than standard filter numbers or designations. I personally don't think these filters are worth the extra cost.

Protecting Your Lenses With Filters.

I recommend using clear UV or very slightly warm Skylight color filters on all your lenses as protection from scratches, dust and fingerprints. With a filter as a lens cover, you are ready to shoot at all times, and your lens mount is protected to some degree if dropped. It has saved me more than once. A couple of years ago, a student of mine went to Switzerland with a new long zoom lens. She was so thrilled by her first views of the Alps that she left the new lens on the roof of the rental car when changing to wide-angle. She and her husband drove off slowly to snap some goats. Of course there was a horrid clink as the zoom hit the road, and they feared the worst. Fortunately, she had installed a filter. It was smashed to smithereens but the lens survived undamaged!

Professional Filters for Travel/Location Photography

Still-life, fashion/beauty and product photography require extremely accurate color reproduction. Merchandise reproduced the wrong color in a catalog especially might be returned in large quantities. Travel and location requirements are a little less stringent, but there are many situations where the color must be very good (in food photography for instance).

Filters are used to modify, correct or balance color for all these situations. Most professionals own several blue and orange, red and yellow, green and magenta gelatin filters in different strengths, plus a technical filter holder.

Color-Compensating (CC) Filters

CC filters come in .025, .05 and then in .10 increments to .50, of the photographic additive colors red, blue and green, and subtractive colors, yellow, cyan and magenta. They are designated by color (R, B and G, and Y, C and M) and strength. A common filter pack for fluorescent lights is a 5Y or 10Y plus a 30M, for instance. Kodak gelatin CC filters are the professional photography standard for use for in front of lenses. They are dyed to extremely precise specifications and sold individually wrapped. Most lenses take 3" square gelatin filters; 5" filters are available also. A metal filter holder is also needed. Most studio pros own a full set of each color.

Light Balancing (LB) Filters and Gels

Light Balancing filters (and gels) are various strengths of blue and orange. Filters are available in glass, plastic or gelatin, and are used, (along with magenta and green CC filters) to balance the color of the light source to the film being used. A set of these filters, along with a color temperature meter is almost indispensable today for the location photographer who must reproduce color accurately under difficult lighting conditions.

Light Balancing filters are used in front of the lens; gels are used in front of lights, for the same reason as light-balancing filters, to modify the color of the light reaching the film.

Blue filters bring tungsten light up in color temperature (make it bluer) for use with daylight film. They include the 80A (3,200K to 5,500K daylight) 80B (3,400K to 5,500K daylight) and the pale blue 82 A,B and C filters which are used when a slight increase in color temperature is needed. The 82B filter is used to bring household lamps from 2,900K to 3,200K to balance with tungsten film for instance.

Orange filters reduce (warm) the color temperature and are used if tungsten film must be balanced with daylight. The most useful one is the 85B (5,500 K daylight to 3,200K). The very light orange 81A, B, C and EF series of filters are often used for a slight warming effect in combination with flash/strobe light (for artistic effect or because some units have slightly higher color temperatures than 5,550K). Of course they can warm overcast or rainy day bluish light too, and they make average sunlit scenes look warmer, resembling early or late light.

Kodak CC filters currently cost about $11 each, in New York, discount; a complete set of 36 different 3" CC and LB gelatin filters will therefore cost you about $400.

Note: CC filters can be combined to produce the same effects as light-balancing filters; if you have all the colors and strengths; the LB filters, though, reduce the number of filters required in a filter pack.

Filter Packs

A combination of two or three CC and LB filters used together is called a filter pack. Packs may be needed to correct difficult mixed lighting situations. Photographers who specialize in location work where difficult lighting conditions are the norm usually use a color temperature meter. (I use Minolta's; see later in this chapter, and also Chapters Four and Fourteen. When using it I carry a lot of CC and LB light balancing gels.)

Use fewer CC/LB filters of deeper intensity to avoid degrading any image with too thick a filter pack. You should not use more than 3 gelatin filters in a pack.

Special Effect Filters

Diffusion, graduated, starburst, multi-image etc., filters are quite popular today. Cokin, a French manufacturer, popularized these filters. In my opinion they should be used with great caution; they can too easily become clichés, especially when bright color is also added.

Note: Moderate diffusion filters with clear centers are flattering to older subjects, and people with skin problems.

Neutral Density Filters

Neutral density filters reduce light without affecting color. A square neutral density-to-clear graduated filter can be extremely useful for cutting the light from the sky in backlit landscapes. I carry these filters in gray-to-clear; muted blue-to-clear, and reddish/orange-to-clear.

Polarizing Filters

Polarizing filters work (in very simplified terms) by filtering out some scattered light waves and passing others on in a specific direction. Polarizers are rotated so you can actually see the effect this has when looking through the lens. They are used for darkening blue skies and reducing glare. As they are neutral gray, and reduce exposure by up to two stops (see manufacturers' directions for specifics), they can also be used in place of neutral density filters (with a Polarized effect).

Note: I think that the over-use of Polarizers often results in rather "dead" looking pictures. Be discreet when you use them.

Testing Professional Film and Filters

Professional slide/transparency films are manufactured to very close tolerances (plus or minus 10CC of filtration).

Many studio photographers test many emulsions of their favorite film, and when they find an emulsion they like, buy it in quantity and freeze it until needed.

Test exposures should include Kodak color control patches and separation guide and gray scale, or a Macbeth color checker and an 18% gray card. Test your favorite slow/medium speed and fast daylight film(s) and tungsten films if you use them.

A thorough test set-up for travel photographers should include a person for skin tones. Shoot under daylight, tungsten light, and fluorescent light conditions, and with flash/strobe and hot lights if used. Use the filters recommended (if any) in the data sheet included with the film. Note all exposures and filters/filter packs used. (I write these on a small chalkboard included in the test shots.) Judge the results of the tests on a light box, using a Kodak or Calumet color-viewing kit for the most accurate results. A good professional lab will help you to judge the tests if you are inexperienced.

Using Color Temperature Meters

Corporate photographers, who must often work quickly under difficult mixed light situations, rely on color temperature meters to tell them what filter packs to use as a basis for tests. Then they test the film and slight variations in filter packs in advance under the same lighting conditions, using the same emulsion, lighting and processing lab as they will for the job.

When viewing test film to decide what additional filtration (if any) is needed, use the CC and LB gelatin filters you have singly or in combination or, use a viewing kit (a set of filters of different colors and densities mounted together). Calumet's viewing filter kit can be used for color transparencies or prints (about $60), as can the more limited but inexpensive Kodak color print viewing filter kit (about $13).

Professional Data Sheets

Film manufacturers' highly-detailed Professional Data Sheets recommend filtration for different light conditions and exposure times; they are free, get them at professional dealers, or from the manufacturers.

Care of Fragile Filters and Gels

Apart from glass filters used as lens covers (which should be replaced frequently) keep filters in a leather or fabric filter case or they can get scratched and will fade eventually. I keep mine in a fabric case designed for 3" Macintosh computer floppy discs. Store filters and gels in the dark when not being used. Gels used in front of hot lights should be replaced frequently. Some people use the Jelly Roll device to store their gels, it is available from photo stores; I keep mine in an adjustable length plastic tube designed for rolled artwork.

More about Gels

Rosco and Lee both manufacture gels in sheets and rolls for the theater, movie and television industries. They are increasingly used by still photographers. They come in light-balancing and color correcting shades, neutral density increments and just about every color you can think of. (The same manufacturers also make several kinds of diffusing and reflective sheets which have many uses in still photography.)

Gels are used in front of flash, strobe and tungsten-light sources; location photographers often use them in front of lights aimed at dull gray backgrounds in industrial areas. A red gel on a background light will make the background red for instance, but will not affect the foreground if the light is properly directed (and masked with "blackwrap" —black aluminum foil— if necessary).

Balancing Foreground and Background Color and Light with Gels

To balance a flash or strobe-lit foreground subject with a time-exposed background area (when using a glass or gelatin filter over the lens to correct a fluorescent-lit time-exposed huge factory floor for instance) use the opposite color gel on the lighthead; for example if you use 30 Magenta on the lens, use a 30 Green gel on the flash/strobe. If you don't correct the flash/strobe-lit area, the foreground (your main subject) will come out magenta. (See the Color Wheel diagram earlier in the chapter.)

Using Gels as Substitutes for Kodak Filters

When I started in photography, 3" Kodak gelatin filters were very inexpensive. I still have some bought in the mid-'70's, with their price stickers of $1.25 each attached. These filters now cost around $11 each at discount dealers. (Kodak photo mechanical [color-printing] filters, which are cheaper than the camera filters, come in the same shades, and are extremely accurate in color, and may also be used in front of lenses.)

Calumet makes Kodak compatible filters that are less expensive, but still by no means cheap.

Note: When using any gelatin filters (or substitutes; see Gels later in this chapter) care must always be taken to keep them flat or you'll get reflections in the picture. This normally calls for using a standard Kodak 3" gelatin filter holder or equivalent (mine is a Samigon 76x76mm Technical Filter Holder) but I've also taped gel over lenses in emergencies.

As I'm not making eight or nine times what I did in the 1970's (and because I don't usually need extremely precise color correction or color balance) I experimented with using pieces of inexpensive Rosco lighting gel in front of the lens instead of 3" Kodak gelatin filters. These currently cost about $4.50, discount, for a 20x24" sheet. I used Rosco Cinegels for my tests, because Rosco is generous about giving away samples, and is making an effort to woo still photographers. Cinegels are on a thicker gelatin base, and probably their color tolerance is not quite so precise as Kodak filters, nor do Rosco gels come in the very palest Kodak shades. For truly precise color, nothing beats using Kodak filters (and making careful color tests.) But for many general photographic purposes lighting gels used as filters do very well. See the filter/ gel comparison table later in the chapter.

Filter and Gel Sets

Rosco's Jungle Kit is a set of fifteen 10x12" sheets of their light balancing Cinegels cut to fit Lowel Light, Smith Victor and other gel holders. (The Jungle Kit contains most of the gels listed in the comparison table on the next page, and costs about $30 at photo dealers).

Individual Rosco and Lee gels come in 20x24" sheets, and in tubes for use over fluorescent-light fixtures (these are used by some architectural still photographers). They also come in wide, long rolls for use over windows.

The cheapest place I currently know to buy gels is Times Square Theatrical Lighting, 318 West 47th Street, New York, NY 10036. Phone: (212) 245-4155. Fax: (212) 956-6537. They publish a useful lighting catalog, and sell by mail.

Calumet makes a useful set of 15 Kodak-compatible light balancing and color correction filters for use with color temperature meters; about $60 for the set. (See Chapter Three.)

Where to Learn More About Filters and Gels

Filter manufacturers (Tiffen, Hoya, Cokin etc.) put out free or inexpensive leaflets about their products. *Using Filters,* a Kodak Workshop Series book, is useful. Film manufacturers supply free Professional *Data Sheets* listing filtration recommended for their products.

Rosco sample booklets showing their Cinegel line and all their other colors are available from professional photo and theatrical lighting dealers, or from the manufacturer. They are sometimes free, sometimes sold for about a dollar. The booklets are interesting to look at and read. Contact Rosco for samples and leaflets at (914) 937-1300; (213) 462-2233 and (416) 475-1400. Lee sample books are a bit harder to come by, try specialist film/television/theatrical lighting dealers.

Note: The individual samples of gels in both gel booklets are just the right size (1 1/2 x 3 1/4") to tape onto a standard-size bounce flash head.

Some Useful Kodak Filters and
Approximate Rosco Gel Equivalents

Filters for balancing the green look of varying amounts of cool white fluorescent light with daylight films. (For specific filtration recommendations for all types of fluorescents see film manufacturers' data sheets.)

Kodak CC Filter and light source	Rosco gel name, number.
.30 Magenta (full fluorescent light)	Tough Minusgreen #3308
.10 + .05 Magenta (about 50% daylight)	Tough 1/2 Minusgreen #3313
.05 + .25 Magenta (about 75% daylight)	Tough 1/4 Minusgreen #3314
	Tough 1/8 Minusgreen #3318

.25 Magenta (almost all daylight)*

Note: Gels are used on close flash/strobe light sources to compensate for varying amounts of filtration on lens to correct background fluorescent light:

Rosco Tough Plusgreen #3304 gel is opposite the .30 Magenta filter.
Rosco Tough 1/2 Plusgreen # 3315 gel is opposite .10 + .05 Magenta filters.
Rosco Tough 1/4 Plusgreen #3316 gel is opposite .05 + .25 Magenta filters.

Blue filters and gels are used to balance daylight film to tungsten lights, household light to tungsten film, and for general cooling effects. ("Gels" were measured under 3,200°K lights.)

Kodak filter	Rosco gel name, number.
80B (3,400°K to 5,500°K)	Full Blue # 3202
80A (3,200° K to 5,500°K)	Full Blue # 3202 plus Eighth Blue # 3216*
	Half Blue # 3204 (+ 900°K)
	Third Blue #3206 (+ 600°K)
	Quarter Blue # 3208 (+ 400°K)
82C (2,900°K household lamps to 3,200°K Type B film.)	
82A (cools; + 200°K)	Eighth Blue # 3216 (+ 200°K)
82 (cools; + 100°K)	

Orange/amber filters and gels are used to balance tungsten film to daylight; to balance cool flash/strobe units to daylight film, and for general warming effects. ("Gels" were measured under daylight.)

Kodak filter	Rosco gel name, number.
85B (5,500° K to 3,200°K)	Roscosun 85 # 340
85C (5,500° K to 3,800°K)	Roscosun 1/2 # 3408 (warms; - 1,700°K)
81C (warms; - 800°K)	Roscosun 1/4 # 3409 (warms; - 1,000°K)*
81A (warms; - 200°K)	Roscosun 1/8 # 3410 (warms; - 200°K)
81 (warms; -100 °K)	

*Note: My tests were made using a Minolta III color temperature meter.

I repeat once again that for precise color nothing beats doing your own color tests, because different lights, films, filters, gels and labs all vary slightly.

Chapter 6

Daylight and Available Light

No two travel/tourism/location photographers (or any other kind of photographers) use light in the same way. Some, mostly advertising illustration specialists, go on location with almost the same equipment they would use back in the studio. They take powerful portable strobe power packs and many flash heads; big lightstands; large to huge soft boxes, and reflectors and diffusers originally developed for movie location work. They light everything from scratch. Other photographers do the exact opposite. Most landscape photographers, for instance, specialize in daylight pictures. They have mastered the use of the variations in the color of light at different times and in different weather.

Developing a Philosophy of Lighting for Travel Photography

Many traveling photographers, including magazine and corporate industrial and architectural photography specialists, shoot in daylight where possible, but have learned how to work with existing light, supplemented by judicious amounts of strobe, tungsten or even small flash lighting in the huge atriums, offices, factories and other locations they must make look wonderful on film. These photographer know a lot about filtration, and often "gel" lights and make tests before they shoot, to balance different light sources and make sure everything comes out the right color on the film.

Still other photographers (including many fine-art specialists) work mostly with daylight and existing light, supplemented with small flash. Some of these are photojournalists. You will have to decide which approach to using light is best for you.

One photographer who does a lot of travel/location work and is very well known for his use of daylight is Anthony Edgeworth. See his book *The Marines,* it will teach you a lot about using daylight as well as about the United States Marine Corps. Jay Maisel and Joel Meyerowitz are both acknowledged masters of daylight also.

My Philosophy of Using Light

Most travel photographers who do assignments today though, must know how to use both daylight and existing light, and to use photographic lighting well.

My photographic background is editorial or editorial-style. My philosophy of lighting is to work with the least added light than I can use and still get good photographs. I sometimes use "fill" flash on camera, and sometimes two or more small flash units "slaved" together off camera. Sometimes I use "hot lights" (tungsten photo-lamps) which are quick to set up, and of course, there are times when only fairly powerful "strobe" (electronic flash) lights will do what I want.

I often have time limits, and almost always self-imposed weight limits. I usually work alone, so every pound of equipment that has to be carried down long airport corridors, up old railroad station stairs or to and from distant parking lots has to be worth its weight in photographic gold. My assistant, if there is one, is almost always hired locally, for local knowledge, not for technical expertise. For these reasons, I do all of my location lighting using the lightest, simplest and most portable equipment I can get.

I supplement daylight almost always, because I like the look of natural, rather than very styled lighting. I carry flash units, or a lightweight portable strobe pack with two heads, or sometimes both. I use hot lights sometimes. Everything has to pack into something I can carry by myself if necessary. In many places, luggage porters are an extinct species.

I work with "bounce" light (reflect light back into the subject) umbrellas to diffuse artificial light and direct sunlight, all depending on the time of day, place and subject. I use flash "fill" (that lightens small shadows) outdoors with a dedicated/TTL flash. I use white or silver or gold reflectors to bounce light with sunlight and flash, and flash, strobe or tungsten lights on stands diffused by umbrellas, soft boxes and scrims, all as necessary. All my lights can be hung, taped, or hidden behind furniture and other objects and spread around a large area. I use a flash meter, and a Polaroid camera and film to make tests of lighting set-ups. I use "slaves" (light receptors that set off a flash or strobe)on my off-camera flash and strobe lights, with a light "trigger" (signal device) or small flash on camera to set them off.

Sometimes, in low light, very long exposures alone, or used with just small areas accented by flash fill (see Chapter Seven), give very good, creative results with interesting color.

You will not use light the same way as I do, or as any other photographer does. Everyone eventually develops their own lighting style, part of their overall photographic style.

A Basic Flash Outfit.

You can't always get the picture you want, even outdoors, without knowing how to modify light. Two useful things to know are how to bounce light with a reflector, and how to use a small flash, on or off camera, for flash fill to lighten shadows, outdoors and indoors.

You will need the following to start lighting well with flash:

❑ A camera or cameras with a high flash sync (synchronization) speed, (1/250 of a second is best); fast lenses and in-camera metering. The cameras should have a depth of field preview button, a "B" (bulb) setting for very long exposures, provision for double exposures and a self timer.

❑ A portable flash unit, with a head that bends, to permit bouncing light, and a remote cord or sync cord so you can use the flash off the camera.

❑ A sturdy tripod that extends to at least eye level.

❑ A cable (shutter) release is helpful for minimizing camera shake at long exposures. You can also use the camera self-timer for this. (Program cameras may need a special release, check your camera manual.)

❑ A 36" or 48" round white and silver and/or white and gold collapsible fabric reflector is very helpful for "bouncing" daylight or available light into close, shadowed areas, and weighs almost nothing, and completes your basic lighting kit.

❑ A hand held combination flash/available light meter is very good insurance as a backup for your camera meters as well as for flash metering

❑ Four basic filters are useful in many lighting situations. (See Chapter Five for the basic filter kit.)

Light Requirements for Professional Travel/Tourism/Location Photography

Commercial travel photography, which is mostly done for the huge tourist industry, almost always requires fine weather. This may be a matter of chance and a lot of waiting about in some countries or regions like the Pacific Northwest and the British Isles, but in others the rainy season is highly predictable, and absolutely to be avoided when planning a shoot. Spring and fall have beautiful light and good weather almost everywhere; but, carefully research weather patterns in advance of any assignment, before you travel to a shoot in islands or coastal areas during hurricane season, or ski resorts when the snow cover has not arrived or is fast disappearing!

Almost all travel, or tourism, or location photography for publication or any kind of reproduction today requires the use of lighting. Pictures with heavy shadows on faces, for instance, are not photographically acceptable, they do not reproduce well. Avoid shooting outdoors in high noon sun everywhere, because of harsh lighting, this is especially true in the tropics. (See also Chapter Five.)

Indoor pictures must have pleasant appearing color, whether precisely corrected or not. Food is a standby of travel and tourism assignments; as food can look unappetizing the wrong color, it is usually necessary to add lighting to whatever is available in the dining room, restaurant or kitchen.

Editorial clients too prefer fine weather and well lit, not too shadowy pictures for most of their stories, but the odd misty day or occasional "mood" shot, say of a person in spotted light under a broad-leafed tree are acceptable.

Most travel/tourism/location photographers like myself do some work for industrial and corporate clients. The annual report season is from September to March, and many older industrial giants are still in the Northeastern United States and Northern Europe. This means a lot of shooting outdoors in extreme cold and coping with short shooting days, and poor weather and light. Under such conditions, if you can't make the weather good, you can at least make sure that the light is interesting or beautiful. It doesn't pour with rain in an annual report any more than it does in a travel brochure, but industrial lights at twilight glowing through mist, fog or even drizzle may look elegant.

Airports, railroad stations, lobbies and public rooms, dimly-lit restaurants, concert and banquet halls, theaters, sports arenas, discos and clubs almost all have one thing in common, whether shot for editorial, corporate or tourism clients—difficult to almost impossible light—and will test your knowledge of filters and your lighting skills to the limit.

Using the Qualities of Light to Convey Mood

Beginning photographers, and some who are not beginners at all, take pictures outdoors, or indoors with available light, or even flash or strobe or tungsten lighting, without giving any thought to the light except to worry if there is enough of it to get an exposure.

But light quality is one of the most important elements in any photograph, sometimes it is the reason for the photograph. The ordinary can be made beautiful, and the beautiful made truly extraordinary, in the right light. Light can be soft and flattering from a diffuse or large, close source; hard or harsh from a single small or distant source; or bright and sparkling from a multi-light source. All of these kinds of light are useful, depending on the mood you want to achieve.

Light from the sun and direct artificial light looks hot when it shines down from right overhead, directional light from the side brings out texture. Diffused lighting from clouds or indoor fluorescent lighting give even, often flat, illumination. Such light is reasonably pleasant on people. Indoors, in factories, hospitals and schools it may convey cleanliness, efficiency etc, or it can read as grim and institutional. Soft pinkish lamplight is used in department stores and restaurants for a warm, flattering, relaxing effect. Lots of bright lights can convey fun and entertainment (the Las Vegas strip for instance) or danger (flashing lights at an accident).

As well as studying light, serious travel/location photographers must know about filtration, because color often records differently on film than to the eye, and correction filters are required to make color photographs look normal. Some colors when transformed to black and white tones, look lighter or darker than you think they will, in the printed picture. (See also Chapter Five.)

To learn how to really see and to use even daylight well, you have to look at light at lot, especially at first. And to augment existing light, or create your own, you will need to know at least the basics of photographic lighting. Anyone can plug in the lights after a ten minute indoctrination, it's creating with light that's hard.

Note: Lighting courses are given in photo and film schools; lighting workshops are listed in *The Guide to Photography Workshops and Schools* (see Chapters One and Twenty).

Looking at Light

To master both daylight and available light and eventually be able to create the effects you want with photographic light, start by studying light, and the lighting effects you like and hate, and think about light quality wherever you go, even when you don't have a camera with you.

Look at light in large dark spaces with tall windows like churches and courthouses and railroad stations, and small dark spaces lit from above like elevators. Watch the sun come up. Stand under a tree in bright sunshine at noon. And study light on swimming pools, lake and rivers in the late afternoon. If you live near the ocean, look at waves in late winter light.

Looking at Daylight

The quality and color of daylight is not the same at different times, different seasons, in different weather or even different places. With the aid of a tripod, you can photograph from the first glimmer of dawn to the last afterglow of sunset. Color records on film differently to how our eyes see it; by photographing at different times of day, and, year, you will learn the variations.

Imagine noon on the flat desert of Utah or North Africa with the sun vertically overhead. White nights in Scandinavia where you can read a newspaper outside at midnight. Think of a drizzly gray fall day in the caverns of New York's financial district—or London's. Mist coming off Pacific ocean surf early in the morning, making the cliffs recede in ever paler bands of blue. Long blue shadows on a Vermont ski-slope late on a sunny winter day. A Kansas wheatfield glowing against a deep blue sky with the sun behind you on a late August evening. Or perhaps just stripes of morning sunshine slanting through a farm kitchen window blinds, painting a still life of dishes, coffee pot and fruit with bands of gold. At night, imagine the neon lit bustle of Times Square or Piccadilly Circus or the Ginza during a damp winter rush hour. Fireworks at a small town or big city Fourth of July celebration. You probably have seen some or most of these things, but never really analyzed what made them beautiful. Often, it was the light. If you can capture these things on film you will take fine photographs, and have come close to mastering the use of available light.

Time of Day

The single most important outdoor photography commandment is to carefully choose the time of day you shoot. The variation in the color and quality of daylight over just a few hours can make all the difference between a mediocre or just average picture and great shot. All professional travel, location and architectural photographers spend a lot of time waiting around for the light to be just right. Low, warm early morning and late evening sunlight is almost always best for photographing landscapes, architecture and any outdoor scenes.

Sometimes this means getting up at four in the morning, because you must be where you want to shoot before the sun comes up—the pre-dawn glow and often brilliant color of a good sunrise may only last from five to fifteen minutes. At Cumberland Island in northern Florida in August I rose at five every morning to get those red sunrises on sand and sea, and then the long pink and blue shadows revealing the texture of undulating dunes and even birds' footprints on the otherwise pristine beach that became a trampled, flat, blinding white at noon.

Many cityscapes and building and monument pictures are "morning shots" rather than evening shots because they face east. Try and work out the best time to photograph important buildings in advance, and plan your shooting schedule accordingly. Many popular tourist attractions are best photographed very early in the morning, before the crowds arrive, and before any litter has accumulated. You should try to get permission from the press or public affairs department in advance to go in before the public, but if this is not possible, the first half hour or hour in the morning is usually fairly quiet. Many colorful activities, like the return of a laden fishing fleet, the setting up of lush displays of produce in a market or the start of harvesting are also definite "morning shots."

Sunrise and Sunset

Sunsets and sunrise are often spectacular on film. The color temperature of the light is low, exaggerating the warm red and yellow tones on film. Sunsets tend to last longer and look redder than sunrises, because of the dust in the air. Scout the location you want in advance, with the aid of a compass if necessary, then arrive at your previously selected viewpoint well before the sunset itself rises or sets. If you photograph for an hour before to an hour or more after sunset you will get a wide range of sky, landscape and sea color from yellowish to orange to red. After sunset itself, the sky will fade to pink, then to pale blue at dusk. A royal blue mid dusk sky is the ideal for cityscapes with lights, the buildings are silhouettes, and separated from the sky. Again, this magic time lasts for only a few minutes, because the sky quickly darkens to navy blue, then black, which usually records as either slightly brownish or greenish on film.

Very Low Sunlight

Although I'm not primarily a nature photographer I have photographed animals and birds in wilderness areas of the United States, and especially on the plains of East Africa. Most wildlife feeds within an hour or so of dawn and dusk, and those that are around at mid-day are spotted or striped or otherwise cam-ouflaged to be almost invisible in bright overhead sun.

If you are photographing professional or amateur models or people of any kind outdoors in sunlight, warm early morning or evening sunlight is infinitely more flattering than harsh noon glare. When the sun is low, you can "bounce" it back into your subjects' faces with reflectors. These are usually white or gold for a very warm look, or silver, and can be purchased inexpensively in sheets or on foamcore from art stores, or very popular today, the collapsible reflectors stretched over thin wire which are easy to transport. Rosco makes a small, handy folding reflector pack of lightweight, flexible, reversible silver/blue material, it can be taped up and is useful for bouncing flash/strobe and hotlights in confined areas.

If You Must Shoot in Overhead Sun

Sometimes of course, you can't choose the time you photograph (or you can't wait). Then do the best you can, using reflectors, flash "fill" or your picture-design skills to minimize harsh effects. Usually it's possible to plan shooting times, and to schedule location scouting or indoor photography or rest for noon time. This is especially important in mid-summer or the tropics when the over-head sun is very harsh. If you shoot lot of sports (they do come up in travel assignments), and have to photograph scheduled events, remember to save plenty of film for the second half of the baseball game, tennis match or bull-fight. The light will be infinitely more pleasing at 4 or 5 p.m. than it is at 2 p.m.

For close-up people pictures, always use reflectors or small flash to fill harsh, unflattering noon light. (See also Chapter Seven.) And remember don't shoot at high noon if you can possibly avoid it!

Bad Weather

The quality of light caused by weather is always important, especially when shooting landscapes. Bad weather can mean beautiful light. On assignment in Northumberland, on England's harsh Northeast coast, I hit an uncharacteris-tic three days of brilliant blue sunny days and cloudless skies. I shot interiors, and was much relieved when great black and white cumulus clouds blew up on the fourth day and let me take the moody castled hillsides and white-capped seascapes that I wanted. But I had to wait for fine weather in the damp English Lake District, lakes in the rain are just not appealing, and useless for editorial, tourism or stock photography.

Softly lit cloudy days are often flattering to people and are usually good for shooting outdoor portraits, because you avoid the ugly deep shadows on faces you can get in bright sunlight. Just before it rains mountains and distant views are a sharply delineated, deep blue. You can photograph in fog, rain or snow (protect your camera with a clear plastic bag). Blue dusk is a great time to shoot mountain vistas well as cities in any weather, and if you shoot at dusk, you can salvage a rainy day because the rain itself will only be noticeable if it reflects on shiny streets, and it won't show up on long exposures of skyline views. In the country, you can make long dusk exposures of damp landscapes too, I've done it very effectively in Ireland, New York State and the Orient. It is my experience that weather often improves at dusk, the rain may stop as you start shooting. The light in bad weather is low, requiring exposures too long for hand held shooting. The light then is high in color temperature, and looks blueish on film. Use this color for effect mood, or, correct it if you prefer.

A stable tripod with vertical and horizontal adjustments is an absolute must for any serious photographer. You will use it a lot in poor weather.

Time of Year

Some pictures are not just "morning shots," or sunset shots, they are summer shots, or fall, or winter, or spring shots. I'm not just talking about the color of the leaves, but about air quality, and the specific position of the sun on the horizon at different times of year. For instance the famous view of the Statue of Liberty with the sun setting right behind it (it looks great taken with a 500mm lens) can only be done for about two weeks in December when the sun sets almost due south of Manhattan. The spectacular cloudscapes of New Mexico are at their peak in August, in northern Europe it gets dark at around 4 p.m. in November, most mountain ranges are hazy in midsummer and so on. Buildings can't be moved, but the sun moves around them. An architectural photographer may wait months for the sun to illuminate the north side of a building. Rainy seasons are to be avoided almost everywhere. If you can plan a fall or spring trip, these are the best photography seasons almost everywhere, with beautiful, clear, angled light. (Remember though, seasons reverse in the Southern Hemisphere!)

Types of Daylight

The quality and the direction of daylight anywhere, at any time and any season is always very important for photography. Here is a brief description of some daylight situations, and their photographic advantages and disadvantages:

Side Light

This directional light from the low-angled sun early and late in the day is beautiful, and the first choice for most landscapes, panoramic views and cityscapes. For buildings and architecture the direction of the sidelight at different times of the day (or year) is important. Sidelight can be a strong portrait light, it emphasizes facial planes, and is excellent for showing up textures of all kinds.

Backlight

Light from behind the subject (sometimes called rim light) is very low morning or evening sunlight, aimed at the lens but masked behind a person, scene, object or building. Sometimes it can shine directly into the lens. When properly used, this can be the most interesting light of all. Long shadows come towards you, heads are haloed with sunshine, translucent leaves and flowers take on a new beauty and portraits are supremely soft and flattering when the sun is low and right behind the subject. And low backlighting is often spectacular over water. This lighting takes quite a bit of practice; use your exposure meter carefully, bracket exposures, and meter up close on people's faces to avoid silhouettes. Flare caused by the sun's direct rays hitting the lens and bouncing around can cause little blue blips, or orange "spaceships" on the picture and can degrade or destroy the image. Use the stop-down preview button on your camera, you can see any problems caused by too much flare. Sometimes flare effects can add excitement to a shot, sometimes you must change your angle to the sun, or use your hand (or a tree branch or other object) between you and the sun to block excess flare. Meter off the sky, not the sun itself for a picture of the sun itself at sunset, or the sky will be too dark, underexposed. Meter off the sky also, not brilliantly backlit water, or sand or snow, or you will again get underexposure.

"Bounce" Light

Light "bounced" onto a shaded subject is very beautiful, it is the soft, warm, glowing light that is reflected from a nearby white building or other large white or very light surface. If you photograph someone on the shady side of a sunny building or street, or under a white porch, you can get flattering "bounce-lit" portraits even in harsh noon sun. Light that is kicked into people's faces from snow and white sand is effectively "bounce" light too. Make your own flattering bounce light with a portable white or gold reflector. Stand or place the subject so that the sun hits your reflector and "bounces" the light back to the shaded or partly shaded subject.

Flat Light

Low sunlight from right behind you that hits the subject directly in front of you is flat light. You can use this warm light early and late all year everywhere, and most of the day on sunny winter days in Northern climates (when it is very yellow). Flat light can be very dramatic in a posterish kind of way especially when using long telephoto lenses. It is the only way to photograph long reflections on water, and is great for sunlight landscapes (especially red Western landscapes) with storm clouds brewing. It is dramatic for cityscapes, city crowd scenes, traffic, markets etc. though it can be a bit harsh for people (they tend to squint), and looks rather like direct on-camera flash. When the light is flat, you can deliberately underexpose scenics for deep blue skies without the need for Polarizing filters.

Three Quarter Light

Old photo manuals recommended shooting with the sun coming over your left shoulder because light from a high 3/4 angle easily defines almost any subject and is an almost foolproof way of getting good pictures with the simplest camera.

Soft Light

This light can come from different sources. It can be the very low light before sunrise, or after sunset, or light diffused by clouds or mist or even drizzle outdoors. Rainy or snowy days are softly lit, and can convey much emotion. Misty soft light can be lovely for land and seascapes, thin fog gives oriental effects of receding planes of color getting paler and paler. Again, you may need to use a tripod in low soft light. Indoors, soft light filters indirectly from a window, especially from a high north window, or a window diffused by translucent curtains. It is the light chosen by many classic portrait and interior painters, and by the early portrait photographers. The direction of the windowlight to your subject varies the light quality of course. Experiment with moving the subject, and your camera angle in relation to the window.

Use gentle and flattering soft light for portraits and people studies outdoors even on sunny days, by moving your subject into the shadow of a building, or onto the shaded side of the street. (You can also shade them with a translucent white umbrella.) Portable reflectors that are made of translucent white fabrics can be used outdoors to soften light. In the movie business they are called "silks" or "flying silks," and are hung from above the subject/set, or angled from the side on stands.

Low light

You can take pictures as long as you can see. The light may be warm or cool.

Use time-exposures and a tripod, or very fast film. (Be aware of possible reciprocity failure for very long exposures.)

Some top professionals use a gyro-stabilizer in low light when a tripod cannot be used.

Top Light

This hard light comes from overhead summer, midday or tropical sun, and is to be avoided as a rule. It causes ugly shadows under peoples' eyes, noses, mouths and chins. Indoors, top light comes from overhead, unshaded lights. (It's a good light for conveying harsh or primitive living conditions.) On the beach, if someone is lying looking upwards, the top light in effect becomes side light, and can be used for conveying a feeling of heat. (Some light is always bounced upwards from snow or white sand, opening up harsh toplit shadows.) When photographing dark-skinned people under top light, add bounce or fill light to prevent the features from disappearing; underexposed in shadowed areas. Use an angled white, silver or gold reflector, or a small flash for this.

Using Reflectors to Soften Harsh or Contrasty Lighting

The most convenient reflectors to travel with are the round, collapsible fabric ones made by Photek and others. Using a motorized camera, or a camera on a tripod, I can shoot with one hand and use the other to hold and angle a 36" reflector to bounce light and fill dark shadows for a people/portrait subject. If you must shoot from further away, ask someone else to hold and aim the reflector for you, close to the subject, but out of your frame of course. (Or you can use a stand and a reflector clamp also, see below.) White reflectors work well up to about 6 feet from the subject, shiny silver and gold ones "bounce" light further.

Top light from overhead sun is not usually good for landscaps. Sunlight at noon hits only the roofs of buildings, leaving too dark shadows below. In general, go "location scouting" (see also Chapter Fifteen) or shoot indoors or take a short rest in the middle of sunny days. I make it an almost inviolable rule not to shoot outdoors if my shadow is shorter than I am. The only exceptions are if I need to show heat, broiling beaches, tropical languor, etc.

Contrasty Light

Very "spotty" light where part of a scene or subject is very brightly lit, and part in deep shadow is also to be avoided because film, especially color film, cannot record the same extremes the eye can see. About five f/stops difference between the lightest and darkest areas is maximum to avoid black underexposed areas and bleached out highlights; (check lighting ratios with a meter). Reflectors and flash can help fill confusing shadows when used close up; but, be aware that noon sun filtering through distant foliage and grassy landscapes causes patches of dark shadows and bright highlights and the image may look so spotty that the totality is very hard to see (the principal behind camouflage).

Take nature photographs early and late; look for clearings under trees. Also be aware of the color you can pick up under foliage. Early in my career I was photographing a Southern resort. A very grand outdoor wedding took place beneath great oaks covered with Spanish moss. Everyone was in "Gone With the Wind" type costumes. I shot from behind the official wedding photographer, and was very pleased with myself until I got the bright green pictures back from the lab!

Wide-angle lens shots of contrasty big-city street scenes half in sun and half in deep shade are also a problem, because if you expose for the light side, the dark side will go almost black, and if you expose for the dark side the light side will be overexposed, too light to record detail. Change your angle, come back earlier or later or wait for a cloudy day to minimize contrast, especially in New York or any city with very high buildings. Flash fill can help.

Window Light

This usually beautiful light is at its best when diffused; on a cloudy day, by thin white curtains, or when light comes from a high north window (the light beloved by classical portrait and still-life painters). You will often need to use a tripod, for longish exposures. Use a reflector or a white sheet, or white illustration board to bounce some light back into the dark side of the face in a windowlit portrait. Interiors shots of even dimly window-lit churches, historic homes etc., can be made with time exposures, using a tripod of course.

Fleeting Light, or Magic Light

Fleeting moments when the light is truly extraordinary come very rarely, and you must seize those moments whenever you can. Extraordinary light often comes in conjunction with awful weather. I can think of a couple of examples: I went to Cambodia to photograph to the famous temples of Angkor Wat with some difficulty. I had a visa for a week. 1969 was not too good a time to be in that part of the world. I spent three of those days in Phnom Penh, then flew to Angkor. I was trapped in the hotel facing the temple complex by a torrential tropical downpour, for two and a half days. On the evening of the third day, just as I was getting very nervous about having to leave next morning, the rain slackened. I ran out with cameras wrapped in plastic. After a few moments, as I stood photographing a gold-colored cow munching on the acid-green grass in front of the gray temple, the sun crept out from crack in the black clouds and the whole scene was suffused with a watery lemon light. The effect was so extraordinary that I almost wanted to just watch and not take pictures. Almost. In ten minutes the sun was gone.

Another time I was shooting pictures after a lull in the troubles in Northern Ireland. I had rounded up some nice American naval officers (with American golf clothes!) to play on a famous course near the Giant's Causeway. There were intermittent showers and rather gusty winds. One captain was putting on a green opposite a particularly impressive black basalt rock formation when bright sun appeared and a rainbow shone right down into the hole. I got two spectacular frames before the rain resumed. Alas, the troubles started again soon after, and the planned advertising campaign for golf holidays in Northern Ireland never got off the ground.

If you have that kind of pure pictorial luck, shoot your heart out! And never quit because of bad weather. It will change, and when it does, you will get great light. I'm a native of England and I know!

I've lived in the same lower-midtown New York east-facing sixteenth floor loft for fourteen years now, and I still love to look at and photograph the rooftops and water towers, distant high buildings and cloudscapes. The light is always changing, but the best effects of all come before or after storms; winter and summer, spring and fall.

Available Light and Mixed Light

Available light is the photographic term for existing light from lamps of any kind in streets, stadiums, stores, offices, schools, etc., or any mixture of daylight and existing light. You can get good results photographing by available light if you follow a few tried and true principals. Available light is often low, requiring the use of a tripod or fast film.

Mixed light is where several different kinds of light exist in the same area. A fluorescent-lit office or classroom may be near a window, or a shop may have both warm tungsten lights and greenish fluorescents In general it is better to use daylight film for most available and mixed light situations. Daylight film looks warm, or orange with non-photographic lights, green with fluorescent lights. If you don't like these effect there are a couple of useful filters that will give good (not perfect color) under such conditions. If very accurate color is essential (it often is on a job) film testing in advance with one or more filters packs is necessary.

Photographing Sunsets and Sunrises

I list these in reverse because sunsets usually last longer and are more colorful than sunrises (because I think, of heat and dust raised in the day). But effects vary widely; peak effects may last a few seconds or half an hour or longer (especially for sunsets). Use slow or medium speed film. Always meter off the sky around the sun, not the sun itself, or you will get a correctly exposed sun, but a very dark to black sky. (Ideally use spotmeter mode on a program camera or use a hand-held spot meter; otherwise, center-weighted in-camera metering used with telephoto lenses should give good results.)

I always bracket sunset/sunrise pictures. Best sunsets are usually when there is a lot of pollution or haze, making the sun deep orange or red, or after storms. Some places I've been where there are fantastic cloud effects are Arizona, New Mexico, Bermuda and the west coast of Scotland. On very clear days anywhere there is too much contrast for great sunsets or sunrises.

Photographs of sunsets can be clichés, and are usually disappointing if shot with a normal 55mm or wide-angle lens. (The sun will look like a pinhole in the frame.) Sunsets are not worth doing in my opinion unless the overall scene is also worth recording, or the color or cloud effects especially good.

To get a reasonable-sized image of the sun rising or setting you will need at least a 200mm lens; a 300mm or 500mm is often better. My favorite pictures of the Statue of Liberty with the sunset behind it are made with a 500mm lens.

Any silhouetted person/object shot in front of the setting (or rising) sun should have a graphic shape.

Use a flash to "fill" and record detail of a person or object within about 10 feet of the flash, as well as the background sunset. (See Chapter Seven for details.)

If you use a 2x tele-extender with a 500mm lens, you can make a very nice large sun with the 1,000mm focal length that results. (Of course, don't look through the lens directly into bright sun for more than a few seconds.)

Night Photography

Problems to consider in night photography are accuracy of exposure, contrast, the law of reciprocity, and color shift that occurs with long exposures. Meter very carefully when using either an in-camera meter or a hand-held meter under lights at night. (See also Chapters Five and Six.)

The best "night" pictures are usually taken at twilight—I call it "blue time" after sunset, before it gets completely dark. The dusk starts off pale blue, like faded denim, then darkens to a vibrant royal blue (the peak time for great "night" shots) then quickly turns navy blue, then black. I usually shoot the whole sequence.

Totally black night pictures are often not so good. Night sky can look greenish, or brownish or purplish on film sometimes, depending on film brand and emulsion. At night, in Times Square, or the Las Vegas strip, or the Ginza for instance, don't aim your camera or meter directly at the bright neon lights; aim the lens or reflected light meter at something mid-toned, like the sidewalk (and use the "memory lock" button on a program camera), or you will get a picture of only the lights, with a totally black background.

Use the spotmeter setting on an electronic camera, a spotmeter (or a tele-photo lens carefully aimed) for distant night views.

Get night exposure and filtration guidelines from sheets packaged with your film (or printed inside film boxes); also see manufacturers' Data Sheets for professional films. Kodak and Fuji don't recommend long exposures, because of color shifts, but try them anyway, the results can be marvellous, and more interesting than "correct" color. (See table below, which is based on my tests.)

Night Photography Exposures

Bracket (vary) these exposures by one-half to one f/stop whenever possible.

FILM SPEED	25 ISO	50 ISO	100 ISO	400 ISO
Amusement parks, dusk	1/15 f/2	1/30 f/2	1/30 f/2.8	1/60 f/4
City skylines at "blue time"	1/2 f/2	1/2 f/2.8	1/4 f/2.8	1/8 f/4
City center signs at night	1/30 f/2	1/60 f/2	1/60 f/2.8	1/60 f/5.6
Country—pale blue dusk	1/8 f/2	1/15 f/2	1/30 f 2	1/60 f/4
Big firework displays	30 s f/2	30 s f/2.8	30 s f/4	30 s f/8
Floodlighting at dusk	1/2 f/2	1/4 f/2	1/4 f/2.8	1/8 f/4
Sound and Light Shows—night	1 s f/2	1/2 f/2	1/2 f/2,8	1/4 f/4
Laser light displays	15 s f/2.8	8 s f/2.8	8 s f/4	8 s f/8

("s" stands for seconds.)

Photographing the full moon*: Aperture of my 1,000mm lens is f/16.
With 100 ISO film I used exposures of 1/30-60 f/16. With ISO 400 film I use an exposure of 1/125-250 at f/16.
*Based on three tests, because the brilliance of the moon varies. I use a 500mm f/8 mirror telephoto lens plus a 2x tele-extender for moon pictures, to get maximum moon size. Remember you want good exposures of the surface of the moon itself, not the surrounding sky (which may vary from pale blue to black). Don't use slow film to photograph the moon unless you have a very fast telephoto lens, because it moves during long exposures.

Why You Should Use a Tripod
for Almost All Night Photography

A sturdy tripod will make all the difference to most night photography. Of course you can hand-hold a camera at low shutter speeds for blurred night impressions; these are often interesting when combined with flash "fill" which stops motion on nearby subjects.

- You can't meter fireworks; use a tripod, choose medium speed film (100 ISO is good) a wide aperture, say f/4, then try and find a viewpoint that includes more than just black sky, and focus on infinity. Set the shutter speed on 30 seconds (or use B—Bulb setting) and count off the time. Use a cable release to minimize camera shake. Bracket with exposures of 8 and 16 seconds.

- Laser displays too vary considerably in intensity, but you will need a tripod for all of them. For bright laser light displays use 100 ISO film, apertures of f/2.8 and f/4 and bracket exposures. Try two, four, and eight seconds.

- A tripod is imperative for photographing floodlit buildings. As floodlighting intensity and color varies widely, meter off lighter and darker parts of buildings or monuments (not the night sky) and average the exposures. With 100 ISO film, try bracketing around 1/2 sec at 2.8. I sometimes use both tungsten and daylight film in different cameras for floodlit scenes and sound and light shows (which alas never start at dusk but wait till pitch darkness) for the best possible interpretation of colors. I bracket exposures at least a half and a full stop in either direction, more if the lighting is very contrasty. Make Polaroid exposure tests of all these situations for a guarantee of good exposure. (See Chapter Four.)

Photographing Available Light Indoor Night Events

A tripod is usually impractical indoors at crowded events (but use one if you can). Flash is usually not permitted. Use the fastest possible lenses, and medium, fast or superfast film. A program camera is unsurpassed for rock shows and other presentations where the light is not too contrasty but constantly changing. I always use my N8008's on shutter priority with the fastest possible daylight or tungsten films to avoid blur if the subject is moving. With low lighting on medium subjects, I use 1/125 of a second at f/5.6 (with 400 ISO daylight film) as basic exposure. (Of course the colors come out warm, which I like.) A long lens (200mm and up) can function like a spotmeter on an SLR camera, and should give you good exposure if carefully used.

If you do a lot of coverage of situations in large areas where you cannot get close to meter (as in theater, sports, shows) a dedicated/TTL camera with spotmetering option or a hand-held spotmeter will give best results. But, you should still bracket contrasty situations. Remember the acrobat in a white suit may be overexposed if he's small on a large dark background. Remember too that all reflected-light meters (and automatic flash units) are designed to reproduce average subjects, and you will have to compensate for very light or dark subjects, and use average readings for high contrast subjects.

"Sneaking" Indoor Pictures

If desperately needed for a tourism brochure, I sneak the occasional picture in theaters and concerts. (Photography is forbidden on Broadway and in London's

West End unless you can get invited to the pre-opening night photo call, for which the whole company —Actor's Equity members and musicians and stage-hands—are paid.) I am cautious "sneaking," and have never had a problem, but remember you try it at your own risk! The safest time to sneak pictures is during bursts of applause, loud scenes, and the big production numbers that come at the end of the acts in musicals and operas. You can photograph final curtain calls in theaters quite openly if you do it quickly and then move out. I have found that an 80mm lens, Kodachrome 25 exposed at 1/60 at about f/1.8-2.8 does very well from an orchestra seat when there is bright lighting on stage. I have not been thrown out of a theater yet; I've used the technique in concert halls and opera houses too. I'm told this is not advisable in the less genteel atmosphere at some rock concerts and shows, where cameras are sometimes confiscated!

Note: I never "sneak" pictures in slums or other potentially dangerous places.

Reciprocity Failure and Color Shift in Long Exposures

Reciprocity is the correlation between lens aperture and shutter speed. If you open a lens one full stop (from f/5.6 to f/4 for instance) twice as much light will reach the film. At average shutter speeds (in the range of about 1/1000 of a second to about one or two seconds), if you want the light reaching the film to remain constant, double (increase) the shutter speed when you open the lens one stop, or halve (decrease) the shutter speed when you reduce the aperture one stop. But at very high speeds and very slow speeds these correlations no longer apply exactly. This phenomenon is called reciprocity failure. You will need to give a slightly longer exposure, or a slightly bigger f/stop than you thought you needed.

In practice, with 35mm cameras and lenses, I have found that bracketing extensively with the shutter speed takes care of any possible reciprocity problems. (I use a tripod of course.) While film manufacturers do not recommend using exposures of over one second for most films, in practice the color shift which occurs at very long exposures is of more worry to studio and product photographers than to travel/location photographers, because sometimes the warm shift you get with long exposures in low light produces interesting colors. (If you want to try, think in terms of exposures of at least a minute or longer, with correspondingly small f/stops.)

Dr. Harold Sund is famous for his glowing landscapes taken at very long exposures, and Marie Cosindas' long exposure color Polaroid prints are now classics. Long time exposures at night come out different colors according to the film used. They can be greenish (with Fuji films), brownish (with Kodachrome 25 and 64) and purplish (with Kodachrome 200). My preferred film for long exposures is Ektachrome Professional 100 (EPP). It holds a very true blue and black.

Film manufacturers do not recommend very short exposures either, they tend to be slightly blue (at above about 1/4,000th of a second, which you can get when using high speed flash or strobelight).

More About Shooting at "Blue Time"—Dusk

Although no manufacturers recommend using their film for exposures of longer than about 1 to 4 seconds because of color shift, outdoors at dusk there is so much natural color shift toward blue in the sky that any shift in the film color is barely noticeable.

With ultra fine grain Kodachrome 25 Professional and an f/4 aperture I start shooting in pale blue dusk at 1/8, 1/4 and 1/2 a second. At royal blue dusk I use exposures between half a second and one, two, four, eight and even sixteen seconds at f /2.8 and f/ 4. Usually all of these exposures are all very good to excellent, with moody blue color variations that I and my clients like.

I sometimes use exposures of several minutes with slow fine-grain film, or when I want color shift for artistic purposes, or when I use slow, long telephoto lenses. I then bracket extensively. Try one, two, four and eight *minute* exposures with ISO 25 film and f/8, f/11 or f/16 apertures.

A slightly faster, still fine grain film is Fujichrome Velvia Professional. (I use it at 40 ISO) It takes a very nice push of 1 1/3 stops rated at 100. There is no color shift that I can discern at that speed. For night photography, in my experience, Kodachrome 25 Professional gives realistic, sometimes subdued color, Velvia is brighter than reality for lights with very good reds and yellows but the sky runs towards purple at long dusk exposures. EPP has very good, bright blues and holds blacks well too. It's ultimately a matter of your taste, and your client's taste. A travel-magazine art director I know says he doesn't care what film people use, as long as the pictures are good!

If long exposures at dusk make you nervous, use fast "push" (800-1600 ISO) Ektachrome or Fujichrome films to reduce the time needed for good exposures. Meter off the sky when shooting at dusk. Experiment with different types of low light and very long exposures, until you don't feel afraid of any of them. Expose tungsten film in daylight and vice versa just to see what happens. Keep practising and studying. Your travel photographs will benefit from everything you know about exposure, film, light, and lighting.

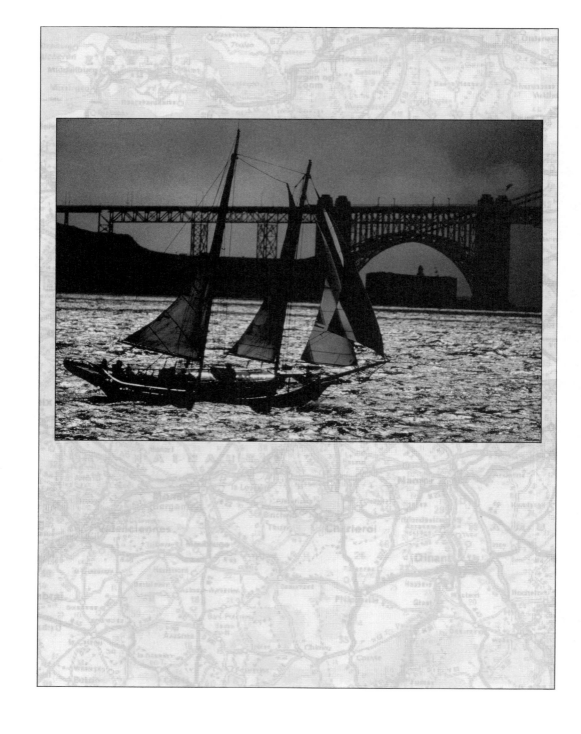

Chapter 7

Photographic Lighting

One of the biggest differences between amateur and professional photographers is a knowledge of how to use added lighting of all kinds. Taking a good course will help shorten the time you need to become competent, but there is nothing mysterious about the process of lighting. As usual, study and practice are keys to progress and success.

Flash, Strobe and "Hot" or Tungsten Lights

The complete subject of how to light is much too large for me to take on in this book. If you don't know anything at all about lighting, I recommend taking a good hands on workshop in photographic lighting techniques. (I give an occasional one myself at the School of Visual Arts in New York!) Photography schools and workshops nationwide, and some individual photographers in their studios, teach practical lighting. Photographers' associations sometimes give advanced lighting seminars. Working as an assistant to a photographer who uses lighting well is of course always a great way to learn.

Some videos on lighting that I have seen are interesting. I especially like those by the well-known advertising photographers Dean Collins and Aaron Jones, but they both require a good knowledge of lighting basics, and are geared primarily to studio photographers.

Of the many books devoted to the general subject of daylight and photographic lighting the best single one I know is called simply, *Light,* by Michael Freeman. It is a very clearly illustrated and lucidly written guide to lighting theory and practice.

A good, clearly illustrated basic guide to lighting with small flash is *Electronic Flash,* a Kodak Workshop Series book.

Evolving your personal lighting style, as usual, comes from a lot of hard practice; from much looking at the daylight and photographic lighting effects you admire and trying to recreate them, and from refining your inner vision of how a scene should look and translating it to practical lighting set-ups.

I will now try to write about travel/location photography lighting specifics, a somewhat technical subject, as clearly as possible.

Small Flash Units

Just about everybody has taken flash pictures with a point and shoot camera at birthday parties or Bar Mitzvahs, weddings or graduations. The photographic quality of many of these snaps, often with burned-out faces, very dark backgrounds and hard shadows, leaves a great deal to be desired to put it mildly.

There are many types of small detachable flash units available for more serious photographers; they range from completely manual (the photographer must use a scale or learn to use Guide Numbers to determine exposures; through automatic (the photographer sets film speed, chooses lens aperture and distance range, and the flash does the rest) to today's computerized dedicated/TTL (Through the Lens) cameras and compatible flash units. Dedicated/TTL cameras and flash units used together measure and control all the light reaching the camera's film plane. (See later in this chapter for details on how to use automatic and TTL/dedicated flash to best advantage.)

Carefully used, even a very small, detachable, manual flash unit can be a tremendous asset to a traveling photographer (using just about any camera) making otherwise impossible pictures possible. Because the light from any single point source falls off very quickly, one flash exposure cannot light large areas successfully. That's the reason for the dark backgrounds in a lot of snaps.

How to Use Flash Fill With a
Point and Shoot Camera

Some (not all) clever point and shoot cameras (like my Nikon Action Touch) permit you to fire the built-in flash even when there is plenty of light for a regular exposure. If you do this, the camera computer takes both flash and available light sources into consideration, and delivers enough flash to fill or soften hard shadows in daylight, open up silhouettes against backlit scenes or sunsets, brighten foregrounds at dusk or on grey days, or record at least some background indoors.

For best fill effects use slow or medium speed film (ISO 50 or 100 is best) and work very close to the subject (no further than ten feet away, maximum; five or six feet is ideal for many subjects; for very bright backlighting you may have to come in as close as three or four feet). Take care to avoid having the flash bounce back into the lens from glass, mirrors or other highly reflective surfaces. That's all there is to it. The fill exposures are usually good, with a bright foreground and slightly subdued background.

But, you can light quite well with only one small flash if you know how to use it. Often, the trick is to use the flash to supplement the available light. Do this indoors by using your camera on a tripod. Then, use long enough exposures and wide enough lens apertures to give correct exposure for the main subject like a large room. Then, add just enough flash to fill dark shadows, dim corners or large dark areas. (The light areas of the picture won't be affected much.) This technique takes the curse off black voids in many indoor and night pictures.

In England recently, I had to photograph poet William Wordsworth's Dove Cottage for a story on the Lake District. There were no wall outlets in the eighteenth-century cottage, tourists were tramping through constantly; the ceilings were so low that I couldn't set up lights on stands and I had to shoot whenever the rooms were empty. These rooms were miniscule, with small windows, and the weather and interiors were very gloomy. (It rains a lot in the English lakes; how Wordsworth managed to write great poetry cooped up in there with his wife, three children and sister I'll never know.) I took 1/2 second exposures with 50 ISO film, at about f/4 and f/5.6 with my camera on a tripod and a 20mm lens. My cigarette pack sized Nikon SBE flash (used off camera, bounced off the ceiling) gave just enough extra light to make the white walls white, rather than blueish in that high Kelvin temperature light. The flash worked especially well in the kitchen where a great black iron stove dominated the room. I aimed the tiny flash directly at the stove from about ten feet away. The direct light made the old stove gleam just enough so that the decorative details on the ironwork could be seen.

Outdoors, even a small amount of flash fill used close to a face greatly improves pictures of people taken in very harsh contrasty light (it softens shadows) or cheers up the picture (it warms the bluish light) when used in grey weather. (See also Chapter Seven.)

The cheapest small, one piece, manual flash units are today made in China (mine is a Ying Yang; it cost under $10). Some cheap or very old flash units are not wired to fire the flash directly from the standard camera "hot shoe" (on top of almost all modern 35mm SLR cameras). These old/cheap units have a sync cord (sometimes called a PC cord) to connect them to the camera's sync outlet. (Note: You can add a sync cord [by using a hot shoe adaptor] to any manual flash unit so that it can be used off camera, and the light bounced; I sometimes use my tiny Nikon SBE flash that way.)

Manual flash exposure (or exposure for automatic or dedicated/TTL flash used in manual mode) is determined by using a distance scale or the flash Guide Number. To find your unit's Guide Number and learn how to use it, see the flash manual, and see the box below.

Camera system manufacturers and the well-known flash manufacturers Vivitar and Sunpak make various flashes that don't require external sync cords. Automatic units cost from about $40 and up, discount, in New York; small dedicated/ TTL models for just about all the top electronic cameras cost from about $60 and up. Any of these units weigh almost nothing, take up little space in a camera bag, and occasionally are worth more than their weight in gold.

Bounce Flash Units

Bounce flashes are two to three times the size of simple units. The flash bends in the middle so that the head can be aimed straight up, straight forward and diagonally forward. This permits bouncing light off a low white ceiling or other surface. This diffuses and softens the light. Some bounce flashes also rotate, making it easy to bounce light from the side as well as from above. Because white ceilings aren't always handy photographers now bounce flash off white 3x5" file cards, or purpose made white plastic "bounce cards" attached to the camera. Light can also be bounced off white umbrellas; white, silver or even gold reflectors; white sheets and even white plastic bags suitably placed. Camera manufacturers as well as Sunpak and Vivitar all offer bounce flash units in automatic and dedicated/TTL models.

Large Flash Units

Large flash units of the so called "potato-masher" type mount the flash head on a handle, and are designed to be used on a bracket attached to the camera tripod socket. A sync cord attaching flash to camera is necessary. They are the highest powered small flash units available, and are favored especially by wedding photographers. Some large off-camera flash units have heads that both bounce and rotate permitting bouncing light from the side as well as overhead. Some off camera units are automatic, some dedicated; with cords for different brands of dedicated camera.

Metz is the best known maker of this type of flash, the classic units have been around for years and now have models with cords for most TTL/dedicated cameras. Disposable batteries or rechargeable nickel-cadmium batteries are used in the handles, or external battery packs can be used. Sunpak also makes several models of this type of flash unit, Vivitar has one. (High-powered battery-portable flash units are listed under strobe, later in the chapter.)

How Automatic Flash Units Work

Automatic flashes have a sensor on the flash unit (they can also be used off camera attached by a remote sensor cord). After the film speed is set on the flash and the camera, a lens aperture and distance range are chosen from a scale on the flash. Within those limits, flash exposure is automatic, the flash cutting off when the sensor has received enough light for a good exposure excess power is discharged or "dumped". Thyristorized models use only the power needed, which conserves batteries.

Most automatic units today have bounce heads which can be used straight up, straight forward or diagonally (some even rotate) permitting bouncing the light off nearby walls, low ceilings or any white surface.

The major camera companies and Sunpak and Vivitar market various automatic flash units. The Vivitar 283 is a powerful, inexpensive automatic bounce flash that is now a classic.

How TTL/Dedicated (Through the Lens) Flash Units Work

If you own a modern TTL/dedicated camera, by all means get a TTL/dedicated flash unit, because this type of flash one of the major reasons for using a TTL camera, permitting many sophisticated flash lighting effects.

Dedicated/TTL camera/flash combinations measure the light from all sources reaching the camera film plane. Computerized circuitry cuts off the flash when there is sufficient light for a good exposure.

Dedicated/TTL flash units are quite easy to use (after you have studied the manual very carefully!), and have their own, often very pleasant, lighting aesthetic. They can be used on the camera hot shoe, or off camera with a dedicated cord attached to the hot shoe. At the time of writing there are no practical dedicated flash units which can be used with slaves (see below).

The popularity of the flash fill lighting effect (combining daylight or available light with flash) is largely due to modern TTL/dedicated cameras combined with dedicated flash units. Today's dedicated flash units have a fill setting which augments the existing light, not overpowers it. (The flash fill technique was first used 60-odd years ago by news photographers, who had to make the necessary lighting ratio calculations manually.) System camera manufacturers and Sunpak, Vivitar and Metz all make dedicated flash units. You must get a unit dedicated specifically for, or with a dedicated module for, your particular brand/model of camera.

Using TTL Dedicated Flash for "Fill"

I use my Nikon SB 24 and SB 23 TTL flash units with N8008 cameras set on the S (Shutter Priority) mode. It permits me to choose any shutter speed I want, not just 1/60 or 1/250 which the camera chooses on P (program) setting when the flash is turned on. I often use a low shutter speed (like 1/15 or 1/8 or 1/4 of a second) in very low light. Of course, you get blurred backgrounds if the camera is not used on a tripod, but the nearby part of the picture lit solely by flash is sharp, stopped at 1/350 of a second (or higher—the actual speed of the light depends on the flash output, and increases as flash power is reduced).

Note: If you use TTL/dedicated flash with a dedicated camera on the P (Program) mode the camera will choose the highest possible sync speed in daylight, which in low light can cause day pictures to look like night pictures.

If your camera has a rear shutter curtain option (as my N8008s do) choose it when using flash fill to minimize "ghost" effects (of the daylit part of the exposure causing blur.when it overlaps with the flash exposed area. You can also "pan" (follow the subject motion) to reduce or eliminate ghosts also.

How Manual Flash Units Work

Manual flash units (or automatic or dedicated TTL flash units when used on the manual setting) put out the unit's maximum power. The aperture/distance table for use with different film speeds which is on the back of most manual flash units is usually reliable.

Alternately, you can determine the lens aperture and distance from flash to subject needed for correct exposure with a manual flash unit (or any unit used on manual) by using the flash Guide Number (see later in the chapter).

Some flash units have built in variable power options when used in Manual

How to Find Your Flash's Guide Numbers

Although today's dedicated/TTL and automatic flashes are a wonderful convenience, sometimes you may want to use a flash on manual for creative control, or you may own a manual flash unit. Here is how to measure your flash's guide number accurately with or without a flash meter.

With a flash meter: First, set the flash on M (manual) full-power mode. Then set the film speed on the flash meter. Stand exactly 10 feet from the camera to meter. You can use the self-timer on your camera to fire the flash, or use a "sync" cord to the meter, or, have someone else fire the flash or hold in the meter button. When the flash fires, the f/stop given on the meter multiplied by 10 will be the guide number for that film speed. (An f/8 aperture will give a guide number of 80.) Repeat this two or three times to make sure of accuracy.

Without a flash meter: Set flash on full-power M (manual). Set the film speed on the flash. Read the recommended f/stop for 10 feet on the flash's distance scale. Multiply the f/stop by 10. That is the guide number for that film. If the indicated f/stop is f/5.6, for instance, the guide number for that flash/film combination would be 56. (When using a flash meter, if the 10' distance indicates a full f/stop, everything above applies, but if a stop and a fraction is indicated, alter distance until a full stop is indicated, and multiply that distance by the f/stop to get the guide number.)

It is always a good idea to verify guide numbers by making tests with real film!

mode, permitting bracketing of flash output. Others (like the Vivitar 283) have an optional variable power attachment.

Using Flash Guide Numbers for Correct Exposures

To get the aperture needed: Divide the distance from your subject into the Guide Number. If you want to stand twelve feet from your subject, and the film/flash combination you are using gives a Guide Number of 80 for instance, divide 12 into 80, which equals 6 plus 8 remaining. This is two thirds of a stop over an f/6.3 exposure (6x12 = 72). An f/stop between f/6.3 and f/8 is thus called for. You can bracket with the f/stop slightly if the main subject is small and light-colored against a large dark area (close down) or small and dark-colored against a large light background (open up the lens slightly).

To get the distance needed for a certain f/stop: (Required for a flash fill effect you may want in daylight for instance.) Divide the f/stop into the Guide Number. The resulting number will be the distance from flash to subject required for correct (or desired) exposure.

"Slave" and "Trigger" Units

A "slave" unit fires a remote flash/strobe by responding to a "trigger" signal from the camera. Most slaves are light sensitive cells that sense flash or strobe light set off from the camera, or by an invisible infra-red light "trigger" mounted on the camera. Other slave/trigger devices are radio-controlled.

Using Two or Several Flash Units Together

Anyone can take several large portable strobe units on location if they have assistants to carry them (and clients willing to pay excess baggage charges) but if you work alone most of the time, especially in remote places, you need to keep the equipment you must lug around as light and uncomplicated as possible.

Today increasing numbers of professional photographers are working with several small flash units, equipped with slaves. The technique was first popularized by the very successful photographer Gregory Heisler, who is known for his innovative lighting.

Carefully placed, multiple, slaved flash units can light large areas. They are especially useful to travel photographers, because they can be used in the many remote places where no electric power outlets exist.

Note: Dedicated/TTL flash units must be joined with dedicated cords for use in multiples. To me this is inconvenient. The expensive cords, which are not very long, permit lighting at close distances only, and they get in the way. I think it is much better to use the classic automatic Vivitar 283 (or similar unit) in multiples with slaves, and measure exposures with a flash meter or Polaroids. This way you can space slaved flash units far enough apart to light large areas evenly. I use up to six slaved Vivitar 283 units to light a 20'x30'x12' room.

Working in Crowds with Slaved Flash/Strobe

Some highly sensitive slaves respond only to an infra-red light trigger, this combination is very "secure" against casual flashes nearby, a problem at weddings and news and public relations events. (Another advantage of infra-red is that the trigger light does not show up in photographs.)

Some slaves and triggers are radio controlled. They are favored by wedding photographers (who must work with lots of flashes popping off around them) and nature and scientific photographers and others who must work very long distances from their subject.

Even radio-controlled slaves are not totally proof against being accidentally set off. Neil Selkirk, a top portrait and corporate photographer, told me he nearly had a disaster when shooting the carefully strobe-lit top floor of the World Trade Center from a helicopter at dusk using radio-controlled slaves. The strobes kept going off without his signal, and he got only one (luckily good) shot. He found out later that a cleaning lady's vacuum was setting off the strobes!

The only truly interference-proof method of firing multiple flash or strobe lights together is by connecting them with "jumper" cords (long electric cords with two male plugs joining the strobes' sync outlets) to a sync cord connected to the camera.

"Triggering" Slaves When You Work Alone

Any flash on camera triggers any off-camera slaved flash/strobe units just fine when no-one else is flashing around you. (Average slaves work within a reasonable distance, say 20-30 feet, see manufacturer's specifications.)

Because of the speed of light all slaved flash/strobe units go off simultaneously when the on camera flash signal is received. Photographing people or other moving subjects lit totally with flash/strobe without "ghost" images (or background blur) is therefore no problem.

Recommended Slave and Trigger Units

I like Wein's various trigger and slave units, and use a WP SSR IR Trigger Model XT (around $60) on my N8008 cameras (earlier models do not work with electronic Nikons; check your own system with Wein triggers before you buy).

This very weak infra-red flash unit's signal does not show up in photographs. I use tiny Wein Peanut slaves on my Vivitar 283's (around $14 each, they snap into the unit's sync cord hole) and a Wein SSR slave on my Dynalite strobe unit. I also use three of Wein's super-sensitive tiny Micro-Slave/Flashes (model SF 200) to trigger the less sensitive slaves on my old strobes; they can also be used as small accent lights. Very secure triggers/slaves are Wein's infra-red Pro Sync series; they have two or four channels which means you can select one that won't be set off by even another professional's flash/trigger; this is essential for news, wedding and party photographers. (A two channel unit costs from about $280 for one trigger and receiver.) Consult manufacturers or lighting dealers for details; model designations and features change quite often.

Quantum, a well-established company best known for its rechargeable battery packs, also makes radio controlled slaves and triggers which are used where light signals from other sources are a problem, and especially to trigger slaves beyond the reach of any kind of light signal. They are often used by scientists and nature photographers. Around $250 for one trigger/receiver.

Calumet Universal Flash slaves are inexpensive (about $20) and can be used on any standard modern strobe, or with small flash units with household type (2 blade) receptacles like Armato and S.A.I. modified Vivitars (see later in this chapter).

Sunpak makes inexpensive, reliable slaves for just about all flash units too.

External Battery Packs and Rechargeable Batteries for Small Flash Units

If you take a lot of flash pictures, disposable batteries have a short life, don't recycle the flash very fast, and soon become expensive. (Realistically, allow about one battery pack per roll of film.) External rechargeable and disposable battery packs which can be attached to flash units will save you money in the long run, and—very important—they shorten recycle time and permit at least couple of hundred flashes without stopping to change batteries (more if the flash-power is reduced). Flash manufacturers offer their own rechargeable packs of different types; and Jackrabbit, Protech NY, Quantum and Speedotron make rechargeable units for most makes of flash.

Armato makes Pro-Cycler rechargeable batteries, and custom modifies Vivitar and other flash units to take them. Perma-Pak, a division of Mamiya, makes 6v and 9v rechargeable modular power systems for most flash units. I use Perma-Pak battery-to-flash connector modules for my Vivitars and home-made battery packs, they come complete with a handy replacement cut-out plates for Vivitar 283/285 model battery chambers. (See later in the chapter for directions on how to wire up you own rechargeable battery packs.)

Disposable Batteries

Don't ever forget to carry enough! I have seen tourists almost weeping at missed photo opportunities in remote (and not so remote) places when their batteries went dead. Start any trip with fresh batteries in cameras, meters, flashes and everything else electronic or electric you carry. I always carry a couple of spare Vivitar flash battery chambers, as an emergency backup for my rechargeable 6v gel-cels (and dual-voltage chargers) and several packs of alkaline AA batteries too. AA's also run my electronic cameras, but are easy to find almost everywhere (though sometimes expensive) if you run low.

Carry spares of hard-to-find size batteries for meters, slaves and triggers too. Carry more batteries in cold weather, and keep them as warm as possible. Batteries are much less efficient in temperatures below freezing.

The Versatile Vivitar 283 Flash

The Vivitar 283 automatic flash unit, originally designed for amateurs, has become a classic lighting tool widely used by location/travel photographers, news photographers, public relations specialists and photojournalists. The unit has a bounce head, is powerful for its size; and is lightweight, inexpensive and simply and quite strongly made.(The current price is around $65.00 at New York City discount stores.)

As a start use the 283 on your camera, direct or bounced. (See the flash manual.) When you are good at this, try using it as a second flash (with a "slave") —for instance as a hair light behind a portrait subject, or as a background light. (This works with fine with a strobe, and even with a dedicated flash as the main light. The dedicated flash will not take the light from the 283 into account, and the 283 must therefore be placed so it is weaker than the main light.)

How Professionals Use Vivitar 283s

283s are used on the camera hot shoe, off-camera with a long or short sync cord. They are bounced off white cards, or special bounce attachments, or off low, light ceilings . Two 283s can be joined in as a pair and bounced out of an umbrella, or they can be aimed through a small or medium-sized portable light bank. Several 283s can be slaved and scattered around small or large areas to augment existing light. 283s can be taped (with "gaffer"—film electrician's— tape) to walls or ceilings, pipes or fences and used indoors or outdoors. Because the 283 is so popular, Vivitar and some other companies make accessories, adaptations and modifications for it.

Two very useful 283 accessories are made by Vivitar. Get them if you take a lot of flash pictures. The SC2 off camera sensor-adaptor has a 6' coiled cord and is threaded for a standard flash bracket/lightstand (or tripod) screw, (1/4-20 size) permitting easy automatic use of the flash within 6' of the camera. (About $30.) The MVP-1 Vari-Power module replaces the 283's removable automatic sensor, and permits firing the flash manually at full, half, quarter, 1/8, 1/16 and 1/32 power, making it very easy to bracket flash exposures, and making subtle lighting ratio adjustments possible. When the power is cut back the resulting very short flash durations are useful for stop motion photography at close distances. At quarter-power the flash duration is only about 1/4000 of a second, for instance. (About $22.00.)

Warning: It is inadvisable to use any older 283's with modern electronic cameras. They could damage the delicate circuitry. The newest model 283's have been modified to avoid this problem; but to be safe, check with your camera manufacturer, or any of the companies listed in this chapter that modify 283's.

Some Modifications for Vivitars

- Armato's Photo Service of Queens, New York is famous for being the first to customize and increase the power of Vivitar 283s (they work on 285's and Sunpaks too.) Rechargeable batteries and custom light poles also. If it can be done to a Vivitar, Armato can probably do it.

  Armato units are sold by certain professional dealers around the country; for prices, the names of dealers in your area, and for custom work, contact Armato at 87-29 Myrtle Avenue, Glendale, NY 11385. Phone (718) 441-6888.

  Protech makes Pro Eliminator 1 and 2 units based on the 283. Contact them at 127 West 30th Street, New York, NY 10001. Phone (800) 223-6051 or (212) 239-8689.

- S.A.I. Photo Products, a new company, makes a unit based on new Vivitar 283's. S.A.I.'s NVS-1 flash unit doubles the basic 283's power output by installing an extra capacitor in the battery chamber. (It must then be used with an external battery pack; see below.) The unit includes a standard and a bare bulb head and a bounce/diffuser panel. The same company is making a Surefire unit—a "strobe on a rope"—actually a standard or bare bulb flashhead attached to the modified 283 body with a ten-foot cord for hiding the light source easily, or hanging it from those weird places you sometimes need on location, like old-fashioned overhead ceiling lamps. S.A.I. is in New Jersey, and guarantees fast turnaround for cash. For details, contact them at (609) 778-0261.

  S.A.I.'s units are recommended by photographer and lighting expert Jon Falk. Jon is the the author of *Adventures in Location Lighting*, a professional book I highly recommend, most especially to Dynalite strobe and Vivitar flash users.

- Holly Enterprises make permanent replacements for Vivitar feet (which are rather fragile). These are available in many photo stores and you can install them yourself. Holly's foot includes a standard tripod thread and a female socket for two blade sync cords for connecting the flash to a battery pack. (These are used on Armato and S.A.I. Vivitar modifications.)

- Armato, Jackrabbit, PermaPak, Protech NY, Quantum and Speedotron are companies that make rechargeable gel-cel battery units. Each comes with a battery-to-flash module and cord. All vary somewhat. (You can make your own rechargeable battery packs, see later in this chapter for directions.)

- Cougar Design makes a plate that replaces the fragile Vivitar 283 foot. It has a 1/4 20 screw receptacle for mounting the flash directly on a Norman or Armato or similar flash bracket; or onto a tripod, or onto a 1/4-20 threaded lightstand stud, and most especially, onto Cougar's own T-Bar mount. The Cougar T-Bar is a clever fixture which joins two Vivitars (with the feet replaced by Cougar plates) together securely. They can then be mounted on the stalk of a photographic umbrella and perfectly balanced on a lightstand with Cougar's Umbrella Tilter.

How I Use My Vivitar 283s

I mostly use my 283s joined in pairs with the small, neat, beautifully made Cougar Design attachments. (Cougar is the brain-child of a good friend, the noted strobe-motion and sports photographer Phil Leonian.)

To fire two joined Vivitar 283s, you can use a flash (bounced if you don't want frontal flash to show in the picture). I use a purpose-made trigger (a Wein SSR infra-red) on the camera, and two Wein "Peanut" slaves which are specially designed to be snapped into Vivitar sync cord holes on the flash units; or I use a long sync cord from the camera to one Vivitar, and one "Peanut" slave on the second 283.

I use this quick to set up, stable, and very light and portable bounce light combination for location portraits and still lifes (like food on a table) and as a main or fill light outdoors (I weight the light stand at the bottom in breezy weather). Two standard, combined, bounced 283s have a guide number of 40 with 100 ISO film used with a 36" Photek umbrella. (This is the photographic way of saying the light output is f/4 at 10 feet; it's f/8 used at five feet, a distance which I recommend for a pleasant portrait light).

I also use Cougar modified Vivitars with Lowel Light's Scissor Clamps and Hama's ball joints and hang them from metal ceiling grids such as those common in boardrooms, offices and factories. You have to install Cougar items yourself; it's not difficult and directions are included. They are available by mail only; contact Cougar Design for details.

Accessories Available for Many Flash and Strobe Units

Tilting adaptors, with a hole for an umbrella stalk, are made by Profoto and Hama for any flash unit with a standard camera shoe. Domke Enterprises make a fixture to join any two bounce flash units with standard hot shoe feet so they can be used in tandem.

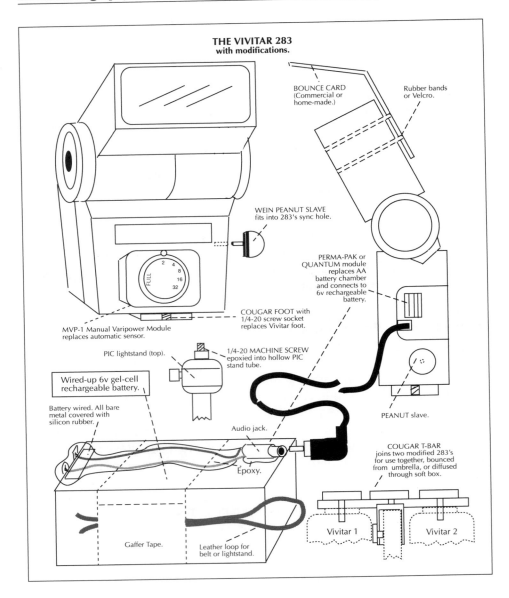

THE VIVITAR 283
with modifications.

BOUNCE CARD
(Commercial or
home-made.)

Rubber bands
or Velcro.

WEIN PEANUT SLAVE
fits into 283's sync hole.

PERMA-PAK or
QUANTUM module
replaces AA
battery chamber
and connects to
6v rechargeable
battery.

COUGAR FOOT with
1/4-20 screw socket
replaces Vivitar foot.

MVP-1 Manual Varipower Module
replaces automatic sensor.

PIC lightstand (top).

1/4-20 MACHINE SCREW
epoxied into hollow PIC
stand tube.

Wired-up 6v gel-cell
rechargeable battery.

Battery wired. All bare
metal covered with
silicon rubber.

PEANUT slave.

Audio jack.

COUGAR T-BAR
joins two modified 283's
for use together, bounced
from umbrella, or diffused
through soft box.

Epoxy.

Gaffer Tape.

Leather loop for
belt or lightstand.

Vivitar 1

Vivitar 2

Sync (synchronization) cords

Sync cords (sometimes called PC cords) for just about all flash and strobe units are made by Paramount and Minicam. Be sure to get the right one for your camera and flash/strobe. Long cords, and custom cords are made by Paramount. As sync cords are temperamental, and can get lost, carrying at least one spare is wise insurance.

Bounce and Diffusing Accessories

The light from a direct flash on camera is harsh, white walls and ceilings are not always available, or may be too far away. Modify and soften on camera flash somewhat as follows:

> ## Bouncing Flash in an Emergency
>
> I often use my left hand cupped over my angled TTL/dedicated flash head as a bounce device when using an auto-focus lens (or with a prefocused subject) There is minimally less light than with a white card; and possibly the light is a trifle warmer, which I like. This works so well I now use the technique often. I discovered this when I had to photograph a formal ball in a huge hall, and had failed to pack a bounce card.

- Sto-Fen Industries makes a neat, tiny, correctly-angled white plastic bounce card and a diffusing dome which fit over many small flash units. I use the card quite often.
- LumiQuest makes a larger, folding white vinyl Ultrasoft bounce device (about 4x7') which Velcros to flash heads, and folds flat when not in use. It gives quite a pleasant, soft light.
- News photographers use 3x5" white file cards taped or rubber banded to flash heads to bounce light.

Note: Bouncing any flash off any white card usually costs about 1 1/2 to 2 stops in exposure. This difference in exposure is allowed for with dedicated or automatic flash. With manual flash (to be super-safe) make tests before taking important pictures.

Reflectors
A collapsible round Photek (or similar) reflector is easy to carry, and use, and a flattering surface to bounce flash light from.

Small Soft Light Banks
These are white in front, black behind, and give a soft, directional light. (See also Scott Geffert's Options in Professional Lighting Equipment, at the end of this chapter.) The smallest Chimera soft light box is designed to be used with a sturdy camera/flash bracket like a Norman or Newman, both are available from professional dealers.

Phil Leonian's Modifications—You Can Make Them Too

Modifying Pic Stands: Pic light stands are inexpensive, sturdy, small and light. (I use the compact PP6-8SU model.) These stands come with a hollow tube top. To adapt them for light heads and camera brackets with standard tripod screws with 1/4-20 threads (like Vivitars with feet removed and Cougar plates attached), Phil taught me to buy 2" long 1/4-20 machine screws and carefully coat 1" at the end of each screw with epoxy. Insert the screws into the tubing at the top each of each Pic stand you want to adapt,they fit neatly. Let set for 24 hours, then cut the heads off the screws, allowing about 1/4" of each screw to remain protruding from the stand.) File the cut screw smooth.

How to Wire Your Own Rechargeable Batteries:
If you use several small flash units together, and are at all handy with wire strippers and soldering iron, you can save quite a bit of money by wiring your own rechargeable batteries. Phil taught me how. Buy 6 volt rechargeable gel-cell batteries from wholesale electronics dealers, or from Digi-Key, a mail-order electronics company. To buy 6.3v Panasonic lead acid batteries from this company, call them at (800) 334-4539; the Digi-Key part number is P129. Single batteries cost about $14 each.

Then, buy battery-to-flash connector modules with cords to fit your Armato, PermaPak, Protech NY, or Quantum unit if you already own one. If you do not own a rechargeable flash unit already, I suggest buying the PermaPak module (compatible with Quantum also). This comes complete with a cut-out replacement plate for the Vivitar battery chamber and costs about $30, at professional photo dealers. (If you don't buy PermaPaks, you must mark, and with a small soldering iron, burn out a hole for the module cords in each Vivitar—or other flash battery chamber cover.)

Then, you must buy appropriate female audio or telephone jacks (about $2-3.00 each) for your modules from Radio Shack stores. Solder these to the batteries using two strands of electrical wire trimmed to the size of your battery. (Of course match the positive and negative terminals on batteries and jacks.) Use epoxy or hot glue to secure the jacks and wires to the batteries.

Then, coat all bare metal with ShooGoo, a silicon rubber sneaker mender from athletic shoe stores (or use something similar). Allow everything to harden for 24 hours before use.

Use Gaffer tape to attach a leather bootlace loop to hang the battery from a belt or lightstand. (See the diagram of the wired-up battery on page 120.)

Warning: Phil does not recommend using home-made battery packs with any dedicated electronic cameras or flash units; they could damage the circuitry, and are meant to be used with slaved flash units used off camera.

Testing Battery Voltage
If you wire your own batteries you will need a charger. Buy an inexpensive 6 volt charger from electronics dealers. (Get a 110-220v dual-voltage charger from PermaPak if you travel overseas.) Charge batteries with AC current for about 24 hours before use.

Measure battery voltage with a Micronta battery tester from Radio Shack. (When first charged, a 6v battery reading should be about 7.20-7.30v, it will drop in a few hours to a normal full-charge reading of about 6.50v.) When the battery is fully charged, insert the connecting module into the flash's battery chamber, and plug in your flash. (If the flash ready-light does not go on almost immediately, unplug the battery and check the polarity of the wiring.)

With a Vivitar 283 (or 285) on full power with a fully charged battery, you should get about 100 flashes with a two second recycle time. Recycle time will then slow down. When the battery reads below six volts recharge it immediately if possible, though it will continue to give flashes until exhausted at about 5.5v.

You will get faster recycle time (useful for light "painting"), and shorter flash duration (useful for stopping motion), on half and quarter-power settings.

Note: Always recharge all gel-cel batteries and battery packs fully, as soon as possible after each use. Fire each flash you own and charge gel-cel batteries at least every three months to keep the flash capacitors and batteries in good condition. I travel with six of these batteries, and two dual-voltage chargers.

Umbrellas and Portable Light Banks

The larger the light source, and the closer it is to the subject, the softer the light. Therefore I generally use the largest umbrellas and soft boxes I can easily carry. I use 50" Calumet umbrellas (about $40, a bargain) in my studio or when I take strobes on location.

I take Photek 36" folding umbrellas (which collapse to 14") when travelling light.

Chimera portable light banks are budget-priced and come in all sizes, from a 16x22" model designed for use with a flash on a bracket, to humongous ones used to light cars. I have a medium-sized (36x48") Chimera, and a narrow striplight (9x36") which I use for portraits. Both set up quickly, fold easily into my tripod or lightstand cases and weigh little. I use them with my Vivitars since I discovered that two 283's joined with a reversed Cougar T-Bar mount can be neatly pushed into a Chimera blank mounting ring.

The Plume Wafer is a very shallow, portable light bank, designed with an internal baffle, that sheds a very even light, and is great for use with strobes.

Two Indispensable Lighting Aids— Gaffer Tape and Black Cinefoil

Gaffer is a heavy duty 2" wide adhesive cloth tape, which can be torn or cut. It is sold by photo and TV/movie lighting dealers. It was developed for movie electricians (or "gaffers") to help hang lights, reflectors and backgrounds, secure and waterproof lighting connections, tape electric cords to stands and floors and is indispensable for location lighting. It is very strong, yet does not take off paint when removed within reasonable time. Gaffer tape comes in grey, black, red and yellow. It costs about $12 for a 100' roll. Most stores carry grey only. Do not confuse it with the similar looking silver duct tape sold in hardware stores, which does take off paint, and doesn't hold things to walls. With gaffer tape you can repair equipment temporarily, tape luggage locks shut, fix a torn hemline in an emergency and more. I roll a few feet around a Magic Marker and carry it in my camera bag at all times.

Black Cinefoil—heavy black aluminum foil—is made by Rosco. Cinefoil can be cut, torn, folded, molded, taped and can be used to hide small lights and light leaks, and made into flags, gobos, snoots, barn doors (these are all light modifiers) and more. It cost about $27 for a 100' roll; I always carry a few feet in my lighting kit. (It comes in white and silver color too.)

Lowel's pioneering Soft Boxes are part of a great lighting system that is widely used by professionals and at many photo schools; Lowel equipment is very rugged, and they publish a useful lighting newsletter also.

Reflectors

36" and 48" round folding reflectors made by Photek fit neatly into my luggage. They collapse to 12" and 14", weigh little and are especially useful to fill shadows opposite an umbrella set-up in portraiture, are handy for bounce-light fill in contrasty light outdoors, especially at the beach, and can be clamped, hung or Gaffer-taped from lightstands, walls or ceilings. They come in white (soft) silver (harder, more directional) and gold (warm, directional.)

You can make your own reflectors out of virtually anything white or silver, from Mylar to plastic bags to newspapers to shower curtains to sheets to special-purpose materials. (See also Chapter Six.)

Lightstands

Bogen, Lowel and Pic make portable lightstands and clamps in different sizes. I own several Pic stands, two large Lowels with separate booms, and assorted, handy Bogen clamps. I often take two Pic PP68SU stands on location, they fold to 17 1/2", and extend to about 80".

Cougar Design also custom-makes the ultimate in lightweight stands with extensions for getting light up high. Modular Cougar "Sticks" extend these, and/or can be used as light poles, or as a monopod. (A super-lightweight tripod, that can double as a lightstand, will emerge from Cougar's workshop soon.)

Using Multiple Flash Set-Ups

Small flash is not just for use on the camera. It is extremely versatile. As many flash units as needed can be used together if each is equipped with a slave unit and triggered from the camera. Mount modified Vivitar 283's or other bounce flash units singly or in pairs on a tripod or lightstands; bend them and stand them on the floor aimed into dark corners, hide them behind furniture or equipment, or gaffer tape them to walls or ceilings. Use Lowel's scissor clamps to hang small lights from metal ceiling frames common in offices and factories. Add color gels over some flash heads if it pleases you (see Chapter Five).

For location portraits, people pictures and even food shots and still-lifes I often use two joined Vivitar 283's, bouncing them out of a white umbrella, or aiming them through a small or medium portable Chimera soft box. Both these methods give me soft light, as well as control of the height and angle of the light. A flash meter and/or Polaroid camera or back will make such lighting set ups much easier. (See Chapter Four.)

Lighting Large Spaces With Small Flash

Several slaved small flash units triggered from the camera can be used to light large areas. Because the flashes all go off simultaneously, you can use this technique when people are in the room. (You can light an empty room by "painting" it with one flash; see later in this chapter.)

Time and Flash

Flash/strobe light can be combined with a time exposure of any length to record daylight or available light and bring indoor and outdoor light into balance. You will need a flash meter. Meter the outdoor light, set the camera shutter at sync speed or below, and add enough flash/strobe indoors to bring the light into balance. You need less strobe/flash indoors at dusk when outdoor light is low. Of course, use the camera on a tripod. Polaroid tests make this technique quite easy.

Using Flash in Remote Areas

The advantage of small battery-powered flash or strobe units is most obvious in the many places where there is no electrical power available, or where A.C. cords cannot be hidden. Carefully placed off camera flash units can fill dark corners of a room (or a cave); separate foreground from background behind a portrait subject's head, or can be used with colored gel over the flash heads and aimed to give "snap" to a dull background.

   With several flash heads spaced evenly, you can do an excellent job of lighting a long narrow boardroom where lightstands and cords would show. In a medium sized room, hang four or six flash units up high (with Gaffer tape or clamps) and direct the light around the room. Two flash units will do in a very small room like an actor's dressing room. (Tape up white paper, cloth or even aluminum foil if the ceilings and walls are not white, or bounce light out of white umbrellas at ceiling height on tall stands.) In a large room, I space six flashes around evenly, or down one side if I want a directional "windowlight" effect. I use shower curtains as reflectors if the walls are not white. Hang flashes (or lightweight strobe heads) spaced evenly from dropped ceilings (like offices and corporate boardrooms) using Lowel scissor clamps.

Using Cumulative Flashes

Still-life photographers who need more power sometimes use cumulative strobe exposures with an open camera shutter in a darkened room. (Firing a strobe several times permits them to use the extremely small f/stops needed for sharp focus with large format cameras when long bellows draw is used for close-ups.)

   You can this technique with cumulative flashes on location when you need a small f/stop, or when there is no other way of lighting with the power at your disposal. Hold the camera shutter open on B (Bulb) setting with a locking cable release. Then, flash as needed, releasing the shutter immediately when you have finished.

   The calculations are quite simple. Each time you want to decrease the aperture one f/stop you must double the amount of light reaching the film. If f/8 requires one flash pop, f/11 will require two pops, f/16 four, and f/22 , eight pops. (Of course you can do the same thing with strobe also.) After about eight flashes, the light becomes less efficient, and you will have to more than double the number of flashes to double the light output. (You will need seventeen, eighteen or even nineteen flash pops for f/32 for instance.) It's the same principle as the law of reciprocity. (See also Chapter Four.)

How to "Paint" a Room With Flash

To "paint" (coat with light) with one small flash in a big space, or nearby objects outdoors at night, first set the camera on a tripod, and level it. The camera shutter must be open while you make multiple flash pops, so you will need a locking cable release. First, lock the shutter open, then aim your (off camera) flash head as evenly as possible to paint the desired surfaces with flash. (Take care not to aim the light towards the lens or yourself.) Note: dedicated flashes that must be attached with a cord to the camera won't work well for this.

My studio is white and 20x30x12' high. To paint it evenly, I used 64 ISO EPX film, a 20mm lens at a lens aperture of f/5.6, and the camera shutter at 30 seconds, the longest automatic exposure my camera delivers. I used a Vivitar 283 with a Vari-Power module and a gel-cel battery. I cut the flash back to 1/4 power for very fast recycle time. I held a black card near the flash to prevent light hitting the lens. I "popped" off the flash with the test button, aiming it at walls, ceiling and floor, while walking quickly round the completely darkened room. I didn't register on the film because I kept moving, and made sure the flash was aimed away from me. I made about 40 or 45 flashes per picture; some using red and blue gels, all the exposures were pretty good, the exact number of flashes is not critical. You will need more or fewer flashes for a larger or smaller space. (If a room is not totally dark you will need to cover the windows with black cloth or plastic bags to shut out all extraneous light, which builds up quickly with long exposures.)

If you have a Polaroid camera or back, tests will help you get good results . Practice light painting in different sized spaces, and use some color gels on the flash like Chip Simons if you wish. I like some white light with the color effects. You may find this technique very useful in crypt or cavern, hut or hogan.

Light Painting With Small Flash

Painting means moving light around (while the camera shutter is held open during a time exposure) to coat a surface with light. This technique has been used by architectural photographers for many years. They generally use tungsten lights. Light painting is a rediscovered, currently popular technique with both tungsten and flash/strobe lights. Aaron Jones developed the Hosemaster fiber-optic tungsten light, and paints with light very precisely, mostly on advertising still lifes. The young photographer Chip Simons made his name with very funny pictures of animals outdoors using small Sunpak flash units covered with color gels. Now he paints people and rooms, cemeteries and industrial scenes with gelled flashes and battery portable strobes (as well as with crazy devices like French gas lighters!) The fine-art photographer Jim Dow uses flash or strobe to paint large mysterious dark rooms.

Balancing Indoor Flash/Strobe and Outdoor Light

To do this, use the camera on a tripod. First measure the outdoor light and set the camera aperture for the highest possible sync speed and widest possible aperture. Then add enough light indoors to equal the outdoor light. You can use either slaved multiple flash units, or better, because more powerful, one or more strobe units and several heads. Outdoor and indoor exposures are most easily balanced when the outdoor light is comparatively low, at dusk or on a very grey day.

A Polaroid camera and a sophisticated flashmeter are a big help for this technique. My Minolta III flashmeter (the current Minolta IV replaces it) measures available light, flash exposure, and cumulative flash exposures, singly or in combination.

Multiple Exposure Flash Pictures

With a black background indoors (black velvet is best) in a darkened room (you can also work outdoors in the country at night against a completely black sky) you can do multiple portraits or exposures of movement on one piece of film. Try it for yourself by setting your camera on a tripod with the lens locked open on "Bulb" setting. Use a medium lens aperture of say f/5.6 with 100 ISO film (exact exposure depends on film speed and number of flashes used) and as many "pops" as you wish different movements. Of course, allow for the cumulative exposures. (If you want four poses underexpose each by three stops.) Note: Repetitive strobes for motion-stopping photography are made for a price.

Color Film for Use With Flash and Strobe

Flash and strobe units are balanced to emit light at 5,500K. Use daylight-balanced color transparency film with flash and strobe lighting. Because the color of flash/strobe light may very slightly (some units produce a higher color temperature than 5,500K) testing a new unit for color is a good idea. With transparency film, you may need to use a CC filter on the lens, or gel over the lighthead(s) for the best possible color. With color negative film, minor color correction can be done in printing. (See Chapters Four and Five.)

Battery-Portable Electronic Flash Units

Battery-powered strobes, as these units are often called, are especially popular with fashion photographers and also with travel, corporate and industrial photographers, who must often light outdoors, or in places with undependable electricity where even a line-voltage step-down transformer (from 240v to 120v) is no guarantee that problems won't arise. Chargers for battery-portable units are available in 110-220v dual-voltage models. High-power battery-portable units (1,000 watt seconds and up) are expensive, ($1,000 or so and up) but worth it if you need the light where electricity is unavailable.

Disadvantages of these units are slow recycle time (some units take up to six seconds on full power) and relatively small number of flashes obtainable from one charge. At least one spare battery is therefore a must.

It should be noted here that two Vivitar 283's joined together and used as a unit, on full power and used with two 6 volt rechargeable gel-cel batteries, with 100 ISO film and bounced out of a white umbrella, has a guide number of 40, and recycles in about five seconds. A popular 200 watt-second battery portable strobe puts out only about 50% (half a stop) more light than this.

Balcar, Comet, Minicam and Norman all make battery powered portable units in different price and power ranges.

How Strobe Power is Rated:
Strobe power is measured in Watt Seconds (ws) in the United States, Canada and some other countries; in Europe and other places the rating is in equivalent Joules. Maximum power of studio strobe units is about 20,000 ws/Joules.

Facts About A.C.-Powered Strobe Lights
Here are a few facts to demystify "strobes," more correctly called portable electronic flash units. (True stroboscopic light, which was invented by the late Dr. Harold Edgerton at the Massachussetts Institute of Technology in the 1930's, is related to electronic flash, but the flash output is very low, repetitive and of extremely short duration.) The use of electronic flash in photography was pioneered by Gjon Mili of *Life* magazine, working with Dr. Edgerton.

An interesting and well-illustrated book about stroboscopic and stop-motion flash photography is *Moments of Vision* by Harold E. Edgerton and James R. Killian, Jr.

Studio Strobes
These units are not at all portable, they continuously require main A. C. power, transform it to very high high voltage (about 4,000v) and store this energy in oil-filled capacitors, which are extremely heavy.

Portable A.C.-Powered Strobes
These strobes need a continuous 110v A.C. power supply (or 220v in those countries where 220v is standard) which is usually drawn from "the mains"—a main electric power outlet. In remote spots, a gas or diesel-powered portable generator, or a 12v D.C. to A.C. power inverter can be used. (See later in the chapter.)

The A.C. input is transformed in the strobe to higher-voltage A.C. power, then rectified to D.C., and stored in electrolyte capacitors. (Portable strobe voltage varies from about 350v to 900v depending on the model and make.) The power range of portable strobes is from 200 ws/Joules to an average of about 2,000 ws/Joules (a few higher powered A.C. portable units are available).

Portable strobes are inherently low-voltage; the flash duration on full power is typically about 1/350 of a second, higher if the power is turned down. "Stop-motion" portables with very short flash durations are available for a price.

1,000 or 1,200 ws/Joules units are are often used by travel/location photographers; they are of a convenient size and weight, and give a reasonable f/stop. Even the smallest portable strobes are bigger and heavier than flash units, which usually prevents them being used on camera. The heads of Norman, Comet and similar lightweight battery-powered strobes can be mounted on a camera bracket if desired.

Portable strobes however, are mostly used on light stands, and often bounced from white ceilings, walls and umbrellas, or diffused through portable light banks.

Advantages of Portable Strobe

Portable strobe is the workhorse of professional photographic lighting. It draws virtually no current after the capacitors are full until the instant of use, gives an immense amount of light at the moment of need, and can stop much motion. You do not need to use a tripod for many strobe-lit situations.

A.C.-powered strobe is much faster-recycling than most battery-powered flash (or strobe) units, average recycle time is about one to two seconds to reach full power. Portable strobes that use power from the mains or a generator have the advantage over battery portables (and of course small flash units) in that they have built in tungsten modeling lights that burn continuously, which makes controlling lighting effects fairly easy. Strobes are very cool in operation unlike hot tungsten lights. Many strobehead designs, accessories and light modifiers are made to vary the quality of strobe light output. Literally hundreds of different reflectors, screens, optical snoots, scrims, barndoors, umbrellas and soft boxes and more can be selected to get your desired lighting "look" with strobe. (See also Scott Geffert's diagrams at the end of this chapter.)

Disadvantages of Strobe

There are only three. Strobes are expensive. A good 1,000 watt second unit with two heads costs around $1,500. They require a continuous power supply. And, strobes are heavy, but thank goodness, getting lighter all the time. Balcar, Broncolor, Comet, Dynalite, Elinchron, Norman, Profoto and Speedotron are top A.C.-powered portable strobe brands. Some of these manufacturers offer dual-voltage (110-220v) models and compact monoblock (one-piece) models. Both are extremely practical for traveling photographers.

Which model strobe you choose will depend on your lighting needs and budget, and on the service facilities available where you work most. I strongly suggest you compare strobes and features by renting a few times from a professional lighting dealer before investing in any strobe system. (Again, see Scott Geffert's **Options in Professional Lighting Equipment**, at the end of this chapter.)

The Strobes I Use

I have two very heavy, old custom-made 1,000 ws strobes which won't quit (they are no longer made). I now use them mostly for studio portraits and set-ups. I recently purchased a very lightweight 800 ws Dynalite unit with two heads to take on location. (I usually use any or all of these with two or three slaved Vivitar 283's for accent lights.)

Packing Strobes for Travel

Get a good bag or case to take your strobes on location. Tenba and Lightware make strong, lightweight shock-absorbing fabric bags. Anvil and Calzone cases are lockable, rigid (and heavy) for shipping equipment as freight.

Safety With Strobe

All A.C.-powered strobe units store high voltage electricity (enough to kill you in every case). It is therefore imperative to learn how to use them safely.

- Read the manual first when you buy or rent any strobe.

- Always attach heads and sync cords to the strobe power pack before connecting it to the main electricity supply.

- Never work with strobe in a damp or wet area, or outdoors in rain or snow.

- Never use a strobe head with frayed wires, or cracked flashtubes.

- Remember that high voltage electricity is always in the wires of the strobe tube, so never, ever stick your finger into the ventilation holes of the tube.

- Strobe heads/monoblocks are heavy; light stands should be weighted at the bottom. Portable weights that can be filled with sand/dirt or water are available.

- Gaffer-tape strobe cords to light stands and floor to avoid tripping.

- When a shoot is finished, always switch off the strobe right away, and immediately bleed out the stored high-voltage electricity by firing the strobes test button. Then you can safely disconnect the unit from the main electric power source and disassemble it.

- Allow strobe tubes to cool after use before disconnecting them from heads for packing.

- Allow all tubes and bulbs to cool for serveral minutes before touching or disconnecting them from strobeheads. Always use cotton gloves or Kleenex when handling them,This will minimize the chance of burns, and prolong the life of the expensive strobe tubes and modelling light bulbs. (Oil residue from fingers is not good for them .)

Strobe tubes are fragile and very expensive, always handle them with care. Wear gloves to avoid skin moisture that is on even the cleanest hands. (Touch strobe tubes [and photo lamps] as little as possible; it will prolong their life.) When shipping strobes, many people take removable strobe tubes out of the heads, and pack them, and the modeling lamps separately. Wrap tubes and modeling lamps in bubble pack, then cardboard and tape tight. I hand-carry fragile tubes and modeling lamps with my cameras. For car travel, it is usually sufficient to put the strobe heads in a good case without removing the tubes.

Using Strobe
Strobes recycle quickly, which permits very fast shooting to catch fleeting mood and motion. The higher power the unit, the smaller the f/stop that may be used.

Most studio portable strobes permit the use of several heads at a time, some permit asymmetrical distribution of light between the heads, and continuous power variation. The duration of the burst of light from most portable strobe units is about 1/350 of a second at full power; as with small flash, when the power is turned down, the duration of the flash decreases, permitting more motion-stopping power. (Multi-tube heads are available for some strobes also, using them decreases flash duration.) Optical lenses and templates, scrims, gels, screens, snoots and barn doors are used by many location photographers, especially fashion, architecture and interior specialists, to modify strobes for different lighting effects.

How I Use Strobe on Location

I try to light as simply as possible, and usually photograph with one main light, using the strobe head bounced out of an umbrella or diffused through a translucent umbrella or a portable soft box. I keep the light about six feet high, fairly frontal, and as close as possible to a seated subject. If needed shadows can be controlled by reflectors. I sometimes use a reflector to add a white, silver or gold "fill" to open shadows on the dark side. (If in a small, light space with too much light "return," I darken shadows with a black reflector opposite my main light.) For portraits, I may use a direct light, aimed slightly down on my subject, as the main light, "filling" with a reflector or second diffused strobe shone through an umbrella. That is very close to the classic Rembrandt portrait light! A small (slaved) flash directly behind the head as a rimlight gives a "halo" hair effect; aimed down it can be a subtle hairlight; a flash/strobehead aimed onto the background separates front and background planes and gives an illusion of depth. Sometimes I bounce a strobehead off a white wall or ceiling or I use it "bare bulb" without a reflector to light a large area. (This technique gives defined but very soft shadows.) Current fashion is to use color gels to light backgrounds of drab industrial scenes, but I don't do this much.

Determining Strobe Exposure

Strobe exposure can be measuredwith a flash meter, (made by Minolta, Sekonic and Gossen); by the use of Polaroid film in a camera or camera back and by guide number.

When you've worked with your strobes for a while you will know the basic exposure for light set-ups you use frequently.

As I've said, the Polaroid method of determining exposure is popular with studio photographers, and those who can travel with a lot of equipment. The advantage of Polaroids is that you can quickly preview the complete photograph. (Do not use Polaroids for color tests unless you have previously run differential color tests.) The disadvantage of Polaroids for a long trip is the additional weight and bulk of camera/back and film that must be carried, and of course, extra cost.

Always make tests for critical color when using any unknown or rental strobe to determine if filtration is needed or wanted. Some strobe and flash units, especially older ones, run a touch blue.

Using Strobe on Location

There are a few pitfalls to watch out for when you travel with strobe. In American towns and cities, 60 cycle (Hertz) 110v power is standard. Note: Nominally 110v power is never 110v, but usually around 120-125v in the United States. Modern 110v and 110-220v dual voltage strobes are designed to cope with minor voltage fluctuations, but you can never be too careful. Find out from your dealer or the manufacturer exactly what your strobe's operating tolerances are. Play it safe, check line voltages with a meter (see later in this chapter) before you plug in your strobe in strange places.

Note also: Never plug European 220v strobes (or dual-voltage strobes used on 220v) into American/Canadian 220v outlets. 220v strobes are meant for use in Europe and the many other countries in the world where 220v is standard power. In the United States and Canada, 220v outlets are designed for running air conditioners, stoves and machinery, and single-phase 220 outlets may deliver an actual 250 volts of power which may be excessive for your unit. (Europeans travelling in the Unites States/Canada with 220-240v strobes should acquire a step-up 220-110v line voltage transformer.)

Using Strobe in Remote Areas

Generators (gasoline or diesel powered) are frequently used to run strobes where there is no electrical power. Professional lighting dealers rent generators. Homelite and Honda are well-known generator manufacturers; contact them for more information if you are thinking of buying. You must use only voltage-stabilized generators with strobes (so-called auto-regulated generators are not suitable), and you must use a volt-meter to assure that the power output is regulated to within about a 2-3% tolerance. The frequency is also very important. A good check before you rent or buy any generator, is to plug in an electric clock (before you plug in your strobes) and check the second hand against your watch to see if the clock (and the generator) is running fast or slow.

Power inverters convert current from 12v D.C. (golf-cart type deep cycle) batteries to 120v A.C. Inverters can be shipped by air or UPS, unlike generators. UPS won't take those. According to Ken Haas in his invaluable book *The Location Photographers' Handbook* (see Chapter Fifteen), Federal Express will ship generators if they are emptied and sealed.

Power inverters are mainly used in RV's and campers, cabins and boats, and by emergency squads and fire departments. They can also be used to power strobes. Inverters are used by photographers who go into remote areas a lot; most have the inverter wired into a car or van; so they recharge from the vehicle's alternator (otherwise spare, charged, heavy batteries must be carried).

Location lighting expert Jon Falk is a power inverter enthusiast, he has one installed in his vehicle. Vanner inverters (discussed in depth by Jon in his excellent professional book *Adventures in Location Lighting*, see the end of this chapter) and LTM inverters are widely used by still photographers.

If you are seriously thinking about inverters you might also want to check out Trace Engineering inverters, which have been recommended by my electronics guru as being especially rugged. I am told by the Trace sales department in Seattle that they are used by San Francisco TV station KGO for all its location vehicles.

Note: Power inverters are usually more expensive than generators. My electronics guru also says that if you can transport a generator and gasoline or diesel fuel to your location, you will get a great deal more power (and shooting time) for a given weight than you will with an inverter that is not wired into a car like Jon Falk's. One charged A.C. battery is good for an hour or two of shooting at most.

Warning: Never, ever rent any generator or inverter or use it for a job without having time to test it out first with your volt-meter and under actual working loads with the strobes you will be using. Not everything is compatible with everything!

Using Strobe Overseas

If your 120 volt strobe is not a 110-220v dual voltage unit, you will need a transformer in Europe and the many other countries where standard power is 220-240v. Be sure and get a transformer with a high enough VA (volt-amperage—equivalent to watts) rating for your unit and the modeling lights combined. A 500 watt 50-60 cycle step-down (110-220v) transformer should cost from around $50.00. They weigh about seven lbs. For high powered portable strobe units (1200 watt seconds and over, plus modeling lights), a step-down isolation transformer of the proper capacity is the safest way to go. Signal, Stancor and Triad are all very reliable brands of line-adjusting, auto-step-down transformers (which can also be reversed and used as step-up transformers for European equipment used in the United States/Canada).

Again, consult a professional lighting dealer, wholesale electronics dealer or the manufacturers direct, for specific recommendations for your strobes and modelling lights.

I carry a Stancor 120v/220v auto transformer, 50-60 Hz, rated for 150 VA. It can be used with 60 or 50 cycle power, (which is common in Europe). It is 4 1/4x3 1/4x3 1/4", weighs only three and a half lbs, and I have used it for many years with no problems (I don't shoot particularly fast), either with an 800 ws strobe (with two 250 watt modeling lamps turned off to shoot), or an old 1,000 ws strobe with a 100 watt modeling light left on while I shoot. This is because any strobe draws full power only for a second or so while recharging its capacitors. If you want to leave all your modeling lights on when you shoot, or if you shoot very fast, you will need a transformer rated for the highest combined voltage of strobe rating and modeling lights; check with strobe manufacturers' and professional lighting dealers and *The Location Photographer's Handbook* for specific recommendations for different strobe models.

Caution: I also use my transformer with my 6v battery chargers for my small flash units, when overseas. I specifically do not recommend using the small transformers that are fine for hairdryers etc., with any strobe or battery recharging device or any other lighting equipment. If these small transformers fail while in use because of a surge (spike) in the (often unreliable) local electric current, your strobes or chargers and batteries could be ruined. Use heavy-duty transformers.

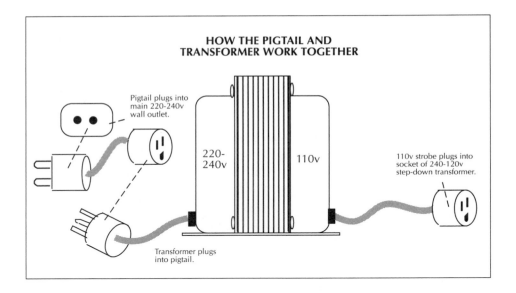

HOW THE PIGTAIL AND TRANSFORMER WORK TOGETHER

Pigtail plugs into main 220-240v wall outlet.

220-240v

110v

110v strobe plugs into socket of 240-120v step-down transformer.

Transformer plugs into pigtail.

Foreign Electric Pitfalls

There are three main problems to contend with when you travel with lighting equipment:

D.C. power still exists, especially in India and other third world countries, and will destroy your strobes if you plug them in to it (if they are not protected by correct fuses). Carry a tiny neon tester (available from electric stores) and check everywhere before plugging in. Both electrodes will glow for A.C. power, but only one if it's D.C. Don't even think of plugging in if it's D.C.!

Too high or low a line voltage can affect your strobe recycle time and maybe power output. A voltmeter such as a Micronta Digital Voltmeter from Radio Shack stores will not only tell you if your disposable and rechargeable flash batteries are okay, but will also tell you if the mains power is A.C. or D.C. and the line-voltage is within the tolerance limits of your strobe equipment. The meter I recommend costs about $30, mine has long since paid for itself by telling me when disposable batteries are still good.

The shape and size of electrical plugs and receptacles varies considerably in different parts of the world. Rather than try to explain all this in words, I created some diagrams on my computer!

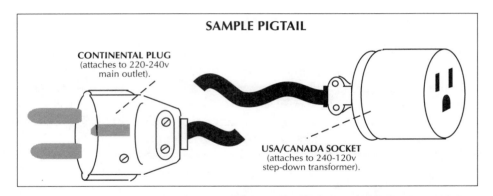

SAMPLE PIGTAIL

CONTINENTAL PLUG
(attaches to 220-240v main outlet).

USA/CANADA SOCKET
(attaches to 240-120v step-down transformer).

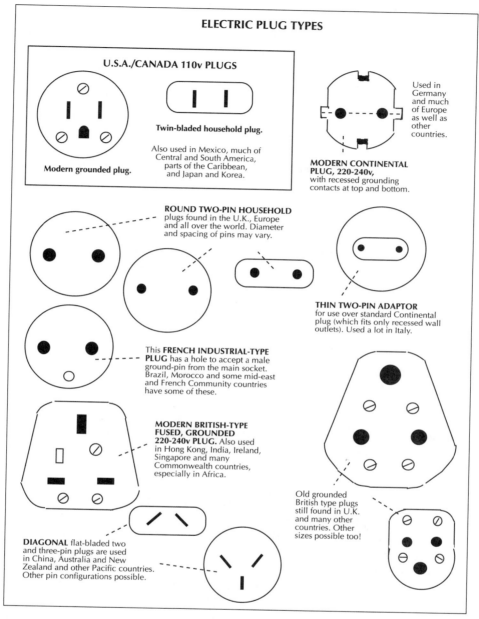

ELECTRIC PLUG TYPES

U.S.A./CANADA 110v PLUGS

Twin-bladed household plug.

Modern grounded plug.

Also used in Mexico, much of Central and South America, parts of the Caribbean, and Japan and Korea.

Used in Germany and much of Europe as well as other countries.

MODERN CONTINENTAL PLUG, 220-240v, with recessed grounding contacts at top and bottom.

ROUND TWO-PIN HOUSEHOLD plugs found in the U.K., Europe and all over the world. Diameter and spacing of pins may vary.

THIN TWO-PIN ADAPTOR for use over standard Continental plug (which fits only recessed wall outlets). Used a lot in Italy.

This **FRENCH INDUSTRIAL-TYPE PLUG** has a hole to accept a male ground-pin from the main socket. Brazil, Morocco and some mid-east and French Community countries have some of these.

MODERN BRITISH-TYPE FUSED, GROUNDED 220-240v PLUG. Also used in Hong Kong, India, Ireland, Singapore and many Commonwealth countries, especially in Africa.

Old grounded British type plugs still found in U.K. and many other countries. Other sizes possible too!

DIAGONAL flat-bladed two and three-pin plugs are used in China, Australia and New Zealand and other Pacific countries. Other pin configurations possible.

"Pigtails"

You can carry a foreign plug adaptor kit (sold at electrical dealers and airport shops) for common foreign outlets, but, if you go off the beaten track in my native England for instance, you will find some plug shapes still around that Thomas A. Edison would recognize.

Therefore, carry a pair of wire strippers, a set of small Hama screwdrivers, a roll of 3M electrical tape and a couple of "pigtails" (different type power plug connectors) with you overseas, and save grief. Make the pigtails about twelve inches long, with a North American female connector wired to one end. At your destination, buy the appropriate male plug or plugs from any electric store, and wire them in. Insert your strobe plug to the female connector in the transformer, the male transformer plug into the female pigtail connector, and the male pigtail plug into the wall outlet. Plug a dual-voltage strobe (check that you have set it to the correct voltage first!) directly to the pigtail, and connect pigtail to wall outlet.

In desperation, when photographing in an ancient Stately Home or Palazzo, you can always unplug Milord's or Commendatore's TV set or lamp, disconnect the exotic plug, wire it to one end of your pigtail, and then connect the North American end of the pigtail to your transformer or dual-voltage strobe to take his portrait. Of course, you'll restore everything afterwards.

Renting Strobes on the Road and Overseas

220-240v strobes, portable light banks, and other photographic equipment can be rented in many major North American and foreign cities. It may be cheaper to rent than to carry your own equipment plus transformers, plugs etc. But, call first to see what is available and to reserve what you need, and be sure to test any rental equipment thoroughly before you depend on it for a job!

The commercial department of many foreign consulates may be able to give you the names of professional photo equipment dealers. *The Location Photographers' Handbook* by Ken Haas lists foreign strobe and other professional equipment rental sources, as well as giving extremely detailed information on voltages, electric plug shapes and the specific transformers needed for different brands and models of strobes.

Tungsten and Other "Hot Lights"—Great for Learning Lighting, and Fashionable Again

Tungsten lights draw A.C. power that heats a tungsten metal filament so that it glows white-hot and emits light. Household lights, flashlights and car lamps are all low-wattage tungsten lights. Some tungsten lights are inexpensive (to begin lighting, a photographer can start with a reflector, a clamp and a 500 watt photoflood bulb for about $25). Hot lights burn continuously, so lighting effects are easy to see and control. For these reasons, tungsten lights are the perfect way to learn or improve photographic lighting techniques. Hot lights are in style again with portrait and fashion/beauty photographers. Tungsten lights are balanced for use with 3,200°K Tungsten film (Type B). Type A film is balanced for 3,400°K lights. Either requires filtration for good color with household and other low Kelvin temperature lamps. (Also see Chapter Five.)

Fluorescent and Other Commercial/Industrial Lights

Fluorescent lights are not tungsten lights (they heat a gas that fluoresces), but street and industrial sodium vapor and mercury vapor lights are. All these special purpose lights are normally used with daylight film, but require heavy filtration for acceptable color (they look green, yellow green or yellowish on film if used without filters). Some special-purpose tungsten industrial lights cannot be filtered, and always look very green on film. (See Chapter Five.)

Safety With Tungsten Lights

Handle all "hot" light bulbs and fixtures with care, they can burn you. Weight the bottom of lightstands (and tape cords to the floor) when using hot lights around models. Allow bulbs to cool before changing them, and prolong the life of bulbs by wearing cotton gloves or using tissue when touching them.

Note: The newest " High-C" lights are tungsten lights that burn at extremely high temperatures, and are balanced for daylight 5,500°K film. At present, they are mainly used in the movie business and are extremely expensive. As they are currently of no concern to travel/location photographers, I won't mention them again.

A Basic Tungsten Set-Up for Learning Lighting

- Two 250 or 500 watt 3,200 K photoflood bulbs (under $5.00 each at most photo stores) they are for use with tungsten-balanced (Type B) color slide film.

- Two ceramic inserts for use between bulbs and lighting fixtures; they cost about $1 each. For safety, use these ceramic inserts between any high-wattage bulbs and photographic lighting fixtures. (Caution: Even with ceramic inserts, 250 watts is too much wattage for most household lamp fixtures and wiring for anything other than a very short period.)

- Two garage-type light clamps and reflectors (about $10 each in hardware stores) or, stronger, two Testrite clamps (about $15 each) and aluminum reflectors ($7 each) from photo stores plus plugs and wire. (Assemble these yourself.)

- Two portable 6' to 8' Pic or Bogen lightstands ($10 up, used; $40 up, new).

- One or two 36" to 50" white umbrellas. ($20 up.)

- One or two umbrella clamps from a photo store. ($10 up.)

- Two 20' standard three-prong grounded extension cords and two three-to-two-prong outlet adaptors. These complete a basic tungsten-lighting kit.

Using the Basic Tungsten Lighting Set-Up

You can carry a basic tungsten lighting kit like the one above, plus a tripod, in an inexpensive nylon duffle bag over your shoulder when you go on your first location shoots.

This set-up can be used for direct light on a subject, or to "bounce" light when lamps are aimed at a white wall or ceiling or umbrellas. A white or silver reflector (see Chapter Six), white sheets, shower curtains, plastic bags and aluminum foil are other inexpensive materials that make excellent reflectors. (Don't use them too near hot lights!) Black cloths, reflectors or boards (which absorb light) are used opposite lights for high contrast and deep shadows.

Practice lighting at first using only one light plus a reflector. I still do a lot of lighting this way. You can use more elaborate set-ups if you wish as you gain experience.

What Are Photographic Tungsten Lights?

They are controlled color-temperature lights, usually much higher in wattage than household lamps. The range is from 200-250 watts to 1,000 watts (higher in the case of large movie tungsten lights). Quartz lights are tungsten halogen lights. The tungsten filament is enclosed in quartz (rather than glass) bulbs and is burned with a halogen gas, reaching a much higher temperature and thus giving off a brighter light. (Quartz lights are much smaller, and burn hotter than regular tungsten lights.) As quartz bulbs are much more efficient than conventional tungsten bulbs, they are the most commonly used "hot" photographic lights today. They are very portable—a quartz bulb is only about 10% of the size of a similar wattage standard photolamp, so it uses a small fixture.

Film Used with Tungsten Lights

Most photographic bulbs of all types and wattage are controlled to burn at a color temperature of 3,200K and are used with 3,200K (Type B) color slide films (marked T after the film name on the box). 3,400K photolamps are balanced for Kodachrome 40 (Type A) a film used only in studios today. Daylight films look orange under tungsten lighting. (See also Chapter Five.)

Recommended Tungsten Lights

Three quartz lights I use and recommend are: the tiny Smith Victor 700 (a tiny 600 watt video-light, which takes up no room in a bag), and the professional Lowel Tota Lights and Omni lights. (Get them all with 3,200K bulbs.) The Omni has many light-modification options, and takes 110v or 220v bulbs without a transformer, so it is great for travelling. I have two of each.

Disadvantages of Hot Lights

Disadvantages of quartz lights are that they draw a lot of power, and burn very hot. When using more than one be sure not to use more than a total of 1,200 watts on any one electric line—make sure no other lights or appliances are operating when you plug in your lights.

Caution: If the wiring at a location looks old, use one 600 watt quartz light per circuit as a maximum, or you may blow fuses, or overheat the wiring.

Quick Tungsten Lighting Tips

- Use a tripod for sharp pictures when shooting under tungsten lights, because you usually have to use rather low shutter speeds.
- When learning how to light, don't forget to try photographing very light and very dark subjects as well as average ones. Bracket such exposures.
- Shiny surfaces present special problems; you may bounce the light or angle it very carefully to avoid unwanted reflections, or do as studio photographers do and aim your light(s) through a translucent "tent" (of opaque plastic or paper).

Tungsten Lighting Techniques Easily Translate to Strobe

Once you have learned to use tungsten lighting well, strobe lighting will come easily. It is the kind of reflector or diffuser, bounce surface, distance of light from subject etc. that influences the "look" of your lighting, not the type of light used. As long as the light is balanced for the film, the same type of strobe and tungsten lighting looks pretty much the same on film. The exceptions are that fast strobe/flash light stops motion, and permits the use of smaller f/stops.

To improve your technique using any lights, try to analyze the lighting you see in TV commercials, magazine ads, and photographs you admire. Attend photographers' seminars, look at light and practice, practice what you learn.

Recommended Reading on Lighting

Electronic Flash, by the Editors of Eastman Kodak, is a clear guide to the subject. *Light*, by Michael Freeman, is the best single book I know on all types of lighting. It includes diagrams of lighting set-ups.

Adventures in Location Lighting, by photographer John Falk, has very specific information and lighting diagrams for Vivitar and Dynalite users, and gives much useful general information on professional techniques for strobe and tungsten lighting, power inverters and more.

Two books on "hot lighting" techniques, with diagrams, that can be adapted to location still photography are: *Film Lighting* by Kris Malkiewicz and *TV Lighting Methods*, by Gerald Millerson.

The Photo District News (see Chapter Two) has an annual lighting issue.

Choosing Major Lighting Equipment

Lighting equipment, especially strobe, is expensive. Don't get too much at first. Wait and see what you need and use often. Invest in quality equipment that has a high resale value.

When you are ready to buy (or lease), visit dealers, talk to photographers and study lighting expert Scott Geffert's HyperCard stack *Options in Professional Lighting Equipment*, which follows this chapter. Scott has edited this for travel/location photographers, and has generously given me permission to use it in this book.

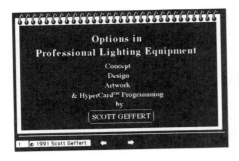

Options in
Professional Lighting Equipment
Concept
Design
Artwork
& HyperCard™ Programming
by
SCOTT GEFFERT

1 © 1991 Scott Geffert

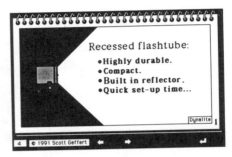

Dear Photographer: Thank you for taking the time to look at this material. I hope it is useful as a reference. The products covered are the most popular on the market for location and studio work. Since specifications change, and my diagrams may not be totally accurate, I suggest you consult a professional photographic lighting dealer for information on specific items. This HyperCard™ stack will run on any Apple Macintosh™ computer. It has been edited for travel photographers. The complete stack of 104 frames is available on disc as shareware. Call me at (212) 924-5943 for a copy. Thanks, Scott Geffert.

02 © 1991 Scott Geffert

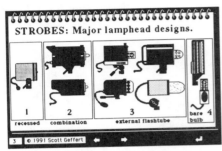

STROBES: Major lamphead designs.

1 recessed   2 combination   3 external flashtube   bare bulb 4

3 © 1991 Scott Geffert

Recessed flashtube:
- Highly durable.
- Compact.
- Built in reflector.
- Quick set-up time...

Dynalite 1

4 © 1991 Scott Geffert

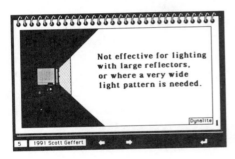

Not effective for lighting with large reflectors, or where a very wide light pattern is needed.

Dynalite 1

5 1991 Scott Geffert

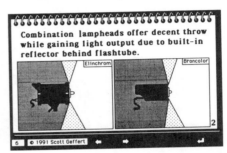

Combination lampheads offer decent throw while gaining light output due to built-in reflector behind flashtube.

Elinchrom   Broncolor

2

6 © 1991 Scott Geffert

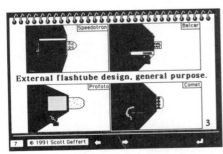

Speedotron   Balcar

External flashtube design, general purpose.

Profoto   Comet

3

7 © 1991 Scott Geffert

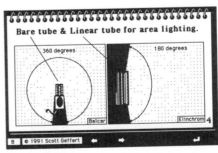

Bare tube & Linear tube for area lighting.

360 degrees   180 degrees

Balcar   Elinchrom 4

8 © 1991 Scott Geffert

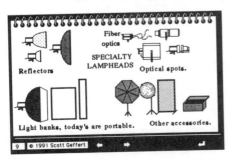

Fiber optics
SPECIALTY LAMPHEADS   Optical spots.
Reflectors
Light banks, today's are portable.   Other accessories.

9 © 1991 Scott Geffert

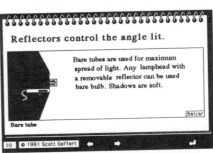

Reflectors control the angle lit.

Bare tubes are used for maximum spread of light. Any lamphead with a removable reflector can be used bare bulb. Shadows are soft.

Bare tube   Balcar

10 © 1991 Scott Geffert

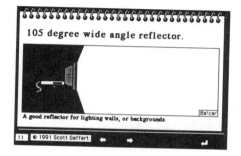

105 degree wide angle reflector.

A good reflector for lighting walls, or backgrounds.

Balcar

11 © 1991 Scott Geffert

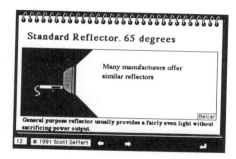

Standard Reflector. 65 degrees

Many manufacturers offer similar reflectors

General purpose reflector usually provides a fairly even light without sacrificing power output.

Balcar

12 © 1991 Scott Geffert

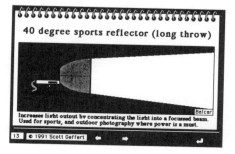

40 degree sports reflector (long throw)

Increases light output by concentrating the light into a focussed beam. Used for sports, and outdoor photography where power is a must.

Balcar

13 © 1991 Scott Geffert

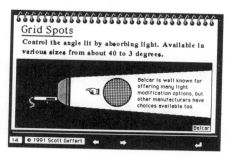

Grid Spots

Control the angle lit by absorbing light. Available in various sizes from about 40 to 3 degrees.

Balcar is well known for offering many light modification options, but other manufacturers have choices available too.

Balcar

14 © 1991 Scott Geffert

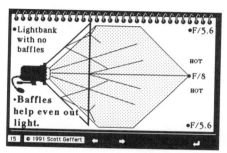

• Lightbank with no baffles

• F/5.6

HOT

• F/8

HOT

• Baffles help even out light.

• F/5.6

15 © 1991 Scott Geffert

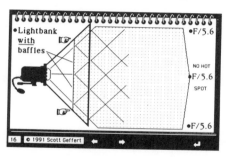

• Lightbank with baffles

• F/5.6

NO HOT

• F/5.6

SPOT

• F/5.6

16 © 1991 Scott Geffert

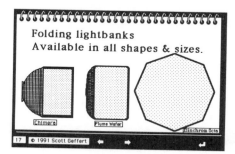

Folding lightbanks
Available in all shapes & sizes.

Chimera   Plume Wafer   Elinchrom Octa

17 © 1991 Scott Geffert

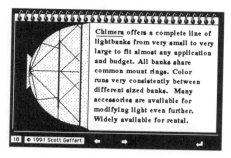

Chimera offers a complete line of lightbanks from very small to very large to fit almost any application and budget. All banks share common mount rings. Color runs very consistently between different sized banks. Many accessories are available for modifying light even further. Widely available for rental.

18 © 1991 Scott Geffert

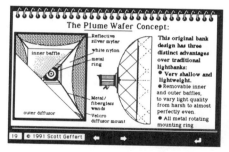

The Plume Wafer Concept:

Reflective silver mylar

white nylon

metal ring

inner baffle

Metal / fiberglass vands

outer diffusor

Velcro diffusor mount

This original bank design has three distinct advantages over traditional lightbanks:
• Very shallow and lightweight.
• Removable inner and outer baffles, to vary light quality from harsh to almost perfectly even.
• All metal rotating mounting ring

19 © 1991 Scott Geffert

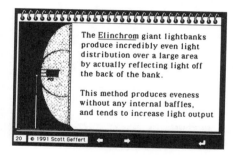

The Elinchrom giant lightbanks produce incredibly even light distribution over a large area by actually reflecting light off the back of the bank.

This method produces eveness without any internal baffles, and tends to increase light output

20 © 1991 Scott Geffert

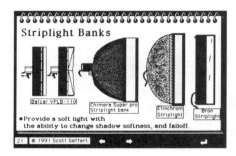

Striplight Banks

Balcar VPLB-110
Chimera Super pro Striplight bank
Elinchrom Striplight
Bron Striplight

• Provide a soft light with the ability to change shadow softness, and falloff.

21 © 1991 Scott Geffert

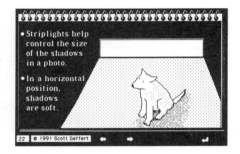

• Striplights help control the size of the shadows in a photo.

• In a horizontal position, shadows are soft.

22 © 1991 Scott Geffert

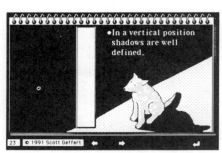

• In a vertical position shadows are well defined.

23 © 1991 Scott Geffert

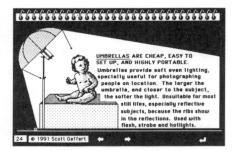

UMBRELLAS ARE CHEAP, EASY TO SET UP, AND HIGHLY PORTABLE.

Umbrellas provide soft even lighting, specially useful for photographing people on location. The larger the umbrella, and closer to the subject, the softer the light. Unsuitable for most still lifes, especially reflective subjects, because the ribs show in the reflections. Used with flash, strobe and hotlights.

24 © 1991 Scott Geffert

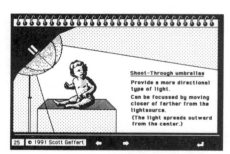

Shoot-Through umbrellas

Provide a more directional type of light.

Can be focussed by moving closer or farther from the lightsource.

(The light spreads outward from the center.)

25 © 1991 Scott Geffert

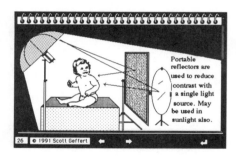

Portable reflectors are used to reduce contrast with a single light source. May be used in sunlight also.

26 © 1991 Scott Geffert

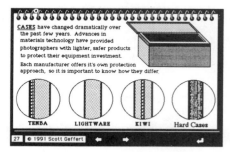

CASES have changed dramatically over the past few years. Advances in materials technology have provided photographers with lighter, safer products to protect their equipment investment.

Each manufacturer offers it's own protection approach, so it is important to know how they differ.

TENBA   LIGHTWARE   KIWI   Hard Cases

27 © 1991 Scott Geffert

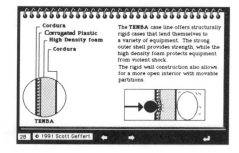

— Cordura
— Corrugated Plastic
— High Density foam
— Cordura

The **TENBA** case line offers structurally rigid cases that lend themselves to a variety of equipment. The strong outer shell provides strength, while the high density foam protects equipment from violent shock.

The rigid wall construction also allows for a more open interior with movable partitions.

TENBA

28 © 1991 Scott Geffert

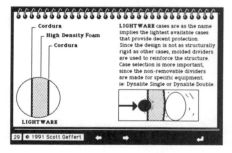

— Cordura
— High Density Foam
— Cordura

LIGHTWARE cases are as the name implies the lightest available cases that provide decent protection. Since the design is not as structurally rigid as other cases, molded dividers are used to reinforce the structure. Case selection is more important, since the non-removable dividers are made for specific equipment. ie: Dynalite Single or Dynalite Double.

LIGHTWARE

29 © 1991 Scott Geffert

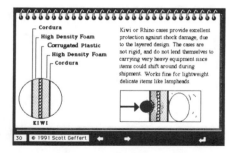

— Cordura
— High Density Foam
— Corrugated Plastic
— High Density Foam
— Cordura

Kiwi or Rhino cases provide excellent protection against shock damage, due to the layered design. The cases are not rigid, and do not lend themselves to carrying very heavy equipment since items could shift around during shipment. Works fine for lightweight delicate items like lampheads.

KIWI

30 © 1991 Scott Geffert

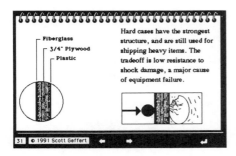

Fiberglass
3/4" Plywood
Plastic

Hard cases have the strongest structure, and are still used for shipping heavy items. The tradeoff is low resistance to shock damage, a major cause of equipment failure.

31 © 1991 Scott Geffert

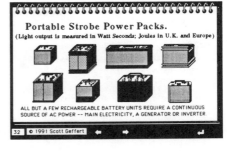

Portable Strobe Power Packs.
(Light output is measured in Watt Seconds; Joules in U.K. and Europe)

ALL BUT A FEW RECHARGEABLE BATTERY UNITS REQUIRE A CONTINUOUS SOURCE OF AC POWER -- MAIN ELECTRICITY, A GENERATOR OR INVERTER.

32 © 1991 Scott Geffert

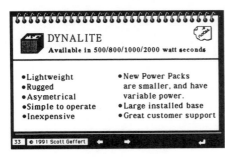

DYNALITE
Available in 500/800/1000/2000 watt seconds

- Lightweight
- Rugged
- Asymetrical
- Simple to operate
- Inexpensive

- New Power Packs are smaller, and have variable power.
- Large installed base
- Great customer support

33 © 1991 Scott Geffert

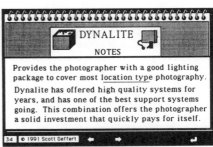

DYNALITE
NOTES

Provides the photographer with a good lighting package to cover most <u>location type</u> photography. Dynalite has offered high quality systems for years, and has one of the best support systems going. This combination offers the photographer a solid investment that quickly pays for itself.

34 © 1991 Scott Geffert

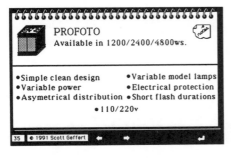

PROFOTO
Available in 1200/2400/4800ws.

- Simple clean design
- Variable power
- Asymetrical distribution

- Variable model lamps
- Electrical protection
- Short flash durations

- 110/220v

35 © 1991 Scott Geffert

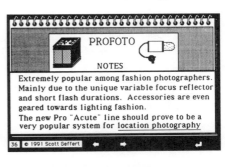

PROFOTO
NOTES

Extremely popular among fashion photographers. Mainly due to the unique variable focus reflector and short flash durations. Accessories are even geared towards lighting fashion.
The new Pro "Acute" line should prove to be a very popular system for <u>location photography</u>

36 © 1991 Scott Geffert

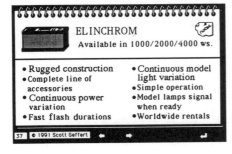

ELINCHROM
Available in 1000/2000/4000 ws.

- Rugged construction
- Complete line of accessories
- Continuous power variation
- Fast flash durations

- Continuous model light variation
- Simple operation
- Model lamps signal when ready
- Worldwide rentals

37 © 1991 Scott Geffert

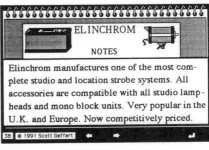

ELINCHROM
NOTES

Elinchrom manufactures one of the most complete studio and location strobe systems. All accessories are compatible with all studio lamp-heads and mono block units. Very popular in the U.K. and Europe. Now competitively priced.

38 © 1991 Scott Geffert

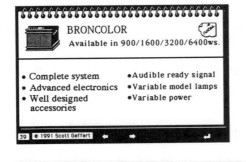

BRONCOLOR
Available in 900/1600/3200/6400ws.

- Complete system
- Advanced electronics
- Well designed accessories

- Audible ready signal
- Variable model lamps
- Variable power

39 © 1991 Scott Geffert

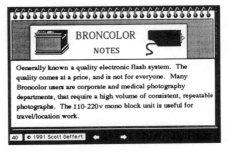

BRONCOLOR
NOTES

Generally known a quality electronic flash system. The quality comes at a price, and is not for everyone. Many Broncolor users are corporate and medical photography departments, that require a high volume of consistent, repeatable photographs. The 110-220v mono block unit is useful for travel/location work.

40 © 1991 Scott Geffert

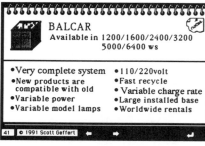

BALCAR
Available in 1200/1600/2400/3200
5000/6400 ws

- Very complete system
- New products are compatible with old
- Variable power
- Variable model lamps
- 110/220volt
- Fast recycle
- Variable charge rate
- Large installed base
- Worldwide rentals

41 © 1991 Scott Geffert

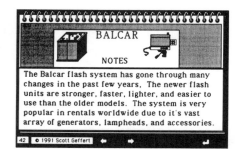

BALCAR
NOTES

The Balcar flash system has gone through many changes in the past few years. The newer flash units are stronger, faster, lighter, and easier to use than the older models. The system is very popular in rentals worldwide due to it's vast array of generators, lampheads, and accessories.

42 © 1991 Scott Geffert

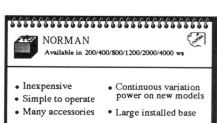

NORMAN
Available in 200/400/800/1200/2000/4000 ws

- Inexpensive
- Simple to operate
- Many accessories
- Continuous variation power on new models
- Large installed base

43 © 1991 Scott Geffert

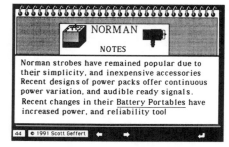

NORMAN
NOTES

Norman strobes have remained popular due to their simplicity, and inexpensive accessories Recent designs of power packs offer continuous power variation, and audible ready signals. Recent changes in their Battery Portables have increased power, and reliability tool

44 © 1991 Scott Geffert

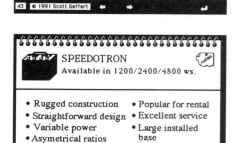

SPEEDOTRON
Available in 1200/2400/4800 ws.

- Rugged construction
- Straightforward design
- Variable power
- Asymetrical ratios
- Popular for rental
- Excellent service
- Large installed base

45 © 1991 Scott Geffert

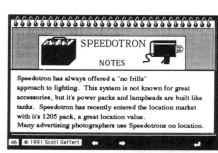

SPEEDOTRON
NOTES

Speedotron has always offered a "no frills" approach to lighting. This system is not known for great accessories, but it's power packs and lampheads are built like tanks. Speedotron has recently entered the location market with it's 1205 pack, a great location value.
Many advertising photographers use Speedotrons on location.

46 © 1991 Scott Geffert

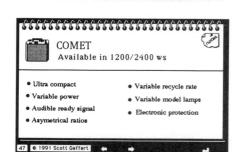

COMET
Available in 1200/2400 ws

- Ultra compact
- Variable power
- Audible ready signal
- Asymetrical ratios
- Variable recycle rate
- Variable model lamps
- Electronic protection

47 © 1991 Scott Geffert

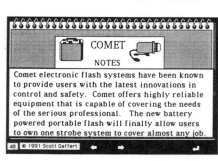

COMET
NOTES

Comet electronic flash systems have been known to provide users with the latest innovations in control and safety. Comet offers highly reliable equipment that is capable of covering the needs of the serious professional. The new battery powered portable flash will finally allow users to own one strobe system to cover almost any job.

48 © 1991 Scott Geffert

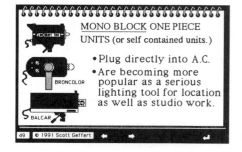

MONO BLOCK ONE PIECE UNITS (or self contained units.)

- Plug directly into A.C.
- Are becoming more popular as a serious lighting tool for location as well as studio work.

49 © 1991 Scott Geffert

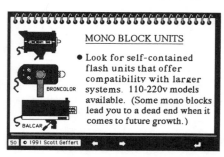

MONO BLOCK UNITS

- Look for self-contained flash units that offer compatibility with larger systems. 110-220v models available. (Some mono blocks lead you to a dead end when it comes to future growth.)

50 © 1991 Scott Geffert

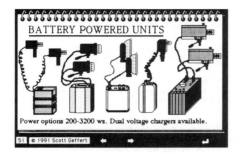

BATTERY POWERED UNITS

Power options 200-3200 ws. Dual voltage chargers available.

51 © 1991 Scott Geffert

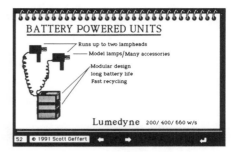

BATTERY POWERED UNITS

Runs up to two lampheads
Model lamps/Many accessories
Modular design
long battery life
Fast recycling

Lumedyne 200/ 400/ 660 w/s

52 © 1991 Scott Geffert

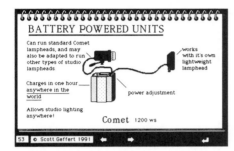

BATTERY POWERED UNITS

Can run standard Comet lampheads, and may also be adapted to run other types of studio lampheads

works with it's own lightweight lamphead

Charges in one hour anywhere in the world

power adjustment

Allows studio lighting anywhere!

Comet 1200 ws

53 © Scott Geffert 1991

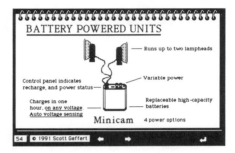

BATTERY POWERED UNITS

Runs up to two lampheads

Variable power

Control panel indicates recharge, and power status

Replaceable high-capacity batteries

Charges in one hour, on any voltage. Auto voltage sensing

Minicam 4 power options

54 © 1991 Scott Geffert

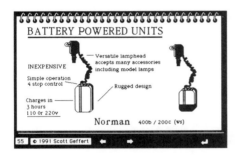

BATTERY POWERED UNITS

INEXPENSIVE

Versatile lamphead accepts many accessories including model lamps

Simple operation 4 stop control

Rugged design

Charges in 3 hours 110 or 220v

Norman 400b / 200c (ws)

55 © 1991 Scott Geffert

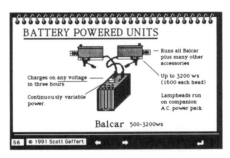

BATTERY POWERED UNITS

Runs all Balcar plus many other accessories

Charges on any voltage in three hours

Up to 3200 ws (1600 each head)

Continuously variable power.

Lampheads run on companion A.C. power pack

Balcar 500-3200ws

56 © 1991 Scott Geffert

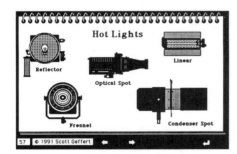

Hot Lights

Reflector

Linear

Optical Spot

Fresnel

Condenser Spot

57 © 1991 Scott Geffert

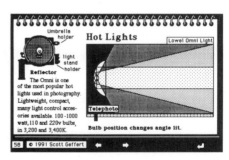

Hot Lights

Umbrella holder

light stand holder

Reflector

The Omni is one of the most popular hot lights used in photography. Lightweight, compact, many light control accessories available. 100 -1000 watt, 110 and 220v bulbs, in 3,200 and 3,400K.

Lowel Omni Light

Telephoto

Bulb position changes angle lit.

58 © 1991 Scott Geffert

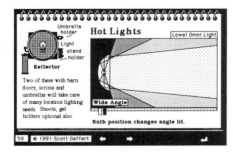

Hot Lights

Umbrella holder

Light stand holder

Reflector

Two of these with barn doors, scrims and umbrellas will take care of many location lighting needs. Snoots, gel holders optional also.

Lowel Omni Light

Wide Angle

Bulb position changes angle lit.

59 © 1991 Scott Geffert

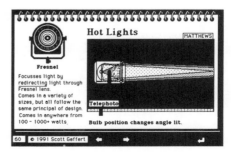

Hot Lights

Fresnel

Focusses light by redirecting light through Fresnel lens. Comes in a variety of sizes, but all follow the same principal of design. Comes in anywhere from 100 - 1000+ watts.

MATTHEWS

Telephoto

Bulb position changes angle lit.

60 © 1991 Scott Geffert

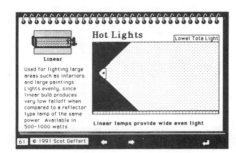

Hot Lights

Linear

Used for lighting large areas such as interiors and large paintings Lights evenly, since linear bulb produces very low falloff when compared to a reflector type lamp of the same power Available in 500-1000 watts

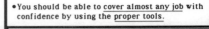
Lowel Tota Light

Linear lamps provide wide even light

61 © 1991 Scot Geffert

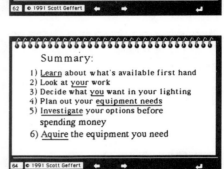

• Take an honest look at the weak, as well as the strong points of your work
You are the best judge of your capabilities.

• If you find that you lighting technique is determined by your equipment, you should look into finding equipment that won't limit your work.

• You should be able to cover almost any job with confidence by using the proper tools.

62 © 1991 Scott Geffert

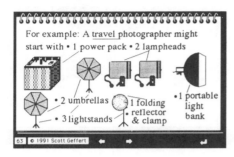

For example: A travel photographer might start with • 1 power pack • 2 lampheads

• 2 umbrellas
• 3 lightstands
1 folding reflector & clamp
• 1 portable light bank

63 © 1991 Scott Geffert

Summary:

1) Learn about what's available first hand
2) Look at your work
3) Decide what you want in your lighting
4) Plan out your equipment needs
5) Investigate your options before spending money
6) Aquire the equipment you need

64 © 1991 Scott Geffert

Chapter 8

People, Landscape, Architecture & Location Still-Life

If your travel photographs are for personal or fine-art use, what you choose to photograph when you travel is, of course, entirely up to you. Some people take only landscapes and natural scenes, others like to make "people pictures" of locals in exotic places, or loved ones enjoying the vacation. Few non-specialists think seriously about architectural photography, but for balanced coverage of a place every serious photographer should be able to photograph buildings and interiors at least occasionally.

Professional and would-be professional travel photographers must be able to handle landscape, people and architecture equally well, they are the mixture that make up the bulk of all photographic travel features, illustrations for travel stories and travel stock. (For top professional work you should be able to shoot location still-life too.) Just check any issue of the *National Geographic*, *Condé Nast Traveler*, or *Travel and Leisure* magazines, or any Sunday newspaper travel supplement to see the varied subjects they cover.

I have written about light, for people, landscape and architectural photography in Chapters Six and Seven, and about compositional skills in Chapter Two. Now I will discuss technique and content requirements for travel subjects.

People Pictures

In reply to the question I am most often asked about people photography: Yes, you do need to get releases when photographing people wherever possible if you hope to sell the pictures for advertising or stock. Stock prices are higher for advertising than for editorial use, and all advertising and promotional use of pictures of people requires releases. Pictures of property and pets require releases for advertising also. (For more, see Chapter Thirteen.)

But, even if you can't or don't want to get releases, you can sell people pictures for many editorial uses without releases. And, I do hope that even if you are a professional photographer you sometimes photograph people for personal reasons, because you think them handsome, interesting or beautiful, or just for the joy and fun of it. Selling isn't everything. (See also Chapter Eleven.)

Photograph People for Complete Travel Coverage

In my opinion, to really understand a place you should get to know some of the local people. For many personally shy travel photographers (I am one) the best way meet people is to photograph them, sometimes you get great opportunities because of your camera. For instance, I spent a marvellous day at a peasant wedding in El Salvador when their photographer didn't show up; and was able to get pictures of then British Prime Minister Margaret Thatcher, because I did a photographic favor for a London Police Inspector, again when his photographer didn't show. Though not a news or celebrity photographer I have made portraits of famous painters in China, Poland and Haiti, and I have shot singers at the Covent Garden Opera House and actors in London and Stratford-upon-Avon. I've also made pictures of the presidents of two of Japan's mightiest corporations and of three aimiable mayors of New York among many other notables. Also in New York, where I take pictures continually, I have photographed bicycle messengers and bus drivers, sculptors and bakers, real estate tycoons, philanthropists, chefs, Wall Street whiz kids and the gentleman who is the president of the Coney Island Polar Bear Club. (He invited me to the clubhouse for hot tea one frigid day in January after I took pictures of him and six other shivering fanatics braving a 42 degree dip in the Atlantic!) People to me are as much a part of coverage of any country or city as great landscapes and monuments.

People are People, Everywhere

It seems to me that some photographers approach people, especially "exotic" people, with the same spirit they would use in hunting an elephant. They "bag" the person from a distance with a telephoto lens, and often shoot the head, without any background surroundings or landscape, and then display the picture head later rather as they would an animal trophy. They make no attempt to record the person's inner qualities.

I am a people photography specialist, and I always strive for a feeling of intimacy in my travel pictures of people. However colorfully someone is dressed or however superficially different a person seems to be from me, I am always conscious that they probably have kids, spouses and occupations, and joys and problems that are not so very different from my own.

I almost always start by asking people, by word or gesture, if I can photograph them, unless they are part of a large crowd. (You can often feel people's reaction to you, by standing nearby holding a camera very obviously, after a few minutes you will have a sense of when they are open to being approached; ask verbally or by pointing at your camera and the person and smiling the request).

Of course, some people don't want to be photographed, and show this by turning away; occasionally someone actually refuses a request with words or a gesture or a shake of the head; I always respect the refusals, and peoples' right to privacy (I'm not a photojournalist, remember) and just approach someone else. Even if you are more of a "candid camera" type that I am, I still suggest that you always ask parents' permission to photograph kids, and ask very poor peoples' permission everywhere.

The most important thing to remember when you ask any stranger about photographing them is that if you are comfortable about the whole thing, they are much more likely to respond positively, and to be at ease in front of the camera.

Work Close for Intimate People Pictures

Permission for photography secured, I usually work very close to people, using moderate focal-length to wide-angle lenses for portraits. (I like showing people in their environment.) I often end up as close as two or three feet from the subject, so getting their cooperation is obviously absolutely necessary. Once you have a good subject, don't take just two or three frames. It takes time for people to warm up, and unless you are in peak practice, it will take you a few frames to warm up too.

I usually keep my left eye open when shooting (this takes some practice), so I can watch for intrusions into the background and I talk to people, even people whose language I don't even attempt to speak, all the time that I am photographing them. (I'll try a few words in any language, however badly pronounced. If I know any, this often causes gales of mirth.) If people understand, they respond; if not I talk in English, which usually amuses them too, and always takes their mind off the discomfort of having a lens pointed in their faces.

Talk to Your Subjects When Photographing Them

Think about it, do you feel comfortable when someone is photographing you? If the photographer doesn't talk to you, and walks around looking at you while muttering about f/stops and apertures, you feel stiff, and wonder where to put your hands and feet, and worry about pimples (if young) or wrinkles (if middle-aged) or how you hate the way you look now (if old). My mother, who was very good-looking, told me that she felt like a very old turtle in front of the camera. I'll bet that Annie Leibowitz's mother—or Herb Ritts'—have to be talked into letting their kids take their pictures!

So, empathize with peoples' private agonies about their appearance, and talk to them about almost anything while photographing them. Even in the street they will be distracted and relax after the first few clicks; they will probably settle into more comfortable, natural positions, and may smile or laugh, or even come up with creative poses themselves. After the initial clicks of my shutter—the warm-ups—I feel free to ask people to move, or to put something down (a plastic shopping bag for instance) or to pick something up (some fruit or beads in a market, a tool for a worker, artist or craftsperson, a book for a student). After a while, I will ask someone to take off a jacket, or reverse a tee-shirt with an intrusive design, or to repeat an activity that's sometimes difficult to capture on one frame (like the peak of a dive, or a kiss between young lovers). My rule is never to be embarrassed to ask anyone to do almost anything. People will immediately let you know if you are overstepping their limits of distance, time or propriety.

Be Aware of Clothing

I like to take pictures of people in national, regional or traditional costumes. These are often good as symbols for a place or a way of life. In America, cowboys wear blue jeans, western shirts and broad-brimmed hats, lumberjacks wear thick red and black wool shirts, New England fishermen yellow slickers and rubber boots, and farmers overalls and long-peaked caps with mesh tops. Relaxing yuppies of both sexes wear polo shirts, tan pants or skirts and loafers; old hippies wear headbands, denim and tie-dye. Even if reality is not quite like that, these stereotypes do have some truth, and especially are useful for tourism pictures and for stock, because they don't date. Austrians in dirndls, Britishers in tweeds (or pin-stripes and bowler hats), Germans in lederhosen or red-checked shirts and olive hiking knickers, Indians in kurtas and saris, Africans and Arabs in beautiful robes and similar classics are all much more long-lasting for picture sales than people wearing very trendy clothes which very soon look only dated.

The Vagaries of Fashion

In the summer of 1989, everyone in the south of France was wearing bright green and purple bathing suits, tank tops, shirts, shorts, dresses, even shoes. Those colors look awfully out-of-date now. In summer 1991 in New York a tee-shirt that said Button Your Fly in 8 inch letters was in vogue. Don't bother to photograph people wearing such stuff. Ten days after you've taken the shot it looks old-fashioned. Look at last year's fashion magazines to see what I mean. (Of course, you may want to make personal photographs that comment on the vagaries of fashion, but that is altogether something other than plain travel photography.) Check when photographing people in traditional or national costume to see if some discordant modern element could be removed to improve the shot. Fancy wristwatches, fancy eyeglasses, sneakers and loud tee-shirts are my pet hates. People are usually willing to take them off or change if you ask nicely.

Formal Portraiture

Formal portraiture is people photography too. Pre-plan your backgrounds and lighting to a large extent before your subject comes on the scene. Use a substitute or stand-in to refine the lighting if necessary. That way the subject won't have time to sit around and get too nervous before you start. Work with more than one camera and lens so that you won't have to break into the rapport and mood you achieve with your subject because you need to change film. Ask your subjects to avoid very extreme or trendy clothes, and bright colors or jewelry that will compete with the face for attention in the picture (unless of course that's part of their basic personality, or style).

Quick Tips for Portraiture

- Ask men to shave an hour or so before you take the pictures.
- Be sure women don't wear too much make-up, and have a soft hair-style, not one that looks as if they emerged from the beauty parlor ten minutes ago.
- A filter with a clear center but slightly soft at the edges flatters many middle-aged and older people, women especially prefer to have wrinkles played down.
- Soft, diffused lighting is flattering to almost anyone.
- Talk to your subjects when photographing them formally, just as you do when working with people on location. Compliment people and tell them they look nice, because saying something like "Oh, that angle makes your nose look big" will kill a portrait session stone dead, instantly. It's your job as a photographer to solve the nose problem, not to make your subject worry about it. For the big nose, use a moderate telephoto lens (in the 80, 105 or 135mm range) and photograph the person looking directly into the camera. Use shadowless lighting.
- If you want to try different poses to improve any portrait, say, "Could you please try so-and-so, I think it would look nice" or to an executive, "I think it would look appropriate if..." or for an unusual pose "Is it possible...?"
- If any pose doesn't look right in the viewfinder, take a couple of shots without comment, then try another variant.
- Remember that photographing two, or three people, or a group, is much more difficult that photographing one person (because they all must look good at the same time); shoot plenty of film.

Finally and most importantly, if you ever promise to send prints in exchange for posing and signing model releases, always send them, and as soon as possible.

Landscape

We live in a very crowded and stressful world, and most of most people's lives today are spent in suburbs, towns or big cities. Almost everyone, even a dedicated city-dweller like myself, has a deep-seated need for space and light. Green unspoiled countryside, wilderness areas, high mountains, peaceful lakes, untouched seashores and even beautiful empty desert lands satisfy that hunger. Therefore good photographs of these things are very popular, and can be big stock sellers in the United States and Canada, and especially in crowded, highly organized countries like Germany and Japan which are top-paying markets for photography. If you photograph for stock, landscape has the merit of being timeless; good pictures of redwoods or rain forests, mountains or moorlands, will be as saleable in twenty years time as they are today.

Some Problems of Landscape Photography

Photographing pristine landscape is not as easy as taking off to a national park or sparsely populated area. Signs of civilization (or sometimes, lack of it) intrude in even the very remotest places today. Scientists and increasing numbers of tourists are causing litter problems in the Antarctic for instance; we all know about the depredation of various forests, including some in just about all nations; and oil drilling, mining, hydro-electric production, as well as population increase, tourism, overdevelopment and even recreational diving are leaving ugly imprints on more and more once unspoiled places.

Pleasures of Landscape Photography

I am not a landscape or wildlife specialist, but I have photographed in North, East and South Africa, in the American desert states, the Adirondacks and in English national parks, the Norwegian fjords and the French, Swiss, Italian and Austrian Alps. I have camped in unspoiled West Virginia, by the roaring tide of the Bay of Fundy in Nova Scotia, and on remote beaches in the Greek Cyclades islands. I love to look at clouds, the changing play of light on water, the movement of leaves in the wind, and tumbleweeds and sand blowing in the desert. I have risen before dawn to catch animals feeding in the Serengeti; and photographed migrating birds at wildlife refuges at Brigantine, New Jersey; Chincoteague, Virginia and in the Farne Islands off England's Northumberland coast. One of my favorite places to vacation and photograph is the remote island of Ouessant off the coast of Brittany, part of the land and sea Armorique National Park in Northwestern France.

Beautiful scenery exists everywhere, even in densely populated countries like my own dear England, and surprisingly close to even very crowded areas like my adopted home in New York City. The closer to population centers of course, the more the landscape photographer has to watch for unintended things that can intrude, break the mood of peace, solitude, oneness with nature, and ruin an otherwise beautiful picture.

Emphasize the Positive

I am not, as I have said before, a photo-journalist. There is pollution, overdevelopment, overpopulation, exploitation of the land, and destruction of natural beauty everywhere. Some wildlife is near extinction, and much is endangered. I do not usually make photographs that emphasize these things. I think that people respond to positive messages as well as negative ones, and we all see so much horror on the small screen every night between 6:30 and 7:30 p.m., that we want the other side of life also. I believe that showing the very many beautiful things that still exist will make people more likely to want to preserve them, even at the cost of jobs, convenience and money. Man does not live by bread alone. So, I don't apologize for showing landscape and nature at its best. If you feel moved to make photographs that show how our planet is being ravaged, I salute your efforts. You will probably even find there is a good market for such photographs.

What I Don't Include in My Landscape Photographs

In many areas of the world lines of electricity towers are a problem for landscape photographers. They run down beautiful Alpine valleys, meander smack through the middle of bucolic New England vistas, slice through many scenic Western views and intrude in many, many other places, usually on the wrong side of the view as far as photography of the landscape is concerned. (England is, I think, the world capital of electric pylons, as they are called there.) Local electric wires, TV transmitters, oil derricks and ski and other cable car towers are related problems. All the photographer who wants unspoiled landscape pictures can do is angle the camera to avoid such things. (But take a few pictures showing them for stock or protest purposes only!)

Railroad lines and highways should be avoided for pristine landscapes, but for tourism photography especially, a distant road or railroad with a well-placed train (or tourist bus!) or a distant single car in the scene, imply that the viewer can be there also to enjoy the vista. I photograph such landscapes whenever I see them, as well as empty ones. Sometimes I specifically search for scenic overlooks, and arrange to be there when a train or bus is due below. With buses, if you are working for a tourist client, arrange with the driver to go extremely slowly along a previously chosen stretch of road, so that you will have plenty of choices of pictures for the client. Dirt roads look romantic in landscapes too, if they are not too bumpy.

Local electric poles and wires, TV antennas and satellite dishes, advertising billboards, gas stations and highway directional signs, even road stripes, are also problems for the landscape photographer. I usually leave those things out if it's possible, but again, a few shots for stock purposes are sometimes useful. Some road and other signs are unintentionally funny, and worth photographing for their own sake.

Garbage, litter and related containers are always out. So are most picnic tables, camp and RV sites and beachfront shacks. The occasional mountaineer's hut, shepherd's shelter or fisherman's cottage can give scale. I take shots of mountains, green landscapes and beaches with and without these things. (I'll also photograph the climber, the fisherman and the shepherd close-up in their landscapes if I can.)

Giving Scale to Landscapes

Sometimes one small sign of human life adds to a grand scene and gives it scale. If you go on the Great Wall in China and walk up to the right from the main entrance, it is crowded with people, and looks ugly and unromantic. But if you climb to the left for a couple of hundred yards, you can see the wall rolling along, slowly diminishing for miles and miles over green mountains. If you wait for one tiny figure to appear, that person makes you fully appreciate the scale and immensity of the wall. (It is said to be the only man-made thing clearly visible from space.)

A distant small boat in a seascape, one or two people far away on an otherwise empty beach or skiers carving trails down a snowy mountainside are useful variations on empty landscapes. Keep these people and objects very small; ski-

and bathing suit fashions change, so do hair styles for both men and women; cars and trucks go out of date; even people on yachts need model releases for advertising uses if they are large enough to be recognizable in a seascape. (You will also need a property release for the yacht to use it for advertising.)

Show Geographic Features for Stock Sales

Landscape photographs that show geographic and geological features of all types are needed for textbooks and encyclopedias. Look for strata and graphic shapes as well as more obvious things like famous rock formations, waterfalls, glaciers and trees and dunes shaped by prevailing winds. "Generic" tropical beach pictures, clean green and blue lake and mountain scenes, beautiful sunsets, cloudscapes, rock formations and bountiful farmland pictures are all sold for advertising stock. (See also Chapter Thirteen.)

Take a Risk—Do it Your Way

Rules are always broken by talented people—Jay Maisel has made some great landscapes including utility poles in the west, and Richard Mizrach has done wonderful pictures of bombed western landscapes. Look for their modern landscape photographs and also those of the early masters, O'Sullivan, Muybridge and Watkins.

Architecture

Many photographers who aren't at all afraid of tackling people balk at doing serious architectural photography. They will take the odd snap of a skyline or church, probably tilting the camera to get the tops of buildings in, and then, thinking they can't do any better without specialized equipment, will leave it at that. But the outsides and insides of historic and modern public buildings, hotels, restaurants, monuments, formal gardens especially in Europe and Japan, and religious buildings and just vernacular housing everywhere all contribute to complete travel coverage of a place, and are usually requirements of magazine and tourism and corporate travel/location clients.

Equipment for Architectural Photography

While architectural specialists almost always do use technical and large-format cameras with elaborate shifts, swings and tilts, the well-equipped 35mm or medium-format photographer can take good architectural and interior photographs with the cameras and lenses they normally use. It is just necessary to understand how to use 20 and 28mm lenses (or the equivalent wide-angles for medium format) as well as moderate telephoto or zoom lenses and know how to place them correctly for good results.

A sturdy tripod that extends to about 7' high or higher is indispensable for almost all architectural and interior photography. I use a Gitzo tripod with a ball head which is very easy to level. (You may also find a small spirit-level handy to help you level your tripod and camera accurately.)

You will need a stepladder to photograph very large interiors; usually you can borrow one at the site, but carry a lightweight aluminum ladder with you if you know there won't be anything to stand on at the location. If you wear glasses, or have astigmatism, a special grid in your camera viewfinder will help you to line up horizontals and verticals so that perspectives of walls and ceilings, floors and furnishings do not unintentionally converge.

What you must remember always in architectural/interior photography is that if you tilt the camera from exact horizontal or vertical, the lines of buildings will tilt to the exact same angle. If you point your camera up, buildings and rooms will appear to lean backwards. If you aim the camera down, vertical lines will appear to lean toward you. And if you tilt the camera sideways, even a tiny bit, as well as up or down, the whole scene will lean sideways too; walls will tilt, and the picture will appear totally skewed for a "Cabinet of Doctor Caligari" effect—not recommended unless you are making horror movies.

How to Photograph Buildings Without Tilting Them Backwards

While this is not always possible, the answer can be as simple as shooting a vertical picture rather than a horizontal composition, or moving further away; getting up to a higher viewpoint, or using a wider angle lens, or a combination of all those things. Sometimes, you will have to go much further away, and photograph the building from a distance with a moderate telephoto or zoom lens. (Zooms are great for precise framing from a distance; I often use my 35-75mm and 80-200mm zooms for architecture and cityscapes.)

The secret of tilt-free architectural photography with a 35mm camera is to always point the center of the lens at the center of the building. If you are going to photograph a 30 story building, the very best place to do it from is the fifteenth floor of a nearby building. That way, equal parts of the building are above and below your lens. Providing it is of wide enough angle to include the top and the bottom of the building, there will be no tilting of lines if you level the camera exactly. There will be slight elongation at the top and bottom of any vertical wide-angle lens picture (or at the sides of any horizontal one), but this is an inherent feature of these lenses and will be scarcely noticeable in your architecture shots.

Special 35mm Lenses for Architectural Photography

Nikon makes 28mm and 35mm perspective correction(P.C.) lenses that shift vertically and horizontally to include the tops of buildings without tilting the camera. Canon has just introduced a 24mm Tilt and Shift lens for its EOS line of dedicated/TTL autofocus cameras, and has offered T.S. lenses for older models for years. Olympus has a 24mm P.C. lens. All these specialist lenses are expensive; worth it if you need them. They can be rented for occasional jobs.

What You Cannot Do in Architectural Photography

Some things just cannot be done, even with view cameras with full swings, tilts and shifts. For instance: it is impossible to photograph the famous 102 story Empire State Building here in New York from immediately below it, on 34th or 33rd Streets between Fifth and Sixth Avenues. You can't see the top.

Most 35mm pictures of the Empire State are taken with telephoto lenses from the top of the RCA building on 50th Street looking downtown, or from the top of the World Trade Center, on West Street, looking uptown. From about ten blocks away (up or down Fifth or Sixth Avenues, or Broadway) you can shoot the Empire State easily from any midsized building, on about the fifteenth floor. From twenty blocks away (near where I live) you can shoot the Empire State from ground level without tilting it, by using a short (43-80mm) zoom lens. The landmark looks especially nice at "blue time" when different colored floodlighting illuminates the top.

Take the PATH tube train across the Hudson River to photograph the Empire State from many parks along the New Jersey shore, both for backlit sunrise pictures, and for the reflected light from sunsets which often stain it gold, sometimes orange and occasionally, blood red. (Weehawken, NJ is directly opposite 34th Street; the view from the Hudson riverfront park by the Exchange Place PATH station in Jersey City puts the Empire State in a New York skyline that also includes the World Trade Center.) In the other direction, shoot the Empire State from across the East River. Get early morning light, or sunset back light on the Empire State from the Brooklyn Bridge walkway, or piers in Long Island City, Queens, close to the Hunter's Point Avenue subway stop. The Empire State Building is also visible from the Staten Island Ferry, the Statue of Liberty, and Ellis Island, to name just three of many interesting views. You will discover your own if you seriously photograph New York.

You can apply the same principals to photographing skyscrapers, cathedrals, and even quite small buildings anywhere, from Sydney to San Diego, Paris to Pernambuco. (Pernambuco is in Brazil, and in case you remember my previous reference to it, I did follow my mother's footsteps and go there; but the city is now called Recife.)

Photographing Interiors

For interiors, again you must get your lens up to the midheight of a room, by standing on a stepladder if necessary. A P.C. (or I'm sure, a Tilt and Shift lens but I haven't tried one) is especially useful for correcting perspective of interiors where it's not too easy to get up high. (Try to get permission to shoot church interiors from choir lofts; other large spaces from similar high vantage points.) P.C ./T.S . lenses can't make enormous corrections; just appreciable ones. It's usually best to use a tripod when working with them.

You will probably need to make quite long time exposures of interiors if you do not specifically light them. These long exposures may affect film color, and the laws of reciprocity failure may apply. (See Chapters Four and Five.)

"Light Painting" with multiple flash exposures can be useful in dim churches or other public buildings (if the ceiling is not too high). About 20' high is probably the practical maximum with a Vivitar 283 or similar-power flash. Light painting takes practice. (See Chapter Seven.)

Architectural photography, and interior photography, will reward you if you persist, and learn how to do them well. They are requirements for professional travel photography.

Still-Life on Location

The subject of still-life photography is so large that I won't attempt to tackle it in this book. Although I am no specialist, I have done quite a lot of still lifes on travel and location assignments; specifically of food, fine-art objects and paintings, precious relics in stately homes and industrial tools. I approach the whole subject in the same way I do architecture, I always use the camera on a tripod and compose the subject through the lens. 20mm lenses work well for me when photographing food in the foreground of a restaurant or dining-room or market or kitchen. Soft back-lighting is usually a good light on food.

When arranging precious relics of authors and other greats in a setting indoors or out, I owe a great visual debt to Arnold Newman, a master of location still-life as well as of portraiture. I once saw a picture of his in Holiday magazine. It was of two immense and frightening helmets, from medieval suits of armor, arranged on either side of an English castle's gates; the scene was photographed with a wide-angle lens so the castle looked small in the distance. The change in scale was very powerful.

A problem you may run into in photographing shiny or metallic objects is that they reflect everything, including the lights, you, and the camera. The really professional way to approach that is to either "tent" the still-life—surround it with a cone or circle or even dome of translucent diffusion material (made in sheets and rolls by Rosco and Lee) or, to partially surround it with non-reflective black. Shine the lights into a "tent" from outside and just cut a tiny hole for the lens. (Set up the still life before "tenting" it of course.) An easy way to solve a glare problem is by liberally applying dulling spray (from photo stores), which I do myself whenever I can get away with it. This requires solvent to remove afterwards and cannot be used on precious relics.

When photographing any complex still-life, if you can work with an assistant or even a totally untrained helper, it will shorten your set-up time considerably. You can then direct the placement of the small objects without constantly having to move from the camera position.

Recommended Books

Photographing Buildings Inside and Out by Norman McGrath is a comprehensive, technically superb and artistically generous book by a master large-format camera architectural specialist.

High on New York by Peter B. Kaplan is a great picture book, and shows his highly personal point of view.

Jake Rajs is one of my favorite landscape and architectural photographers, his book *Manhattan* is a classic, and his book *America* a great tour of all the 50 states.

A good book to read on still-life photography in general is *Secrets of Studio Still-Life Photography* by Gary Pertweiler. Even location still-life photographers will benefit from some of his techniques. (See more discussion on still life in the next chapter on self-assignments.)

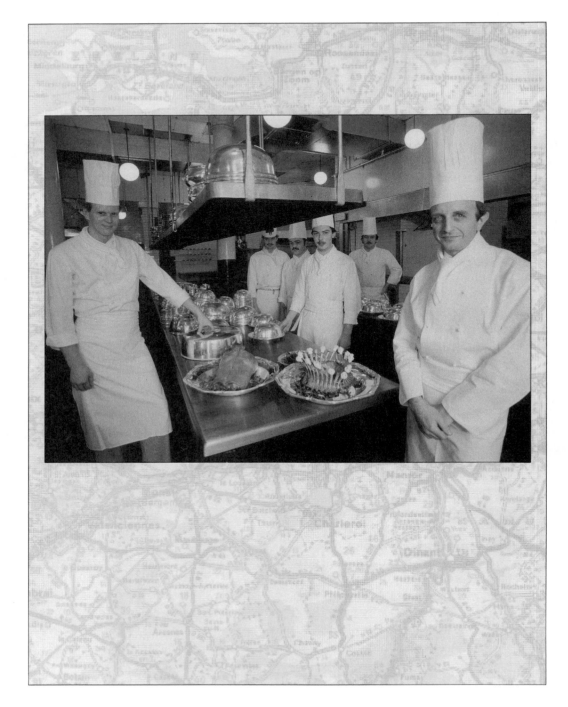

Chapter 9

Ten
Travel/Location
Self-Assignments

This is the "teaching" chapter of the book. It is intended for anyone who need more practice in photography in general, or in the skills specific to travel/location photography. It can also be used as a guide for professionals on how to approach travel, tourism and location assignments.

What You Should Know Before Shooting Travel Assignments

Before any photographer can accept or solicit assignments (paid work) from clients, obviously he or she must be able to deliver what the client needs. The best way to learn is to practice with self-assignments. That way you can go back and reshoot anything you don't like (more than once if necessary), make corrections, and sharpen your point of view. When you have done all of these self-assignments well, you will be able to handle just about any travel, or travel-related, job that you are offered.

The self-assignments given are very typical working situations. Choose the subject matter carefully, so that the photographs will provide you with good travel/tourism/location portfolio material, and will be available for stock as well. (See also Chapter Thirteen.)

You should also be able to market at least some of the pictures directly to "clients"—the subjects of the photographs. If some of these "clients" are businesses and corporations, you may well develop assignment clients who will use you regularly, because art directors, etc. give work first of all to people they know, trust and like.

When someone does want to buy some of the work from the self-assignments, be sure and ask for at least enough money to recoup your out-of-pocket expenses, even if you are a relative beginner. It took time, skill and money to make your pictures good enough for exhibit or publication—don't undervalue them, or your skills.

If you are a photographer for fine-art or pleasure, some of these self-assignments should help your "seeing" skills, and the practice should help your fluency and refine your technique.

Style for the Self-Assignments

Your "look" is your signature. Be proud of it, and work to develop it. Photographic fashions change; currently a rather fine-art, grainy or soft-focus style is in vogue, but if that is not your style, never mind. Your own particular look may become the next fashion.

Black-and-white photography is now being used again by some of the most sophisticated travel clients. Corporate, tourism, public relations and stock picture users are usually more conservative. The assignments suggested for this type of subject are best approached in a straightforward manner, in color. Be as creative as you wish, in your own way, with advertising/editorial subjects.

 Assignment #1 — A Working Portrait

Photograph someone in his or her working environment; outdoors or indoors. This is a very frequent assignment request, and could be shot in either color or black-and-white.

The object of this assignment is to both make a good portrait, and show clearly the person's job, either literally or symbolically. Choose someone who works for a typical local industry or an outstanding individual. The "look" should be editorial, not too stiff or posed, for a magazine, newspaper, corporate brochure or annual report.

Possible uses of the photographs: a) sale to a magazine or newspaper; b) sale to the individual; c) sale to the company or corporation; d) stock. (For stock, get a model release before you shoot.)

Equipment: You will need as a minimum a camera with a normal lens. A moderate wide-angle lens and a medium telephoto lens are useful also. (I like to use a 28mm lens for environmental portraiture, and usually include quite a bit of the surroundings.) Try a "normal" 50-55mm lens for a waist-length portrait and an 80-105mm lens for a tightly framed head—clients like choices.

Very important is a tripod to precompose the background—a cable release for this is helpful but not essential. Carry a reflector, or improvise one (see Chapters Six and Seven) to supplement available light.

Film: Use slow or medium-speed slide or print film (25-100 ISO) outdoors; appropriate film and filters for the lighting indoors (see Chapters Five and Seven.) If the shot is being done indoors, you will probably need supplemental lighting (bounce flash, tungsten or strobe.) Take along a sync cord or trigger/slave combination if you use strobe; a long extension cord or two for tungsten lights.

Professionals will need: Color Compensating (CC) filters and/or light balancing filters, or the approximately equivalent gels (see Chapter Five) if using fluorescent or industrial lighting as the main source (make advance color tests for such situations).

Research: Finding a suitable subject, and the best place to photograph him or her. Choosing any tools, books or other objects to be included in the portrait that best symbolize the person's job. When you have your subject, try to find out as much as you can in advance about his or her job, family, interests or background, also his/her hobbies. If your subject is a writer, read some of his/her books. If you can get a portrait subject talking about themselves or anything else, you will get better pictures (but keep shooting when they stop talking also).

Suggested subjects: A mayor, innkeeper, chef, craftsperson, technician, farmer, medical or legal professional, law-enforcement or fire officer, factory manager, ordained member of any religion, writer, mother of large family, teacher, etc.

Possible locations: Inside or outside City Hall (include flags, etc.), interior or exterior of a pretty inn, hotel or resort; a barn or silo or bountiful field of crops; a hospital operating room or ward; a classroom in a school or college; a police station or firehouse with action in the background; an interior or exterior of a church, synagogue, mosque, etc. Inside locations are usually better for portraits of business executives, managers, lawyers, computer programmers, teachers, nurses, homemakers, chefs, etc. because that is their normal working environment.

Variables: Availability of good location, the subject's schedule and clothing. (Ask him or her to wear quiet colors unless a special uniform or typical costume dictates otherwise. You may need to ask executive men to shave before a late-afternoon shoot. Carry a comb and some flesh-colored face powder for any subject, just in case.)

Permissions: From a company, school, hospital, etc., may be needed to shoot on their premises. Get a model release from your subject, also from any other people you may choose to use in the background of the shot, so you can use the pictures for stock later.

Transportation: If you choose to take the person somewhere to best express personality or occupation, be sure to arrange for a car or taxi beforehand.

On the shoot: Before posing the subject (or before he/she arrives), set up your tripod and compose the background, and approximately arrange any lighting where you want to place the subject. Of course, compose through the lens! You will then be free to concentrate on the nuances of the portrait. It is important to talk to the subject throughout the session so that he or she doesn't "freeze"! Be sensitive to your subject's personality, allow them to contribute to the portrait, but don't let them take over the shoot. Include your subject's face and hands, and some relevant background, in most shots. Think about feet. Do you want them in or not? Some people just don't notice feet, but the way they point or turn can be expressive.

Get the portrait subject actually working, not just pretending to work. Make some pictures with him or her looking straight into the camera also. Don't be afraid to ask anyone (tactfully) if it's okay to clean up a messy desk, move tools, shift an intruding piece of furniture. Watch out for ugly shadows on the face or intrusive objects in the background.

Take plenty of pictures (36 shots as an absolute minimum). When you do this, you will find that most subjects soon get used to the camera and relax. You will warm up too, and achieve a relationship with the subject which is not possible when you take only a few shots. Classic portrait photographers sometimes spend hours or days getting to know a subject! Results: An interesting photograph that tells a story about a person or way of life; also a saleable portrait.

Look At: *In The American West* by Richard Avedon; *Portraits* by Bill Brandt; *The Man Who Shot Garbo* by Clarence Sinclair Bull; and *I Dream a World* by Brian Lanker—these books are examples of wonderful portraiture.

 Assignment #2 — Landscape or Cityscape

Choose a truly beautiful, unspoiled landscape (or seascape) or a very dramatic town or cityscape. Photograph it at different times on a sunny day. Start shooting just before sunrise to the very early morning, take a few comparison shots at noon, and photograph seriously again in the very late afternoon/sunset through "blue time"—dusk.

The object of this assignment is to show how changing light, color temperature (and sometimes weather) affect a scene; and, to make the most beautiful landscape possible.

Possible uses of the photographs: Part of an editorial travel story; a corporate promotion of a city or region; regional or national tourism promotion by airlines etc.; stock pictures; post cards; calendars; portfolio pieces; fine-art/wall decoration.

Equipment: You will need as a minimum one (or better two) cameras to shoot fast in changing light; wide-angle and zoom telephoto lenses. (I like a 20mm lens for most landscapes, but sometimes use moderate zooms—say 43-80mm or 80-200mm—for precise framing and to bring, say, distant mountains or buildings closer.) A sturdy tripod for long exposures is a must (use one that extends at least to your eye level) and a camera cable-release is handy. Carry spare batteries, a backup meter if possible.

Film: At least two rolls of 35mm slow to medium-speed film (or equivalent amount if you use medium or large format). I use Kodachrome 25, Fuji Velvia (ISO 50; I rate it at ISO 40) and Ektachrome 100 Plus (all in professional versions) for landscapes.

Research: Do some driving/traveling around and choose the most beautiful landscape you can find, or the best view you know of a downtown skyline. My definition of a pristine landscape includes no man-made objects.

Variables: Weather and time of year. Check weather forecasts and wait if necessary; a very clear day with sunshine and nice white clouds in a deep blue sky would often be ideal. Before or after storms you often get dramatic cloud effects. Check the position of the sunrise and sunset in advance. Fall is good for some landscapes; and winter especially good for many cityscapes; for instance then, lights go on in Manhattan office buildings before sunset, making for great views towards the lit-up financial district with the setting sun behind them.

Alternate Approaches: You can include highways, railroad lines, small farms, distant hikers/climbers/skiers, a boat, a lighthouse; but all these should be used very small in the overall scene. For cityscapes, no single building should predominate—you are out to show the spirit of the city as a whole. Look for the best possible vantage points: bridges, hilltops, cliffs, fire towers, scenic overlooks, rooftops, high office windows, observation towers, piers, river and lake fronts.

Permissions: Arrange in advance to arrive very early, return and then stay late, at a building observation tower, rooftop with a great view, national, state or local park, private property etc.

Transportation: A car is normally a must to "scout" locations (see Chapter Fifteen) and to move equipment, but city dwellers can sometimes manage using public transit.

On the shoot: Arrive at your chosen vantage point half an hour before sunrise, and well before sunset; set the camera on a sturdy tripod and be ready to shoot in the rapidly changing light very early and late. Make sure your horizon lines (and vertical building lines if a cityscape) are level. (If you have difficulty with this because you wear glasses consider getting a grid-style viewfinder for your camera; a small spirit-level is also helpful.)

Take all your pictures from the same spot for maximum comparison of changes in light effects. (Mark your tripod position with tape, stones, etc., so you can find it again.) Of course you can also do variations on the theme for art purposes.

Meter off the nearby sky, not the sun itself, during sunrise and sunset or you will get underexposure. (Use a 135mm lens or longer on camera as a substitute for a spotmeter.) Shoot from about half an hour before until about fifteen minutes after sunrise; half an hour before sunset through the pink afterglow and then the darkening blue sky of dusk.

Bracket your exposures. You need not bracket the midday exposures if you generally get good daylight exposures. If fast-moving clouds are present, photograph different cloud effects.

Results: You should have a great variety of mood in these landscape pictures; the color range will be from reds, warm oranges and pinks at sunrise and sunset, to palest blues at noon through royal blue and midnight blue before sunrise and after sunset without the use of any filters. That is because the color temperature changes from very low to very high at different times of day.

Note: the noon pictures are for purposes of comparison, only very rarely are they better than the early or late ones, but there are always exceptions to every rule, so don't skip them.

Look At: All the landscape photography books listed in the bibliography.

 Assignment #3 — Architecture/Interiors

Make a series of five to ten carefully composed interiors and exteriors of any important historic public building or major new building you can easily reach. Include people in some of the shots.

The object of this assignment is to show off the architecture, important design features, and the building when it is in use.

Possible uses of the photographs: Sales to architects, contractors, developers, owners, municipal and other authorities, as well as for the same uses as Assignment One.

Equipment: You will need: Camera, sturdy tripod, cable release, wide-angle, normal and medium zoom or telephoto lenses. A small spirit level may be helpful. Possible added lighting for the interior shots. Film to balance with principal lighting sources. Basic filters.

Professional equipment: Perspective-correction (PC) or tilt-and shift lenses for 35mm SLR cameras. Architectural specialists use technical and large-format cameras with shifts, tilts and swings for correcting perspective.

Film: Slow or medium-speed daylight or tungsten film, or both, as appropriate.

Research: Choosing the building. Note: find out the angle of the sun especially in relation to the main entrance. Select good viewpoints from other buildings and nearby sites, as well as more distant views. Avoid ugliness in backgrounds.

Permissions: Getting permission from the necessary authorities to photograph interiors, and/or from the owners of nearby buildings to use as vantage points.

Transportation: You will need a car or taxi to take yourself and your equipment to and from the location. Big-city dwellers can use public transit.

Variables. Weather, time of year, time of day, traffic activity in the area. If the main entrance to the building faces north, this usually means photographing early or late on a mid-summer day, when the sun illuminates that part of the building, or choosing a cloudy day. Dusk shots from outdoors showing the warmth of lighted interiors are often excellent. Find out the time of the building's maximum use—people in architecture pictures brings them to life. Avoid parked trucks outside the building.

On the shoot: Design your photographs carefully, keeping lines level, etc. (see Assignment Three). Watch the light. Try early and late shots. If tilting the lines of an interior or exterior is unavoidable, do so very carefully and symmetrically. Bracket indoor exposures, adding light when needed, and perhaps try light painting (see Chapter Seven). Use filters if needed for mixed-light or fluorescent-lit interiors.

Take pictures both with and without people. A new college library should should show some students, churches need worshippers, a historic home usually has a curator, a few tourists, and so on. Take some (but not too many) close-up shots of special design features, ornamentation, lobby art etc. to finish your assignment.

Result: You should have well-designed pictures suitable for use in a publication, brochure, annual report, or to decorate an office or boardroom wall. Other possible uses are as fine-art, covers of religious bulletins, and postcards as well as stock and portfolio pictures.

Look At: *Architectural Digest*, and "shelter" magazines like *HG* for examples of top professional work. *Photographing Buildings Inside and Out* by Norman McGrath is a truly excellent reference book.

Assignment #4 — A Location Still Life

A carefully-styled picture of food and drink with an appropriate scenic or interior background. Would-be corporate photographers can use products or industrial artifacts in suitable places instead.

Subject for inexperienced photographers: A simple picnic lunch or a formally presented outdoor luncheon setting. Anywhere with a nice view; a beach, for seafood; a country garden, or pretty city park for a picnic; a restaurant terrace with a nice view, or formal garden for a buffet lunch.

Subject for the experienced: Formal food presentation in a restaurant or hotel, with lighting on the food for correct color. Use strobe (bounced out of an umbrella, or through a collapsible soft box) and daylight film, plus time exposure for the background if necessary. See if a local inn/hotel/restaurant/caterer will trade food and "styling" (food arrangement) services in return for pictures to advertise their business.

Equipment: You will need the following as a minimum: A camera, wide-angle lens, tripod, cable release. Indoors, you will usually have to add strobe or multiple flash lighting. Outdoors, a large white and silver reflector is helpful for bouncing light. (See Chapter Seven.) I use a 20mm lens for most location food shots to get maximum depth of field.

Film: Slow or medium-speed film, daylight or tungsten type, as appropriate.

Props for the outdoor shot: A picnic cooler and ice for carrying food if the shoot is far from the food source. For a picnic, as with most still lifes, you will have to "style" the shot. Choose a big good-looking wicker basket, a bright plain or check tablecloth (don't use white, or flowery designs that will clash with the food). Use contrasting or complementary napkins, china or plastic plates. A universally appealing picnic spread includes bright fruit, attractive raw vegetables like tomatoes, carrots, scallions and cucumbers. Use a ham or cold roast chicken for a centerpiece. Don't forget French or Italian bread, wine and glasses.

Picnic suggestions: A clambake or lobster dinner at a beach; a barbecue in the South or Southwest; corn, steaks and hamburgers in a city or suburban backyard; a poolside spread of cool salads; a campfire dinner in the mountains; a kids' picnic of hot dogs and cookies in a park with swings, etc., in the background. Use your imagination together with local culinary traditions, and beauty spots.

Props for the indoor shot: Food prepared by the restaurant or hotel. It could be the chef's specialty or something very photogenic. A decorated lobster platter is almost always safe. The place should be styled to look elegant, rustic,

Italian, etc., depending on ambiance and price range. Flowers and wine give a festive feeling everywhere. Little flags are fun props for casual "foreign" places. Guests used as models (or models you bring along) should be mostly couples—mix up the ages. Bear in mind that picnics are casual; very formal places call for very well-dressed guests. Ask models to wear appropriate, non-fussy clothes.

Permissions: From owners of private property outdoors; restaurants, chefs, etc. indoors. Get model releases from all models, chefs, waiters, etc. for possible later stock or advertising use of the pictures.

Transportation: A car (or taxi) is normally a must to scout locations, carry equipment, props and models, etc. for this type of shoot.

Logistics: Buying, cooking and food, and getting it and other props, to your picnic site. Keeping food fresh; setting up the still life. Rearranging a room slightly for the camera, putting room back together afterwards. Cleaning up everything, outdoors or in. If you can take an assistant or helper, or best, a professional "food stylist" who knows how to arrange food for the camera, you will be able to work much faster. If you have only limited time to set up indoor lighting , and position food/props/furniture, an assistant is almost a must. Direct the food arrangement and placement from camera position.

If you are going to include models as diners, arrange for them to arrive fifteen minutes before you plan to shoot.

Variables: Outdoors: time of day, weather, angle of the sun. Plan the shoot for about two to three hours before sunset on a pleasant day.

Indoors: Chef's availability. You will have to set up, shoot and get out fast. Chefs, kitchens and restaurants have tight schedules. About one hour before the place starts serving lunch or dinner is usually good for photography.

On the shoot: Set up your camera with a 35mm, 28mm or 20mm wide-angle lens on a tripod. Make a background composition, and light the food area if necessary, then place the food close to the lens so that it dominates the picture. Arrange the food and drink carefully by alternately looking through the lens and placing platters etc. for best effect. I often mask holes in the table setting with casually dropped flowers or leaves; you can also use wine bottles and glasses, or anything else you like. The critical factor is always to get fresh, appetizing, beautiful food, with correct color. Shoot both horizontals and verticals.

Alternate Approaches: Take some attractive people to enjoy the picnic and photograph them eating, after you have done the still lifes. Include the chef, owners, and waiters in formal indoor photographs.

Results: A useful and appetizing "location still life" and possible eating/dining pictures as well for your travel/tourism portfolio.

Possible uses: Summer feature on a local beauty spot (possibly using local produce) in regional magazine or newspaper; possible feature on a restaurant, stock. Of course, if you live on Cape Cod, or the bluffs of the Mississippi, or close to a great California beach, the picnic shot or series may have more than local interest.

Look At: Magazines like *Bon Appetit, Family Circle, Food and Wine, Gourmet* and *Woman's Day*. These will all help if you feel unsure about your food styling abilities, and they show current top professional work.

Assignment #5 — Abroad in America/Canada

This is a "picture story" about an ethnic or immigrant neighborhood.
The object of this assignment is to practice for photographing in foreign countries, and to produce a feature (illustrated piece with no time deadline) for a local or regional magazine or newspaper (or for a foreign magazine or newspaper). Travel stock.

Equipment: A camera (two are much better) and normal, wide-angle and moderate telephoto lenses. (Fast lenses are helpful.) A small flash for fill light is useful. Appropriate filters to correct color in indoor pictures.

Film: Slow to medium-speed daylight film for outdoor shooting, fast daylight or tungsten film (400-1600 ISO) for available light indoor shooting.

Research: Selecting the neighborhood; try if possible to locate one or two members of the community to focus on. A family, who will let you photograph them is an especially good subject.

Suggestions: Try to find little-known or less-photographed ethnic groups. Enclaves of Afghanistanis, Iranians, Laotians, Koreans, Pakistanis, Portuguese, Romanians, Sikhs, Vietnamese and West Africans are among those that are seldom photographed. Pictures of the life of these groups will sell more easily than those of larger, old-established communities like the Chinese and Japanese.
Try to make intimate pictures of the life of the people, not just a superficial "tourist" view. Visit homes if possible. Show people at work and in their leisure hours. Include the obvious, like storefronts and foreign-language signs and foods, and, of course, celebrations for special holidays, as well as lesser-known features of the life of the group. What sports do they favor? What religion do they practice? (Get a wedding if you can.) Try to include contrasts between younger, American/Canadianized people and their parents and grandparents. Don't ever forget to take an "establishing" or overall shot that gives a feeling for the whole neighborhood. A busy crossroads, thriving market, etc., from a high vantage point, may be useful for this and will do if you can't find something original.

Variables: People's schedules, national/religious holidays, time of day, weather.

Permissions: From individual home and store owners, etc., to shoot inside. (If you can get model releases the pictures will have additional value for stock.)

Transportation: Public transit or a taxi may be best; parking is often impossible in old immigrant neighborhoods.

On the Shoot: Smile, be patient, ask permission before photographing, and accept the fact that some people will not want to be photographed. You will almost certainly have to make several visits to get good coverage. Bring along some small prints on your second or subsequent visits, or carry a Polaroid Spectra camera and film, and give away prints as "thank yous" and in return for poses.

Professional tips: This is a travel feature, keep it upbeat. Aim for one or two strong pictures that sum up the place—a feature story today rarely runs more than four or six pages. A cover shot is almost always vertical with clear light or dark space at the top for the publication's "logo" or title. Covers are often, not always, of attractive people looking into the camera. A "spread" goes across two pages, and the center of interest should not fall into the "gutter" (the join down the middle). Important one-page pictures are often run vertically on the left side of a spread, therefore the center of interest usually faces right. If you shoot important pictures as both horizontals and verticals you give the art director maximum choice. Detail shots only complement, but never replace, strong establishing shots. Evening shots are kind to cities.

Variation: A feature on the life of one attractive member of the community.

Results: An editorial story that may be saleable locally or nationally, even internationally; stock, portfolio material, fine-art.

Look At: *Condé Nast Traveler, Geo* (in German or French), the *National Geographic, Travel and Leisure* and *Travel/Holiday* as examples of top current work, and subjects/places chosen by different travel magazines. Look at regional magazines too.

 Assignment #6 — A Tourist Resort

A good motel, hotel, country club, dude ranch or other resort, with sports facilities—a nice pool, or lake or beachfront; a golf course, tennis courts, horseback riding etc. Alternatively, shoot a ski resort in winter. The object of this assignment is to advertise and/or promote the facility as a place for active vacations.

Equipment: A camera (two are better), normal, wide-angle and telephoto lenses. A tripod. A small flash and a collapsible reflector for fill light will probably be useful. Lights if planning to shoot interiors of bedrooms. If this is a beach or lakeside resort, a water-resistant camera may be helpful for pretty shots taken from water-level. (See also Chapter Three.)

Film: I take plenty of fast and slow, daylight and tungsten film, for this type of assignment. You never know exactly what you will encounter.

Research: Locating the facility, possibly finding a good-looking young man and woman, or 50-ish couple, with sports clothes to take with you as models.

Permissions: From the owners/management of the resort. You may have to agree to show them the photographs before publication. (Promise to offer them a good price if they want to use any.) Agree that you will not photograph any guest without the guest's permission, or that you will take your own models and photograph early or late when no guests are about. Get all the people you use as models to sign releases in exchange for photographs.

Transportation: Car or taxi.

Variables: Weather, time of day, season. (Plan to shoot both early and late outdoors on sunny days; do any indoor shots in the middle of the day.) Timing is important; find out when the resort's facilities are busy or empty.

On the shoot: Wait for great weather! Don't forget overall views of the main building from a good vantage point, showing the surrounding landscape. Then show sport/fun against a background of the place. Have people actually diving into the pool (shoot from low down, with your camera over the pool edge; it will make it look larger). Show people actually playing tennis and golf, not just pretending to. If the place has extensive grounds or gardens show the space and peace of the natural setting. Views from a boat are great for seaside, lakeside and riverside resorts. Pictures showing water are always very appealing. Low sunlight from behind you onto the subject is best for reflections and the bluest possible water. Do some "after" pictures of people relaxing with cool drinks, lying in hammocks, reading in a quiet spot, dancing on a patio, etc. Don't forget to photograph any special sports or unusual features offered. Always make dusk shots lit from inside, of buildings, and romantic "mood" shots of couples in the evening (the one of people on the beach, barefoot but in formal clothes, is a cliché, but clients still seem to use it).

Possibilities for good vantage points: On a horse at dude ranches, on a ski-lift, on or close to a diving board, on a boat for a waterside resort, low and close to the green at a golf course, at netside for tennis.

Professional tip: Consider showing a beautifully-situated resort from the air.

Have the pilot fly as low as is safe, use high shutter speeds and possibly a gyro-stabilizer (see Chapter Three) and work early or late when long shadows define the landscape.

Results: Coverage that can be used for advertising, brochures, public relations and magazine/newspaper features, and also (with releases from the property owners and models) stock. Portfolio material.

Look At: *Travel and Leisure* magazine, any issue. *Aerial Photography* by Harvey Lloyd is an excellent illustrated manual by a master of this subject. And if you can get hold of a used copy of *Great Resorts of America* by Chuck Lawless, published in 1983, you will get a very good overall feel for resort photography.

 ## Assignment #7 — Bright Lights at Night

A Disco, Circus, Amusement Park at Night, or Downtown Entertainment Area. The object of this assignment is to improve your "available-light" photography. It will provide personal/fine-art pictures, a possible picture story, portfolio material and stock.

Equipment: You will need: Two cameras, fast lenses of different focal lengths (or zoom lenses), tripod and cable release, flash. A TTL/dedicated camera, a TTL/dedicated flash and a spotmeter (or long telephoto lens on dedicated camera) are all especially useful in the rapidly changing light of such places. A cord for using a TTL/dedicated flash off camera may be helpful.
　　Carry everything in a backpack, army-type, or other inconspicuous bag. I like to work with an assistant, or other companion, in big cities at night.

Film: Take plenty. For "available light" shooting I use fast daylight films. (Use tungsten film if you wish also.) When using "fill-flash" I like 50-100 ISO film.

Permissions: Amusement park management will have to be approached for permission to take a camera on rides. Some will require you to furnish them with proof of liability insurance. You may need permission from artistes for circuses and similar indoor events. Carry model releases and a pen. Your best bet is to try not to be conspicuous—just shoot as a "tourist."

Transportation: Any way you can get there.

Variables: Lighting conditions can be extreme. The ideal time to photograph is at "blue time"—dusk before it gets quite dark. In midsummer in the United States this is between about 8 and 9 p.m. depending on location and exact date. If you wish, take a couple of models (boy/girl having fun never goes out of style; of course get model releases if you do this).

On the shoot: Take some conventional pictures to show the overall scene, using fast film and available light. Bracket exposures or mark rolls and plan for clip tests (see Chapter Five), then use medium-speed film at longer exposures adding flash fill to stop nearby motion; or try "panning" (moving the camera with the action) while shooting at a slow shutter speed like 1/15, 1/8 or 1/4 or a second. Use any other technique you like to try to capture the fun of the place rather than a literal representation of it. If you use models, have them run, laugh, play the games, etc.

Results: Exciting, somewhat abstract pictures to complement the factual ones in your portfolio. Editorial features. Brochures. Stock, postcards, fine art, pictures of family fun. Sales to management, performers, musicians. Wall art.

Look At: *Existing-Light Photography*, a good manual by Eastman Kodak.

 Assignment #8 — A Formal Event or Meeting

This is a very typical "meeting" magazine, newspaper or public relations assignment. Make a series of about twenty color or black-and-white pictures on print (negative) film, of the guests and speakers, happenings and audience at any formal indoor party, meeting, conference or similar event.

Equipment: You will need: Two cameras and wide angle lenses for quick "party" shots (preferably one should be a wide-angle zoom lens). Moderate telephoto or zoom lenses for pictures of speakers. A flash unit, with a bounce card. An external battery pack or plenty of disposable batteries (allow one pack of disposable batteries per roll of film for fastest recycling.) A TTL/dedicated flash is very useful here, as is a flashmeter. Many pros use an automatic flash like a Vivitar 283.

Film: Use 400 ISO print (negative) film for maximum depth of field. I would tend to do this assignment in color unless the client dictates otherwise; color negatives can be quickly processed at "one hour photo" shops, and speed is often important for this type of job. The color negatives can be printed as black-and-white if needed. Keep prints and negatives together in separate envelopes for each roll.

Professional tip: If you shoot Fujicolor 100 DX-coded film, some professional labs will number each print on the back, which can save you a great deal of trouble when reprints are ordered later.

On the shoot: Use the flash bounced if possible; use flash direct if distances are too great for bounce. Use flash together with a low shutter speed (about 1/30 of a second is good with 400 ISO film) in order to record at least some of the background of the room. (See Chapter Seven.)

Talk to groups of people as you photograph. Try to make them smile. Don't be afraid to ask them to pose or to arrange special groupings. Some people may prefer not to be photographed holding drinks or cigarettes. Keep notes of people's names.

Be very discreet when photographing speakers (best time for unobtrusive shots is at the beginning and end and during applause). Never interfere with the speech, or block the audience's line of vision. (You can always ask for a couple of extra shots after the speech is over.) Take shots of every speaker, and of groups of people together on the podium.

Results: Good samples for a public relations portfolio, possible future assignment work, highly probable sales of prints to individuals or the event's sponsors.

Look At: "Hospitality" (in-house and hotel) meeting, business and trade magazines (see Chapter Eleven) to see the standards for "meeting" pictures. A friend of mine gets up to $1,000 per day for taking top-quality ones!

Assignment #9 — An Outdoor Tourist Event

Photograph the largest, most interesting "people-related" event you can easily reach. It could be a parade of any kind, a huge outdoor market, a boat race, local or national sporting event, a balloon festival, a concert or cultural gathering. Use wide angle, normal and telephoto lenses for complete coverage. Include overall views, medium and closeup shots in both horizontal and vertical formats. Show participants, and audience and the performance or game, or race or whatever, from a good vantage point. Try to get pictures of key people and peak moments.

The object of this assignment is to produce a magazine or newspaper feature, personal pictures, travel stock, tourism promotion. (For very specific directions on how to approach this type of subject, see also the sample letter of assignment in Chapter Eleven.)

Equipment: Ideally, at least two cameras, better three (to have different lenses quickly available at all times), and fast wide-angle, normal and zoom-telephoto lenses. A small flash for fill light. Plenty of spare batteries. Carry all this in a sturdy backpack or other inconspicuous bag.

Professional tip: A small, light aluminum stepladder is sometimes helpful to get above crowds (where permitted).

Film: Depending on weather, I use slow or medium-speed daylight transparency film. (If you want prints for an album, personal or fine-art pictures, and don't care about possible future stock usage, use print film.)

Permissions: In large cities, or for major events, you may need credentials from the police and event organizers to get close. Apply well in advance. Otherwise, get there very early. I walked unhindered onto the middle of the Verrazano Narrows Bridge between Staten Island and Brooklyn at six a.m. to photograph the start of the New York City Marathon, because I did not have an assignment or a photographers' badge from the NYPD. The race starts at ten. I got great shots which sold well as stock later. It is not normally easy to get model releases at such events, but carry a few forms with you just in case.

Results: Portfolio, personal and stock pictures, possible editorial feature.

Look At: Newspapers, magazines, and travel magazines for "event" coverage.

Assignment #10 — Travel/Tourism Promotion

The object of this assignment is to produce an advertising-style feature about the most famous tourist attraction that is within your reach. Take models with you—have them sign a model release first, and reward them with pictures. Find models among your good-looking family, friends and acquaintances, and at modeling schools, acting workshops and little theaters. Consider paying actors, students or retired people a small fee; or, promise them a percentage of any stock sales. The models could be a young couple (yes, boy/girl is ever popular) or a mature man and woman (who should be fit and active) to symbolize older tourists, a major part of that market.

If you go to a theme park, take a nice-looking family with kids. Models of any race are O.K. Minorities are especially needed for stock.

Equipment: Two cameras, wide-angle, normal and short telephoto lenses. A reflector and/or a small flash for fill light are helpful.

Film: Slow or medium-speed film.

Permissions: Some museums and other attractions require a photography permit and do not allow flash. Suggestion: Offer a "first look" at the take and promise reasonable photographic use fees to management in exchange for privileges. You will almost always need permission to use a tripod or set up lights.

Variables: Know best times of day for posed shots, times of biggest crowds.

Styling: Think about what your models will wear. Clothes should be casual classic: a sportshirt, loafers and slacks for the man; blouse and jeans or skirt for the woman. Ask all models to avoid wearing anything with strong patterns, or black-and-white, or any extreme fashion that will go out of date quickly. Have kids wear plain colored tee shirts, and jeans or plain shorts or skirts.

Transportation:
You will need a car or taxi to get models to the site.

On the Shoot: Show the couple or family together enjoying the facility, talking and laughing with staff, enjoying the sights, looking at souvenirs, etc. Buy them a few hot dogs and sodas to loosen them up! Take plenty of pictures. Your models will soon forget you and the camera and have fun. Don't have people stand stiffly and point at things. Feel free to direct subtly, looking through the viewfinder all the while. "Could you look over here for a minute please," or "that was great, could you try it again, but slower" are two directions I use a lot!

Professional Tip: Pick up any litter that might show in your photographs, and visually eliminate anything or anybody unattractive. Make the whole feeling very lively and upbeat.

For personal/fine-art photographs, choose any point of view you like!

Results: Model-released pictures that can be used for advertising and promotion, for public relations distribution to accompany press releases, as well as for editorial features. Stock/portfolio material. Personal/fine-art pictures. Practice in directing for those who wish to improve skills in working with models.

Look At: The ads and "advertorials" (editorial-style ads) in the travel sections of newspapers, and consumer and trade travel magazines.

General Considerations for the Self-Assignments

Think very carefully about where to do all these self-assignments (which are all based on similar ones I have done many times). Check local amusement attractions, resorts, new hotels, etc. and any photographs they are currently using. One of my students recently did "Assignment Ten" for himself at a scenic railroad near his home in western New Jersey. The railroad bought the rights to reproduce several of the shots in its brochure and he is currently negotiating prices with them for public relations uses.

When you have done each assignment, edit it very carefully. Did you get what you wanted or hoped for? Should you go back to improve the take? Are you honestly proud of the pictures? When the answer to that question is yes (it may take one or more reshoots to get there) show the take to the owners, managers, organizers, etc., and you will probably sell some work. Even if you are 100% unsuccessful at selling anything immediately, you will have gained experience, have good pictures for your portfolio and stock, and will have made some useful contacts that you may hear from later, especially if you periodically remind them of your existence, and show new work. (See Chapter Ten.)

Also see the Travel Highlights chapters for suggestions on how to approach and improve wildlife and underwater photography. The suggestions below should help anyone improve any photography.

Ten Quick Ways to Improve Your Travel Photographs

1. Photograph as many different people as possible. If you are shy, start by getting family and friends to act as models; learn how to get them to do what you want (or "direct" them) before you leave on a trip. On trips, use your travel companions and acquaintances as models. Photograph them in natural positions, not just gazing at the camera or pointing at something. Don't be afraid to approach strangers; a smile that says, "Please, may I?" will go a long way. (Look at any travel magazine to see how many "people pictures" are used.)

2. For sharp pictures of any fast-moving subject, and pictures taken from moving vehicles, use a high shutter speed to avoid blur caused by subject movement—1/250 of a second or higher is good. On program cameras, use the Shutter Priority setting to choose shutter speeds. Also use high shutter speeds with telephoto or zoom lenses, to minimize camera shake. A tripod is a necessity for consistently sharp pictures with long lenses (200mm and up), and with all medium-format cameras.

3. Be aware of backgrounds in all your pictures. Inexperienced photographers tend to overlook them, but a sign right behind someone's head, a garbage container or litter in a pretty park, or utility lines in a panoramic landscape can ruin an otherwise very nice shot. Stand on a bench and shoot slightly down, or hunker down and aim the camera up to avoid some background problems, and provide a different point of view.

4. Be keenly aware of prevailing light conditions at all times and with all subjects. Especially avoid hard noonday light and subjects that are part in sun, part in shade. (Keep a manual camera set for prevailing light conditions, so that you are ready to take a picture without adjusting the f/stop.)

5. Take several pictures of any good subject, human or otherwise. You need to make quite a few shots to get a human subject to relax and show their personality. Try several different angles or arrangements of people, landscapes or architecture, to get the most creative possible composition. Bracket (vary) exposures slightly whenever possible for optimum color. Vary lenses—a telephoto shot of someone in a landscape is very different from one taken from the same place with a wide-angle lens, and it's not just difference in the relative sizes of the main subject. Remember that labs—even the best—occasionally scratch or mark film, and extra frames may save the day. On really great subjects, take pictures with another camera, or at least on another roll of film, for extra "insurance."

6. Don't forget to take some "establishing" pictures that show the overall scene and give a sense of place. These are all too often forgotten by neophyte travel photographers in both city and the countryside. Get up high, move farther away and/or use a wide-angle lens. Try taking three overlapping shots to show a sweeping view or mountain panorama. Use a tripod if possible, and aim the camera to the left, center and right, using something as a reference point where the pictures join. (Professionals often use specialized panoramic cameras (they are expensive) to do the same job in one picture. For amateurs there are surprisingly inexpensive Kodak and Fuji "throwaway" panoramic cameras. (See Chapter Three on equipment.) Pictures of signs can help pace a slide show, and caption a family album of vacation prints.

7. Don't be afraid to photograph in bad weather for your own travel pictures, even if these are not always wanted by editorial or other assignment clients. Gray skies, mist, fog, rain and falling snow can make evocative personal and fine-art images, and overcast light is good for shadowless portraiture. Protect your camera from moisture with a clear freezer bag or dry cleaners' wrap. Poke a hole for the lens (covered with a Skylight or UV filter), and tape it tight leaving a hole for your hands. Select a fast film if you are uncomfortable with slow shutter speeds (400 ISO is good), and fire away. Flash "fill" works well on overcast days, use the same technique as you do at dusk. (See Chapter Seven, Photographic Lighting.)

8. Think about what you want to say with your pictures. They should do more than record "I was there." Perhaps a place is over touristy for your personal taste— a well placed sign in the foreground can emphasize that point of view. You may love or hate a city. New York City, for instance, can be photographed looking glittery and glamorous or run-down and desolate; both approaches are valid, and both can make strong pictures.

9. Be very patient, especially when photographing people. Wait, camera ready, for a child to giggle, an old man to look up from his card game, a worker to change the angle of his hammer. Wait also for a sailboat to go under a bridge, ducks to settle on a pond, a distant skier to appear on a mountain, the sun to come through scudding clouds. The resulting pictures will be worth the extra time spent.

10. Compose all your pictures "through the lens." This sounds elementary, but many people view a subject with their eyes, then quickly put up a camera and take a snap, not stopping to look through the viewfinder, or move around and study what the lens covers, or whether a different lens would be better, or how a scene translates into two dimensions. Try to keep both eyes open when looking through the viewfinder (this takes practice) so you are aware of what's happening outside the picture area.

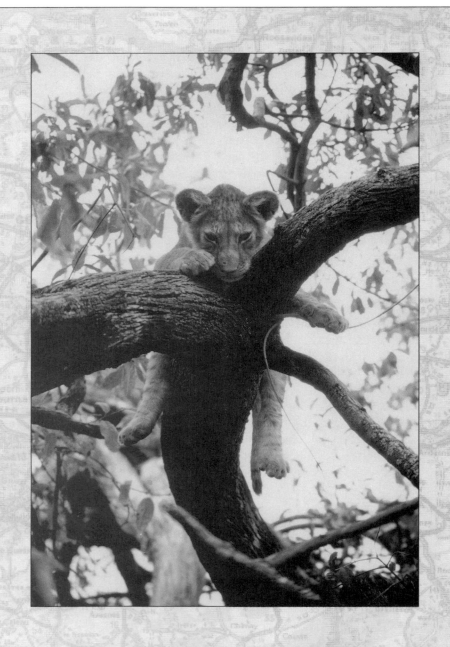

Chapter 10

Editing, The Portfolio and Self-Promotion

Editing skills are important for serious amateur photographers, and critical for professionals and would-be professionals. Editing takes some practise, but you will be amazed at the difference it will make to your presentations. Most beginners, and many inexperienced professionals, show far too much, and weaken the effect of their best work. Don't make this mistake.

How to Edit Photographs

Whatever the final use of your photographs, your work is incomplete until it has been edited. Good picture editors are highly skilled, and can look at work with a dispassionate eye, which the photographer who made the shots cannot. However, since at the beginning of your professional career (or for your personal pictures) you won't normally have access to the services of a trained editor, you should learn editing skills yourself. Everyone, including superb photographers, sometimes takes dull or technically lousy pictures. They just never show them to anyone.

Whether you are making a professional portfolio, a school thesis, prints for an exhibition or a quality family photographic album, you need to carefully choose and limit the photographs you show to gain maximum effect. At first anyway,the best way to edit is to look at all your pictures a lot. Pin black-and-white and color prints to a wall and let them stay there for a while. Ideally, look at slides projected in a darkened room, where you can see them big. Study each picture carefully. (Use a Kodak Stack Loader to eliminate having to put each slide individually into a Carousel projector wheel.) Or, use a light box, illuminated from underneath, and a "loupe"(a small magnifier that fits the eye). See below for directions on how to make a light box inexpensively.

However you edit, be realistically critical but not self-destructive. It is easy to start—just remove pictures that are unintentionally too dark, too light, blurry or just plain boring. After studying your initial selection for a while the best pictures usually jump out, but sometimes, on a second or third look, one's choices change. For that reason, I never throw anything but bad mistakes away; I just store pictures I don't choose to show.

Put your "selects" aside for a few days if possible, then look at them again. Then decide which of the photographs look the way you wanted them to look, and say what you wanted to say. If you have several very good but closely similar shots, study the exposure, small gestures, composition and color of each, carefully. You will almost always find one that is just a little better than the rest, even if only you can tell the difference. Mark these special pictures on the mount. You may choose as I do, to save them for your "private stock"— photos that you hope to use for a book or exhibit one day.

How to Make a Light Box

You can save quite a bit of money by making a light box yourself.

Buy two fluorescent lamp fixtures about 6" shorter than you want your box to be; and a sheet of 1/4" opal true-white plastic of the correct length and width.

Make an open 12" high box of the right size for your space (and the fluorescent fixtures) from 1" lumber (or use an existing box).

Paint the box white inside. Drill a couple of ventilation holes on each side of your box, put the fluorescents in and wire them together.

Drill holes, and screw the plastic down, use clips, or, rout out the lip of the box to fit plastic.

If possible, make your light box big enough to take a couple of 36 exposure rolls of 35mm slides, or long enough for uncut rolls of 120mm transparencies.

Sequencing

After you have edited a group of photographs, arrange them as interestingly as possible. The purpose is always to entertain or hold the viewer's attention.

Editing Transparencies on a Light Box

For the second stage of an edit, professional editors always lay out transparencies on a large light box. Buy a professional daylight-balanced light box if you wish.

With a light box, it's easy to sequence pictures so that each relates visually in some way to those preceding and following them. This is essential for a professional portfolio where you must entertain and impress potential clients. Pacing is very important for audio/visuals and even good vacation slide shows.

Editing Tools

- A loupe by Agfa (inexpensive) or Schneider (the best, adjustable to your eye).

- White and red china markers (grease pencils) from stationery stores to mark black-and-white contact sheets.

- A light box (see earlier in the chapter for directions on making one).

- A Carousel (or compatible) projector; an 80 or 140 slide Carousel wheel.

- A Kodak Stack Loader for the Carousel projector (permits loading a stack of 36 slides at a time).

- A rubber stamp with your name and the international copyright symbol (it's easy to copyright stamp pictures while editing, and then you won't forget to do it later. (See also Chapters One, Two and Thirteen.)

Plastic or cardboard sheets or sleeves that hold twenty 35mm slides, (or other format sheets/sleeves) and individual, nonharmful Kimac plastic slide/transparency protectors. (See Chapter Thirteen.)

Editing for Albums and Slide Shows

When sequencing large or small prints for an exhibit, print portfolio, or public relations or family album, lay out the prints on a large table or a clean floor. Sequence album prints for "spreads" (of two facing pages).

If you are editing slides from an assignment or trip to say, Bermuda, you might start with beach pictures, then architecture, then people shots and finish with interiors. Or, you can group pictures by color or by shapes that dissolve into each other. (Turn off the sound on your TV and study commercials to see how top professionals edit. After you have done this for a while, you will understand why no one today can sit through long disorganized slide shows.)

The Professional Portfolio

You probably will need to have at least 50 pictures that you are proud of before attempting to make a portfolio to solicit assignments for publication. When you have selected them, think about who will be looking at the photographs and choose material that is appropriate for each client. This does not mean that you have to change your individual style—that may be why you get hired— but only that you use that style on subject matter that clients can relate to. It is (normally) next to useless to show location portraits of children to an architectural client for instance, but if a new school has to be photographed, you might add such pictures to your selected architectural shots. The child portraits mixed with the Bermuda travel shots might be perfect for someone who operates family-oriented tours. Think creatively, and vary the portfolio with each client if you wish.

Portfolios for Assistants

People seeking a job as a professional assistant in a top photo market need a sharp-looking portfolio that demonstrates their interests, talents and, most importantly, their printing skills.

The strongest portfolios of any kind are done by photographers who show originality, passion and conviction as well as technical skills.

Specialized vs. General Portfolios

New York City photographers (and probably most Los Angeles and Chicago and Toronto area photographers, too) who are established in the profession are nearly all specialists and show portfolios that reflect this.

Advertising illustration, fashion and beauty, still life, photojournalism, corporate/industrial, travel and location, and portraiture are some specialties. An increasing number of photographers are stock specialists.

Beginning photographers and those in smaller cities/markets often do a variety of work. While their portfolios are general in nature they should still have a unified look—the prints should be the same size, and have the same finish and same borders.

Slide Portfolios

Twenty to 40 slides may be shown, either sequenced on a wheel that fits a Carousel projector, or mounted on black cardboard presentation sheets.

Print Portfolios

Subject matter should be grouped in two or three areas—travel, corporate/industrial, and architectural/interiors for instance, and should flow from one section to the next. Color prints, black-and-white pictures and published tear sheets are usually shown in separate groups.

Set-up or posed advertising illustrations or stock pictures using models and photojournalistic and editorial "real" people pictures should always be shown separated in my opinion. Show prints all the same size, and with the same borders and finish, for a nice effect. I often show prints in a "press book" type of presentation case (available at art and photo suppliers). I show prints unmounted.

I also show prints and tear-sheets (of published work) laminated (encased in clear plastic) in a good-looking hard portfolio case.

Fine-Art Portfolios

Fine-art prints may be of different sizes but almost always look best in my opinion if they are uniformly mounted and/or matted. Choose the color of the mount or matte carefully. Black or white isn't always best. I like the look of a medium gray mount for many color and black-and-white prints.

Portfolio Cases and Boxes

Whether for commercial or fine-art presentation, always get the best looking portfolio book or box you can afford. Sign, date and number prints for exhibition on the mount if you wish, but don't do this for a commercial portfolio.

Albums for Personal, Public Relations and Fine-Art Prints

For a print album, edit and sequence carefully and don't make the prints (or the album) too big. Prints from 3 1/2 x 5", 5 x 7" to a maximum of 8 x 10" size are good for meeting and party shoots, weddings, etc.; standard 3 1/2 x 5 1/2" (snapshot size) prints for a personal family album are economical.

Choose only your best pictures for a personal vacation travel album; be strong and set bad shots aside. If you only have one picture of Aunt Minnie at the Taj Mahal and it's a poor one, store her away in a box if you want the album to look excellent. It's well worth the expense of buying an archival album; cheap ones discolor quickly, smell like plastic, and may harm your prints eventually.

Fine-Art Exhibition Prints

I have said elsewhere that you should learn to print (at photo schools or workshops) if you want to exhibit. But if you have the funds for large exhibit prints, I can personally recommend three New York labs who do great work and will ship anywhere.

Ken Lieberman Labs specialize in making box-mounted prints for corporations, museums, decorators, and many top photographers. A 20x30" box-mounted Type C print (which needs an internegative from a transparency), currently costs about $260; from a negative about $225. Lieberman also makes dye-transfer prints and (extremely expensive but virtually permanent) Carbro-process prints. Contact them at (212) 633-0500.

Newman Photographics specializes in high quality Cibachrome (direct positive) enlargements from transparencies. Cibachromes are very fade-resistant. Newman uses highlight masks to reduce contrast (often a problem with Cibachromes). Contact Newman at (212) 505-1840.

Modernage Labs specialize in large to mural-size black-and-white prints. Contact them at (212) 997-1800.

Locate professional labs in your area through classified phone directories.

Inexpensive enlargements

Small prints from color negatives are made by one-hour photo shops everywhere. Kodalux labs (currently in Fairlawn, NJ; Atlanta, Dallas, Palo Alto and Honolulu) and Kodak labs in Canada, make inexpensive prints and 20x30" posters from slides.

Canon and Kodak thermal transfer (color copier) prints can be made on the spot from prints or slides at "quick copy" shops just about everywhere. They cost about $6 for an 11x17" copy here in New York. Many professionals use these for "drop-offs." I like them for promotion pieces as well as for "wall art".

Framing Prints

In my opinion, frames for gallery exhibition, or home or office decor should be plain, narrow and all the same color. You can choose light wood, aluminum or you may prefer frameless plastic or glass covers held together with clips.

Filing and Storing Photographs

Do not use inexpensive, thick polyvinyl chloride (PVC) sheets to store your slides for any length of time. (The plastic can be identified by its strong smell, and will eventually adhere to, and damage transparencies.)

Sturdy DW Viewpack transparent archival storage sheets (available with dust covers and metal file hangers) are the best, and are used by many stock agencies including my own. They are made in England and sometimes sold (in the Northeastern United States anyway) by the Sam Flax chain of art supply stores. Phone (212) 620-3010; fax (212) 633-1082. If you have difficulty getting them from Flax, order direct from DW Viewpacks Ltd., Unit 7/8, Peverel Drive, Granby, Milton Keynes, England MK1 1NL. Phone (44-0908) 642323; fax: (44-0908) 640164.

Thinner, less expensive Perma-Saf archival storage sheets (which also come with metal hangers that can be hung in file cabinets) and which are used by the Library of Congress among others are marketed by Franklin Distributors, P.O. Box 320, Denville, NJ 07834. Phone (201) 267-2710.

Kimac makes archivally safe, transparent, plastic slip-on covers for individual 35mm slides. I use them on every slide I send out, and all my favorite pictures that I store. Kimac covers are sold at just about all good photo dealers.

Store prints in boxes, envelopes or albums to prevent damage.

All slides and negatives should be stored in a dark, cool, dry place.

I keep my "super selects" in Kodak cardboard boxes in a safe. I keep stock in Kimac slide covers, then in DW Viewpak archival sheets hung in standard metal file cabinets.

My filing is by country or by subject. I store "outtake" (rejected or spare slides) in the original boxes in filing cabinets with shallow drawers. (I found mine very inexpensively; they were originally used for cancelled checks.)

Presenting Professional Assignments

For your final choice of pictures for any kind of assignment edit, my best advice is to rely on your instincts for what you want to show. Asking advice will only confuse you, as no two people, even professional editors, will choose alike. An assignment edit will probably contain hundreds of pictures to give the art director plenty of choice (don't forget to include horizontal and vertical versions of the same shots, except for audio-visuals, which use horizontals only).

Present edited shots in 20-slide plastic sheets or in Kodak Carousel wheels, whichever the art director or picture editor prefers.

Always number and copyright stamp all slide/transparency mounts (or each print on the back) and include related numbered caption sheets with the take.

Supplies for Editing, Presentation and Archival Storage

Kodak Carousel projectors, wheels and Stack Loaders are industry standards available at photo dealers everywhere. Get the cheapest autofocus projector you can afford. If you are fussy, Navitar makes fine lenses that replace the plastic ones that come as standard with Carousels.

Acculite light boxes are excellent, as are Kaiser's, which also look very handsome. A Schneider (top-of-the-line) or Agfa (budget) loupe for viewing contact sheets and transparencies is essential. Kimac slide protectors will save you grief and damaged pictures. All these are available at photo dealers.

How To Start Promoting Your Photography

Great pictures are at the heart of great self-promotion. Show only your very best work, immaculately presented. Show the work that you want to do at first, and mix it with the best of what you have done for clients as you get more experienced. The first step is to edit your pictures well, the second, to have a business card printed. This can be a simple card in tasteful type from a local printer at first.

Most experts agree that the portfolio size should be limited. A projection portfolio should probably contain no more than about 30-40 slides (you can mix color originals with slide copies of tear sheets or black-and-white prints if you like). Carry the work in a standard Kodak Carousel slide wheel. (Carry your own projector if the client doesn't have a Carousel or compatible projector.) You can also show transparencies of any size in black cardboard presentation sheets, available in all formats from art and photo dealers.

I repeat, keep the portfolio small. A print portfolio should have no more than 15-20 black-and-white or color samples (or combinations of both) in a smart press-book type folder or box or zippered case with glassine sheets.

If you have a lot of published work, laminated tear sheets of published pages in a nice case or box look very professional. Original prints can also be laminated. All laminated material should be backed (with stiff, opaque plastic) to make them the same size. Laminall Plastics, 11-42 46th Road, Long Island City, NY 11101; Phone (718) 786-6480 does an excellent job; I have twenty-year-old laminated sheets from them that have not yellowed (this is not true of some other laminators).

Some advertising photographers use 8x10" duplicate chromes of original transparencies or tear-sheets. These, while expensive, look great in uniform black mounts. Get the dupes made by professional labs, or, if you are skilled, dupe them yourself onto film made for that purpose. (Consult Kodak and Fuji about this; I have never done it seriously myself, and there are new duping films on the market.) There are even portfolio cases with built-in 8x10" lightboxes.

Two Archival Storage Suppliers

Two companies that sell portfolio boxes and cases; albums, mounts, sleeves, storage boxes and many other archival supplies which are used by museums, and that publish free catalogs with much information on photo storage are: Light Impressions, phone (800) 828-6216, and University Products, phone (800) 762-1165.

Showing Your Portfolio

Beginners often try to show too much at one time. The portfolio should be limited in size for three reasons. First, art directors are very busy—you don't want to bore or overtax them; second, any good art director can see what you can do by looking at very few pictures. And, most importantly, even if someone likes your work a lot, they may have nothing to offer in the way of jobs at the moment. Sometimes it may take several visits before work is offered, so you need some pictures in reserve for when you call back.

Always carry your business or promotional card and a few photo copies of pictures to leave behind when you show work.

Stock photographers should keep a "Stock Picture Delivery Memo" (see Chapter Thirteen) handy when they see clients, just in case someone is interested in holding work from the portfolio. (Be certain what you leave is copyright-stamped!) If you have stock pictures, make an alphabetical listing of them by subject and leave it with your card. Remember too, that stock clients can turn into assignment clients.

Promotional Mailers and Cards

The very first promotional tool any photographer needs is a business card, as I have already mentioned. These can cost as little as about $25 for 100 all-type cards, from jobbing printers. Resist the temptation to have cutesy "clip art" designs on this basic card!

5x7" photo cards, with your name, address, phone number and a photograph can be produced quite reasonably. I send them out as mailers periodically, and as Christmas cards. Studio X here in New York does a nice job on such cards they cost about $200 for 100 cards. Call them at (212) 989-9233.

Some postcard printers catering to photographers: MWM Dexter, Inc. (800) 431-1995; fax (417) 678-3626. Postcard Productions, (207) 236-0703; Serbin Communications, (805) 963-0439. (Other card printers advertise in the *Photo District News* . Also see classified phone directories.)

If possible, mail out a different promotional card every six weeks or three months. A Christmas or Seasons Greetings card is always a good way to keep in touch with old clients, and bring your name before new ones. Do not use "family" type greeting cards unless the picture is a fine photo of generic holiday interest!

Mailing Lists

A good mailing list is a very important promotional tool. It is cheaper, and perhaps better to start by building your own mailing list. Use local contacts, do research in libraries, and use classified telephone directories (*Yellow Pages*) as sources. A good magazine store will provide much useful browsing. Two groups of professional directories are expensive but exhaustive, and may be consulted at good libraries. The *Standard Rate and Data Guides* and *Bacon's Media Directories* list newspapers and consumer magazines, business publications and more.

Photographer's Market (published by Writer's Digest Books) is an annual directed at photographers. It lists many buyers of all types of photographs

> ## The Travel Industry Personnel Directory
>
> A travel agent friend told me about this useful directory, published by Fairchild Books. It lists national and state tourist offices, tour wholesalers, airlines, cruise and ship lines, car rental companies, hotel and motel chains and more. I use it both to locate possible clients and as a research tool when planning a trip. It currently costs $22.50. To order call (800) 247-6622.

(these are often in the lower paying end of the market). It sells in bookstores for around $20.00. (See also Chapter Twenty.)

Commercial Mailing Lists

Lists of photo buyers, including publishers, large and small advertising agencies, graphic designers, etc., on pre-printed labels and broken down by region and specialty can be purchased from professional list brokers, including Creative Access, phone (800) 422-2377, and Steve Langerman Lists, phone (212) 466-3822.

Photo District News carries ads for mailing-list sellers in its classified section. The American Institute of Graphic Arts (AIGA) has chapters nationwide and sells lists of its 1,700 members (good sources of annual report and corporate work) on preprinted labels or computer disc.

Send out your promotional mailing pieces fairly frequently. Every two to three months is probably not too often. There seems to be a consensus that it is more effective to mail (or hand deliver) a new promotional to 100 carefully chosen people several times a year than to scatter one card to 1,000 people once a year.

Fax Services and Newsletters

If you subscribe to a service that provides stock request (want) lists, you can advertise your travel plans and add selected buyers' names to your promotional mailing list. (See Chapter Thirteen for more on these services and stock business newsletters.)

A newsletter distributed free to picture buyers and catering to editorial photographers is being published by AG Editions Inc., publishers of the respected *Guilfoyle Report*. Photographers can inexpensively advertise their travel plans, stories available for syndication, stock specialties etc. several times a year in the United States, biannually in Europe. It is a new venture, I haven't seen a copy yet. For details, call (212) 929-0959.

Promotional Directories

The Creative Black Book, American Showcase, New York Gold Book, Direct Stock and several other national and regional directories where photographers advertise, are expensive (upwards of about $2,000 per page) but worth it if you are moving into high-paying advertising and corporate assignments, or if you have very good model-released stock that may command high advertising prices. These directories are distributed free to a carefully selected list of proven art buyers. They also provide reprints to the talent who advertises with them, for use as mailers/promotional pieces. These directories are not for those on a tight budget, but are generally considered by top experienced and established photographers to be part of a long-term promotional strategy. That strategy also includes regular mailing pieces, ads in magazines read by art directors (*Select* and *Photo Design* are two) and extensive circulation of one or more portfolios, often by the photographer's representative or agent.

Working With Professional "Reps"
A few photographers are lucky enough to have a dedicated spouse or friend who is able to carry their portfolio around and represent (or "rep") them to art directors and other art and picture buyers early in their careers.

Most photographers start by "repping" themselves, because it is difficult to get a good rep until you have an established business. Reps live on a percentage (usually, but not always, 25%) of the sales they generate for a photographer, so it is obvious that they either have to be paid a salary or have a large-grossing photographer in order to survive.

Repping is not an easy way to make a living, especially in these days of "dropoffs" (leaving the portfolio for a short time) and the fact that art and photo buyers in big agencies and magazines screen portfolios, making it more difficult for reps to establish relationships with art directors.

Competitive bidding for big-money advertising jobs is routine today, and only a few very well-established reps get to see top art and creative directors regularly, so the business is tough for new reps without contacts. But, as in any field, some people have the talent and persistence needed for selling, and if you are clever or lucky enough to find one, treasure him or her.

In fact, most top reps who stay in the business not surprisingly end up working with the photographers who make the most money, usually those who do high-paying corporate annual reports, or advertising or fashion work.

To try to find a rep, you can advertise in the *Photo District News* or in the Society of Artists and Representative's (SPAR) newsletter. Reps seeking talent advertise in both.

Working With a Rep
To get on well with any rep, your understanding with him or her should be clearly spelled out in writing in advance, and the agreement should be to the satisfaction of both parties.

Edith Leonian, a good friend and a former board member of SPAR, says that it is very important for you and your rep to have similar goals for your career, and that these should include where you want to be working, and how much you want to be billing within a certain amount of time. She advises that photographers confer with their rep frequently.

If the arrangement does not work out after a reasonable trial period of about one year, you should be able to end the relationship without costly arguments.

Representing Yourself

Most travel photographers will almost certainly have to rep themselves, at least at the beginning. Don't think of this as boring; you can learn a lot from the people you meet. The three most important criteria in selling yourself are: Great pictures, good follow-up and a personal rapport with potential clients.

To start, make a list of publications, designers or other clients you would like to work for, whom your style "fits." Mail or hand deliver one (or several) promotional pieces, and follow up with phone calls a couple of weeks later. If you can't get in to see the person you hoped to, don't give up. While many magazines, design firms, etc. have a "drop-off" policy, they will call you for a personal interview if they like your work. Of course, if you can use someone's name to get in to see a potential client, do so. (This does carry an obligation to show only truly good work!) Don't sniff at seeing assistant art directors, associate art buyers or junior editors; because they will pass you along to the boss if they think you are good, and they, themselves, like to get to know new talent. In the fast-paced communications industry people move up quickly and assistants can soon be in a position to give out work themselves.

Networking—Probably the Best Way to Find Clients

Your "network" is everyone you know—family, friends, people you know from work, social activities and professional colleagues. A great deal of photography work is given to someone the art director knows, likes and trusts.

- If you go to any kind of art school or college which graduates future art directors, be sure to keep in touch with their careers.

- If a client moves to another job, keep in touch with him or her.

- Ask clients to refer you to other people who might use you.

- Remember everyone you meet potentially has a cousin who is an art director! Carry your business card wherever you go.

I went to art school at night, and worked as a guide in the United Nations Headquarters here in New York, for two years. I did paste-ups and mechanicals for the Scholastic Magazines group, and I was a Student Travel Officer for the British Tourist Authority before becomimg a photographer. Contacts made at all of those places later resulted in assignments when I turned professional. Knowing people will get your foot in a door, but you must have a good portfolio and skills, and do good work if you want to be hired more than once!

Making Sales Calls

When you locate a possible client, telephone for an appointment— you may have to be politely persistent. When you get in, it's good to remember a few points. Representing yourself is selling yourself, no doubt about it. This has nothing to do with photography of course, but you should dress appropriately when calling on potential clients (photography is after all an "image" business). You are always to some degree judged for yourself as well as for your pictures when you make calls, and you must usually impress new clients that you would be a good person to represent the publication, or company, as well as be the best photographer for the assignment. Dress more formally for a call on the corporate/public relations world (after all, they wear suits) than you might for a visit to a magazine, advertising agency, graphic designer or book publisher.

Today is most emphatically not the sixties, when I for one went around in jeans and safari jackets. A good rule when seeing any client is to wear what you would wear to dinner at a good but not too formal big-city restaurant.

When You Get the Assignment

Once you have an assignment, you have the obligation to do it well, and on schedule no matter what it costs you in time. Art directors', sales directors', and picture editors' jobs (and repeat assignments) depend on your performance.

When you have done any job, always thank the client for the work. Top photographer Nancy Brown used to be a busy model. I used her two or three times some years ago. She was not only pleasant to work with but the only model I ever used who always sent me a note of thanks afterwards. I don't know exactly how she made the transfer to photography, but now she is a very good and very successful advertising illustration photographer. I am quite sure that she still thanks all her clients, and that this has contributed to her success.

How to Thank a Client

Send a thank-you note by all means. It never hurts to take a client who has given you a job out to lunch, or to send someone who uses you regularly a small gift at holiday times. (Clients don't normally want framed photographs!) Entertainment and small gifts are tax-deductible to professional photographers.

Promoting Fine-Art Photography

I haven't tried this, but I have read *Photography for the Art Market* by Kathryn Marx. It gives a lot of information about the fine-art photography business, and should be helpful to those interested in the field. The Photographic Arts Center publishes a newsletter—*The Linked Ring Letter*—and distributes books about self-promoting, exhibiting and selling fine-art prints; Contact them at 163 Amsterdam Avenue, New York, NY 10023. Phone (212) 838-8640.

If at First You Don't Succeed

Be patient and keep showing and improving your portfolio. Never, never underestimate the importance of persistence. Many good people in all artistic fields don't make it because they don't hang in there. The people that do succeed in photography, as well as in every other art, do so because they are both talented and persistent.

I truly believe that if you do good, honest work, and love doing it, and don't get discouraged by a lack of easy success, eventually you will find enough people to hire you to make photography support you. Whether you will ever get rich is another matter!

Further Reading

Four good books on the whole subject are *The Perfect Portfolio* by Henrietta Brackman; *Promoting Yourself as a Photographer* by Frederick W. Rosen; *How to Sell Your Photographs and Illustrations* by Elliott and Barbara Gordon; and *Selling Your Photography* by Arie Kopelman and Tad Crawford.

The Creative Black Book, American Showcase, Corporate Showcase, Stock Workbook and other creative directories can be studied at good libraries.

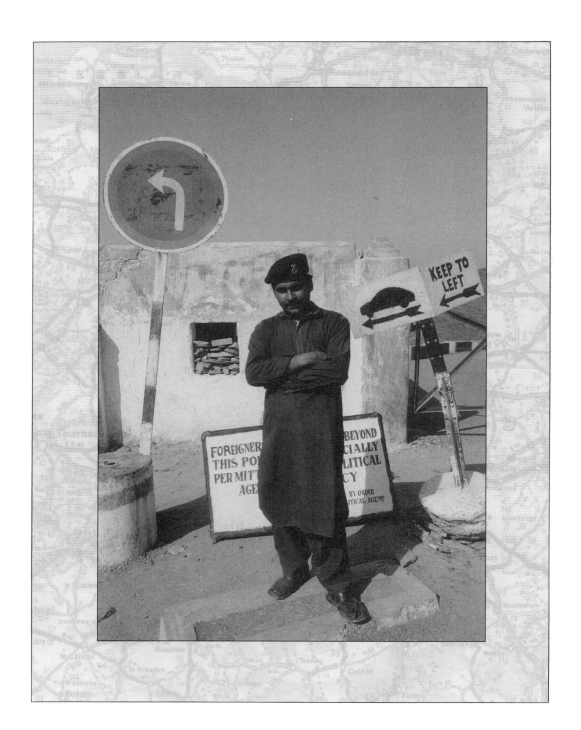

Chapter 11

Magazine and Editorial Photography

For me, travel magazine assignments are the most fun of all. You are given a framework for a job, but usually nothing is too specific, and as a rule you are selected for a particular assignment because the art director likes your point of view. On a magazine assignment you must cover the main points of a story, but are also free to wander off and find things on your own. The ideal magazine art director wants photographs that complement, not merely illustrate, a writer's work, and appreciates what you bring to a story. Occasionally, photographers originate travel essays, which are run as picture-stories with short text captions. Obviously, this is ideal from the photographer's point of view! A nice layout of several pages in a top magazine is a terrific portfolio piece.

For top magazines, travel photography is quite well paid. Pay is either per day or per page, with a minimum guarantee, and is to some extent negotiable. The American Society of Magazine Photographers suggested minimum editorial day rate for its members is $350, which has not increased for ten years. Only a few photographers command very high fees for magazine work today.

Magazine photography is prestigious, as most magazines give credit lines on the same page as the work appears, and is a good way for up-and-coming photographers to get name recognition, and for established photographers to keep their name visible. For the above reasons, it is competitive, and not too easy to break into. Almost no magazines today employ staff photographers (except the *National Geographic*), though some have contract photographers, who are guaranteed a certain number of days' work, published pages or sum of money, for the length of the contract. Freelance photographers do most magazine assignments. Therefore, good new photographers always have a chance, especially if they have a fresh and personal viewpoint, are pleasant and persistent, and most especially if they have good ideas for features and stories. Avant-garde and small magazines are most likely to take a chance with new talent.

Skills Needed for Magazine Photography.

I will go out on a limb here and say that the skills needed for magazine photography are social as well as photographic. Most travel magazine readers are well-educated, and quite sophisticated. Magazine editorial staffs reflect this, and want the people they hire on a free-lance basis to be presentable, pleasant and self-sufficient. They aren't there to hold your hand in Timbuctoo or wherever, and although they will give you all the help possible before the shoot, a lot of the on-the-spot negotiations and persuasions are up to you. This is not the type of work for the inarticulate photographer who is only happy in old jeans. (Jeans are fine on some occasions but on others must be supplemented with more formal dress so that you "fit in" to the scene.)

If you would like to work for national travel magazines, realistically appraise your portfolio and skills. It is a given that a magazine photographer will be excellent technically, have a point of view that fits with that of the publication, and the something extra that will bring life to the story, location portrait or whatever. If you feel that your work meets those standards, the next step is to do some research at a good magazine store or library. Art directors' and photo editors' names are listed on magazine mastheads (opening credits). When you have found a publication you think you will fit, and the picture editor's name, call to find out how to show work. Almost all magazines look at portfolios regularly, but "dropoffs" are the rule for people they don't know. You will get a call back if they are interested.

How to Find Travel Magazine Clients

Browse in a good magazine store. Many magazines today are part of a larger publishing group. For instance: American Express Publishing (*Travel and Leisure, Food and Wine, L.A. Style*); Condé Nast (*Condé Nast Traveler; Vogue, Mademoiselle, Glamour*, etc.); Rodale Press *(Backpacker, Organic Gardening).* Publishers of both travel magazines and many books are the National Geographic Society (*National Geographic, National Geographic Traveler* and *World*) and Reader's Digest Publications (*Reader's Digest, Travel/Holiday*). New York City and environs are still the nation's publishing capital. You certainly don't have to live here in this age of fax and Federal Express, but you will probably have to make periodic visits or get very good at shipping your portfolio of prints or duplicate slides if you want to work for top magazines. Los Angeles and California in general are the second publishing market in the United States (and is the "hot" art center in the country) but almost every state has at least a few publishers. The publishing centers in Canada are Toronto and Montreal.

Don't overlook foreign publishers. In Europe, Germany's giant Gruner and Jahr of Hamburg is one of the biggest. They put out *Geo* magazine (in German and French editions) among many other publications. Most of the big European and Japanese magazine publishers pay very well, and many have New York offices or representatives.

Where to Learn More About Magazine Photography

Attend meetings of chapters of the American Society of Magazine Photographers (ASMP). Phone (212) 889-9144 or fax (212) 779-9446 for membership information and a list of chapters nationwide. Get a list of their current books and monographs on the photography business. The *Standard Rate and Data Guide* series of directories (called the *"Redbooks"*) list consumer and trade magazines that accept advertising. *Bacon's Publicity Checker* is a similar exhaustive list of publications directed at public relations professionals (Bacon's 1991 directory lists over 60 consumer travel magazines and over twenty major travel-trade magazines). These directories all include magazine circulation figures, and may be consulted at libraries. There are overseas editions too. (See Chapter Ten for more details on these directories.)

Photographing Assignments on Location by Adrian Taylor, (formerly art director of *Travel and Leisure* magazine) is a collection of interviews with some great magazine photographers, and insights into how they approach assignments.

A Guide to Travel Writing and Photography by the successful writer/photographer team of Ann and Carl Purcell is recommended reading for people who want to try combining writing with their shooting. (Also see the Bibliography.)

The Smaller Magazine Market

Travel magazines break down into international, national, regional, city and local. Specialized travel magazines exist for backpackers or RV owners or doctors, for instance. "In house" magazines are distributed free to airline and cruise passengers, as are hotel/resort publications. Regional magazines serve a city, state, county or popular tourist area. Local photographers have a good chance of getting published in well-known regional publications like *Arizona Highways* or *Vermont Life*. Even better opportunities exist in lesser-known regional publications, such as *Down East, The Maine Magazine* or *Wonderful West Virginia*. (All of these use excellent photography). There are regional magazines published all over the United States and Canada which are always on the lookout for good new pictures and especially for appropriate feature ideas and stories. Check your own state, province, or area to see what's published. In the region of upstate New York where I have a house for instance, there are *Hudson Valley Magazine, Kaatskill Life* and probably other publications too. Of course regional and local magazines don't pay what the big ones do, but working for them is good experience, gives you tear sheets (printed pages) and can serve as a stepping-stone. If you can write well too, you have an excellent chance for publication in smaller magazines.

Some major manufacturers have a natural interest in travel and publish glossy magazines that use travel features. *Ford Times* and *Amoco World* are just two examples. Quite a few magazines of all types have regular travel features, with the picture emphasis towards food, wine, gardens, the outdoors, the mature person, or whatever is the main focus of the magazine.

Sample Letter of Query to a National Magazine:

Photographer's Letterhead

Mr. Mrs. or Ms. Trendy Editor
High Flying Travel Magazine
200 Prestigious Avenue
The Great Apple, NY 100??

Date

Dear Ms. Trendy:

"Carnival" is celebrated with enthusiasm in India's only predominantly Catholic state, Goa, a former Portuguese colony. It begins this year on (date) with religious parades by its Catholic population in the towns of Margao and Parlim and continues for three festive days. What interests me most is what people wear: elaborate embroidered silk saris and tunics with headdresses. There are statues of saints decorated with flowers, and much pleasant revelry.

I intend to be in India in (month) and will go to Goa to shoot the festivities in Margao, Parlim and possibly Old Goa as well. I see this as a lively photo essay focusing on the traditions of the Goan people in which Portuguese and Indian traditions make a fascinating blend. Goa is also famous for beautiful unspoiled beaches, and has decent hotels. It is the burial place of St Frances Xavier, who has an elaborate tomb at the Basilica of the Born Jesus, and there are many other interesting ancient churches many of which have special feast-days. I think the extraordinary customs and costumes and the traditional foods—specially decorated fiery Vindaloo curries, cooling vegetable platters and ornate cakes—would make a vivid picture story for High Flying Magazine.

So that you'll have some idea of my work, I include tearsheets.

OR

I'm enclosing a promo piece that shows some of my more recent work (to editors who know your work).

OR

I enclose a few sample copies of recent work, and will be glad to bring or drop off a portfolio at your convenience.

I look forward to hearing from you.

Yours sincerely,

Phantastic Photographer

Sample Letter of Assignment: (on Magazine's Letterhead)

To: John/Jane Photographer
Your address
New York City/Suburb, USA

Date

Dear Mr./Ms. Photographer (or John/Jane):

This letter will confirm Gotham City Magazine's assignment for you to photograph the Union Square Greenmarket near East 14th Street in Manhattan. We will guarantee you four pages at our customary rate of $?.00 per page, plus film, processing and local expenses for this local assignment.

This popular market has been in operation only since 1985. Farmers from upstate New York, New Jersey, Connecticut and Pennsylvania come in for the Wednesday, Friday and Saturday market days and sell vegetables, fruit, flowers and plants. Eggs and chickens, meat and fish are sold on the weekends. New York State gives a dispensation to its vintners, so upstate winemakers sell their wares also. As we have not scheduled when the feature will run, we would prefer that you avoid any highly seasonal pictures. (Or: this is for a fall issue, show pumpkins; Christmas issue, show trees and holly etc.)

You will need to try for a colorful cover (vertical). Most of our covers are of people who are likely to appeal to our (upper middle income) readers. An attractive young woman with a basket of goodies in front of a vendor in overalls selling appetizing produce, and with eye contact with the viewer, would be a good bet. Allow light or dark space on top for our logo.

We will also need a strong horizontal picture for the opening spread. It should say "farmers' market and Manhattan" at one glance. Allow for type on the top left quarter of the picture. We definitely DON'T want to see anything dirty or ugly. Make a few overall shots from a height or distance showing the whole market in its urban setting. This is the only place where it's okay to show cars, traffic etc. Minimize these in all other shots. We want a "country" feel as much as possible. Show abundance and beauty. There will probably be families buying, sampling, checking produce, the more attractive and sophisticated looking the better. If you set anything up, it should look candid and unposed. Not more than a couple of elegant close-ups of massed vegetables/fruit etc. Our writer likes cheese—he recommends Charley Cheesemaker in the piece—so try and get some good shots of him and his wares. If you find a subject that you think would make a great cover, shoot plenty of film on him or her, and try to get a model release. At least get the name, address and phone number, so we can get a release later.

We don't like to crop pictures, except very slightly at the edges to make the shots fit the magazine's format. Needless to say, pictures with highly contrasty light, heavy shadows on faces etc. are not acceptable. We prefer you to use (Kodachrome or Fujichrome Velvia) film where possible.
Keep notes for captions, especially note names. Keep all receipts for local expenses, film and processing. We cannot reimburse expenses without receipts.

Enclosed is our letter of introduction. The market manager is Harry Smith, phone (718) 449-2122, evenings. You might want to call him in advance.

I very much look forward to seeing your take. With kindest regards,

Jerry/Mary Picture Editor (or Art Director, Photography Director etc.)

Sample Letter of Introduction:

Magazine's Letterhead

Date

To Whom It May Concern:

This letter will introduce Mr. John/Ms. Jane Photographer, who is on assignment for Gotham City Magazine to produce a photo feature on the Union Square Greenmarket.

This feature, which is planned for publication this fall, will be part of a special issue on the best places for families to enjoy Manhattan, and we think will appeal strongly to our readership of 1.2 million above average income New Yorkers, and another 300,000 New York lovers around the country and the world.

We would appreciate your giving Mr./Ms. Photographer any and all assistance that you can, so that he/she can show this delightful part of the city in the best possible light.

If you have any questions about Mr./Ms. Photographer's assignment, please feel free to contact me at any time.

With thanks in advance for your help.

Yours sincerely,

Jerry Picture Editor (or Mary Art Director etc.)

Sample Magazine Assignment Contract for Photographers:

PHOTOGRAPHY CONTRACT

This agreement is between, _____(the PHOTOGRAPHER) and Super Terrific Publications, Inc.. (the PUBLISHER), for the acquisition of rights to photographs to be used in Super Terrific Travel (the MAGAZINE).

1. ASSIGNMENT. PHOTOGRAPHER agrees to photograph the subject_____

_____ for publication in MAGAZINE.

The due date for this assignment is _____.

2. RIGHTS. All photographs taken/created under this agreement will be considered as specially commissioned for use by MAGAZINE, subject to the following provisions:

(a) PHOTOGRAPHER grants PUBLISHER exclusive first worldwide periodical rights to the photographs, beginning with date of your signature and continuing until 90 days after their first publication in MAGAZINE.

(b) Any photographs not selected for publication will be returned to PHOTOGRAPHER along with all rights to these photographs except that none may be made available to anyone for publication until 90 days after the MAGAZINE has first published its selections. PHOTOGRAPHER will not authorize the use of any such photographs in any publication that could be deemed competitive without first notifying MAGAZINE in writing.

(c) In the event that any of the photographs are used on the cover of the MAGAZINE, the PHOTOGRAPHER agrees not to authorize such photos to be used on the cover of any other publication without prior approval of the PUBLISHER.

(d) PHOTOGRAPHER grants PUBLISHER the right to use PHOTOGRAPHER's photographs, name, pseudonyms, biography and likeness in publicizing, advertising and promoting the article containing PHOTOGRAPHER's work. There will be no re-use fee when photographs are used in the context in which they originally appeared.

(e) PHOTOGRAPHER grants PUBLISHER the right to use any of the published photographs for the advertising and promotion of the MAGAZINE, it being understood that such use shall be subject to a re-use fee.

(f) PHOTOGRAPHER grants PUBLISHER the right to select material from the assignment and use/re-use it in any of its other MAGAZINES, domestic or foreign, or anthologies or collections of magazine material for the full NINETY (90) DAYS of the agreement, subject to a re-use fee.

(g) PUBLISHER agrees to print PHOTOGRAPHER's credit line in the following manner: (i) If PHOTOGRAPHER is author of all the pictures in the article, credit line shall appear on the first page of the article in a type size no smaller than writer's credit line. *(Sometimes you may wish to defer to a famous writer and say 75% of writer's credit line. This is a negotiable item—you may wish your credit to be larger than writer's credit if this is a major essay originated by you.)* (ii) If the work of other photographers also appear in the article, PHOTOGRAPHER's credit line shall appear adjacent to each of his/her pictures, in type size of no less than 7 points.

PHOTOGRAPHY CONTRACT, CONTINUED

3. PAYMENT. In considerations of the rights granted by this agreement, PUBLISHER agrees to pay PHO-
TOGRAPHER the sum of $_____ upon acceptance of the photographs. This fee is an ad-
vance against the PUBLISHER's standard space rates applicable to the North American edition of the MAGA-
ZINE. The balance of such rates, if any, shall be paid at the time of publication of the photographs upon
receipt of your invoice. Payment will not be processed until photographs with clear, accurate caption information have been submitted.

4. EXPENSES. PUBLISHER will reimburse PHOTOGRAPHER for reasonable expenses (including travel,
film and processing, lodging, meals and miscellaneous) not to exceed $_____ as submit-
ted in an estimate by PHOTOGRAPHER. (See MAGAZINE's Expense Policy, attached.) If actual expenses
exceed the estimate, only those expenses approved in advance will be reimbursed. All expenses must be
itemized and substantiated by receipts.

5. ADVANCE ON EXPENSES. PUBLISHER agrees to advance $_____ against expenses
(and/or day rate or space guarantee), provided PHOTOGRAPHER signs a receipt for the full amount of the
advance.

6. WARRANTY. By delivery of photographs to MAGAZINE; PHOTOGRAPHER warrants (i) that they are original;
(ii) that PHOTOGRAPHER owns all rights to them free of any prior assignment; (iii) that they have not
previously been published in any form; (iv) that they will not be published prior to the on-sale date of the
issue of MAGAZINE in which they are published; (v) and that the publication or other use of your photographs will not, to the best of your knowledge and belief, infringe upon or interfere with any copyright,
proprietary right, or other right of any kind.

7. LOST/DAMAGED PHOTOGRAPHS. PUBLISHER agrees to take every care of PHOTOGRAPHER's work,
and to use insured/bonded carriers to transport work. However, PUBLISHER is not liable to loss or damage to photographs at any time that they are not in the PUBLISHER's immediate possession or control. In
the event the photographs are lost or damaged while in the magazine's possession or control, the amount
to be paid to you is subject to negotiation, but PUBLISHER's liability shall not exceed
$_____ in the aggregate.

This agreement sets forth the entire understanding between the parties. Please confirm by signing and return

ing copies to: _____ (title), by: _____ (date).

Signed for SUPER TERRIFIC PUBLICATIONS (name and title).

_____ Date:_____

SIGNATURE OF PHOTOGRAPHER:

_____ Date:_____

PHOTOGRAPHER's SOCIAL SECURITY NUMBER: _____

(Remember that all contracts are negotiable until they are signed!)

Sample Expense Account Policy Statement:

Information for Super Terrific Travel Magazine Photographers

(Note: Similar policies may be used by other clients.)

1. When you return the signed Photographer's Agreement to Super Terrific Travel Magazine, please send an invoice for an advance against the assignment guarantee as stated in the Agreement.

2. Expenses should be kept to a minimum. They should be reasonable and should be directly related to the story assignment.

3. Super Terrific Travel Magazine will pay for economy airfare directly related to the assignment. Upon accepting the assignment, contact the Super Terrific Travel Magazine photo department, and they may be able to make the travel arrangements for you. If not, you will make them and be reimbursed by submitting a photocopy of the original airline ticket.

4. Super Terrific Travel Magazine will pay for a single or double room, as appropriate. Lodging will be reimbursed by submitting the hotel invoice(s) for the days covered.

5. If a personal car is used the allowance is (.00¢) per mile, which includes gasoline costs. *(This at time of writing is 27.5¢ per mile; consult your accountant for current standard I.R.S. mileage deduction.)*

6. Please submit all expenses promptly and include an itemized report for the dates involved. All receipts must be taped to sheets of 8 1/2"x 11" paper, and must be submitted with the expense report.

Note: The Accounting Department carefully scrutinizes all expenses and will not process those that are not properly completed or substantiated.

7. If the assignment requires more than _____ (often 10) rolls of film per day approval must be obtained from

_____ (name or title.)
(This restriction, which I do not like, has been added because some photographers shoot stock at a magazine's expense. When a magazine trusts you, they will relax this inhibiting stricture.)

8. Super Terrific Travel Magazine will pay (no more than) $ 00 *(currently around $16.00)* per roll for film and processing. Rush processing fees must be approved in advance. It is possible to make arrangements to purchase film through the Super Terrific Travel Magazine *(or other client)* photo department and have it processed at the lab they use.

9. You must submit complete written identification of the assignment photographs, sufficient to enable Publisher to write accurate captions and agree to verify all facts as stated in the written identification material. Additional space rate will not be paid until this information is supplied.

Note: Some publishers (and all commercial travel clients) may include a paragraph like this: Photographer will secure model releases from subjects wherever possible on Publisher's or photographer's standard model release forms. He/she will in all cases obtain name, address and phone number of people featured in photographs, in the event that Publisher later determines that a release is necessary before publication of subject's picture(s).

10. Publisher may request photographer to bring back current material that will help their fact-checkers, including menus, event lists, programs listing names of performers, ferry schedules, etc., etc.

Trade Magazines

Trade magazines are targeted at packagers, photographers, planners, plumbers, programmers and almost any other trade, industry group, craft, organization or profession you can think of. They usually have smaller circulations and are lower paying than national magazines, but the biggest of them pay more than local or regional travel magazines.

Some trade magazines use travel features (especially those directed to affluent professionals); the travel story must always have a slant toward the magazine's audience. All trade publications need photographers with the skills of a good travel/location photographer from time to time. Don't overlook even small trade magazines. Working for them is a good way to gain experience and help you eventually make it to national magazines.

To find trade magazines, see the directories mentioned earlier in the chapter, at a good library. Ask business and professional people you know what specialized magazines they read. Consider concentrating on one trade area that interests you: hospitality, transportation, or food-service oriented publications, for instance, or some major industry you know something about. Some trade/company publications are: *Aviation Week, Ford Times, Food Technology, Travel Weekly*. You get the idea. They are all included in the directories.

Books

Book publishers use a lot of photographs. The biggest and best paying market is high school textbooks, because textbook print runs may be very large. Many of these picture needs are filled by stock and most are not particularly travel related except for social studies and language texts. The usual need is for shots of families, teen-agers, workers, professionals of all nationalities, ages, races and religions. Some assignments are available, and a good way to meet picture editors is to send in a stock picture list. Encyclopedias, guidebooks and trade (general) books all use travel pictures from time to time.

Getting a photo essay or travel picture book published is not easy, especially if it's in color, as color photographs are very expensive to reproduce. The photographers that succeed do careful research into the marketplace, and make and present well thought out "dummies" (physical mock-ups of the book). This is relatively easy to do today with Kodak and Canon color copiers. You might be able to improve your chances by working with a graphic designer. Possibly you can trade photography for design services. Even a student graphic designer today almost certainly has access to a computer, can set type and help you with your portfolio in general. And designers you meet that way are always potential clients. People like to work with those they know.

A few photographers publish their own books, which obviously is wonderful from the point of view of doing what one loves best; but equally obviously involve big risks and expense. Sherman Hines, perhaps the top Canadian travel photographer, is one person I have met who is very succesful indeed at this.

"How to Self Publish" seminars are given by individual photographers and ASMP chapters from time to time. Check the photo trade papers and photoschool announcements. If you have a unique, terrific idea or access, or an in-depth marvelous collection of pictures for a specific travel picture book, and if there is nothing like it around, you should try and find a publisher. Search in libraries and good bookstores, and if you see something in the same general area as what you want to do, trying that publisher is a good bet. Publishers very rarely take books that come in unrecommended.

Try and find a picture book agent or consultant (they advertise in the *Photo District News*) and dummy a section or chapter of the book, and start showing the dummy around. You may be able to find a sponsor. Kodak's Professional Photography Division now sponsors quite a few books it feels are important, as to a much lesser extent do other photographic manufacturers, as well as printers, paper companies, and major corporations. Books that involve art and culture, the environment and social issues, and that reflect positively on a business or geographic area, are more likely to be sponsored than others.

Newspapers and Travel Photographs

Newspapers of all sizes use local travel features and pictures illustrating places, events and attractions within easy range of their readers. You might start by doing a picture story on a tourist attraction close to home (see Chapter Nine, Self-Assignments). A golf resort, a ski-area, or an amusement park are good bets, or you might prefer a quiet scenic area, state park or historic village or town. If you can produce a feature of about six to ten good photographs illustrating different aspects of the place, you have a good chance of selling it because the resort or attraction, or theme-park, are advertisers in local publications. Most newspapers publish foreign travel pictures periodically, some have regular travel supplements. The biggest papers often use travel pictures and stories, though some may be supplied as a feature from a public relations firm or national tourist organization. Some major papers have regular travel supplements. *The New York Times*, to give just one example, uses black-and-white pictures every week to illustrate stories from around America and the world in its Sunday travel section, and has a biannual *Sophisticated Traveler* magazine.

Newspapers normally employ staff photographers, but use "stringers" (regular contributors on call) and freelancers as well. General newspaper work gives editorial photographers a tremendous variety of experience; many world-class photojournalists started that way, before going on to freelance magazine and other types of photography. Several young photographers I know started by shooting sport or "paparazzi" pictures on a part time basis. Local papers need lots of local sports pictures, even including coverage of high-school games. Newspapers are always interested in "picture feature stories" in their area. Show your portfolio to the photo editor. If you can come up with a few picture story ideas, you will probably get some work. Some newspapers offer photography internships to young photographers. Inquire if interested. You could also contact the National Press Photographers Association (NPPA) to see if they have any leads.

Advice on sports photography from a non-expert

I often have to photograph sport as part of travel/tourism coverage. I use my usual range of lenses (see Chapter Three) but after taking overall shots, I rely mostly on telephoto-zooms. I always use the widest apertures and fastest shutter speeds. (Specialists use super-fast lenses in the 300-600mm range.) The aim as a rule is to bring your subjects close, separate them from the background, catch peak action, and usually to stop motion. (You can also use slow shutter speeds—try 1/8 and 1/15 and "pan"—move with the action to show motion.) You don't need to be able to ski to do good ski pictures (take cable cars and ski-lifts and walk around to find good vantage points); but to do great ski pictures almost certainly requires at least good skiing skills. In fact, the more you know about any sport the better, because then you can anticipate action. Prefocus on places where you think you will get good shots. Autofocus lenses help sometimes, but not always. Motor-drives help a lot. Shoot a fraction before any peak moment to capture it on film.

Many sports events start in hard noon light, but continue for quite some time, so save film for later in the day when light is more interesting. Shoot high-speed film for all night games. To light sports events is for specialists, getting the lights up high enough is just the beginning. See Jon Falk's *Adventures in Location Lighting* for specifics.

I do not know of any major book on sports photography, but Kodak's *Pocket Guide to Sports Photography* contains many useful hints. Study *Sports Illustrated* magazine or specialist magazines about skiing, yachting, track, horseracing, etc. for a look at what top specialists do.

Chapter 12

Tourism Photography

I am a specialist in tourism photography. For twenty years I traveled around the world as the official photographer for a major tour operator, a contact originally made through my British connections. I have also worked for a big student tour company, and photographed cruises in the Caribbean, Aegean and the Orient, and canal-barge cruises in Europe. I've shot national advertising campaigns for airlines, and promotions for national tourist offices.

Tourism clients often require specific pictures not available as stock. The best need very beautiful pictures to enhance their quality image, so there is nothing compromising about working for tourism. Tourism photography, however, is always commercial and not personal photography. This should not (ever) mean bad or hackneyed photography. What it does mean that you will usually be working to specific guidelines, even to detailed "layouts" (art directors' sketches of what something should look like). You may have to show technicalities, such as hotel rooms or golf course layouts, and you will quite often have to work with professional models.

Requirements for Tourism Photography

The most important single skill for photographing for tourism is to be able to work well with all different kinds of people. It is possible to be a fairly reclusive travel photographer and make a living (you would have to shoot and sell a lot of travel stock landscapes). It is not possible to be a solitary photographer of tourism. You must not only be able to photograph people well, you must never forget that you are very often photographing your client's clients, and never get in the way of their enjoyment. I'm proud of the fact that none of my clients'

clients ever complained about me. I have often asked tourists to pose, occasionally usurping a free day by asking them to return to a locale in better light, and had clients "model" in set-up scenes. All this without payment, except for the odd drink or meal, and they signed model releases (usually limited to the tour company's use). The secret is appearing relaxed, competent, well organized and totally in control while having good rapport with the person running the program, and being pleasant, flexible, polite, up front, quick and patient with the clients on tour, all while bearing in mind the often tight schedules of organized groups. John Lewis Stage, a great people photographer, who shoots the rich and famous and powerful, once told me his magic formula for getting the poses he wants from important people: He always asks the aide, publicist or assistant, etc. "Is it possible...?" (for so-and-so to do so-and-so). I've used the phrase ever since, it works with ordinary subjects too! And my English upbringing taught me to always say "please" and "thank you" and to "sir" and "madam" people at frequent intervals.

How Tours and Cruises are Operated

If you have never taken a tour you might like to know how they work. On arrival, clients rest, and then on the first evening there is an introductory cocktail party (or Captain's cocktail party on ships) where clients dress quite formally. Events proper usually start (early) the next morning.

On bus tours, there is a lot of riding around in a bus, with short breaks for meals and sightseeing en route, and about every third day, a full day or two in one important spot.

On cruises, days at sea usually alternate with days in port.

To do a really good job as a photographer, it is imperative to have your own car, or local transport, because what you need and the group needs are not exactly the same. The tour or cruise always ends with a gala farewell dinner where everybody gets dressed up. (To photograph this well, be there the day before to get acquainted if possible.)

I have found that three days is the perfect amount of time to be with a particular group—one to get to know people, two days to photograph them. I then leave to avoid "upstaging" or taking the limelight away from the tour director. The tour director or cruise host or hostess is your most important ally in this work—be nice to them always!

Working for Tourism Clients

I always ask the tour director/cruise host to introduce me to the clients as the "official photographer" (or photographer on assignment). I always say I'm photographing for the client (or brochure or magazine), and that I will not take anyone's picture without asking them first.

I never, ever take "group shots" to sell on the spot. (There are photographers on ships who do this. Remember Ace in the *Love Boat* TV series?) There are also plenty of group photo specialists at major monuments around the world who bring back prints in an hour. I never promise to send tourism subjects pictures I have taken, but ask them to contact the client's head office for "out-takes" if they are available. I will give away the odd Polaroid print, or take people's picture on their own cameras if requested to do so.

Working With Staff

It is very important on any tourism assignment to remember, and be considerate of, the hard working and not very well paid people who work in the industry. Many depend on tips for a large part of their income. While tour managers are well-paid professionals and colleagues if you are photographing groups, waiters, stewards, drivers, local tour guides and many more should be well-tipped. They are your allies and enjoy the fun and recognition of being photographed. You should explain clearly what you need in advance, respect their need for keeping schedules and be aware of their problems. Be as courteous to them as you are to the clients and of course reward them at the end for their assistance. The amount to tip will vary according to the help they have given; if in doubt, be generous, you may need their help again!

I have learned a lot from professional tour managers in particular. Some of them have become good friends. The thing they are always concerned about is the dynamics and well-being of the group as a whole. Good tour managers do not show the overt favoritism they may feel, especially to clients who are more physically appealing than others. Therefore, when working with a group of tourists for a day or several days, it is important for the photographer not to cause jealousy within the group, and to pay attention to (and even make a point of photographing) the less attractive members of a group, even though you are fairly sure the pictures will not be selected. If a tour leader or manager asks you privately to single out a particular person, couple or group within the group it is almost always for good reason, and you should do it.

The client too is always aware of the market base, and if they do good business with, for instance, older women traveling alone, you must make a point of photographing such clients (or older men) in pleasant situations, and with the tour director. Show friendly people of both sexes, and, where possible, show some younger people having a good time too.

Working With Professional Models

Find professional models through agencies (see the classified phone books again) and through actors' agents, modeling schools, etc.

If you book through a big model agency, be sure that you (and the client) fully understands the financial terms. Top models are usually booked on a "weather permit" basis, which means some part of their fee is payable even if a shoot is cancelled for poor weather. Travel time, make-up time and more may also be charged for.

I often use actors as models, they are usually nice-looking, or interesting, and know how to move, and act, and react, and will work for quite reasonable fees. (You can sometimes find aspiring actors who are willing to model in exchange for pictures. Theater groups are a good place to find them.)

Before you start shooting, always get model releases signed by all paid and unpaid models if you have any intention of marketing the shots.

If you get to the very top of the still photographic tree, and shoot major advertising assignments, or produce stock designed for travel/tourism advertising, you will probably be working with top models, and will probably employ stylists to worry about the "look" of clothing, food, the room or other setting. You may even employ hairdressers and make-up artists. (These specialists run ads in professional photography publications.) You won't have many problems to deal with. Experienced models know how to move, and act, and can work quite well even with inexperienced photographers. Stylists will take care of the "look" of everything.

Working With Non-Professional Models

Most travel photographers, at first anyway, use attractive people who are not professional models, and use a client's clients as models on occasion. They have to learn to do their own styling. Here are a few suggestions:

- Make sure that women don't wear too much make up. If in doubt, less is better. Hairstyles are almost always best simple and natural.

- Men should shave before a shoot, unless a very casual laid-back look is what you and/or the client want.

- You may have to help models to choose clothes, which should be casual to dressy as appropriate, but unfussy. Sportswear, bathing suits, and nice dress clothes may all be useful on the same shoot.

- Clothing colors should usually be rather muted in my opinion—but some other travel photographers disagree with this! Avoid all visible brand names on clothes or shoes.

- Avoid photographing anyone whose body is not superb in shorts or miniskirts, tank tops or bathing suits.

- Have models actually doing something, not just pretending to do it.

- If the subject is a sport, it is essential that the models be at least reasonably proficient at the sport. On a golf course, they must know how to hold the clubs correctly, and how to make real shots. (You can have them do the shots over and over in a certain place if needed.)

- If the models are supposed to be eating, drinking a toast, or jogging, have them really do so (but a bit slower than usual). Shoot a scene over and over again, if necessary, to be sure you have what you want. (I try to make the clients laugh about all this.) Many otherwise good commercial or stock travel/tourism photographs fail because the models are not quite believable. (Partly of course, all of this falls into the area of personal taste.)

- When you include people in pictures of rooms, or at poolside etc. be sure they are not just standing around, or sitting stiffly, pointing, or otherwise looking awkward.

- The best way to get people to relax is to talk to them the whole time you are shooting. I do this with the camera to my eye, but other people work with the camera on a tripod. I never take my eye from the viewfinder, because fleeting gestures can make all the difference to "people" pictures.

- Photograph rooms both with and without people, and have models look towards the camera, or ignore it, as appropriate or as called for in the layout. There are no rules about this. I usually like eye-contact but cover myself by shooting people looking away from the camera also.

Working With Professional Assistants

Professional freelance assistants, almost always to be found in the biggest cities through photographers' associations, ads in the *Photo District News*, photo schools etc. in the United States and Canada and overseas, can be a big help. I usually hire assistants who have their own car or van, who are well-dressed, polite and intelligent.

Assistants are human beings, treat them as such! If an assistant does foul up on a job, or you get very tense (which can happen) and you yell at them, apologize afterwards if humanly possible!

Assistants are paid by the day, and cost more if they are specialists in, say, lighting. (A few lighting assistants know more than some photographers who hire them!) Assistants get overtime after eight hours, extra pay for weekend work, and of course if you use their vehicle, that costs extra too.

You must have Workmen's Compensation Insurance if you use models and assistants. (See also Chapter Fifteen.)

What the Tourism Client Wants in Photographs

There are a few points to keep in mind at all times when you are photographing people for tourism. One is that if they are guests who have paid for the vacation (on a tour, in a hotel or on a cruise), in that tourist's mind you represent the facility's head office. You must never interfere with their enjoyment. If you do, the client will certainly get to hear of it.

When you are photographing a tour group, you will probably be told about any large or small difficulties with the tour, hotel, ship, restaurant or whatever. My way of dealing with that is to say to the guest, very politely, "I'm so sorry to hear about your problem, but I'm only a freelance photographer here and have no influence. Why don't you take it up with the head office?"

An extremely important thing to remember at all times is that no tourism client wants you to show that the client is a part of a herd or crowd. Your photographs should reflect this. People in pairs or congenial small groups is the effect you want to achieve. In the case of an extremely popular tourist site for instance, which can be packed with people during the high season, the best solution is to arrive as soon as it opens, when you usually have a half hour to shoot a few people enjoying the place before the big crowds arrive. This rule applies to beaches, pools, museums, etc. as well as monuments. Failing that, lunchtime or just before closing time are possibilities, though later in the day the site is usually not so neat or clean. In restaurants, clubs, etc. and at festivals, of course, you want a good crowd.

Another rule is that some people who are very willing to have their picture appear in a tour brochure are not willing to sign a model release authorizing unlimited use of their likeness. A release is necessary, or you can't use the image, so a simple limited release is needed. It can even be handwritten by the client if he or she prefers. (See later in this chapter, also see Chapter Thirteen, Travel Stock, and the sample Limited Model Release form in Chapter Twenty.)

The last commandment for tourism photography of places—both landscapes and city scenes—is to remember is that it never, ever rains in a tourism brochure. Probably not even in the rain forest! The late Barry Hicks, chief photographer for the British Tourist Authority (a government body), was for many years a generous mentor of mine. The first thing he taught me was the importance of always waiting for the sun. As there are always plenty of interiors to shoot for tourism, you can do those in poor weather; or you can use the time to scout locations and note the exact spots and angles you want when the weather improves. The sun always comes out eventually, even in England.

Although this is not a commandment, the good photographer of tourism (and of travel in general) always remembers that travel is to some extent the realization of a dream or fantasy for everyone. It is an escape from the responsibilities, pressures and realities of everyday life; it is romantic in both the literal and metaphorical senses of the word. To show ugliness, which exists alongside beauty almost everywhere, is to destroy the dream. One does not have to lie in travel/tourism photography, but merely to omit sometimes. Pollution, and poverty exist almost everywhere, there are overcrowded spots in many countries; they are not what professional travel photography (as opposed to photojournalism) is about, and there is no point in including them in your views.

Capturing the "Dream" on Film

Tourism photography may be for international, national, regional or local advertising or promotion. Tourism assignments are usually shot in color, but may occasionally be shot in black-and-white for newspaper use.

Major tourism brochures often use very high quality photography, but the style is not so important as showing lovely places, attractive people, friendly staff and locals and good weather.

Model Releases and Tourism Clients

Some tourist clients who have paid a lot of money for a trip, cruise or whatever, may not be willing to sign a standard model release, but you must legally have a release to include pictures of people in a tourism brochure, which is a form of advertising or promotion. A limited release, usable only by the particular client, is the answer for this one. Ask your client's legal department to draft one. (A sample, limited "group-tour" release is included in Chapter Twenty.)

Conferences, meetings and parties are usually held in resorts and big hotels, and the organizers usually need good, sharp, clear photographs.

Cruise and tour operators, airlines, car rental companies, large and small hotels, motels and resorts, and even the people who design, construct and furnish new tourism facilities are among possible tourism-related clients who need good photography.

As to expressing mood in your travel photographs, that comes with a great deal of practice, with awareness of light and composition, and with your own sensitivity to your surroundings. Heavy usage of soft filters or other tricks to show romance are clichés and should be avoided. If you feel that a place is romantic and beautiful it probably is, and if you trust your own instincts you will be able to convey that feeling of beauty and romance in your photographs.

A Useful Directory
To pinpoint tourism clients, a good sourcebook is *The Travel Industry Personnel Directory* which lists national, state and regional tourist offices, air and cruise lines, hotel chains, wholesale tour operators and more. I also use it to help plan trips. (See Chapter Ten.)

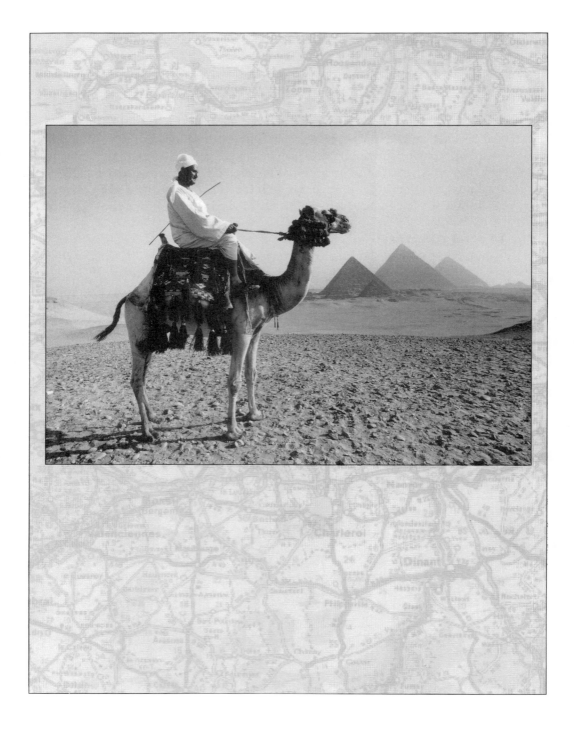

Chapter 13

Travel Photography and the Stock Picture Business

Most photographers who travel, professional and amateur alike, would like to earn recognition and money for all of their hard work and wonder if they too can sell and sell again the pictures they've taken around the country and around the world; make big bucks, get published in the best magazines, or at least cover some of the costs of their travels.

The true answer to these questions is not simple, and nothing like the inspirational "I was a simple housewife in New Hampshire but now I lean out of my kitchen window every few days and shoot the sunsets and I'm making $3,000 a week from my stock photos" school of writing about stock.

I can only say that books and videos which imply that stock shooting and selling is easy are what the British call a lot of codswallop! (There are a few good books on stock, I'll list some I like at the end of this chapter.)

You probably can sell some travel stock pictures, if your work is very good, and if you are prepared to invest a serious amount of time and even money producing stock, and spend time finding clients, and studying how the stock business works. To market any appreciable quantity of stock, you must match your pictures with potential buyers, keep your name in front of them, and keep your stock files up to date. In other words, to make stock a business. (I personally see absolutely no point in shooting stock if you can't make a decent long-term profit.) To make a profit, you must carefully keep track of all costs incurred producing stock, and figure out what you have to charge to cover photographic and administrative expenses, as well as travel expenses. You must then add your profit margin!

To make stock pay, you must have good paperwork and follow-up. (See later in the chapter for more on pricing and paperwork.) You should also be realistic about the stock picture industry.

The Big Business of Stock

Today's stock photo industry is a very big business, grossing millions of dollars world-wide. About 90% of stock pictures today are marketed by midsize to large stock picture agencies (sometimes called picture libraries).

The biggest agencies are getting bigger and more international every year, absorbing smaller agencies and forming international affiliations. (The stock business, like any other, is not without its pitfalls; there have been some insolvencies of stock agencies in the last few years which have caused their contract photographers big problems and loss of income. As I have said, about 90% of stock is leased by agencies, on behalf of individual photographers.

The remaining 10% or so of stock pictures is almost all leased either by individual photographers with large or highly specialized stock files (scientists fall into the latter category) or by places like art museums and zoos who employ staff photographers, and who market photographs of their collections.

How Do Buyers Locate Stock Pictures?

Picture researchers are employed by corporations, design companies, book and magazine publishers, travel companies and anyone else who needs existing (or "stock") pictures. Some picture researchers are on staff, others free lance. All researchers' time is limited, so they usually prefer to go first to places where they can be pretty sure of finding a selection of pictures that will fit their needs. Some stock need lists are circulated to agencies and some photographers directly. Many textbook publishers, for instance, work primarily in this way. Some stock needs/wants are listed by services that send out bulletins regularly by fax, computer modem or the mails. Photographers and others pay to subscribe to these services.

Stock agencies and, most recently, individual stock photographers, can advertise their wares in promotional directories that are distributed free to proven stock buyers. The American Society of Picture Professionals (ASPP) has many picture researchers as members; the society publishes a monthly bulletin that accepts ads from individual photographers. (See also Chapters Ten and Twenty.)

Where Do Stock Agencies Get Pictures?

Agencies get pictures from individual photographers (almost all under contract with the agency), from other owners/copyright holders of specialized collections who don't market their own material, and from their affiliate agencies at home and overseas. Some photographers today specialize only in producing stock; they either set up an organization to market it themselves, or market through a few or many stock agencies, or do both. At least one, probably several, major stock agencies have owners/partners/principals or photographers on salary who produce stock images owned by the agencies.

How Are Stock Pictures Sold?

Stock pictures are almost never "sold" outright. The images are leased, for specific and clearly-defined uses and for limited time periods, either by the agency on behalf of the photographer (who retains ownership of the copyright) or by the photographers themselves.

Some stock images are extremely valuable and are leased many times over. Very rarely, a client wants a "buyout" (outright transfer of the copyright, ownership of the image). They can expect to pay a very high price.

What Travel Subjects Are Best for Stock?

Stock pictures can be on almost any travel or travel-related subject; from Anatolia to Zanzibar, anthropology to zoology, aardvaarks to zebras. New cityscapes, pristine wilderness scenes, tropical beaches and good wildlife shots are in constant demand. The big textbook market uses many pictures from around the world of families, geographic features, industry and agriculture.

What Styles Work Best For Stock?

Stock can be generic (with the "feel" of much television advertising) or quite journalistic/editorial or very personal in style. There are no absolutes. Study some stock directories (see the end of this chapter and Chapter Twenty) to get an idea of what's currently being offered if you wish.

I personally don't think a photographer should alter their style for stock, but others may differ.

What Formats Are Used For Stock?

All formats, with the vast majority at present being color transparencies in the 35mm format. However, people who produce stock directed at the advertising market tell me there is an increasing demand for medium and large-format pictures.

At present, only a few stock agencies handle black-and-white stock, but that may change soon, as black-and-white images are becoming fashionable again, and new four-color electronic scanners can be used to reproduce black-and-white transparencies as well as prints. Color prints (from negatives) are only very rarely used as stock. (See also Chapter Five.)

How Stock Agencies Function

Agencies get almost all their pictures from the photographers who have contracted with the agency which must use its "best efforts" to market the images. The photographer retains the copyright, and normally receives no money until the images are leased and the agency has been paid. (Every rule has exceptions, I know of at least one agency that makes small payments to photographers when a large body of new work is accepted.)

An agency will usually ask its photographers to submit new work, edited to some degree, in 20 slide plastic sheets for easy viewing. The agency's staff then further edits or selects pictures. The "selects" (and the rejects) are then returned to the photographer.

Captioning, and copyright stamping of all selected images, is necessary. There are some computer programs that can be a help with captioning chores (see

Copyright

This is a very short overview. For more, see the books recommended at the end of this chapter.

Why Copyright Ownership Is Basic to Photographers
Only the owner of the copyright of a photograph (usually the creator), or his/her authorized agents, can lease, sell (or even give away) the right to publish it (or of course reproduce any kind of other creative work from it) in any country that is party to the international copyright conventions. In the United States, violation of copyright is a federal offense.

How To Protect Your Copyright in Your Photographs
As a general rule, never sign any so-called "work for-hire" agreement transferring the ownership of your pictures to a client. If a client needs outright ownership of your pictures badly enough, you may be able to negotiate a high fee, acceptable to both, that would make it worth your while for a transfer of copyright. In such a case, I prefer a more limited agreement that allows me to retain at least some interest in my pictures. I have negotiated this type of agreement when photographing clients of a client on tourism shoots for instance (see Chapter Twelve).

If you want to make residual "sales" of any kind, including stock sales, it is crucial to keep control of your copyright, and ownership of your images. Income from residual sales, including stock, can exceed the fee for the original assignment; this is especially true for editorial photographers.

Always Use a Rubber Stamp (or Other Imprint) to Help Protect Copyright
Although it is not technically necessary according to the copyright laws of the United States or Canada, you should physically protect your copyright (and identify ownership) by always marking your name and the international copyright symbol on the back of prints, and on the mount of all slides and transparencies. Get one stamp for prints and large format mounts, and another, small stamp to fit 35mm slide mounts. (You can use a computer program for this, and there are also in or out of camera devices that mark permanently.) The wording should read:

Photograph © copyright 199—
Name of Photographer
All rights reserved.

You can use Roman numerals if you prefer. Some photographers omit the date altogether, fearing to limit the life of the image. Many top photographers use a stamp requiring that a copyright notice be published with the credit line.

later in the chapter). Selected, captioned, copyright-stamped pictures go back to the agency, where they are logged in, sorted, classified and entered on the agency's computer, microfilm or other retrieval system. Finally the pictures are filed, ready for inspection and possible selection by stock clients.

How Do Big Agencies Differ From Small Agencies?
Most big agencies today market with four-color catalogs and outside sales-people. They employ picture researchers and have space where clients can come to view what is available. Most big agencies are affiliated with others, in the United States, Canada and around the world. Some agencies are market-ing with video hookups. CD-Rom discs which store large numbers of pictures are being used by a few agencies. (Stock photographers are currently worry-ing about this trend; there are possibilities for unauthorised use of images.)

Most big agencies have some kind of computerized accounting system, and furnish print-outs giving details of sales to their photographers.

How Stock Agencies Pay, and Get Paid
All agencies, large and small, get a commission from their contract photogra-phers for their services. The commission is negotiable, and usually, but not always, 50%. The commission is deducted from the license fee negotiated with the client on behalf of the photographer. The agency gets paid on or soon after publication of the photograph, and pays the photographer his or her royalty, less deducted commission, according to a schedule negotiated in the photog-rapher/agency contract.

Note: All contracts are negotiable until signed. If you have a valuable pic-ture collection, study the model contract in the *ASMP Stock Picture Hand-book* carefully. My best advice is to consult a competent lawyer before signing any agency contract if you have a major collection of good pictures.

How Individual Photographers Market Stock
Individual photographers whose work is widely published, who are known for a speciality, or promote their work aggressively (or all three) often do very well by marketing their own stock directly. They frequently do the business chores involved with the help of a spouse or partner. Picture buyers contact these photographers directly for their needs.

Professionals who market their own stock have carefully organized and in-dexed files, and they send out promotional mailings, which are often listings of their photographs by subject. Some individual stock photographers now ad-vertise in stock directories. (See later in the chapter.)

Can Part-Time Photographers With a Few Good Pictures Sell Stock?
Some serious amateur or part-time photographers may, if they are very lucky or persistent, sell some stock pictures; the problem is always matching pic-tures to buyers. A few "semi-pro" and part-time photographers I know have sold some stock through the services that advertise stock buyers' wants via fax or computer modem, for a fee. (For more on these, see later in the chapter.)

My Philosophy on Stock

Although I have made quite a bit of money from stock images (more than $150,000 to date) I do not consider myself a stock photographer. I have done a lot of travel magazine assignments, and tourism assignments, a fair amount of industrial and corporate work, and some portrait and still-life photography, both in my studio and out of it. I own the rights to 99.5% of this work. I also make quite a lot of "personal" photographs for pleasure, to record my daughter's growing up years; and some just for art (I hope). Sometimes I take pictures for fun, or to test film, or to experiment and practice new skills—and because life doesn't seem complete to me if I'm not photographing.

Luckily, some of all of these personal pictures sell as stock, so I don't feel I'm squandering money on film. But the bulk of my stock comes from assignments where the travel expenses are paid for by clients.

My stock agency chooses from the pictures I submit which they think suitable (I rarely guess correctly which ones they will pick). I write captions, and stamp my name and copyright on the mounts, and let the agency market them. Gradually, sales have built up, but stock has never been anything but a slow, steady source of income to me.

I don't give my agency everything; I keep my most cherished pictures as "private stock" because I plan to publish a book of favorite pictures one day, and I feel that some images are too personal for stock use. You have very little control, in reality, of your images once they are in an agency's files.

I also use some of my best photographs in different portfolios to solicit assignments. Sometimes a client, or someone who has seen work of mine they like, buys stock from me direct, or I sell a stock image from my portfolio. Sometimes, such stock sales lead to later assignments. I always try to make that happen!

Why I Do Not Shoot Specifically for Stock Very Often

I am a single parent, and do not have much spare cash to finance self-assigned stock picture shoots at this point in time. If I did have it I'm not sure that stock would be what I would want to photograph. The longer I make pictures, the more I am interested in on-going personal projects, with the intent of getting a photography book or books published eventually. Much travel stock is very generic, and I don't have a very generic turn of mind. For instance, I go to London often and I quite often photograph red double-decker buses as graphic objects, because I like them. I don't think I've ever sold one as stock. I just received a nice American Express flyer with their usual world-wide photographic illustrations. One picture was a full frame vertical of the front of a London bus with ads for the musicals "Miss Saigon" and "Les Miserables" on either side of the destination sign on the top deck. I was in London last fall and saw those ads on the fronts of many buses. It just never occurred to me to photograph them, and I am saying this with some regret.

I literally don't seem to have much sense of what appeals to "middle America," and therefore really don't know how to shoot pictures of the kind shown in many current stock catalogs and directories.

But I always shoot plenty of extra film (at my own expense) whenever I travel—of beautiful landscapes, current cityscapes, interesting people in different countries—with stock sales in mind. Happily, some of these pictures do sell as stock. You will have to decide for yourself what approach, if any, to stock is right for you.

Other reasons I am not as enthusiastic about stock as some other photographers are that I very rarely even see any of my stock pictures used, and when I do see them, I am often disappointed. When several photographic styles are mixed, as they often are when different photographers' stock is used together, the patchwork "look" achieved is not as good, in my opinion, as when your work is used alone in a nice layout, nor is it especially creatively satisfying.

But, I most certainly do appreciate the income I get from stock and I respect people who know how to shoot stock well, because I do know quite lot about the stock business. I will try to honestly answer questions I've heard many times about travel stock, as best I can.

What Exactly Is a Stock Travel Picture?

A travel picture that has already been taken. A picture buyer or editor can play it totally safe and view stock images before spending money, as opposed to commissioning pictures on assignment, where of course results depend on the skill of the photographer (as well as weather and a bit of luck) and can never be absolutely predictable.

Travel stock is especially useful to buyers who need pictures out of season— New York in a snowstorm can't be assigned in June for December publication; if a magazine did not assign it the previous winter, searching out stock is the only answer for the art director or picture editor. Ephemeral conditions anywhere, like thunderstorms in New Mexico, or rainbows in Ireland, or the eruptions of volcanoes in Hawaii, cannot be given out as assignments with any guarantee of success.

I will now call a spade a spade and say that stock is used by some clients to save money. They think of stock as the budget solution to a visual problem, and try to get pictures as cheaply as possible. Photographers who value their work (and who want to remain in business) should know how much it costs to produce good stock pictures, and should never sell (or more correctly lease) their stock pictures too cheaply.

Relative beginners should be aware that (after the first time perhaps) the mere "glory" of publication is not reward enough. Be extremely skeptical if someone tells you how reproduction in a small publication will be great for your career! It certainly seems to me that if a picture is good enough to be used, it should be paid for.

I might give a worthy charity or cause permission to reproduce an image of mine free, but I won't ever sell stock at a ridiculously low price. Any photographer, even an amateur in my opinion, deserves a fair payment. (Amateurs who can afford it can always donate the fee to a charity in the country where they took the picture.) Professionals of course need a profit! (For more on this whole subject, see Pricing Stock, later in the chapter.)

What Travel and Other Stock Pictures Usually Sell Well?

Beautiful generic travel images of say, turquoise lagoons, sparkling mountain peaks, pristine landscapes and Western scenery of all kinds, and rolling farmland and cornfields, etc., are often used as backgrounds for ads. Rather idealized travel "people pictures" of, for instance, young lovers on palm-fringed beaches, and silver-haired joggers on golden-leafed New England lanes and the like, are much in demand for travel advertising and promotion.

Travel stock pictures can be, and often are, of very well-known subjects. I've sold plenty of pictures of Big Ben, the Statue of Liberty and the Eiffel Tower for instance, and so has every other travel photographer in all likelihood. (They must of course be very good pictures of Big Ben, not just snapshots.) Familiar tourist icons, if done well, are in demand by the many stock users who don't have the budget to send a photographer on assignment for their brochures. Visit any travel agent and pick up some literature to see what I mean.

Other travel stock staples are model-released "people pictures" of youthful, healthy, good-looking, interesting people of all races, ages, nationalities, religions and social classes; vacationing, studying, working and doing "family" things. Current leisure and "lifestyle" pictures (model released) are always big sellers; excellent nature and animal shots, science, industry, agriculture, business and sports pictures do well too. Major city skyline shots, especially at sunset/dusk, are always needed. Landscapes of all types in all seasons showing geographic and geologic features, as well as ecological and ancient historic subjects, are all classics that don't go out of date.

Obscure "fine art" type pictures, commercial-product shots, and ordinary portraits of the wedding and baby variety are not normally useful as stock.

What Style and Subjects Do Stock Users and Stock Picture Agencies Look For?

Technically, this is an easy question to answer. All stock pictures should be easy to "read," well composed and uncluttered, well lit and correctly exposed, without heavy shadows on faces or other important areas. The center of interest should normally be in sharp focus, with no unintentional blurring of the main subject, and the finer the grain the better, as a rule.

As to specific subject matter, that is not so easy. Pictures should convey emotion and mood, and/or contain information. Photographs that can imply

---

Model Releases

Model releases (legal permissions to publish photographs) are needed for many, not all, stock uses today. Get them signed whenever and wherever you can; model-released pictures (of people, and even recognizable private property) are more valuable than pictures without releases. For much more, read the books listed at the end of this chapter. (Also see the English and foreign-language releases in Chapter Twenty.)

contentment, well-being, strength, security, purity and so on have many potential markets. Pictures that show how people live, work, worship, etc., are widely used by textbooks, as are scientific, nature and geographic shots.

The contemporary "look" of much stock is brightly colored, with an upbeat mood, rather similar to that of much advertising. Fine grain film is preferred. Some stock specialists are now shooting medium format to make their work stand out; I think that great pictures stand out in any format.

Where Should a Travel Photographer
Go to Shoot Stock That Will Sell?

I have met a few amateur travel photographers who seem to think that just by going anywhere overseas and shooting a lot of film, they will sell a lot of stock pictures. Successful photographers who shoot professionally for stock know better, and are quite selective—they have to be, travel and film is very expensive. They tend to specialize, and carve special niches for themselves in stock.

You will have to decide what you want your niche to be. Some photographers sell stock that is mostly a by-product of assignments, like me. (My stock specialty if I have one, is famous tourist spots.)

As to place, further ahead than next year, "hot" destinations are hard to predict. (And constantly changing world events could upset any predictions.) One photographer I know of reads *The Wall Street Journal* regularly for leads to new travel stories—if the financial writers like a place, he reckons that tourism will soon take off. But it's safe to suggest avoiding areas of war, famine and pestilence, civil unrest (all the bailiwick of the photojournalist) and anywhere that everybody with a camera goes to.

I love Venice for instance, it is one of the wonders of the world; go there to see and enjoy it by all means, just don't count on selling stock pictures of the city because there are so many, many pictures of it already out there. I have been to Venice about twenty times, taken hundreds, if not thousands of pictures of it (some I think are beautiful) and have only sold three or four.

But I went Macchu Picchu only once, for one day, and the pictures have sold again and again. However, check with the U.S. State Department, or Canadian Department of External Affairs, if unsure of the political climate in any unfamiliar foreign destination. At the time of this writing, there is a U.S. State Department travel advisory (warning) on travel in Peru. (See also Chapters Fifteen and Seventeen.)

Where to Start Shooting Travel Stock

I would suggest that anyone planning to build a travel stock file now specialize in less traveled regions, smaller countries, and places where there are not too many top local photographers. Anywhere pleasant that you have special access to is a very good bet. Anywhere warm and lovely by a not too crowded ocean, anywhere green and peaceful and beautiful, anywhere that's real wilderness might also be good for starters.

People are enjoying more short, active vacations than they did in the slower-paced past, like the '60's, when just seeing a new place was still sufficient.

Are Model Releases Always Needed to Sell Travel Stock?

The question of releases is tough for travel photographers. In today's litigious climate, get releases of people whenever you can. Model releases make all pictures more valuable.

Many of the biggest stock agencies today will only accept released "people" pictures because then they can be used for advertising and promotion, and on travel magazine covers (which are used to advertise/promote the publication).

Today, even some textbook publishers are asking for releases.

Stock images used for editorial (story or article) illustration inside a book or magazine, or for other purely editorial uses (like educational audio/visuals), do not normally need releases.

Current news pictures are protected in the United States by the First Amendment to the Constitution, but just what constitutes other purely editorial use is sometimes blurry, so get releases whenever you can if you want to sell stock.

Privacy laws in other countries, including Canada, vary. If you are making important stock pictures using paid or unpaid models, get a release.

To sum up, professionals should get releases wherever possible.

If you are doing a job, pay the models a fee for the release, and bill the client. On a stock shoot, even using unpaid models, if you are investing a lot of money on film, get "short form" model releases before you photograph people, and trade the releases for pictures. (Examples of these in English and a number of other languages, which you may copy and use, are included in Chapter Twenty.)

If you photograph people in remote places, where they are very unlikely to ever see their likenesses reproduced, you are probably safe even if you don't get a release. But if you expect to make money from the images, in my opinion you should give your models pictures, gifts, or money in recompense. It's exploitation otherwise.

Recognizable pictures of pets and private property must always have releases for advertising use in the United States and Canada and some other countries.

If people are not recognizable, and if a pet or property is not recognizable, you do not need a release.

Good Stock Sellers

Pictures of rafting down the Colorado, hiking in the Himalayas, scuba diving, snorkeling and shell collecting off the Virgin Islands, Great Barrier Reef or Costa Rica will probably all sell. These and other pictures of people enjoying leisure should do well, especially if you can get model releases.

Classic (and long lasting) landscape stock pictures are of mountains, water of all kinds, deserts, bountiful agricultural land, the rainforests of the world and pristine snowscenes. Nature pictures are ever popular.

Excellent pictures of the world's most historic buildings and monuments, like the Pyramids or Stonehenge, geographic features like the Grand Canyon or the Rock of Gibraltar are always in demand and never go out of date, because they are symbols—of permanence, mystery, strength, or man's insignificance for instance—as well as great travel destinations.

Keep a Watch on Trends

Follow current news for subjects that are "hot" and those that are definitely not. Travel shots of the Middle East are not doing well at the time of writing!

Foreign tourism to the United States, especially the west, and most recently to "mid-America"—including Iowa, Kansas, Kentucky and Nebraska—is booming according to a recent front-page story in *The New York Times*. Alaska and Hawaii, and Canada's west coast and Maritime Provinces are "hot" too. U.S. and Canadian tourists are visiting seaside and cultural areas of Mexico, and just about everywhere in the Caribbean in big numbers. Australia and New Zealand are definitely "in." In fact, I'm sure that troubled world conditions will result in the expansion of tourism to all these places.

Golf resorts and golfing holidays are big. Japanese life in all aspects is selling well, especially for textbooks. Eastern European travel scenes are still in demand.

By the time this book is printed, Western European pictures should be selling again after a weak period (because of unfavorable exchange rates with the American dollar among other things). Europe is currently in the news, because of its movement towards a closer economic union and a reduction of national barriers. The 1992 Olympics mean a need for pictures of Spain (especially Barcelona), and the Haute Savoie region of France. Euro Disneyland, at Marne-la-Vallée just east of Paris, opens in April 1992.

Most stock pictures of all these things were taken well ahead of time by photographers who planned carefully.

I've met one photographer who is seriously shooting Atlanta stock now, in preparation for the 1996 Olympics!

If You Work Closely With a Stock Agent

Good agents can be very helpful in identifying needed subjects. For those that wish it, they will often make specific recommendations. But, I've never heard of an agent who would guarantee sales from any stock shoot. If they do, then it's an assignment, not stock.

Who Shoots Stock Pictures?

Most professional travel/location photographers must shoot assignments as well as stock to earn a living. Some well-established, well-financed travel photographers also take a lot of stock pictures.

A few photographers who are in constant touch with the needs of the stock-picture marketplace function quite like advertising illustrators, or TV or even movie-production companies. They finance big stock "shoots" and travel to special locations.

East Africa and the Caribbean are popular with travel stock specialists because animal pictures and tropical beach scenes are always in demand. These big-time stock photographers often travel with assistants, professional models, stylists and more.

Some stock agencies have salaried or contract photographers that produce pictures according to current demand.

A moderate number of successful stock photographers combine their shooting with a related business or profession; they include scientists, naturalists, airline personnel and a few photographer/writers who can of course produce complete features for publication.

Use your Special Skills, Knowledge or Access to Shoot Stock Successfully

I strongly suggest that you incorporate your "strengths" into your stock shooting. Successful photographer Michal Heron, for example, specializes in people and family life. She has built up contacts with Native Americans over many years, and does very well with her stock pictures of their festivals, home life and ceremonies. Busy travel photographer Robert Rattner shoots a lot of nature and underwater pictures, and he also has good friends in the English Channel Islands, and spends quite a bit of time there. (These islands are a handy jumping-off spot for both Britain and France, where Bob does a lot of shooting.) My own contacts in England mean that I can stay there free, or at low cost, and I can spend enough time there to go to places the average tourist never sees.

Think about what and where you know best, and build your stock taking on these things.

Who Uses Stock?

The market for stock today is very large and apparently still growing. But, possibly because of the large number of photographers and agencies competing for this business, stock prices at present are static at best.

Almost all magazines use at least some stock; so do advertising agencies, publishers and graphic design firms. Corporations and business organizations of all kinds who publish annual reports, in-house magazines and brochures; and use audio-visual sales aids are also big stock customers. The high school textbook market is the biggest and best-paying book market, and textbook publishers constantly need released pictures of nice-looking, believable people; especially school-age children, teens, intergenerational families and the handicapped, in both America and the rest of the world. Travel shots showing how people live in other countries or regions are more useful than pictures of monuments for this market.

Book publishers use pictures illustrating scientific subjects like biology and geology, and scenes that show people talking for language texts. Newspapers, trade (consumer) books, greeting card publishers, catalogs, travel wholesalers and resorts are among quite frequent stock users also.

How to Start Marketing Stock

You can work with a stock agency (see later in the chapter for how to locate major agencies) or promote your own stock, or do both.

I do both, and try to turn stock sales I make directly into future assignments.

To market your own stock, you will need as a minimum:

- Good, clearly identified and accurately captioned pictures, that are classified or filed so that you can locate them easily.

- A list to mail out summarizing the pictures you have. (Stock lists can be a simple typed sheet of the main subjects of the pictures you have in your file, though today they are usually more elaborate cross-referenced computerized lists.

- A mailing list of people who use your kind of stock. (See also Chapter Ten.)

- Persistence, enthusiasm, energy and patience.

- A good book or two about the business of stock (see recommendations at the end of this chapter.)

Commercial Sources of Stock Users

Commercial mailing lists of picture buyers are available for a fee, some list brokers advertise in the *Photo District News* (see Chapter Two). There are several fax/computer network services that list stock wants for a subscription fee. Approach such services with a mild degree of caution. While most are legitimate and provide plenty of leads (many of which are low-paying), monthly fees for these services are quite high (currently, in the range of about $25 to $65) and there may also be sign-up charges. You will need a fax machine or computer modem. Hundreds, perhaps thousands of people (and some stock agencies) subscribe to these services, so you will have a lot of competition for specific picture calls.

Suggestion: negotiate with a service for a reduced sign-up fee or a trial period, or both. If you are thinking about marketing stock, and producing it, you may find the want-list services useful as a research tool, to learn what buyers are looking for, and to find names to add to your promotional mailing list (see also Chapter Ten). If you do this, the money for such a service will not be wasted, even if it doesn't generate a lot of stock sales.

I know four professional or part-time professional photographers who subscribe, or have subscribed, to PhotoSource International, an established stock-want listing service in Wisconsin. All have made some sales from leads provided by the service. None have made a lot of sales. (See also later in the chapter.)

Paperwork and the Business Side of Stock
If you want to deduct your stock expenses for tax purposes, keep careful records of what you spend producing and marketing it. In addition to the obvious costs of making stock pictures (film, labs, dupes, props, assistance, travel, camera repairs, etc.), telephone, computer network, fax and packing and Federal Express and mailing costs for submissions to potential users are high. The IRS will want to see a profit within three to five years, and substantial evidence of business activity before that.

Record everything you spend, keep lists of who you contact and, of course, keep meticulous records of all stock submissions and returns. Learn about your state's sales-tax laws and regulations. Send out all invoices promptly.

A sample stock submission form, and a sample stock invoice follow.

Model release forms for travel photographers, in English and foreign languages, are included in Chapter Twenty, and may be photocopied if you wish.

There is much, much more detail about stock paperwork in ASMP's *Stock Photo Handbook*, and in *How to Shoot Stock Photos That Sell* by Michal Heron. (See also later in the chapter, and Chapter Twenty).

Computer "Stock Photo Management" Programs
There are several programs for Mac and IBM users advertised in the *Photo District News*. I don't use one because I don't market stock extensively myself.

How Seriously Should a Professional
Travel Photographer Take Stock Sales?
Very seriously indeed. If you have a good stock file, and take care of it, the income is fairly stable, and comes in regularly. It is a big help for free lancers, including myself, whose income fluctuates, but whose bills must be paid each month. It takes time and continuous work, though, to build and maintain a good stock file. Travel photographers must keep some stock images current (others are classic) because city skylines, cars, advertising and theater signs, fashions and even hairstyles change. When I do an assignment in an interesting city or town, I almost always take some skyline and downtown pictures (at my own expense of course), and I look out for situations that lend themselves to stock shooting. It's sometimes worth staying a few extra days at your own expense to get good stock coverage of an important place.

SAMPLE STOCK PICTURE DELIVERY MEMO:

Photographer's Letterhead

Att: Mr George Photobuyer
Worthy Tool Company
25 Greanleaf Avenue
Nicetown, IN 12345

Date:

Notice: The pictures listed below are submitted, at your request, for examination only. They may not be reproduced, duplicated, photocopied, electronically scanned, digitalized, stored on disc or used as artist or photographer reference without a signed licensing agreement from photographer or his (her) agent. The client agrees not to project these valuable images, or expose them to sunlight, heat or dust, or to subject them to damp or humid conditions. Client (named above) is responsible for loss or damage from moment of receipt until returned to the photographer.

The pictures may be examined free for two weeks *(or period of your choice)*. After two weeks a holding fee of $1 *(or other fee)* per picture per day will be charged, unless noted to the contrary below.

Please check count and acknowledge receipt of images by signing below. After five days, count will be assumed correct, and pictures acceptable for reproduction.

QUANTITY	SUBJECT	FORMAT	COLOR/B&W	AGREED VALUE
1	*Basalt Rocks at Giant's Causeway Northern Ireland, UK	35mm vert	color	$2,500
2	Andes Mts, aerial views, Chile	35mm vert	color	$1,500 each
1	Dents du Midi Mts, France; snow	35mm vert	color	$1,500 each
1	*Rock of Gibraltar, sunset, backlit	35mm vert	color	$4,000
1	Foothills and Himalayas, Gulmarg	35mm vert	color	$1,500
2	Vertical faces, Shawangunk Mts, NY	35mm vert	color	$1,500 each

As per our agreement, a research fee of $60 *(other amount)* will be charged if no images are used. This fee is deductible from license fees of over $500.00.
*Denotes especially valuable image, as per our telephone agreement.

Return: This submission is conditioned on the return of all items, undamaged, unaltered and unretouched.

Client (named above) assumes all risks for the items listed from the time of receipt by client to the time of receipt by photographer, or his (her) agent.

Your carrier loss or damage: Reimbursement for loss/damage shall be amounts(s) indicated indicated above. Do demand a receipt from your carrier, and insure shipment.

Receipt acknowledged for client: (Signed)_____Date:_____

SAMPLE STOCK PICTURE LICENSING AGREEMENT:

Photographer's Letterhead

Date:
Client Purchase Order #
My Invoice #

Att: Mr. George Artbuyer
Worthy Tool Company
25 Greenleaf Avenue
Nicetown, IN 12345

LICENSE TO REPRODUCE THE FOLLOWING ORIGINAL COPYRIGHTED PHOTOGRAPH(S) SUBJECT TO THE CONDITIONS LISTED BELOW AND ON THE REVERSE OF THIS INVOICE:

Terms and Conditions: Client assumes all responsibility for loss or damage to this original transparency until it is returned to the photographer. The value of the image for insurance purposes is: $4,000.00. Payment of licensing fee shall be made within 30 days of the receipt of this invoice, or upon publication, whichever is sooner. 1 1/2% interest per month will be charged on unpaid balance. Photographer's name and copyright notice shall be reproduced in no less than 7 point type, adjacent to the image, in the form prescribed on the reverse.

(Note: A well accepted valuation standard in the industry, that has stood up to court challenges, is $1,500 per good-quality image. In this case I have valued the excellent shot at $4,000 because it has sold before, and has future sales potential. Different photographers have differing requirements about publication of copyright notices/credit line, but by asking for them, your copyright is protected.)

Picture is described as follows: One vertical 35mm original Kodachrome color transparency: The Rock of Gibraltar at Sunset, # SM 24251. *(Use a file number.)* Photograph is not model released.

Rights Granted: Use is limited to front cover of catalog for drilling tools, size 8x10", 20 pages, print run 50,000, distributed in the United States of America only.

(Note: Be as specific as possible; the ASMP Stock Picture Handbook and other recommended books detail how to negotiate stock prices for advertising, annual reports, packaging, greeting cards, TV, etc. Specify a time-limit, size limit, additional usage rights (use on the drill packaging for instance) and foreign language uses if applicable [An additional fee (often 50%) may be charged for re-use in a Japanese-language version of the catalog, for instance.] For books and magazines, the print run as well as the size the picture is reproduced are among factors determining the price.)

LICENSING FEE: $850.00

No New York State Sales Tax due for Indiana (out of state) delivery.
(Note: Consult an accountant for details of sales tax laws.)

Thank you.

(Signed) Phantastic Photographer
(or Rosemary Representative)

Plan Your Stock Shooting Very Carefully

Travel can cost big money these days, so if you are going to totally finance stock-shooting trips yourself, you must have a well thought out business plan to maximize your returns. You might specialize in one country that you really love. (Even much-visited places have wonderful spots where photographers rarely go, and pictures showing the daily life, industry and geography may sell well for textbooks). Be sure and go to areas that are not overphotographed.

To specialize in in-depth coverage of a major country, concentrate on subjects that are important or interesting to you. Focus on national parks, religious or historic sites, or the life of any group within the country. That way, you will enjoy your stock shooting, and may come to have a serious body of work that will lead to assignments or even a book, later on. If you persist, you should soon become known as a person to call for images of that place.

For myself, being English originally, and because I love the country, I will go on photographing the British Isles (though the many excellent photographers who live there make the competition stiff). I am now photographing the modern, racially diverse Britain—new developments such as the enormous Docklands project in London's East End. I also photograph literary and artistic Britain, when I get a chance.

I'm also currently expanding my United States coverage, because it's a "hot" destination and because I love the West especially, and haven't traveled there as much as I would like to. Of course I know there are some great western landscape photographers working today—too many to list them all actually—but I hope that my specialty of photographing people in their environment won't compete too directly with the likes of David Muench.

I have already confessed, though, that I don't have the mind of a true "travel stock" photographer. I can't think in terms of the boy/girl on the beach or happy senior citizens at play featured in so many stock catalogs. Why? It's hard to put into words. Those pictures don't seem worthwhile to me I guess, or perhaps I just don't have the illustration talent needed to make them ring true.

I personally think every ambitious or aspiring travel photographer should aim first and foremost to do as many assignments as possible. You get stimulating input from good art directors, picture editors and even writers, as well as immediate feedback, creative gratification and recognition, and most importantly, money that pays the rent next month, not two or three years down the road!

The ASMP Stock Picture Handbook

A "must" for anyone who is serious about stock is The American Society of Magazine Photographers *Stock Photography Handbook*. It the definitive source of information about all aspects of the stock business, including marketing your own stock, working with stock agencies, and resolving problems. It includes a prototype photographer/agency contract from the photographer's point of view, and many different sample stock forms and model release forms. Most importantly, it contains detailed information on necessary paperwork, how to figure out what it actually costs to produce stock, and how to arrive at fair prices for various stock uses.

Pricing Stock

There are no set, or officially recommended prices for stock pictures. That would be against United States law and many other countries' laws.

Professional photographers and stock agencies obviously must and do charge high enough prices to make a decent profit. Stock prices are negotiated (very carefully) according to use. The same picture used 1/4 page small in a textbook or very large on a 36-sheet advertising billboard would command very different prices, for instance.

To me, it is elementary common sense for any good photographer—including part-timers, photography students or starting professionals—to only lease stock for a fair price.

At one time the ASMP published specific stock price guidelines, based on surveys of its members. (This was discontinued because of the difficulty and cost of keeping the surveys constantly updated.)

A book that gives reasonably current and very specific stock price guidelines is *Negotiating Stock Photo Prices* by Jim Pickerell, a well-known stock specialist. If you are really serious about marketing your stock, this book is a "must" investment. It is available by mail order only for $17.95 plus shipping from Pickerell Marketing. (See below.)

How I Price Stock

To be specific about my pricing, I market directly only to a very few customers who contact me. They are advertising agencies, tourist companies and magazines who know me and my work. I never lease any of my "private stock" of selected best pictures for any use whatever for less than $300; some fees are considerably higher.

My stock agency leases my work to companies I do not have the time or inclination to market to on my own, or who I would never be able to locate on my own. Most of my agency "sales" are for editorial reproduction, and are in the $150-$500 range (I have had a few advertising sales for considerably more than that, but they are the exception. (For much more detail, see the publications recommended at the end of the chapter.)

Stock Newsletters

Jim Pickerell, who knows a great deal about stock, publishes a newsletter called *Taking Stock,* six times a year. For a sample and details write Suite A, 110 Frederick Avenue, Rockville MD 20850. Phone (301) 251-0720.

The *Stock Photo Report* is a well-regarded monthly newsletter edited by British photographer Brian Seed, who was a cofounder of the Click agency in Chicago (now owned by Tony Stone Worldwide, a big London stock agency). This report costs $60 to $195 a year depending on services/features chosen. Get a sample copy, details and subscriptions from 7432 Lamon Avenue, Skokie, IL 60077. Phone (708) 677-7887; fax (708) 677-7891.

Fax/Modem Stock Want Services

PhotoSource International is a well-established stock want list service, using fax, computer modem or the mails. They have a daily, weekly or monthly service. Contact Ron Engh at Pine Lake Farm, Osceola, WI 54020. Phone: (715) 248-3800; fax (715) 248-7394. They will send a free sample listing and prices on request.

Stock Catalogs and Directories

Most big stock agencies publish catalogs showing some of the pictures they have on file. (They are for distribution to stock users.) If you want to study a couple to get an idea of styles, request them from stock agencies you hope to be associated with. There may be a small charge.

Direct Stock is a catalog which was published for the first time in fall 1991 It is a medium for individual photographers to advertise their stock. It is distributed free to art directors, picture editors and other stock buyers. Price per page starts at around $2,000. Reprints for self-promotion are available. For more information contact Arie Kopelman (also the publisher of the New York Gold Book directory). Reach Direct Stock at 10 East 21st Street (14th Floor) New York, NY 10010. Phone (212) 979-6560.

The *Stock Workbook* is a thick catalog of stock pictures (mostly ads placed by stock agencies).

Black Book Stock is similar. It is published by the same people as *The Creative Black Book*. Some individual photographers advertise here. You can buy these big directories in major photo stores, or study them in libraries. (See also Chapter Ten.)

Do Stock Agencies and Clients Accept Duplicates (Dupes) of Slides?

Yes, if they really want the pictures, no if they can get originals.

More and more photographers are having "dupes" made to protect the fragile originals, especially as new electronic scanners tear the corners of 35mm slides rather too easily. (Two of my pictures were torn by scanners this year, I got reimbursement, but was still sorry to lose the images.

A very good lab that specializes in 70mm dupes from 35mm originals is A & I Color, 933 North Highland Avenue, Los Angeles, CA 90038. Phone (800) 544-3016.

How To Locate Stock Picture Agencies

The Picture Agency Council of America (PACA) publishes a directory that lists its approximately 100 stock agency members' specialties and wants. The directory is often given away free at major photo shows, and is available for $5 from any member agency, or from the PACA president, currently Marty Loken, c/o Allstock Agency, 222 Dexter Avenue, North Seattle WA 98109. Phone (206) 282-8116; fax (206) 286-8502.

Recommended Reading on Stock

The *ASMP Stock Picture Handbook* (mentioned above) is the business "must" on this subject; it costs $29.95 plus $3 shipping, order from 419 Park Avenue South, New York, NY 10016. Phone (212) 889-9144; fax (212) 779-9446.

How to Shoot Stock Pictures That Sell by Michal Heron (a good friend of mine and a successful assignment and stock photographer) is a detailed, explicit, and clear-eyed manual for making money with stock pictures. Michal specializes in people photography for book publishers. An adjunct is her collection of stock forms (both are put out by my own publisher).

Negotiating Stock Photo Prices by Jim Pickerell (see earlier in the chapter).

One of the earliest books that got people enthused about stock was *You Can Sell Your Pictures* by Henry Scanlon, a brilliant salesman and a cofounder of the successful Comstock picture agency. It has a very positive outlook, an especially good chapter on negotiating prices, and gives the stock agency viewpoint well. Read it in libraries if you can't locate a copy in used bookstores; it was published in 1980.

Chapter 14

Location
Photography

I have already said that travel photography is very competitive and not extremely well paid. Many travel photographers, including myself, also do some location photography, because the same kind of seeing, thinking and skills and equipment are called for when you work for organizations, corporations, large and small business; in factories, offices, schools, hospitals, banks, warehouses, chemical plants, television studios, banquet halls, farms, mines, supermarkets and many other places in cities, towns, villages, suburbs, industrial parks and the remotest country areas.

I have photographed on the deck of an oil tanker, in the clean room of a pharmaceutical factory, on top of a coal slurry conveyor belt and an airport control tower, in hospital maternity wards and operating rooms, college classrooms, and numerous conference rooms, law offices and schools, among other places.

I've been to Perth Amboy, Port Elizabeth and Paulsboro, New Jersey for refineries and docks for an annual report; Arlington, Virginia for an insurance company audio visual; and Columbus, Indiana to photograph the architecture of a whole small city for a magazine. In Montreal the shoot was for an American bank, in Branford, Connecticut a hospice for advanced cancer patients. I went to Oyster Bay, New York to photograph a community constructing an adventure playground (magazine); Sandia, New Mexico to a solar heating research facility (corporate brochure); and San Diego, California (once to do an audio-visual for a company under contract to the United States Army, another time to shoot in a nuclear-research facility). In New York I have photographed in posh corporate offices, in the subways (officially, you need a permit from the NYC Transit Authority in Brooklyn), on tugboats and trucks and backstage at the circus, many theaters, and television programs.

So, location photography is varied and interesting. It is also often educational, challenging, hard work, and fun. It is also well paid. Freelance fees range from about $800 daily for average industrial jobs to several thousands of dollars a day on the level of top-name annual report specialists.

Location photography can be cold (a lot of annual report work is done outdoors in winter). It can be frustrating (there's often a lot of waiting around because to get your pictures you can rarely interrupt or disrupt whatever is going on). Location photography calls for much tact. The people you will be working with have their own jobs to do, because (however well-prepared the high-up powers say they have prepared for your coming) you are only an interruption of the local meeting, production run, safety inspection or whatever. Branch offices are often not well-prepared for the arrival of a photographer in their midst, so you have to convince the people there to help you. Woe betide you if you don't.

Skills Needed For Location Photography

The single thing that almost all location shoots have in common is difficult to terrible lighting conditions. For instance, hospital operating rooms are normally lit with average room-level fluorescent light on the ceiling, which would call for some form of magenta filtration depending on the film you are using. But a circle of very high powered tungsten lights shines on the area where the doctors and nurses are working. Do you shoot tungsten or daylight film? Filtered or unfiltered? (I usually go with unfiltered daylight film.) You also have a contrast problem, because the light-to-dark ratio may be more than five to one, which is all that transparency film can comfortably handle. Hospital safety regulations, which are highly understandable, have always prevented me from adding any of my own lighting. It is possible that ABC, CBS or NBC could get a dispensation. I've never been able to.

While you usually can light most other location situations, the areas to be covered are often very large. If you light them completely, which is certainly possible, it calls for a lot of knowledge, equipment and assistance. I almost always prefer to combine available with added light, using rather long exposures for the background area if necessary. I light the important areas with several flash units, used combined or separately or both; or, I use strobe lights, whichever seems best for the situation. I use daylight film with an appropriate filter on the lens, and opposite colored gels on the lights to bring the color into balance. (See Gels, Chapter Five; and Photographic Lighting, Chapter Seven.)

Working With People on a Location Shoot

A factor that is crucial on most location assignments is to be able to motivate people. Whether it's getting on with the teacher whose class you are inevitably interrupting (or having no nonsense with her students who all seem to think they are on America's Funniest Home Videos), or coaxing shy, reluctant or uncooperative production line workers, it's the location photographer's job to sort out the people problems, get subjects to pose, and bring home good pictures for the client. Time spent getting friendly with people before the shoot is almost never wasted. And don't forget to say "thank you" afterwards (send prints if you have promised them) and to take away any photographic debris.

If you are shooting for an annual report you will have had meetings (probably quite a few meetings), usually with the graphic design firm that is handling the report but also the client's representative—often the Public Affairs Director (or similar title)—about the situations that must be covered. If it is a large corporation with many locations, travel must be scheduled efficiently to avoid retracing steps unnecessarily, and also to coordinate with any irregularly scheduled or seasonal events that the client wants to include in the report. Stockholders meetings, board of directors meetings and the like call for you to dress well; whereas if you are climbing about on a "cat cracker" (catalytic cracker) in an oil refinery in January you must be warm and well protected in layers of clothes that can survive the odd dab of oil.

When you are on any industrial location shoot, you will almost certainly be accompanied by a member of the company's staff. Be very, very nice to this person. They can make or break your shoot. Be understanding about their problems; they have probably been take away from their regular job as a safety engineer, PR assistant, etc. to help you. While it may be a fun break from routine, they will have to catch up on their normal work later. So show appreciation.

Group and Celebrity Portraits

A very frequent business/corporate assignment is the group portrait. Plan the shoot and test film in advance, set up lighting well before your subjects assemble. It is easy to arrange groups pleasingly if everyone is of the same importance or rank—as in "team" pictures. Just arrange people by height and space them. If necessary use stairs, benches or even ladders or scaffolding to stagger the height with large groups. When photographing groups of important people, it is of course imperative that they be placed according to rank, with the company president, chief designer or other principal very prominent. Sometimes, this person can sit down when others stand. It is especially important to have everything well-organized when you photograph a big businessman, prominent politician, or other "star"—your time with them may be very limited.

If you are shooting a real star, they are usually great subjects, but be sure and see their last movie, TV show or play before you meet them! No actor is ever tired of talking about themselves. (I say this from long personal experience.)

Neil Selkirk, the top portrait and annual report photographer, who works with the political and business elite around the world, always does meticulous research before he shoots important people, especially groups. From aides, he gets data on rankings, and heights, and lights the location using "stand-ins" (substitutes). He marks seating or standing positions with name tapes. Everything is prepared for assembling everyone and shooting immediately and quickly when the group arrives.

Business Visas and "Carnets"

All of the major photography shoots that I have done overseas have been for travel/tourism clients. Their offices or representatives handle any necessary formalities and permissions for me. I use midprice range 35mm equipment (see Chapter Three) and in most cases I have had absolutely no problem with customs anywhere. When traveling on my own, I travel as a tourist whenever possible.

A business visa may, however, be needed to do a big shoot. Get details from travel agents, consulates or visa services. (Find visa services in classified phone books.) Importing a lot of valuable camera and strobe equipment may be a problem too, especially to countries where cameras are highly taxed and/or hard to get. A Carnet is an official document, backed by a bond, that is recognized by many governments. Carnets are used mostly by commercial travellers who import, for instance, samples of expensive merchandise to international trade fairs, and then re-export them. Photographers who travel overseas with a lot of expensive/new-looking equipment should get a Carnet also. It will you save having to post a cash bond when entering Canada, for instance. (Note that United States regulations for Canadian photographers are not quite so strict; see Chapter Seventeen.)

Some countries do not recognize the Carnet, and special arrangements should be made through consular/tourism officials to import equipment to those places. A bond or photography fee (or both) may have to be paid.

The number one, two and three rules for dealing with customs officials everywhere are: make and carry a detailed list of everything, with serial numbers. Carry and show letters of assignment. Get all paperwork stamped and signed by customs/other government officials. (See also Chapter Fifteen.)

Inquire of U.S./Canadian Customs Offices (in major cities and at ports of entry) as to where you can get a Carnet and insurance bond. See classified phone books to find customs brokers.

For detailed information on Carnets and where to obtain them, see the invaluable *Location Photographer's Handbook* by Ken Haas, recommended later in the chapter.

Shooting for Audio/Visuals and Public Relations

I have made audio/visuals for banks, furniture manufacturers, insurance companies, textbook publishers, tourist public relations and the United States Army and Postal Service, among others. The cardinal rule with A/V's is to shoot only horizontals. Audio/visual assignments (some are made with stills even now despite camcorders) as a rule call for working from the producer's storyboard and usually you rush from one situation to the next. If you can, try to persuade the producer that slowing things down a bit will ultimately get better results. However, be prepared for a lot of pressure on such assignments. Most of the audio/visuals I have worked on have been for corporate or business clients, but travel clients use them too.

Most public relations audio/visuals (and other PR assignments I have worked on) are low budget, and the time to shoot is limited.

Lighting Audio/Visuals
Audio visuals are the one type of assignment where I usually light with small quartz video lights (see Chapter Seven) because they are very quick to set up and knock down. I shoot tungsten film with these lights (see Chapter Five). Also, the continuous light is easy on your subjects. Of course, if the subject matter is very fast-moving, then you must use multiple flash set-ups, or strobes (again see Chapter Seven).

Location Shooting With Changing Light Conditions
When you are shooting where the light is constantly changing, in such places as rock concerts; theaters; dance, opera, or other auditoriums; or in welding shops, smelting mills and so on; the program camera comes into its own. You are often not allowed to use (or are not near enough to use) flash, so load with fast film (400 ISO or higher) and fire away. The program exposures under difficult, fast-changing light conditions will be good to excellent in most cases, better than if you used manual exposure with spot meter readings. I prefer shooting on S (shutter priority) setting with a program camera, it gives me most creative control.

Hazards and Legalities of Industrial Location Shooting
Quite often location shooting is done under difficult or even somewhat hazardous conditions. I once got very sick (with severe vomiting and diarrhea) after spending two days photographing a refinery in Venezuela, because of an allergic reaction to petroleum vapor ingested through the skin of my uncov-

---

Things You Should Never Do on Location

Warning: never, ever touch any piece of the client's machinery or equipment in an industrial facility, and don't ever plug in a light or even switch one on or off without permission. You could cause problems with union personnel, or create a safety hazard.

If you do run into any serious problem, have or cause an accident or damage, consult a lawyer immediately. You should also carry liability insurance that protects you, in case an action or piece of equipment of yours injures someone, or damages something, while you are photographing. Workmen's Compensation Insurance is necessary if you hire assistants. For detailed information consult the brokers of photography insurance mentioned in Chapter Fifteen, or your own broker. You may also wish to read *Selling Your Photography: The Complete Marketing, Business and Legal Guide* by Arie Kopelman and Tad Crawford.

---

ered arms and legs. You will normally be asked by the client to sign a release from liability when shooting industrial pictures. You may not be able to do the job unless you do sign a release, and you may choose to do so. Obviously, be very cautious always, and obey all safety regulations about hard hats and shoes, protective goggles and earplugs.

Note: If you do a lot of location shooting, you should certainly carry insurance. (See later in the chapter and Chapter Fifteen).

Where to Start in Location Photography

If after reading this, you think that location photography is for you, start in your own area and build up a portfolio. If you have any access to business or corporate or industrial or institutional situations, use that access to shoot pictures for a corporate type portfolio. (See also Chapter Nine, Self-Assignments.) After you have a portfolio and at least some experience, you can approach small business, corporate and other clients like contractors and real estate firms; hospitals, schools, camps and colleges; malls and restaurants; government offices and public utilities. They all need pictures at times. (See also Chapter Ten.)

Freelancing for Corporations

Many larger corporations employ freelance photographers fairly often. This field is very competitive because it is well paid. The better your pictures, and the more businesslike an impression you create, the better chance you will have at succeeding. Prepare a resumé and include it with your portfolio of appropriate samples (don't show pictures of cute kids, or models or colorful travel shots; what corporate clients want to see are good pictures of management and workers, interesting, well-designed photographs of industrial subjects, and of course anything pertaining especially to their field).

Circulate your portfolio to corporations that interest you. Contact the Human Relations Department for names of the individuals who commission photography. Remember that corporations are more formal than editorial or advertising clients, so dress in appropriate business attire when soliciting work.

Annual Report Photography

Some of today's annual report photographers are photo journalists who also do some annual report and corporate work to supplement their editorial income. Increasingly though, photographers specialize only in corporate work. If you aim first at smaller companies in your own area, you will build your portfolio and your skills, and can move up. The specialty of shooting blue-chip companies' annual reports and corporate brochures is highly competitive, because it is very well paid. Top free lancers who work regularly for the biggest corporations make as much or more than top advertising photographers. Most of this top-paying work is given out by graphic design firms who are members of the American Institute for Graphic Arts, or AIGA. (See later in the chapter.)

The Location Photographers' Handbook

For professionals and would-be professionals I highly recommend *The Location Photographer's Handbook* by Ken Haas, a top annual report specialist. This book might just become a bible for serious traveling photographers. It includes an amazing amount of detailed information assembled from experience, and from United States and other government documents and official sources; it gives much information on big-time location shooting, and on working conditions in about 170 countries and territories. A tiny sampling of its facts: where to rent strobes in Bulgaria, what diseases are prevalent in Burma, how to import photographic equipment into Bhutan, the address of a Kodak recommended lab in Berchem, Belgium, and the public holidays in Burkina Faso. It also describes how to get a "Carnet," the best place to sit on a plane, sunrise and sunset times for different latitudes and much, much more.

Reading the four closely written pages on diarrhea should help you to decide whether you are a true traveler or just a timid tourist!

Staff Photography for Corporations

Many of the largest corporations in America and Canada employ staff photographers to produce brochures, quarterly reports, pictures for in house magazine and public relations use, as well as some annual report work, although this is almost always supplemented by the work of a well-known free lancer. Some corporate photo departments are small, some quite large.

Today most such jobs go to graduates of good photography schools, which also provide leads for jobs. Credentials are needed to get ahead in the hierarchy of the corporate world.

About three years ago I had a mature student who was a very good photographer. He was a former Marine pilot who had quit a staff photographer's job at a big aviation company. When I asked him why he was getting a degree he said that he had made $15,000 a year less in salary than a colleague doing the same job for the same length of time who had a Bachelor of Fine Arts in photography!

Further Sources of Information
on Corporate and Industrial Photography

The Corporate Photography Showcase, an annual published by American Showcase, contains portfolios by corporate industrial specialists.

Look at corporate annual reports, at magazines like *Fortune, Forbes* and *Business Week*, and at big trade magazines to see the work of top corporate/industrial photographers.

The American Institute of Graphic Arts (AIGA) is headquartered at 1059 Third Avenue, New York, NY 10021. Phone (212) 752-0813. It has several regional chapters. They sell a mailing list of their graphic designer members, who commission a lot of annual report and location photography. Call or write for more information and the address of the chapter nearest you.

Industrial Photography by Jack Neubart is a well illustrated and researched book on that subject, based on interviews with experts.

Chapter 15

Planning and Preparation for the Travel Shoot

All photographers, amateur and professional, who expect to bring back really good pictures from a travel shoot need to be well organized before leaving. Otherwise, they risk arriving at a destination at the wrong time, wasting a lot of time on arrival trying to find out where things are, or even failing to get what they need because of lack of planning.

When You Plan a Big Trip, Where Do You Start?

First and foremost, professionals should thoroughly discuss with the client (or stock agency) what needs to be covered. For a personal shooting trip, write down your goals in detail.

Then, get a map and guidebooks (see later in the chapter) and work out a reasonable itinerary, perhaps with the help of a travel agent.

Fix dates ahead if possible, you will usually save money on airline tickets.

Professionals should always be ready to travel at short notice to take the rush jobs that often come up.

The more you can find out about any destination and job beforehand the greater your chances of a successful shoot. Much planning and preparation should be done before you leave home; but, you should also try to arrive at your location ahead of time to "scout" for good locations and vantage points, and make local contacts. This is especially important when you haven't done much traveling previously. Later on, you can pull together a shoot based on experience, even if you don't have much time to plan ahead. If you are professional, and you are asked to hop on a plane on one day's notice, take the job (as long as your skills are up to it) and cram on the plane and on arrival at your destination!

Using a Travel Agent

A travel agent's time is valuable. To help him or her, do as much of your research as possible before you talk to the agent. Be as specific as you can about where you have to go and what you have to or want to cover.

Allow the travel agent to do what they do best, use the computer to plan airline routings that will save you time and money, and find options in your price range for hotels, car rentals, etc. These services are free, paid for by commissions from airline, etc. to the travel agent, and do not increase your cost.

Good agents have traveled a lot themselves. They can often offer detailed suggestions based on personal experience, and will knock themselves out to get last-minute reservations or elusive information for established clients.

Of course, if you buy only an occasional cut-rate ticket, and if very extensive research is required, or several overseas phone calls have to be made, or if many changes in itinerary involving extensive reticketing or reservation changes are made, a travel agent may justifiably charge you a service fee.

You should expect enthusiasm, prompt call-backs, and patience if you do have to change an itinerary, from any good travel agent.

How Much Time Will You Need to Photograph a Place?

In general, you need at least a week to get an impression of the highlights of a big city, two weeks or longer for the very largest like London or Tokyo.

One to three weeks should be enough for many regions—and small countries, allowing 200-300 miles a day, plus one to three days each for important towns. There is no way you could cover a large country with many special places of interest, like France, Egypt or Japan, even moderately thoroughly in less than a month; six weeks would be much better. If you are specializing in an area or country, and can afford it, several visits at different seasons will give you more varied weather and events, and will be be less tiring than one very long stay. You won't have to worry about keeping your film refrigerated either.

Professionals should be able to come up with highlights of almost anywhere in just a few days, if that is all the time available, or if that is what the client's budget permits! (See also the next three chapters.)

Scouting Locations

Until recently, I worked almost exclusively for magazine, tourism and corporate clients. They tell me where to go and more or less what to shoot. My job is then to select the most photogenic things from their lists and make the best possible pictures of them. I do my on-the-spot research by walking a lot in cities, and by driving in other areas.

Nowadays I am initiating more of my own travel projects and encounter the same problems as stock photographers, who must choose subjects without detailed guidelines. Stock photographers tell me they plan their trips meticulously, to fill gaps in their own coverage or add to it, or as guided by their stock agencies for needed subject matter.

Location scouting means finding the best places to photograph, and travel photographers do this all the time. For insight on how a professional "location scout" approaches his work, I asked the advice of my neighbor Les Fincher (originally a still photographer on movie sets), who now "scouts" locations for television commercials, feature films and occasional big-budget advertising still photography.

Note: Les suggests than some travel photographers who know an area well may find that "scouting" locations is a useful source of additional income.

Les Fincher's Tips From a Location Scout

- Thoroughly discuss and make sure you understand all the client's requirements.

- Budget and shooting dates should be pinpointed.

- The scout must consider the format—stills, TV, movies—and the scope of the project. How many models/actors and crew are involved, the amount of spaces needed for camera movement, how many days of shooting, etc.

- The scout must then find what is needed. First travel to the general area you think the location will be—farm country, mountains, pretty village, etc.

- Then drive around the area. When you see something that resembles the requirement, approach the owner to clear it for shooting.

- Never lie about or minimize what shooting or filming at any location will mean in terms of problems for the owner. (This is to prepare them for the arrival of a film crew which can have 40 or more people in it, plus lights—not so much of a problem for still photographers.)

- When you have a likely location, photograph the place from all four sides (both inside and out if necessary).

- Note the sun directions at different times of day.

- The position of due north (with a compass).

- The sound conditions if the shoot is for film or TV.

- Then find alternate locations.

- Offer the director, art director or other client several choices (four or five is good)—there are many reasons why a good-looking place may not "work" for filming or still photography.

- When recording the place, shoot negative color film; snapshot-sized prints are the final objective. (Note: Many still photographers use Polaroids for scouting and testing models.)

- Most location scouts photograph in a panoramic style using a 35mm lens to move through the image area vertically (four or five shots for each side of the whole exterior, and of all interior walls in rooms being considered for the project.)

- Prints are developed, then taped together to make strips, overlapping the pictures if necessary. It usually takes four or five pictures to show one side of a building, and it takes four strips of photos to show a building exterior, or a room interior. This method allows the photo-montage to be viewed with a perspective close to normal vision, rather than distorted by wide-angle lenses or panoramic cameras.

- Always remember you are the eyes of the director. Don't leave any visual question unanswered. Photograph inside all rooms that might be used, showing all doors and windows. Photograph looking out of windows, and show surrounding landscape, and buildings. Take close-ups of special architectural features, or possible problem areas.

- Outdoors note carefully on each strip of pictures: orientation, time of day, sun direction.

- Indoors note floor number, ceiling height, room size.

- Also note building height/number of stories, property size, whether nearby roads belong to town, city, county, etc. (for parking permits).

- Then you will need: owners/management/other contact names, business, home phone numbers and local government and police numbers for any necessary permits. (Not often needed for stills.)

- Needed also: listing of local accommodation and restaurant facilities, availability of fax and Federal Express and similar services, and, important for location scouting, a one hour photo lab.

- Finally, the location scout has to negotiate the price for the shoot, if the location is chosen.

- Location scouts almost always work in a hurry. Send the picture montage strips (crazy-glued onto legal-sized manila file folders, with all pertinent data written on individual folders) via overnight express to your client.

- If a location is approved, notify the property owner, and fix a shooting date. (Also notify the owners of places not chosen.) Then you can return home.

A Trip-Planning Exercise

As an exercise, research and plan a trip to a place that you very much want to photograph, even if the trip is not imminent. Dust off the skills you once used to write term papers. Visit a library, make phone calls, and assemble your materials. Read and distill what you need to know about the place (its highlights, people, culture and travel conditions) from guidebooks, atlases, and the latest government advice for travelers (see later in the chapter).

Guide books, foreign government tourist authority offices, consulates, travel agents, airlines, hotel chains, car-rental and cruise companies and the like have the information you need. The American and Canadian Automobile Associations (AAA and CAA) have excellent travel guides and maps, free for members. Travel magazines, chambers of commerce, fellow photographers, and people who've been there recently are also good sources of information. If planning a shoot for a corporation, find out as much as you can about the company, from local contacts with the company, annual reports, business magazines, customers and suppliers and employees.

- Summarize the important things you learn in writing.

- Make a shooting outline, or "story board"—a series of sketches of picture sequences.

- Then, write a proposal to a real or imaginary travel, tourism or location client, outlining the reasons you want to photograph the place you have chosen, and why these pictures would be interesting to their readers/guests/clients. Be as specific as possible. Amateurs should list personal objectives.

Budgeting Travel

Budgeting is an essential part of travel planning for almost anyone. Professionals must often submit written bids or budgets for travel assignments.

Your budget should include the cost of:

- ❑ Professional and personal insurance
- ❑ International and domestic air travel
- ❑ Car rental, gasoline and tolls, parking (per day)
- ❑ Other land travel costs (busses, boats, ferries, trains, taxis, subways)
- ❑ Sightseeing tours
- ❑ Admissions to museums, other attractions
- ❑ Hotels (per night)
- ❑ Meals (per day)
- ❑ Tips and miscellaneous expenses
- ❑ Photography fees, if any
- ❑ Model fees or tips
- ❑ Film (estimate an average number of rolls per day, include test rolls; some photographers mark up the cost by 10%)
- ❑ Processing (allow for extra charges for "pushing," "pulling" and "clip" tests)
- ❑ Shipping film
- ❑ Of course, don't forget to add your fee (by the day or by the job) to the estimate if this is a professional assignment

---

- If you wish to carry the exercise to its ultimate, make a travel budget. Allow for long distance and local transportation, hotels, meals and incidentals. Multiply the amount of film you will shoot by film and processing costs (include test rolls) and add this to the budget. (Note: the ratio of film shot to pictures published is high as a rule, ten rolls of film per day is very moderate shooting.) Add the fee you would like to get. With this professional approach, you just might sell someone on the idea of paying you to do the job, or, you might talk yourself into making the trip. (See also Chapter Ten.)

Researching a Destination—New Zealand

I have never been to New Zealand. For the purposes of this book, and because I want to go there, I researched the trip. First I consulted The New Zealand Tourist and Publicity Office, Air New Zealand (both have toll-free 800 numbers) and the Insight Guide to New Zealand. I called Hertz and Avis and a travel agency specializing in tours to New Zealand. Then I talked to my friend Pat Collyns (who was there in January '91); my neighbor Les Fincher (who was there in February '89); and a former student who moved here from New Zealand only four years ago. I carefully studied two picture books of New Zealand that Les had brought back with him. (The Air New Zealand and New Zealand tourist office brochures that were sent me are well-illustrated too.)

Budgeting a New Zealand Trip

Based on my research, the travel cost at the time of writing for a three-week independent trip from New York to New Zealand would be about $6,000 (excluding film and processing, or the photography fee). Economy class advance purchase air fare from New York to Auckland costs about $1,300 in winter, $1,500 in spring and fall and $1,700 in summer. (Remember the seasons are reversed Down Under.) Air New Zealand, Continental and United are the carriers from the United States at present (you can also fly from Canada and Australia). An automatic transmission car for three weeks with unlimited mileage currently costs about $1,500. (Less if you can drive a stick-shift car.) Single or double midprice motel rooms cost about $40-60 per night at the time of writing. There are plenty of less expensive bed and breakfast, farmhouse and cabin/campground accommodations too. Recreational vehicles (RV's) can be rented, and there are some luxury resorts. Allowing $50 per day for gas, modest meals (most motels have kitchenettes) and incidentals, land expenses should be around $3,000 for three weeks. Add $500 for internal tourist flights, ferries, boat and yacht trips and unexpected expenses. (Two people travelling together would increase the land cost only about 10%, for meals.) A prebooked car and rooms are essential in late December and January. Prices fall somewhat in the spring and fall.

Group tours to New Zealand are of course less expensive than individual travel; a reason many people take tours. About $3,000 is the current minimum basic cost of a three-week tour from New York to New Zealand, including air fare. (Of course your photographic opportunities will be somewhat limited if you take a tour, unless it's a photo tour.)

For student or tight budget, there are local trains and busses. Tent camping sites and walking tours are available.

With this type of estimating, you will be able to decide if personal travel is affordable, or if a stock shoot would be cost-effective. Professionals can present clients with a detailed and accurate picture of expenses.

Highlights of New Zealand

New Zealand has about 3,000,000 people and 70,000,000 sheep. It is comprised of North and South Islands (a few tiny ones too) divided by the Cook Strait, and is about 800 miles long. The peak summer travel season (Christmas through January) is somewhat crowded (by New Zealand standards) at tourist spots because New Zealanders and Australians take their vacations at this time. At other times, you can happily drive around as your whim dictates. Spring and fall (the reverse of ours) are good for photography and travel but coolish in the evenings. Winter in New Zealand is cold in the South with heavy snow in the mountains, and rainy in the North.

Auckland, where flights from North America arrive, is the principal city (population about 800,000). It is famous for yachting and is the largest Polynesian city in the world, with about 100,000 (mostly New Zealand Maori) residents of Pacific island descent. It has good shops, interesting museums, etc. Auckland though, is not the main reason to go to New Zealand. The spectacular scenery is. The "must sees" in New Zealand are:

North Island

The scenic and yacht-filled Bay of Islands, Roturua and the thermal hot springs region, volcanic Mount Taranaki/Egmont and surrounding national park. Most tourists visit the Waitangi Treaty House where, in 1840, the peace treaty ending hostilities between Maoris and European settlers was signed. It is now a national shrine and museum. (I have mixed feelings about such monuments; I don't need to tell you who lost the wars, or their lands.) Many Maori people live in northeast New Zealand. Wellington, the capital, has a population of about 300,000 and is at the southern tip of North Island. This is where car and passenger ferries make the three and a half hour, sometimes rough, crossing to Picton on the South Island.

South Island

This is the more scenic of the two. The 12,350 foot high Mount Cook and the glacier of the same name are in the country's most famous national park; a friend said the small-plane flight to the glacier and a stay in the Hermitage Hotel at its base were very enjoyable. The rolling Canterbury plains have enormous sheep farms and nice pastoral landscapes.

Milford Sound, Doubtful Sound and the Fiord region are world famous. You can take day steamers and make wonderful pictures (but allow time if you need sunshine, because the fjord area has one of the highest precipitation rates in the world, and the fjords are often misty and foggy). The city of Christchurch, founded for Anglicans of good character (and still considered very English), is one of New Zealand's most beautiful. The Otago Lakes, especially Te Anu, are recommended as extremely scenic. Hikers can take the Milford Trek, a famous escorted walk of several days; high-season reservations are needed far in advance. It is possible to stay at a Maori "marae" or meeting house or on a sheep farm in several different places to meet these very different types of New Zealander. The two national sports passions are Rugby football and lawn bowling. Both are played fiercely, and a match or two should not be missed. You can do all or most of the above in a busy three weeks, if you fly between major centers. There are also scenic rail connections between the main cities of New Zealand.

Quite obviously, a deeper look at New Zealand would take longer than three weeks; if I were an ambitious young travel photographer I might backpack around the country for a few months.

If all this sounds very expensive, remember that New Zealand is a long way from New York. The airfare is about $300 less from the West Coast. Compare prices to current costs in Europe or Japan. Foreign exchange rates are currently against the dollar to put it mildly!

Researching Lower-Cost Travel Destinations

All the places listed below will produce fine travel pictures and, at the moment, the U.S. and especially Canada are great travel bargains attracting visitors from all over the world.

In the United States and Canada research a trip to New England (especially Maine and Vermont) if you live in the West; to the the Southwest (especially Arizona, Utah and New Mexico) if you live in the Northeast; to Montana or Wyoming if you live in the deep South; or to the Louisiana plantation and bayou country and New Orleans if you are a Northerner or Midwesterner or a Canadian. Or, plan a trip from anywhere to Canada's Maritimes, or British Columbia, which are both very beautiful; the Canadian dollar is currently discounted 15% against the U.S. dollar. Mexico too, is currently a great bargain, and southern Mexico especially is an attractive travel destination.

Travel "Comps"

If you have a legitimate editorial assignment to go anywhere from a major publication, you may well be able (or the publication may be able) to get discounts, or even "comps"—(complimentary fares, passes, accommodations etc.) for part or all of the trip. This does happen, although most top travel magazines pay their assignees' own way, for obvious reasons.

Bona-fide members of the Society of American Travel Writers, who are well-published professionals, are often invited on trips by national tourist organizations. Membership requirements of this organization are very stringent, requiring extensive publication. There are a few photographer members. For requirements contact them at 1100 17th Street, Suite 1000, Washington, D.C. 20036. Phone (202) 785-5567.

Questions Professionals Need to Resolve
With the Client Before Going on Assignment

❏ Who is going to own the residual rights to your pictures? You should always keep control of your copyright, for residual and stock sales and because your pictures are your legacy that may possibly be valuable as art one day. (See also Chapter Thirteen.)

❏ Are all your travel, film and incidental expenses for the assignment covered? (Professionals should make sure that all legitimate nonpersonal expenses are covered.)

❏ Are travel time and editing time covered? (The ASMP recommends that professionals charge half their photography day rate for this work.)

❏ Are you being offered a guarantee of a certain number of days or pages at an agreed rate, or a flat fee for the job? (Negotiate this with the client. See also Chapter Eleven.)

❏ Will the overseas office supply you with an interpreter/or translator if needed? Normally the answer to this is yes for a business corporate assignment and no to an editorial assignment; for the latter you will have to find your own on the spot. I always prefer students to professional guides.

❏ Will the new cruise ship/other facility actually be completed when you arrive? Be sure about this one, and make sure you will be paid if you have to wait around.

❏ Do you need to photograph all the vessels/hotels public rooms/other subject matter, or just the important ones/part of it? Is the assignment in color or black-and-white or are both needed? Find out before you go. (If ever in doubt, do more, not less.)

❏ Are professional models lined up, or do you have to cajole the passengers/ staff/local people into acting as models? (Make sure to take appropriate language model releases, see Chapter Twenty.)

❏ Are bad-weather time and waiting time allowed for in the schedule? (Be sure airline reservations can be changed if the need arises.)

❏ Is there any limit on the amount of film you may shoot? (Established professionals with good rapport with the client should not have to deal with this one.)

❏ Are there any other conditions?

Written agreements or contracts that spell everything out will save grief and money if you run into any problems later.

My best advice: Never commit your own money to a job without an official company purchase order and a money advance. Ask for a detailed letter of assignment stating the client's requirements, terms, and the payment policy if the work ends up not being used through no fault of yours.

Return a copy of the agreement, signed and dated, marked with the notation "Terms Agreed" before you leave. While some oral agreements hold up in court it's always better to get everything in writing.

Caution: Get a big percentage of your expense money and your guarantee "up front" (in advance). I ask for at least 50% of expenses and a percentage of the fee.

Arrange for periodic "progress payments" on fee and expenses if the job is a long one. You still have to pay the rent at home. (See also Chapter Eleven.)

When all the above is settled you can happily leave on your trip. Now all you have to worry about is doing a great job for the client.

Official Government Advice for Overseas Travelers

We are living in difficult times, and I do not presume to give security advice, except to recommend always keeping a low profile when traveling. If you are planning a trip to any area where unrest may exist, or where travel is difficult, consult the following for any possible advisories (warnings) on travel.

The United States State Department's Citizens Advisory Center is in Washington, D.C. (Phone: 202-647-5225). Call from a touch-tone phone (rotary phones can be used but the service is much slower) and have a pencil and paper handy; the system is automated, you get answers by punching in different numbers. It sometimes takes time for the line to answer, so be patient. Get information about obtaining a United States passport, where to write for background papers on travel in general, and travel to specific foreign countries and regions. U.S. Public Health Service foreign immunization recommendations and requirements, and Consular Service foreign visa advice is also available.

Travel advisories (warnings) are given out by the same number. These too are recordings obtained by punching numbers, and are changed daily or as necessary.

Note: This same telephone number is also the one to call if you have major problems (like the illness or death of a companion, or someone's arrest or disappearance) while overseas. In serious emergencies like those, of course you can talk to a human being.

The travel background information is sent to you by mail, for a small fee, so allow time when using this service.

Booklets on many travel subjects are published by the U.S. Government printing Office. They include Foreign Entry Requirements (#459X; 50 cents; it lists over 200 embassies and consulates); A Safe Trip Abroad (#154X); Tips for Travelers to Mexico (#156X); and Your Trip Abroad (#158X). All of these booklets cost $1.00 each. Order from R. Woods, Consumer Information Center-X, P.O. Box 100, Pueblo, CO 81002.

Canadians who need the same types of information should call the Department of External Affairs, Travelers Advisory Service, in Ottawa. Phone (613) 992-3705.

Note: Take all travel advisories seriously, they are not given out lightly; but if you decide to go anyway, call overseas (to a client's representative, a relative, friend, U.S. or Canadian consulate) to find out more detailed, local information.

Professional Reference Books and Favorite Guide Books

As already mentioned, Ken Haas's *The Location Photographer's Handbook* is "must reading" if you photograph overseas on assignment frequently. It contains information about health, safety, public holidays and more that would be useful to traveling amateur photographers also.

The *Professional Photo Source* is a useful directory. It includes listings of assistants, foreign consulates, labs, permits, rentals, repairs, stock agencies, stylists, travel/tourism information and more. It is especially strong for the New York metropolitan area and East Coast, but has good information about most of the U.S. and some for Canada, London, Paris and Milan.

A good guide book is a friend when you are travelling. For many years I used Fodor's Guides almost exclusively. They are still excellent and cover just about the whole world. My choice now is the Insight series of city, regional and national guidebooks—first because they have lots of well-reproduced color photographs which give a good sense of what a place looks like, and second because they are very strong on cultural and historical background information. They also include enough practical stuff about electricity, climate, public holidays, transport, etc. for my needs, and some information (not too detailed) on accommodations, from international class to campgrounds (with an emphasis on moderate prices).

Birnbaum's Guides are comprehensive, with plenty of information for travellers who like up-market hotels and resorts, and for mature and handicapped travelers too. The cultural/historic coverage is also very well-done.

The famous red *Guide Michelin* (in French only) is of course indispensable for travel in France. Michelin's Green Guides to different regions of France, as well as many foreign countries and cities (some of which are in English) are reliable and good for hotels, restaurants, historic sites and architecture.

Penguin Guides are well-written and researched.

Frommer's guidebooks are good; I used them in my student days. (Believe it or not, young readers, there was once a Frommer guidebook called *Europe On $5 a Day!*)

The Lonely Planet Guide series specializes in Asia and Third World countries. They are now branching out—I own the very comprehensive volume on Mexico.

The Let's Go series of guides compiled by the Harvard Student Agencies have been recommended to me by well-traveled American and British students on tight budgets. *Let's Go USA* is said to be particularly helpful. I own *Let's Go France*, which is excellent. (I list all these guidebooks because sometimes your preferred series doesn't cover where you want to go.)

Maps

I've loved maps all my life. A map can set you dreaming, then will help you plan driving schedules, choose centers and estimate time needed. Maps also help with captions, and make great souvenirs when marked with your travels. AAA's regional maps and guides of the U.S. are excellent and free to members. It's worth joining just to get these, they have Canadian information too. (So, of course, does the Canadian Automobile Association.) Rand NcNally, Hagstrom, and Hallwag maps of foreign countries are widely available in North America. Get a general one for the country/region before you leave; detailed and city maps are best purchased at your destination. Maps as well as guidebooks can be found at many bookstores.

If you don't have a good bookstore near you, try The Complete Traveler, 199 Madison Avenue, New York, NY 10016. Phone (212) 685-9007; fax (212) 982-7628; or the Travelers' Bookstore, 75 Rockefeller Plaza, New York, NY 10019. Phone (212) 664-0995. Both specialize in travel books, guides and maps.

The Travel Industry Personnel Directory is a fairly exhaustive listing of sources of travel information. It is sold by mail .(See Chapters Ten and Twenty.)

Insurance for Traveling Photographers

You have to consider several kinds of insurance:

- Your medical insurance usually covers you overseas (except in wars) unless you stay away for six months or longer—check with your insurance company.

- Camera equipment insurance for amateurs is usually available as a floater on household insurance. Consult insurance brokers.

- Baggage insurance (but not professional equipment loss) and travel cancellation insurance are available through travel agents.

Professional Insurance for Photographers

ASMP offers its members several types of professional coverage:

- "Pro-Surance" covers studio content, including electronic equipment, valuable papers, worldwide camera coverage, and more. Currently, a New York City photographer with $5,000 worth (used value) of camera equipment, and $5,000 of other electronic equipment (used strobes, computers, etc.) would pay about $800 annually for this package. (In other regions this insurance can cost less or more.) Reshoot insurance covers expenses caused by loss of exposed film due to lab damage and camera problems and more. The premium is based on annual billable expenses; it is not cheap—neither is the cost of reshooting a job.

- Other recommended types of insurance are: Liability and Workmen's Compensation (you must have these in the U.S. if you hire assistants or models). Call ASMP at (212) 889-9144 or their broker, Taylor and Taylor Associates at (212) 686-1406 for details. Taylor and Taylor also writes various individual professional policies for members of the Advertising Photographers of America (APA).

- The only group insurance for camera equipment alone that I know of is offered to members of the Professional Photographers of America (PP of A); the current cost is $2.40 per $100 (with a minimum coverage of $15,000) for all risks. The rate is lower for additional coverage. Contact the PP of A at (800) 786-6277 for details of membership requirements and the insurance.

Pretravel Checklist:

(See also the Personal and Photographic Checklists that follow.)

At least a month before your trip get:

❏ Small passport pictures (get/make extra prints).

❏ Passport (if you don't have one already; I keep mine current).

❏ Visa(s) if needed.

❏ Shots.

❏ A "Carnet" for your equipment if needed (see Chapter Fourteen).

❏ Insurance (personal and photographic—see earlier in the chapter; check and make sure all policies are current).

Reservations—Make them all as far ahead as possible, including:

❏ Airline ticket(s)—include domestic or connecting flights, overseas flights, and local flights at home or overseas. (Note: advance purchase air tickets are often cheaper than those purchased at the last minute; but these are not a bargain if you must change plans frequently; unrestricted tickets carry no penalties. Standby tickets are always great bargains, if you can be very flexible. They are often available from New York to London, for instance.)

❏ Car rental reservations. (U.S. and Canadian driving licenses are accepted by rental companies just about anywhere. If you are going to buy, lease or borrow a car abroad, check auto associations or consulates to see if a translation, or a foreign driving license or special insurance is required.)

❏ Train, car, ferry reservations, or local ferry or cruise reservations if required.

Then get:

❏ Hotel reservation confirmation(s)—especially important for the first night or two in crowded cities like London, and in busy tourist/resort areas.

❏ Credit Cards—These are essential for modern travel. (I recommend carrying both an American Express card and either a Visa or Mastercard.) Activate the cash advance numbers if you haven't done so already; there are now cash machines in most airports and many other places overseas. Some overseas cash machines now accept some North American bank cards. An AT&T or other telephone company card is a must. Also, carry your phone company's USA Direct (or equivalent) call-home number card; overseas calls charged to foreign hotels cost a fortune. Take a major gasoline credit card, but it may not be accepted overseas.

❏ Travelers Checks. American Express checks are accepted just about everywhere without a qualm; with some other checks you have to go to banks to cash them, not always convenient. I like $50 denominations. (Record all numbers; store one copy of the numbers at home; keep one copy in your wallet and another in your clothing bag.)

❏ Cash: A few clean US $1, $5 and $10 bills are handy in addition to $50 in local currency. US dollars are widely accepted for tips overseas.

❏ Professionals should take letters of assignment and introduction, and contact phone numbers (make two copies of these). Pack the spare copy safely with your gear.

❏ Business address/telephone book.

❏ Daily planner or diary (or Filofax or laptop computer if you use one).

❏ Guidebook and map.

❏ I carry my important papers en route in a flat courier's purse, with a wrist strap. It has compartments for passport, tickets, credit cards, traveler's checks, different currencies, etc. Or, be like New Yorkers and wear a waist pouch. Carry travel documents with you at all times when staying in cheap hotels or camping. In good hotels, put valuables in the safe while working.

❏ Carry a lightweight plastic file folder to conveniently store important but not vital telephone number/address book, business cards, lists, maps, etc., and receipts and notes as you accumulate them. Store this in your luggage.

Checklist for Personal Items:

❏ Personal address/phone number book.

❏ Glasses or contact lenses if needed; spare glasses, prescription.

❏ Medication if needed, and prescription.

❏ Toiletries, with personal hygiene items, Tylenol etc. (I keep a kit with all this stuff packed in my bureau so as not to forget important trifles; to be stuck somewhere without a nail file can be miserable. I also keep a spare house key in this kit.)

❏ Thin wallet (to keep on your person when documents are checked).

❏ Business cards.

❏ Pocket calculator.

❏ Travel alarm clock or watch.

❏ Felt tip pen, ball point pen, pencils.

❏ Clothes. The less you can carry the better. Avoid anything that has to be dry-cleaned (often bad; usually expensive and slow overseas).

❏ Comfortable shoes, boots or sneakers; lightweight dress shoes.

❏ Plenty of socks and underwear.

❏ A robe/nightwear.

❏ Easily washable working wear. (Mine is usually khaki or black pants, with a turtleneck and layered tops plus a loose wind/waterproof jacket with plenty of pockets.) I don't wear a photographic vest—I feel they make me look too conspicuous, and a possible target for thieves.

❏ Thin gloves, or ski glove liners plus mitts for really cold weather.

❑ One lightweight, hand-washable dressy outfit (mine is a black silk shirt, with flowing black pants or a long batik skirt, black silk socks and black Chinese slippers).

❑ Carry a swimsuit if you wish, but buy summer or winter resort clothes locally if you need them; they look more appropriate than those brought from home, allowing you to "blend" in better, and they make fine souvenirs.

❑ A lightweight raincoat or poncho is a must. (If you get one in a glaring orange or yellow, you can wear it to stand and photograph in the road!)

❑ I don't wear sunglasses (I feel they get in the way of photography), but almost always buy a big hat or long peaked cap locally (they bring me luck).

Photographic Checklist

Well ahead of time, make a complete list of all the photographic items that you carry with you. List all serial numbers, for both customs and insurance purposes. Make several copies of this document, leave a couple at home in a safe place. (Or, obtain a "Carnet." See Chapter Fourteen.)

Thoroughly check out any new or newly-repaired equipment. Test emulsions. (Shoot film for both.) Buy film.

You Will Need to Take:

Copy this list as is, or adapt to your needs.

❑ Film
  • 35mm color transparency. Slow, medium, fast, tungsten; as needed
  • 120; 220; large format film as needed
  • Color negative film in sizes and speeds needed; Amateur, Type S, Type L
  • Black-and-white film, slow, medium fast
  • Polaroid film, as needed for different cameras and backs

❑ Film holders/roll film backs

❑ Sima lead-foil bags for film

❑ Camera bodies with bodycaps as needed
  • 35mm
  • Medium format
  • Large format

❑ Special cameras (Polaroid; panoramic; point and shoot; underwater)

❑ Polaroid backs for camera format(s) used

❑ 35mm lenses:
  • wide-angle
  • normal
  • telephoto
  • zoom
  • macro
  • P.C./T.S.
  • Tele-extender

❏ Medium/large format lenses, as needed
❏ Lens shades if used
❏ Skylight/UV filters (use as protectors on all lenses)
❏ Filters/gels
❏ Gel holder
❏ Gel kits, gel sheets; gel frames for lights
❏ Cable release(s)
❏ Meter(s) handheld: incident, flash meter spot meter, color temperature
❏ Soft fabric pouches or wraps for equipment
❏ Tripod
❏ Cable releases (include special release for TTL/dedicated cameras)
❏ Camera clamp
❏ Flash unit(s)TTL/dedicated, Vivitar 283, other flash units
❏ Spare flash battery chamber(s)
❏ Rechargeable gel-cel battery pack(s) for flash
❏ Battery charger(s)110v, 220v
❏ Miniature flash/slave unit(s) if used
❏ Slave unit(s)
❏ Flash trigger(s)
❏ Flash foot to lightstand adaptor (if needed)
❏ Bounce card for flash
❏ Vari-Power modifier(s) if used
❏ Flash bracket if used
❏ Disposable batteries (of each size used)
❏ PC (sync) cords
❏ PC connector mender
❏ Portable Strobe(s)
❏ Strobe heads
❏ Strobe tube(s) and modelling light bulb(s) and spares
❏ A.C. power cords for strobes
❏ Slaves for strobe(s)
❏ Voltmeter and neon tester
❏ Quartz light(s) if used; spare 3,200K bulbs
❏ A.C. power cords for hot lights
❏ Foreign plug adaptors
❏ Pig tail(s)
❏ 110-220v transformer, rated for your equipment
❏ Lightstand(s)
❏ Umbrella(s)

❏ Portable light bank(s)

❏ Adaptor ring(s) and struts for light banks

❏ Reflectors, collapsible; white, silver, gold, black

❏ White sheet or shower curtain

❏ Small clamps

❏ Small screwdriver set

❏ Vise grip

❏ "Swiss army" type pocket knife

❏ Tape —"Gaffer," electrical, masking, mailing

❏ Magic marker(s)

❏ Model releases: English; foreign language

❏ Large garbage bag(s), Ziplock freezer bags

❏ Rubber bands, Avery labels, 3x5" cards, note book(s)

❏ Camera bag; under seat, sturdy; about 11 x 16 x 9"

❏ Soft camera bag, with shoulder pad

❏ Backpack, or camera backpack (if used)

❏ Equipment case(s) for shipping strobe(s), lightstands, tripod, umbrellas, etc.

❏ Luggage cart and shock cords

❏ Sturdy duffle bag or soft sided bag (for clothes)

❏ Cheap crushable nylon duffle bag (for extras acquired en route)

❏ Large, strong, Army-style duffle bag (I put all unbreakables inside this)

❏ Padlock(s) and chain(s) and spare keys

❏ Specialized professional items:_____

❏ Misc:_____

_____

_____

_____

Tips for Hassle Free Packing

Copy my lists, or make your own, and check off preplanning, personal and photographic items as you do/pack them. It is all too easy to forget something important if you don't.

Your best bet is to make a list of everything photographic you own, and then choose what you will need on the assignment. Pack a day ahead. Take as little clothing as you can get away with.

I hand-carry onto the plane: Cameras, lenses and fragile items; a toilet kit (which I keep packed at all times); enough film for a few days; a good book.

Last Minute Checklist

Professionals should call/check in with the client before leaving. Something may have changed at the last minute.

❏ Leave contact numbers, and arrange how to keep in touch.

❏ Keep the home as well as the business number of the client on hand.

❏ Pay up your personal bills, and arrange for someone to return your business calls and look after your studio, apartment, house cat, plants (not to mention husbands/wives/loved others/kids, etc.) while you are away.

❏ Let other clients/contacts know you are/will be in an area, and for how long, and that you are available for assignment when the primary one is finished.

❏ 24 to 48 hours ahead, order a cab or limo to take you to the airport (if needed).

❏ Don't panic. (If you did forget to pack something it's not the end of the world, you can probably get it locally. If not, and it's vital, you can probably call home and have it sent.)

If you've done all the above, you should be able to sleep well before you take off!

Car Rental

In the U.S. or Canada, I try to get a car rental agreement that does not include a mileage charge. This is usually possible for rentals of a week or longer. In some very popular places, like Florida in winter, you are advised to book ahead for lowest rates. A subcompact car is fine if you don't have to drive long distances, but if you will be driving several hundred miles a day I suggest getting a midsized car with cruise control. (This can be a big saver in energy on long stretches of straight road out West for instance.)

For car rental overseas, when I am going to a country where I know the roads are good, and language no big problem, I am happy to drive myself. I usually rent a car from the local affiliate of the major U.S. car rental companies before I leave. Avis, Hertz, National, etc. offer various types of discounts to members of photographers associations.

You will save a considerable amount of money in Europe, Australia, and most other places outside the U.S. and Canada if you rent a car with a standard shift.

In countries where I am not comfortable with the idea of driving myself, I try to hire an assistant with a car, a local taxi with a driver who speaks English, or a student as a driver. I use chauffeured limousines only as a very last resort (or if a rich client is paying) because they are very expensive, and the chauffeur type is not usually too happy with the hours that a photographer must keep.

Chapter 16

The Travel Shoot

Some people think that doing a professional travel assignment is like going on a lovely paid holiday. It's usually not like that at all. When I am on assignment, photography is just about all I do for eight, ten, twelve or sometimes more hours a day. Far from partying, I usually have room-service meals and watch local TV to unwind in the evenings. On assignment you must sometimes be up before dawn for days in a row—and dawn is around 5 a.m. in many places in summer—to catch the first light or to drive or fly a long way to another destination. On assignment you are spending a lot of someone else's money, and they are depending on you to bring back what they need, when they need it. Sometimes this is difficult. For instance, you may not be sent to a given location or country at the right time of year for the best pictures, but you have to make fine pictures anyway.

There is usually pressure of time on a professional assignment, especially in these days of tight budgets and weak dollars. Quite often, there are problems with scheduling and coordinating the shoot that must be resolved on arrival, no matter how careful was the advance planning. You must allow extra time for poor weather in some places, and occasionally need to be able, as Kipling said, to "keep your head when all about you, are losing theirs and blaming it on you." Travel assignments are challenging, demanding, exciting and interesting almost always, but a vacation almost never. Almost.

Every single travel/location photographer has his or her own ways of dealing with pressures and problems, of getting mentally focused and keeping concentrated on the goal—good photographs. The following is my way.

Getting Started

If the first leg of the trip is by air, I book a car service to the airport to avoid struggling for cabs while dragging my heavy equipment cart. I arrive at the airport two or three hours before check in time. This gives me a choice of seats (I like an aisle seat near an emergency door on the left side of the plane; I get cramps in my right knee on long flights!) and time to get my film hand-examined, not passed through an X-ray machine. (This may not be possible outside the United States and Canada, see also Chapter Fifteen.)

Despite the good advice I give other people, I always rush around a lot taking care of last minute details before I leave home (or when making a long transfer between locations) so I try to schedule a free day before starting work in a new place. I would pay for this day myself if necessary but, luckily, most clients know that jet-lag reduces efficiency and allow you that leeway on a trip. Ideally, make long intercontinental trips by day, arriving in time for dinner, a shower and bed. You can do this trans-Atlantic or to South America. If you have time, long trans-Pacific flights (which are no thrill in a crowded plane with a cramped Economy class seat) can be made easier by a stopover in, say, Hawaii or Fiji, which is certainly no hardship.

On arrival I schedule a free day for meetings with local client representatives, scouting for locations, exploring and acclimatizing myself, and a little relaxation time before starting shooting.

The worst moment for me on any travel assignment is when I have arrived at the destination and settled into the hotel, but have no pictures in the camera. I feel lost, not knowing where anything is, or whether I will be able to make any sense out of the place at all. One may have read all the guide books, talked to people who have been there, and talked to others about the job, but not until I have given a place a thorough once-over, and been out and taken a few pictures, do I feel that I'm in control. This nervousness applies even when I go on assignment to places which I know very well, like London, but of course is much stronger when the place is totally new. Shooting lists and letters of instruction are often made by writers, or editors, or business executives, and not by visual people. Some designers and art directors have such a specific vision, it makes you wonder if you can, or even want to, come close to it. Different people who work for your client may want different things from the same shoot.

At dusk in a strange city, tired after a long flight, sometimes you wonder if any of this is translatable onto film. Of course it always is, sometimes more successfully than others. It is your job as a professional travel photographer to make that translation; to capture the sense, and look and feel of a living breathing place onto little pieces of Kodachrome or Ektachrome or Fujichrome. You have to make people who aren't there with you share what you feel, and also show them what the client wants to express in many cases. You know in your heart that you can do it, that you will do it, but stage fright is always there before you "go on." My father (who was a trans-Atlantic commuting actor) told me that fear before the performance is a mark of a good actor—perhaps it is a sign of a good photographer also.

When I am being paid to photograph, I always stay in a good, centrally located hotel. English-speaking staff, telephones that work at all hours of the day and night, and room service are all important when you are working long hours. I ask for a quiet room with a view, not too close to or far from the elevators.

Minimizing the Risk of Theft When Traveling

In a good-class hotel I am not worried about theft by the staff, but I don't take chances. I have, as I have already said, nondescript luggage, and I keep it and all the photographic equipment I am not carrying that day padlocked in the cases and out of sight in the closet.

- I put my valuable document case with travelers checks, credit cards I won't need, and cash into the hotel safe, keeping only a Visa card and enough cash for a day or two on hand. (I check my passport too, in many places, but keep it on hand in places where a police presence seems to make this a good idea.)

- I wrap exposed film each day in a freezer bag and date it, and put it away (in the hotel "mini-bar" in hot countries).

- When I'm paying the bills, and staying in mass-market big-city or budget hotels, especially those near railroad stations, I keep all documents on my person. (Use secure pockets or a money belt/pouch.)

- I also carry my cameras and other expensive equipment with me. If you must leave tripod and lighting equipment, extra film, luggage, etc. in such a hotel, I strongly suggest tipping (generously) the concierge/hall-porter, or a member of the front desk staff to lock your valuables in the hotel office.

- Caution: In hostels, campgrounds, etc. never leave anything for even a minute, however inconvenient. (Two English college students I know had all their money, checks and passports stolen in a campground toilet at the Grand Canyon. They had left them in their backpacks, outside the stalls.)

- Never, ever, leave luggage unattended at airports, banks, bus stations, car rental offices, railroad stations, or in train compartments. (See also Insurance, in Chapter Fifteen.)

To banish jet-lag and nerves with physical activity, I start by turning my hotel room into a comfortable working environment. I separate equipment from clothes, and cameras from lighting equipment; lay out my notes on the desk, and put film in the mini-refrigerator. I hang my dress clothes in the closet, but never put anything except paperwork in (one) drawer. (I used to unpack completely when I first started traveling, but left behind a lot of nice clothes!) I put my travel alarm, photo frame and books by the bed. Then I have a good soak in a hot tub after the plane ride, go down to the hotel lobby and buy a local map, a few postcards, and a perhaps a souvenir pictorial guidebook to the place.

I usually chat to the concierge or hall porter about local transport and take a stroll in the vicinity of the hotel.

First thing next morning, I make phone calls to let any contacts know I have arrived, and arrange appointments if necessary. Then I drive (or am driven) around for an hour or two in the country (in towns and cities I walk) or take a taxi, subway or bus to look at the "heart" of the area (as recommended by the guide book, client instructions, the concierge or other locals).

If it is my first visit to a great city I will probably take a standard half-day sightseeing tour to get oriented. I'll take a camera on these trips (it would be asking to miss great pictures not to) but use the tour more to orient myself than to photograph. I take a map, and mark locations, the direction of the sun and time of day, and list the positions of high viewpoints and interesting neighborhoods. I make notes of things I need to cover by neighborhood and plan a shooting schedule. Important outdoor locations have priority because of weather. Specific events/festivities obviously can't be moved, so I schedule around them too.

If required, I meet the client's local representative that first day and use him/her to help make appointments for "people pictures" and indoor locations, scheduling them for middays if possible, so I won't lose good early and late outdoor shooting light. As I said, especially on the first evening or two, I try to eat in my room, and like to relax and watch TV. (This can be hilarious, because overseas it's often old, dubbed, American westerns; sometimes these days there's also CNN or a music channel.) Next day I start shooting.

Photographing at Tourist Facilities

To photograph hotel or resort architecture, rooms, and staff you have to co-ordinate with the management. These pictures have to be scheduled for when they won't disturb clients, often at midday. For interiors, I use a tripod always, and mostly 28mm and 20mm lenses, and I usually set up lights to photograph rooms. "Styling" rooms by adding flowers, a book or a picture, or by moving plants, changing a bedspread, or removing little cardboard signs, TV's and little "minibar" refrigerators is often needed.

My favorite quick hotel exterior shot is with a nice line up of staff outside the main entrance. I pose gray-suited management, uniformed front-desk staff, imposing doorman in full regalia, pink-overalled maids, napkin-bearing waiters and aproned luggage porters. This almost always looks good, and implies Service with a capital S, which the client loves. At the pool you can do handsome lifeguards and towel boys—you get the idea. Small hotels, inns and restaurants are best photographed with the smiling, friendly owners out front.

Photographing Food

To photograph inside restaurants is tricky. You always have to go and talk to the chef in person, arrange for him to prepare something for photography (yes, they mostly are temperamental) and arrange a time when he (or quite often she nowadays) can pose. I sometimes draw the chef a picture of what I mean to do, so he or she can visualize the effect wanted. A kitchen usually needs "styling" (which means getting rid of ugly things, rearranging others, and perhaps bringing in special props, like a big fish, lobster or colorful fruit and vegetables). I like a row of big, well-polished pans hanging in the background of kitchen shots. The best times to photograph chefs are usually about 11 a.m. and 5 p.m. because they've finished most of the work of preparing lunch or dinner, but the customers have not yet arrived. There is usually about a half hour lull for them at these times. I never tip chefs (they usually have more money than I do) but do get their name and address and send prints.

For food setups I always use a tripod, and usually use light bounced out of an umbrella, and soft high sidelighting. Sometimes I use tungsten light and film, to blend with the overall lighting, but more often use a portable strobe or two joined Vivitars. (See Chapter Seven.)

I always try (and usually succeed) to find someone on the staff (it's often a management trainee or public relations person) to assist me when shooting in hotels and restaurants, because of the need to set up fast, move tables and food around, shoot, clean up, and pack up and get out smartly.

Photographing Tourist Staff

Although you can usually get off-duty hotel and restaurant staff to pose as clients, they don't often have the right clothes or "look" to be clients, and I don't use them as models unless desperate. I do like to photograph staff doing their work though, and tip them appropriately afterwards.

Sometimes staff will rescue an assignment, as when I had to photograph Harrod's department store in London. I was allowed one hour between 8 and 9 a.m. for two mornings before the store opened, because Harrod's does not permit photography of its customers, who often include royalty and the rich and famous. I photographed the large handsome doorman outside the main entrance and posed the head of the great Food Hall in his tailcoat and gray silk tie in front of shelves of caviar and truffles, marrons glacés and hovering white-capped assistants. Then I made pictures of the butcher and his assistants putting frills onto lamb legs, and elegant young women at the perfume counter spraying themselves with stuff that cost more per ounce than many people earn in a week!

The staff were so pleased to be photographed that for the grand finale I was granted the special dispensation of fifteen minutes to photograph Harrod's famous tearoom in all its glory of massed iced cakes, chocolate biscuits, scones and clotted cream, while a line of hungry people waited not very patiently for me to finish so they could attack the goodies when the tea shop opened at 3 p.m. I had rented a 600-watt quartz hot-light for this assignment, because I had to move around so fast, and bounced the light out of an umbrella and used tungsten film. Hot-lights are very quick and easy to set up and knock down (for more see Chapter Seven). I should mention, though, that the Harrods' cakes were starting to melt a bit as I finished.

Photographing Tourist Guests

At hotels and resorts, you can scout for guests who will pose for you and sign releases (it's usually easy to find nice-looking "models"; you may have to per-suade some by reassuring them that they are very photogenic, otherwise you wouldn't have chosen them). Arrange optimum hours to shoot them at the pool, golf course, beach, etc., all of which look best at uncrowded times. Too many people at any of these spots makes the place look cheap. Buy the guest a "thank you" drink later (on your expense account, of course) and, if possible, send "out-takes" (decent slides you can't use) later as a gift.

Photographing Monuments

You are almost bound to have to photograph the Sphinx if you go on assignment to Egypt, the Great Wall when in China and the Taj Mahal in India. They, along with the Statue of Liberty, the Acropolis and many other places you can easily think of, are symbols for a whole country or culture and are always in demand by tourism and business clients. American Express, Federal Express and textbook publishers for instance, all use all of these "musts" in different ways.

You may find your first sight of a world-famous monument disappointing; the Pyramids for instance, are a flat, dusty beige in overhead noonday sun, and are usually surrounded by crowds. You will have to decide how to make the Pyramids look their majestic best. (I hired a camel and driver and met them next day at dawn in the desert; the sun rose behind the Pyramids, the camel was silhouetted in front for a fine effect.) The Pyramids also look powerful at dusk, and there is floodlighting and a sound and light show just about every night at the Sphinx and nearby Pyramid.

When photographing any world-famous monument or site, you must usually get up early to avoid crowds, or stay late, or do both. Sometimes, special permission is needed. Quite recently I had the Liberty Bell in Philadelphia to myself for an hour before the public was admitted at 9 a.m. (Of course I needed permission from the local National Park Service Superintendant.) At all monuments, look at the light, try new angles and a creative approach. There is always another good picture to be made of even the most familiar symbolic sights; they are almost all truly splendid things.

Capturing the Spirit of a Place

This is the most difficult thing to do of all, and no two photographers will do it in the same way. I can suggest that you be very thorough in your advance research and in scouting the location once you arrive, that you go back more than once to a scene that you like if it's necessary, and that you include as many local people as possible. If you are inexperienced it's very important not to forget photographic basics in the excitement of being there. Your own taste will be your ultimate guide, trust it, and your own talent.

Keeping Track of Pictorial Goals

Whether on a paid or self-assignment, you must be focused (literally and mentally) on what you want to express in your photographs. Think of the pictures you are taking at any given moment as part of a larger whole. Refer to your letter of assignment (or whatever instructions you received, or list of goals you set yourself) frequently to refresh your memory. It's easy to overlook something, especially if you weren't crazy to do a particular shot in the first place.

Try and visualize how a real or imagined art director/designer/picture editor would use your photos.

If you shoot too many all-green-and-blue landscapes for instance, they will look boring laid out together in a magazine, tourism brochure or exhibit or album of prints. Balance landscapes with architecture and people pictures, and make sunrise or sunset or interior exposures on daylight film, for warm color. Mix overall views, medium shots and close-ups. Take verticals as well as horizontals, and make both right and left facing compositions.

Make a Shooting List

- Note what you have to cover on a shooting list, it helps a lot as the assignment proceeds.
- Plan shots in series grouped by location, or by special equipment or assistance needed, or by any other method that makes sense to you.
- Check off items one by one as you photograph them. Sometimes you may want to go back to redo something you have already covered, if the weather improves dramatically for instance.

I personally believe that people who shoot for stock have a bigger problem with balanced coverage that those working on assignment with outlines supplied by a magazine or commercial client. Successful stock photographers tell me that they assign themselves specifics, and make very detailed shooting lists, often with a daily schedule. Many work closely with their stock agencies, to produce coverage the agency feels is needed.

Keeping Flexible

While careful advance planning is extremely important for any successful travel photography, and especially critical for travel assignments and self-assigned stock shoots, a plan should not be so rigid that nothing can be altered. Weather, local conditions and problems with other people's schedules can change the best laid plans. If I can avoid getting locked into reservations, I always do so. If I go on a charter flight or restricted air ticket, I allow some extra time for contingencies that may force a change in plans. If nothing goes wrong (it usually doesn't) a few extra days at the end of the shoot "hanging out" with your cameras are great, I take some of my best personal pictures then. At such times, you can scout for new story ideas, take stock shots or, of course, just relax which is divine but makes me feel rather restless after a day or two!

Locally, be flexible too. You must be able to stop eating in the middle of lunch if the sun comes out while you are photographing in Ireland—the pretty light may only last for fifteen minutes, and if you keep lunching you may miss the shot you have been trying to get for two days. If you suddenly learn about a local festival that will make all the difference to your coverage of Hong Kong, you must change your reservations to Bali, whatever the later problems. Lord So-and-So may cancel three appointments (very politely, and with good reason) before you can photograph him in his country house; the shoot will probably be rescheduled on the one night you had a theater invitation to a hit show in London.

Evenings at the theater are rare, though I love them. When I'm working on assignment, that's usually all I do. If I am photographing on the beach, or at a pool, I don't go swimming. If I'm shooting a market I'm not shopping. If I'm shooting in a restaurant or at a party, I don't drink (I've observed this last rule since an evening, long ago, when I lost some important party shots because I'd had a few drinks and didn't load a camera properly!)

Do the fun things after you've got your pictures—if you have the strength.

Pacing Yourself

When traveling on a long professional assignment, take an occasional complete day off, especially on a trip with several segments. You need it not only to rest, but also to get your receipts and expenses sorted out, organize notes for captions, mark any film rolls that slipped into the corners of bags, get your laundry done, and, especially, mentally assess the quality of the coverage you have so far. People on personal trips can of course take as many days off as they please!

On a day off, run a roll or two of test film through a local lab to check camera function and exposure. You can also use the day to telephone, and schedule appointments and shooting dates. I have been known to cheer for one rainy day, and to revel in doing nothing much then during a hectic assignment. I enjoy room service, television and a few peaceful hours as the raindrops fall.

Choosing a Center

I try very hard not to photograph on days that I fly, drive very long distances, or change hotels, all of which mean mean packing, unpacking and rearranging my equipment for quick access.

Changing hotels is especially disrupting, so I try to work from a center if possible. I would rather stay in one place for a week than move three times, even if it means a lot more driving, because when I am organized in my hotel room it becomes my home quickly. I get to know the staff, who can help a lot; and I learn where my favorite roads and views are, and about local events that often make for good, non-cliché, pictures.

A few years ago I had to photograph the large state of Bavaria in southern Germany. I had been there before, and knew I didn't want to stay in its largest city, Munich, because of city traffic and parking problems, and because the countryside was the focus of the assignment.

I chose a good hotel (the Sonnenblick) on the outskirts of the resort town and regional center, Garmisch-Partenkirschen. Then I planned trips to the castles of Neueschwanstein and Hohenschwangau, the handsome lakeside resort of Lindau and many lesser-known places. I soon got to know the most scenic roads (even back roads are almost all fast and good in Germany) and found off-the-beaten track, half-timbered or painted villages, a beer festival in

July, pretty lake steamers, brooding stretches of the Black Forest, and lots of locals, including a woodchopper with a feather in his green hat who looked straight out of the Brothers Grimm! Of course I also photographed Oberammergau, with its elaborately painted houses, woodcarving shops, and bearded males and long-haired women preparing for the next year's Passion Play.

I have no problem photographing as well as driving 200 or 300 miles in a day if necessary; of course, if you have a driver you cover more ground and it's less tiring. In Bavaria I was alone, and covered more in the nine days I stayed in Garmisch than I would have been able to if I had moved three or four times. I did burn a lot of gas though, but fortunately the client didn't complain.

Keeping Track of Film for Later Processing

As you shoot, mark each cassette or roll with a removable adhesive Avery label (they come in all sizes and colors; available at stationery stores) or black permanent Magic Marker, so that you keep track of your subject matter. Mark each individual film cassette, for instance: Day 1, roll C; Day 3, set-up B, roll D, etc. or whatever system makes sense to you. At the end of a day or take, put the film in freezer bags, squeeze the air out and rubber band the bag closed. Mark date/location, etc. on the bag and then keep it cool until processing.

When you get the film processed (I recommend waiting until you get home for this), you can ask the lab to identify each roll with your removable marked label. First though, divide the film into groups. Then, process the film in two or three separate batches to minimize the slight but real risk of a lab losing or damaging an entire take. (Professional insurance to protect you for this is available from ASMP, see Chapter Fifteen.) Use the identifying labels also to select rolls for any necessary clip tests when developing.

Shipping Film Home for Processing

If you are going on a very long trip with several stops, you may need (or wish) to ship film home for processing. (I don't like overseas processing.) Use a well-known shipping agency like DHL Worldwide or Federal Express (see also later in this chapter). If possible let your lab or representative know beforehand you will be shipping film from overseas. After marking instructions on all the rolls, wrap batches of film in two layers of plastic bags, then wrap the whole package in newspapers for insulation. Tape that together and include detailed instructions for your trusted lab, then put the package in a sturdy box. (You can also use a Sima lead bag or two if you are worried about X-rays; see also earlier in this chapter and Chapters Five and Nineteen.) Hand deliver the film to the shipping agency of your choice. Mark the package "Undeveloped Film, Do Not X-Ray, Keep Cool and Dry." You can ship the film in two or three separate packages to minimize possibilities of loss. (See also Insurance, below.)

The forwarding company will deal with customs forms. Send the film to your lab, client, or other representative. Make sure they know that the film must be processed immediately on arrival. Arrange and if necessary pay for all this before you leave home. Members of Kodak's "Pro Passport Service" get an ID card, a list of DHL Worldwide Express offices with phone numbers, and receive a 10% discount on shipments from most countries. (Contact Kodak Pro Passport at [800] 242-2424, extension 99, for details.) Federal Express also has offices just about everywhere. (See also Insurance in Chapter Fifteen)

Airport Security and the X-Ray Problem
Despite the signs at airports, cumulative X-rays are not good for film. If you carry unprocessed film with you for several segments of a long foreign assignment (and through several mandatory airport security inspections), put your film in Sima lead-foil bags. The "Jumbo" size bag holds about 60 rolls of 35mm film; suggested list is $19.95. They are obtainable at professional photo dealers. I use the double-thickness bags in third world countries. (See earlier in this chapter, also Chapters Five and Nineteen.)

Note: United States federal law and Canadian regulations permit you to ask for hand examination of your film.

If you don't use lead bags, put a few rolls of 1600 speed film on top of your hand-carried film package. That will convince many (not all) foreign security people to hand-inspect your film, and save it cumulative X-rays.

I personally don't know anyone whose film has been damaged by airport X-rays, and have never seen film damaged by X-rays (I am told by Kodak that it looks like wavy shadows on developed film) but you can never be too careful.

Handling Travel Paperwork
When traveling and photographing, professionals must take the time to keep track of all expenses, or you will lose on both income-tax deductions and client reimbursements.

I don't have a laptop computer, but I do note the exchange rate the first day I arrive in a country, and keep a "Daybook" or diary of petty cash spent each day. (I keep all receipts, you never know if you will be audited; see also later in this chapter.) You may like to carry a currency converter; I use a calculator.

Pay all possible bills with credit cards. American Express cards have no preset spending limits, but you must keep your payments current. You may pay at any office abroad if you are on a long trip. Visa and Mastercards are accepted in some places and countries (especially at smaller hotels, restaurants, national railroads and local transport companies) where Amex cards are not, and payments should also be kept current.

Always keep all money exchange receipts. You may need them to change money back into dollars, and the fee is a tax-deduction for professionals. (Take my advice and never deal in black market currency. It is against the law, you will usually be dealing with unsavory people, and you risk being stuck with money you can't exchange back into dollars.)

Returning Home

Don't relax your travel vigilance when you land on home ground (it's easy to do when tired), keep track of all your bags until you are safely inside your own front door. Call your client or stock agency and say you are home. (They do care!) After any assignment/trip always have your film processed as soon as possible when you arrive home; the color can "shift"—and image quality deteriorate quite quickly, especially if you had to keep the film unrefrigerated at any time during your travels.

First sort film into two, three or more batches, identifying rolls by the dates/ numbers/letters you marked on Avery labels; then take a few key rolls to the lab immediately and refrigerate the rest. If you need exposure adjustment or more clip-tests this can be decided after viewing the first of the take. Process the rest of the film in successive batches as quickly as possible.

When you have all the film back, edit, rough-out group captions, stamp it with your name and copyright symbol and rush it over to the client who is almost always impatient for that first look!

Tidying Up Loose Ends

Your last chores will be writing up expenses, making detailed caption sheets for the pictures (I keep mine on the computer), sorting out equipment and getting it checked-out and cleaned after an arduous trip. Then, bill the client as soon as possible.

Billing and Record Keeping for Tax Purposes

Do this as soon as possible, both to get paid quickly and also so that you remember what those funny little pink tickets and diary notations were for. (The United States Internal Revenue Service does not require receipts for items costing less than $25, diary/daybook listings are accepted.) Keep and file the daybook. I advise keeping the pink tickets too, I am super-cautious because I have been audited several times.

Include a statement on all your invoices that your terms are net 30 days. Many businesses today charge 1 1/2% per month interest on any unpaid balance; because final payments can take much longer than the customary 30 days, especially in lean economic times. (See Sample Invoice later in this chapter.)

Planning Personal/Vacation Travel

If I am traveling without an assignment, I plan an itinerary also (but a more relaxed one, of course) to see and photograph places that interest me. I let people know where I will be traveling, and call my answering machine quite frequently, just in case someone wants something from where I will be at the last minute. It happened once when I was "hanging out," as my daughter says, with friends in Rome. That first small assignment blossomed into a client that I had for twenty years.

On a personal trip, I don't usually carry more than two cameras, a lightweight tripod and two small flash units with external batteries and a charger. I take about four lenses, and I search for beautiful landscapes (which I like to photograph more and more) as well as interesting people. I'll also do buildings and interiors if they are important. I do take plenty of my favorite slow and fast film. (See Chapter Five.)

I live very modestly when traveling at my own expense, but that does not mean the trip is not fun or successful. I went to California a few years ago because I wanted to get to know the state better, it was during an air-fare war. I had previously done two assignments in San Diego, so I spent my three weeks mostly exploring the northern part of the state.

First, I spent a week in San Francisco (where I sublet a vacationing chef's apartment through a mutual acquaintance); then I got a good deal on a rental car and drove up through the wine country, cut to the coast at Mendocino, and drove up through redwood country as far as the Oregon border and saw great Victorian "lumber barons'" mansions at Eureka. I returned inland, through the Trinity National Forest, gold-mining and garlic-growing country, then returned to the coast to see the famous sights of Carmel and Monterey, Big Sur, the Seventeen Mile Drive at Pebble Beach and the rest of California Highway One down the rugged blue misty coast. I stopped near San Luis Obispo to photograph William Randolph Hearst's mansion—or palace—San Simeon, one of the greatest houses I have ever seen. Reservations for the mandatory tours are limited, book a few days ahead at (800) 444-7275. Professionals should send a copy of the letter of assignment to the Rights and Reproductions Coordinator, Hearst San Simeon State Historical Monument, 750 Hearst Castle Road, San Simeon, CA 93452 to make arrangements. If it's a last minute assignment, have your picture editor call (805) 927-2020.

I checked out Santa Barbara—the Reagans were not in residence—and was shocked by the oil rigs so close to the beautiful shore. Then I drove across Los Angeles on several freeways (but did not dare stop to photograph) passing the Hollywood sign en route (it's copyrighted). I spent a night in an art-deco first class cabin on the grand old Queen Mary in Long Beach (a far cry from the D Deck closet on the Queen Elizabeth which I had when I came to America) and finished the trip by spending a few days with friends in Anaheim, where my daughter flew out to join me. We saw Disneyland together for three days before returning home.

I have sold quite a few pictures from that trip; of the misty Golden Gate Bridge, redwoods, and my daughter with Mickey Mouse; also of Japanese tourists at Point Lobos, vineyards in the Napa Valley, and even empty California highways. By now stock sales have covered the expenses of this modestly-priced odyssey, which I thoroughly enjoyed. (I want to go back one spring or fall to spend time photographing and getting to know Los Angeles, and to "do" the art scene there thoroughly, and also to see Yosemite and Lake Tahoe.)

Sample Travel Assignment Invoice

Att: Mr. Whizz Bang Sales Director
Sensational Tours Inc..
222 Landmark Avenue
New York, NY 100??   Date: June 14, 199?

Invoice for assignment to photograph hotels, inns and tourist facilities in England, May 24 - June 8, 1991.
Rights granted: Use in tourism brochures from 1992 -199?
(Note: Always set time or other usage limit, this is a negotiable item, and should satisfy both parties.)

Round-trip economy *(but go business class if you can!)* airfare: New York/London *(based on lowest current fare)* $600.00

Local expenses in Pounds Sterling converted at $1.87 to the pound
(use current rate) Photo copies of receipts are attached

Five nights Classy Hotel London @ 50% discount	350.00	
London Meals	104.50	
London Taxis, Busses, Subways	44.25	
London admissions	17.45	
London tips, misc.	24.25	
One week compact car rental	180.00	
Rooms with meals outside London:		
Two nights Ye Olde Spotted Swanne, Stratford	76.00	
One night Royal Inne, Windsor	45.00	
One night Roman Villa, Bath	38.00	
One night The Cloisters, Salisbury	60.00	
Two nights Land's End Hotel, Bude	160.00	
One night Lord Francis Hotel, Plymouth	52.00	
One night Brandnew Motorway Inn, Swindon	55.00	
Misc. meals en route	54.00	
Gas	94.00	
Admissions, tips, misc.	41.00	
Total expenses (in Pounds Sterling)	£1355.25	U.S.$2,544.71

86 rolls film and processing @ $15:   1,290.00
(Note: Add cost of Polaroids, clip tests, "push/pull" and rush charges etc., if used.)

Total Expenses:	4,434.71

Agreed Fee: 14 days @ $500.00 per day (or as negotiated)   7,000.00

Total:	$11,434.71
Received in Advance:	$ 7,500.00
Balance due:	$ 3,984.00

All photographs to be returned, unaltered and unretouched, to the photographer after use; no Sales Tax due.
(Note: check your own state Sales Tax regulations.)
Terms net 30 days; 1 1/2% per month interest will be charged on the unpaid balance.

Thank you,

(Signed) Phantastic Photographer

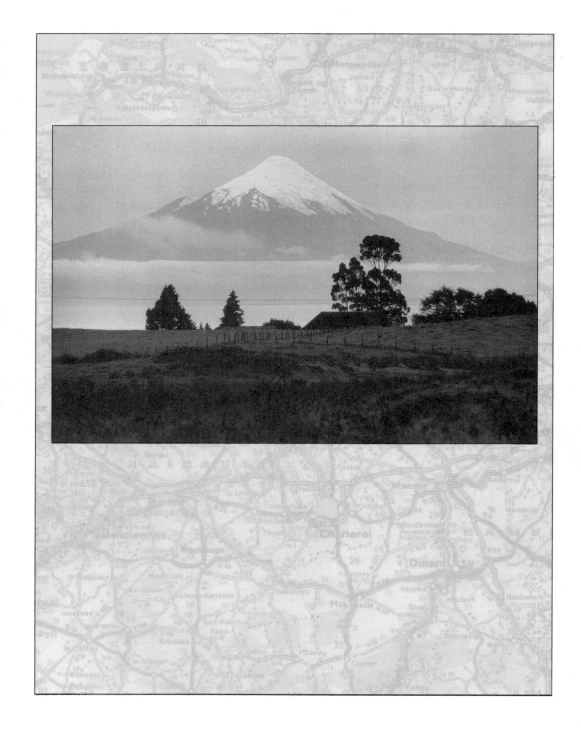

Chapter 17

Travel Highlights: North, Central & South America

Many of my clients are in the tourism business, in one form or another. Most of the places listed below are tourist musts. Of course, I try to go off the beaten track too, and enjoy that more and more. My recommendations are subjective, but what photographer would go to Rome for the first time without seeing the Colosseum, or to Bangkok without spending time at the Temple of the Emerald Buddha? To dig deeper before you go, consult libraries. If you live in a big city, you can visit the many tourist offices and consulates that have specialized libraries. I spent an instructive afternoon at the Australian Consulate library here in New York recently, looking at back issues of the *Australian Geographic*, specialist publications about national parks and the aboriginal people, and reading local newspapers.

The United States—New York City

New York is, with all its problems, the quintessential city. (For me, only Tokyo, Istanbul and Hong Kong come close for sheer energy.) New York is marvelous to photograph, the center is compact and most people are very friendly despite their reputation—but by all means be a bit cautious. Especially don't leave valuable equipment unattended for even a second, and never work outside at night without an assistant or companion to keep an eye on the surroundings. (Actually that's good advice for most cities today.)

Spring and fall days in New York often have exceptionally clear light; at Christmas the decorations are spectacular and especially fun in Italian sections in all boroughs. Fourth of July and other holiday fireworks on the East River taken from Long Island City in Queens give opportunities for great Manhattan skyline pictures, and dusk pictures taken from the Empire State Building, RCA Building or World Trade Center observation towers, and from the walkway of the Brooklyn Bridge, are classic. So is the view east to lower Manhattan from the park which is beside the Exchange Place PATH train station in Jersey City (across the Hudson River).

May, June and September are the months for all kinds of block festivals, great for photographing people. New York's busy Chinatown grows ever larger, the most authentic quarter with superb outdoor food markets is now east of the Bowery and just north of Canal Street. Traditional Italian street festivals are held in Greenwich Village in June and early September, and just about every population group in the city has a parade or festival one day of the year. Take the D subway train to Coney Island in Brooklyn to photograph working New Yorkers (and some tourists) relaxed and at their best. Rides are open June through Labor Day, the boardwalk and beach are there all year. I leave when the family groups do, after "blue time." The Botanical Gardens in Brooklyn are especially lovely in April and May, and early October; or, go to the New York Botanical Garden in the Bronx and combine the trip with a visit to the Bronx Zoo, where most of the animals have lots of room—don't miss the African plains section. Staten Island has New York City's only historic village, the Richmondtown Restoration, and I don't suppose you want will miss the Staten Island ferry ride, a 40-minute round trip—it is one of the greatest travel bargains in the world. The ferry passes the Statue of Liberty and Ellis Island, but not too close.

For on-island views of those national shrines take a Circle Line boat from Battery Park. Be prepared for hideously long lines, spring to fall; tripods are okay outside. (For photography inside with a tripod special permission is required at both sites; write well in advance, with a copy of assignment letter, to: The Superintendent, Statue of Liberty/Ellis Island National Monuments, Ellis Island, NY 10004. Request time before/after the places are open to the public.)

Queens is called the borough of homes, but it has our airports, some of the best cemeteries I have ever seen, a great scale model of New York in the Queens Museum, and the New York Mets whose devoted fans are worth photographing at Shea Stadium.

My own neighborhood of Manhattan, once called the Photo District (nowadays, the Flatiron District or officially, the Ladies' Mile Historic District) has cast-iron architecture and the prototypic skyscraper, the Flatiron Building, which has just been cleaned. There are good shops and restaurants, and pretty houses reminiscent of New Orleans in nearby Gramercy Park (which has a moderately priced hotel of the same name).

The West Village has many tree-lined streets of charming old brick (and a few wooden) houses, full of literary associations from the '20's and '30's. The East Village around St. Marks Place is for students and youth (and especially "punks"). You will find gentrified and ungentrified tenements with fire escapes, and good cheap shops and restaurants. The Lower East Side, made famous by immigrants, still has a lively street market on and around Orchard Street, go especially on Sundays. Soho has Civil War era cast-iron lofts, is the center for expensive art galleries and has good restaurants and shops, too. The Upper

West Side in the 70's and 80's is the best place to find New York's famous rows of brownstones.

For event lists, and a city map, contact the New York Convention and Visitors Bureau, 2 Columbus Circle, New York, NY 10019. Phone (212) 397-8200.

Technically you need a permit to use a tripod on any public sidewalk or park in New York City. Apply to the Mayor's Office for Film, 254 West 54th Street, New York, NY 10019. Phone (212) 489-6710. Permits are issued free. The office is efficient—getting a permit takes only about ten minutes—and you can shoot immediately. (Note: for most purposes in New York, you can actually do as I do, and shoot like an innocent tourist. I have listed the few places where permits are essential below.)

You always need a permit to use a tripod outdoors at Lincoln Center, South Street Seaport and Rockefeller Center; guards will stop you if you try, so apply in advance to the various public relations departments (these places are all privately owned). You need a permit for a professional-looking tripod at Battery Park City, and on the observation towers at the Empire State Building and World Trade Center. (Ordinary tourists with small tripods are not usually bothered at those places.) You also need a permit, and a letter of assignment, to photograph the great city symbol of finance; apply to the Communications Department, New York Stock Exchange, 11 Wall Street, New York, NY 10003. Phone (212) 656-6626 for magazine photographers; others should call (212) 656-6215.

Don't even think of driving in Manhattan unless you have a companion who can sit in the vehicle at all times; legal parking spaces are nonexistent, traffic police and tow-trucks super-vigilant and fines enormous. Public transport is good (busses are safer than the subway at night) and taxis relatively cheap.

New York State

"Upstate" New York is not too well known except to people who live there. A pity; it is green, rolling and beautiful, has nice small towns and interesting old industrial cities that will surely make a comeback one day just because of the architecture. Niagara Falls and the great Adirondack National Park are wonderful to photograph. I have a house in the Town of Shawangunk in the Hudson Valley, an hour and a half from the Big Apple. The area is mostly orchards, there are fields of black-and-white cows, and it all looks quite a lot like parts of England. Across the Hudson River, at Hyde Park, the Franklin Delano Roosevelt home (a large but relatively simple place) is next door to the enormous, ornate Vanderbilt Mansion, one of America's stateliest homes. Advance permission is required for professional photography in both locations.

Farther north and west in NY State, Saratoga (famed for horse racing) and Chautauqua (famed for culture) both have splendid Victorian gingerbread architecture. Our wine producing region, the Finger Lakes, is quite extensive and you can visit wineries. Taughannock Falls and Watkins Glen have charming, rather Victorian looking waterfalls—perhaps I say that because my soft green and gray pictures of them somehow look like antique postcards.

The city of Niagara Falls, New York is not my favorite place (the motel strip on NY 62 is a classic) but the falls themselves transcend their exploitation and are the greatest natural attraction in the Eastern United States. The close-up views of Horseshoe Falls from the west side of Goat Island are spectacular. Niagara Falls, Ontario is quite pleasant, with pretty parks and a floral clock, and has great views of both the American and Canadian falls. There are high viewing towers on both sides of the border, but I prefer the close-ups. For the best pictures of all take the Maid of the Mist boats that go to the foot of the falls—almost under them it seems—and also take the Cave of the Winds walk. (Take an underwater camera or housing, or use plastic bags carefully taped around ordinary cameras on both these very damp excursions; rain ponchos are provided.) Time exposures of the floodlit falls at dusk/night are best taken from the Canadian side. I haven't seen the falls in winter, but there is a festival of lights in November and December. I have seen student pictures taken out of season, and the falls look superb under snow.

Pennsylvania

Go to Philadelphia in May to see crew racing on the Schuykill River (and the crews tending boats along Boathouse Row, which is illuminated at night). This is a good spot for city skyline pictures too. Delancey Street goes across the city. The architecture of this street changes in different districts but it's very pretty to very handsome all the way. The Italian Market in the South End is open air, jammed and terrific. The "center-city" Reading Terminal Market is covered, more sedate but still worth photographing. You need a permit from the National Park Service for professional photography with a tripod at all the historic sites; try and arrange a before-opening-hours visit to the Liberty Bell and Independence Hall which are are always mobbed. Outside Philadelphia, near King of Prussia, is Valley Forge with reconstructed soldiers' log huts, and George Washington's fine stone farmhouse headquarters. I like it in winter under snow, when the shivering army is easily imagined. There is lots of lovely open space in Pennsylvania, another underrated state scenically. Take Route 120 from Williamsport (where the Little League Baseball World Series is held in August) to the edge of the Allegheny National Forest. You will pass below Hyner View; make a short detour to the locally-famous spot overlooking what is billed as the Grand Canyon of Pennsylvania. It is worth photographing.

New England

I sometimes imagine America as many separate countries, like Europe. Some states would be joined with others, but Vermont and Maine are so distinctive (because of their long history, low population and relative isolation) that they would have to be separate countries —my mental equivalents are Austria and Norway. New Hampshire is, to me, less unique. People in Maine, Vermont and New Hampshire are very friendly, despite the jokes made about them. Smaller towns and villages are typically crowned with white wooden churches. Mixed hardwood and pine trees, hills, mountains, lakes and, in Maine, the rocky shore, lighthouses and ocean, make scenery as lovely of its type as can be found any-where. I especially like East Jamaica, Vermont, near Bennington; and Castine,

Maine. The fall foliage season in New England is, of course, world famous. It runs from early September to late October (earliest near the border of Quebec). In late September or early October it reaches Massachusetts where the Berkshires around Pittsfield are very photogenic. Boston has many great buildings, and the charming Beacon Hill district of brick houses and cobblestone streets. Nearby Lexington and Concord, of course, are shrines of the Revolutionary war. Cambridge has Longfellow's mansion, and Harvard; the Harvard Yard is especially good to photograph in fall when it is full of fresh-faced students pushing bikes. Don't miss Cape Cod, part of which is now a National Seashore. Further south, Rhode Island has whaling captains' houses at Bristol, the 19th-century summer "cottages" (mansions) of some of America's most famous families; the yachting center of Newport; and beautiful, misty, Block Island. In Connecticut, Mystic Seaport is a historic restoration with many fine old ships and there are many picture-perfect villages, including Lakeville.

Roads can be very crowded in New England at fall foliage time. I have photographed in Vermont then without advance reservations, because many homeowners rent a room or two to tourists at the peak season. (Find rooms through local tourist bureaus or chambers of commerce.) Make reservations well ahead if you prefer hotels, motels or inns. Don't miss a church supper or two (good and cheap and a way to meet and photograph the locals). They are combined social events and fundraisers. County fairs and music festivals are offered throughout New England in summer. I especially like the area north of a line running roughly from Rutland, VT, Laconia, NH to Bar Harbor, ME. New England is less traveled the further you get from New York and Boston.

Washington, D.C.

To me, this is the most beautiful city in America, with planned vistas that might have been designed for photographers. The handsome new Canadian Embassy across from the new East Wing of the National Gallery of Art completes the view up Pennsylvania Avenue to the Capitol. Reflecting pools seem to be everywhere. The 300mm telephoto lens shot from the Iwo Jima Memorial across the Potomac to the Capitol dome, the Washington Monument and the Lincoln Memorial is a classic. From the Capitol steps (with a tripod permit, see below) shoot fireworks over the Washington Monument on major holidays. It is even photographically worth braving the crowds at cherry-blossom time, but it's hard to predict exactly when in March/April this falls. I like Washington at Christmas when the huge National and 50 appropriately-decorated state Christmas trees are in their glory, and in fall though the colors there are more subdued for some reason than in nearby Virginia.

There are a lot of very good assignment and stock photographers living in Washington and vicinity, including my friends Pat and Wayne Fisher (who help me out a lot when I go there), so though I have both done assignments and shot some (I think) very nice stock in Washington, I haven't sold many stock shots of the place.

You don't absolutely have to have a car to get around Washington, though it's convenient. The subway is good and safe and goes almost everywhere; taxis are cheap (metered by zone). Parking not easy to find downtown or around the monuments. A car (and permits for professional photography from the appropriate National Park Service bureaus) are essentials for photographing George Washington's Mount Vernon and Thomas Jefferson's elegant Monticello, both reasonably near Washington, in Virginia. (These are both highly photogenic.)

If you use a Tripod in Washington

To photograph with a tripod at or near or in just about all the famous places in Washington requires a permit, best applied for well in advance of your visit. The National Park Service, National Capitol Region, Public Events Office handles the city monuments. Call them at (202) 619-7225. The Capitol Police, Sergeant at Arms Office, issues necessary permits for outdoor photography with tripods anywhere in the Capitol vicinity, and for (assigned) indoor photography in both the House of Representatives and Senate. Phone (202) 224-3121. To photograph inside the White House requires a letter of assignment to get a permit; send it (as far ahead of time as possible) to the White House Usher's Office, Washington, D.C. 20500.

New Jersey, Delaware, Maryland, Virginia

No, New Jersey is not wall-to-wall concrete. If you love old-fashioned beach resorts as I do, all along the shore from Long Branch and Asbury Park to Atlantic City (Donald Trump's Taj Mahal casino is world-class visual kitsch) and Cape May—these are all in New Jersey—to Reheboth Beach, Delaware and Ocean City, Maryland; you will find amusement areas, fishing boats, pleasure boats, gingerbread architecture and of course crowds on the fine beaches in summer. Around the Chesapeake, on Maryland's eastern shore, there are still a few practically undeveloped and undiscovered small towns and villages; find your favorites with a car. Try Oxford or Tilghman Island. The Delmarva Peninsula has nice flat farmland. The rather handsome former railroad terminal of Cape Charles, Virginia, is famous among fishermen—the enormous Black Drum fish caught around there have to be pushed around in wheelbarrows. Go in May if you want to photograph them. The Assateague, Maryland, and adjacent Chincoteague, Virginia, National Seashore protected areas are both superb, with booming surf and long, steep, white sand beaches. They are not too crowded even in summer if you walk a bit away from the parking areas. Although the wild ponies of Chincoteague are legendary, they are few and hard to spot at most times. I haven't been there at roundup time in August when there are huge crowds. I have been in mid/late November to photograph the hundreds of thousands of migratory birds. Cape Hatteras, North Carolina, National Seashore is very beautiful but also very crowded in summer; just north is Bodie Island which is much less visited.

The South

The famous restoration at Williamsburg, Virginia, with costumed villagers, craft shops, etc. is a fine place to photograph, but avoid busy holidays. Professionals must get permission, and may be able to arrange private time at the more crowded attractions. The University of Virginia, designed by Thomas Jefferson, is worth photographing at Charlottesville . The Skyline Drive along the Blue Ridge Mountains (start at Front Royal) is lovely, but often too blue—very hazy and polluted. The clear light of fall is best (and foliage color is at its peak) in Virginia sometime in late October. Some roads are very heavily traveled then.

In West Virginia (which is underphotographed) Harper's Ferry is beautifully situated at the confluence of the Potomac and Shenandoah rivers, and has terraces of old stone houses as well as the ruin of John Brown's fort—and famous arsenal.

The countryside of western North Carolina around Asheville is very mountainous, and there is great folk art in the region. I have photographed Cherokee woodcarvers, several quiltmakers and a lady who makes stuffed life-size "Mountain People" that are a cross between Cabbage Patch dolls and serious sculpture. The Biltmore Mansion near Asheville is one of America's greatest houses; it was built to resemble a French château by a member of the Vanderbilt family. The grounds are fine too.

I have three times taken a boat trip along the IntraCoastal Waterway, between Newport, Virginia and Miami, Florida. Some places I liked a lot: the great naval port of Newport itself, full of battleships, tankers and smaller craft; the Dismal Swamp Canal (obviously named before travel public relations; it's not at all dismal) near Elizabeth City, North Carolina; Charleston, South Carolina, beautifully laid out with white wooden Georgian houses (in the harbor is Fort Sumter, where the shot starting the American Civil War was fired). Savannah, Georgia, has lovely gardens, restored cotton warehouses along the riverfront and nice, quiet flowery streets of old wooden homes.

I "did" Atlanta twenty years ago for a magazine, and saw it again recently on another assignment. The place was practically unrecognizable, it has grown so much. The Martin Luther King Memorial (which is always surrounded by groups of solemn kids), the Coca Cola Headquarters, and the panoramic view from the revolving tower are "musts." Old Stone Mountain outside the city has heroic-size carvings of Southern Civil War scenes.

I made an all-too-brief visit to New Orleans before I was a professional photographer, and saw just the iron balconied houses of the French Quarter, the cathedral and Jackson Square and Preservation Hall where the jazz was very good. Not a bad visit obviously; I would love to see these highlights again, and visit the Mississippi bayous around the city, too.

In Florida, where I have been several times, I like Cumberland Island, part of which is a nature refuge, and where there are some rather splendid decaying mansions of 19th-century industrial barons. Some of their descendants still visit. The beaches are almost deserted and white, with wild horses occasionally to be seen. Jacksonville has a fine drawbridge over the IntraCoastal Waterway, Cape Canaveral is a thrill. (There is rampant motel development nearby, great for my kitsch collection.) Rich Palm Beach reminds me of Bermuda, with pink and white houses. I must be the only person living in America who has never been to Walt Disney World. Fort Lauderdale looks rich also, and has a splendid harbor. I have taken fun pictures of almost wall-to-wall small craft just outside the main channel exit from the harbor.

I like the Art Deco District of Miami Beach, where European fashion photographers can often be seen working; some of these 1920's and '30's buildings are attractive small hotels. (A travel agent friend recommends the Park Central and Cardozo hotels.) Start with a look at the Fontainbleau Hotel, a 1950's monument to glitz, whose glories have been immortalized by Elliott Erwitt, and go south for the historic area. Viscaya, an enormous Spanish-style villa with waterfront gardens near Miami, was built by John Deere, the tractor magnate, and will give you some pictures, but it is always crowdwd.

The Midwest

I haven't seen as much of the heartland as I should like, but I very much enjoy Chicago when I go there. I head straight to the Wrigley Building and North River for "instant Chicago" pictures, and have sold some of them as stock—which suggests that Chicago is underphotographed. Columbus, in southern Indiana, is a very small city where a great many of the finest modern architects of the world have designed large and small public buildings. The family foundation created by the Cummins Diesel Engine fortune sponsored all this. I once went to Wichita, Kansas and saw the nearby prairie land called the Flint Hills. It's almost empty and very lovely.

The Southwest

I have been to many parts of the world, and have no hesitation in saying the most spectacular landscapes I have ever seen are in the American Southwest. Fly to Phoenix, Albuquerque or Salt Lake City and drive in a circle through Arizona, New Mexico and Utah and you can't go wrong photographically. I do suggest you avoid high summer if possible, although a lot of fine Indian festivals are held then, because in July and August the most famous places are crowded, and it's very hot. If you do go in July or August, don't push yourself in the middle of the day, go off the beaten path a bit, and you will be all right. Start from booming Phoenix (see Scottsdale) then drive up via Sedona and Oak Creek Canyon to the Grand Canyon. If you can't get a reservation in the park, I recommend the small logging town of Williams about 50 miles south, which is still rather frontierish and relatively unspoiled, but with plenty of motels—two good ones are owned by Britishers!

Grand Canyon National Park is open 24 hours a day, year round. Go in spring, fall or winter if you possibly can. Take the West Rim Drive to Hopi Point for sunset views (in summer you must park and use a shuttle bus); the East Rim Drive is open to cars all year. I like the views from close to the museum at Yavapai Point on the East Rim in the early morning. Take the East Rim Drive out through the Painted Desert to Cameron (you can stay at the historic trading post there) and if you wish see the North Rim of the canyon, where I haven't been. They say the view is fine, and the place relatively uncrowded.

Monument Valley is a Navajo Nation-administered park partly in Arizona, partly in Utah. Yes, it is very well known and much photographed, but it's nonetheless a spiritual experience. The great red rock formations rise sheer from the valley floor, and Navajo gods seem very close. I recommend staying at least a couple of days here, to catch sunrises and sunsets and ever changing cloud effects, and just to soak up the feeling of the place. Don't miss the North Window, Artist's Point and John Ford's Point (where a Navaho and his horse wait to pose for a fee!) If you take a guide, he will show you places not open to unaccompanied visitors. Just outside the park, stay at Goulding's Lodge, a tasteful modern motel that blends with the huge red rocks around it. It is next to the historic Goulding's trading post that is now a museum dedicated to John Ford and his movies. Or, camp in the park itself. Reservations at both places are a must, the valley was full of Europeans when I was there in April. (I'm told that in July and August the area gets very crowded indeed, best plan your photographic visit out of the high tourist season.) From Monument Valley take Route 163 north into Utah—it's like driving through a Georgia O'Keefe landscape of receding round hills striated with red, gray and black layers.

Stay at Moab, Utah for the superb Arches and Canyonlands National Parks. From Moab, drive down into New Mexico via Arizona and wonderful Canyon de Chelley with great Indian pueblos, to Chaco Canyon, Taos and Georgia O'Keefe country, and Santa Fe, New Mexico (which is beautiful but again very busy in July and August). Besides the major attractions, on almost any back road in the Southwest you'll come across almost-abandoned one-gas-station towns, with thin old-timers all wrinkled and dried out by the desert heat. (The young of all races leave, mostly for the delights of Los Angeles.) In late summer in the desert, you get spectacular cloudscapes and sometimes intense thunderstorms. I have never been to Las Vegas, Nevada but it's my next planned trip. The ultimate in kitsch, which interests me right now.

Texas

I have only seen Dallas, Houston and El Paso, and not for long at that. I want to spend more time in these places, and go out into the Texas hinterlands. I particularly enjoyed Houston where I photographed (of course) oil-related things; the Houston ship canal is a fine industrial landscape. Downtown Houston skyscrapers are fronted by open space, which makes photographing them simple. In Dallas I shot a swimming meet, visited the infamous Texas School Book Depository building, and had a fine lunch in the Neiman Marcus store. (I'm told the new architecture in Dallas is spectacular.) I spent only a couple of days in El Paso and vicinity, crossing to Mexico at Ciudad Juárez.

California

I love it. For a description of a personal trip I made there, see Chapter Fifteen.

San Francisco.

Yes—it is very beautiful. I spent about eight days shooting it, and loved the place. The classic view of "painted ladies"—Victorian houses covered in gingerbread against the modern skyline—is taken from Alamo Square. Golden Gate Park gives you the shot of the bridge against the downtown skyline, and there are big ferryboats leaving from the Fisherman's Wharf area all day long for pictures from the water. You must get up early to get good streetcar pictures, because they are usually uncomfortably packed with tourists hanging onto every crevice. I would not want to "do" San Francisco without a car, too much walking uphill, but, parking as usual is a problem in the business district downtown. Go north from San Francisco to see redwoods and wine country, south for Carmel, Monterey, Big Sur and miles of unspoiled coastline.

San Diego
A booming city, with perhaps the world's best zoo, ornate Spanish-style buildings in beautiful Balboa Park (which I'm told today sadly also has a homeless encampment). There is a fine Art Deco District too, the harbor is splendid, with sightseeing cruises. Nearby La Jolla is famous for surfing and theater. I went to San Diego to photograph, believe it or not, for army recruiting and nuclear research. San Diego is two hours from the Mexican border at Tijuana.

Los Angeles
I've driven across it, as a New Yorker I can almost handle the freeways without fear. Hollywood and Anaheim, where the original Disneyland is, are two of the world's great tourist attractions. Absolutely marvellous fun, particularly if you take a cute kid as I did. Contact Disney Public Relations in advance if you are doing an assignment in Disneyland, and they will probably produce Mickey. It's easy to get lesser characters like Goofy (sorry Goof).

California's three great cities each have a real character of their own. My stock pictures of California have done especially well in Japan.

The Northwest and Alaska
I have never been to the Northwestern states or Alaska. These are all great scenic places. Their tourism potential has only just been scratched.

Temporary Importation of Photography Equipment Into the United States

Canadian and foreign tourists and photographers should carry itemized lists, with serial numbers, of all the equipment they bring into the United States. Get them stamped by customs on leaving home, and show them to U.S. Customs on arrival. If you have a "reasonable" amount of equipment, a verbal declaration that you are doing an assignment and temporarily importing used equipment— "tools of the trade"—will satisfy the United States Customs inspector. You may be asked to state when you are leaving.

If you carry a lot of high-priced, new-looking equipment, avoid problems by getting a "Carnet" before you come. (See also Chapters Fourteen and Fifteen.)

Canada

I love Canada, and especially Canadians, who seem to me to combine some of the characteristics I like best of both the British and the American character, with a bit of good French flavoring too! Canadians are very friendly, but it's still polite to ask permission for people pictures.

The Maritime Provinces

Nova Scotia is the province of Canada I know best. I have a theory that in about a hundred years time, when everyone has immense amounts of leisure, the last truly unspoiled beautiful places will have what the English euphemistically call "unsettled" weather. Nova Scotia is such a place. You don't go there to get suntanned (although the last few summers have been very fine). Coming from the south, take the ferry from either Portland or Bar Harbor, Maine to Yarmouth, Nova Scotia, which has a lovely harbor. I've sailed into it three times, it's usually misty and has small gray islets draped in seaweed and a fine lighthouse. Nova Scotia has hundreds of miles of rugged sea coast, a temperate, changeable-to-damp climate (quite like England's, in fact) pretty wooden towns and villages, a very interesting and rather sad history (not exactly to the credit of the British) and is to me another place with haunting spirits lurking in the atmosphere.

Go there spring to fall; see very authentic highland gatherings (many Scots went to Nova Scotia when the English seized their lands in the mid-1700's). You can meet their descendents and also those of American Loyalist families who backed the wrong horse in the Revolutionary War and fled north when King George lost it. Other Nova Scotians are descended from slaves who escaped to freedom; the province was one of the terminals of the Underground Railroad organized by American abolitionists.

Many Nova Scotian French Acadian settlers were ruthlessly expelled by the British at the time of the Napoleonic wars (they went to Louisiana where they became "cajuns") but a few managed to stay; others returned later. Today there are many quaint little French villages, especially north of Yarmouth on the road called "French Shore," which boasts several enormous wooden Catholic churches.

At Annapolis Royal, there is an old English fort; at Port Royal, a recreation of the oldest settlement in Canada, founded in 1604 by the great French explorer, cartographer and bon vivant, Samuel de Champlain. The best place to see the enormous rise and fall of the Bay of Fundy tides (at 50 feet the highest in the world) is close to the town of Truro. I camped nearby at Bass River.

On Nova Scotia's south coast, Lunenburg is picturesque, but pretty Peggy's Cove is usually overrun by tourists in midsummer. Try nearby Blue Rocks instead. Inland are farms, orchards and lumber mills; but coastal fishing is still the main source of livelihood throughout the province.

Cape Breton Island is famous for its scenic coast road; it is joined to the rest of the province now by a causeway. On its north coast I like the French-settled fishing villages of Cheticamp, Margaree Harbor, Grand Etang and Pleasant Bay, on the Cabot Trail scenic drive. On the south cost Keltic Lodge is a famous, handsome white wooden resort hotel located on a piney cliff jutting into the Atlantic.

There is a huge restoration of a 17th-century French fortress city, Louisbourg, near the old mining town of Sydney. The road to Louisbourg is winding and not very good, but it's worth the long drive; locals wear very authentic period costumes and uniforms, you can stay on the site.

In New Brunswick, a place to photograph great tides is the Fundy National Park. St. John is a pleasant city; Digby, a ferry terminal. There are some Loyalist settlements also, most of New Brunswick is farm country. I'm told that the small province of Prince Edward Island is charming, but haven't been there.

Newfoundland is uncrowded and beautiful. Because of plane trouble some years ago I had to spend several days at Gander, en route to Iceland. I used the time to visit the Terra Nova National Park, and drove to nearby gray shingle fishing villages on stilts (one is named Salvage). There were huge wooden racks of salt cod drying in the sun, small fishing boats bobbing in rocky coves and flocks of sea birds. One of my students, Dr. Kim Shaukat, took a ferry in April from Halifax, Nova Scotia (a fine town, see the Citadel guarded by men in kilts) to St. John's, Newfoundland (see the colorful pubs on George Street). His shots of the prow of the ferry cleaving through dark-blue water decorated with thousands of chunks of broken ice were terrific. On another bad plane ride, we stopped to check an engine at Goose Bay, Labrador in midwinter. It was the bleakest place I have ever been!

Temporary Importation of Photo Equipment Into Canada

Canadian customs rules about importing equipment are quite strict. U.S. tourists entering Canada with a couple of cameras, a few lenses and a reasonable amount of film will probably have no problem (but should carry an itemized equipment list, with serial numbers, and have it stamped by a U.S. Customs official before leaving).

In practice, enforcement of Canadian customs regulations seems to depend somewhat on where you enter the country. Thousands of tourists every day cross the border at Niagara Falls, New York for instance, and customs officials at Niagara Falls, Ontario are very easygoing, and I haven't ever had to show my equipment there, or pay a bond there. It is also quick and easy to enter Canada by car from Maine or Vermont. But at Yarmouth, Nova Scotia, Canadian customs officials seem to stick to the letter of the law, and I had to put up a $500 cash bond on one trip. (I got the money back on leaving.) Customs examination at Montreal airport is also quite strict.

Professionals who only occasionally enter Canada with a lot of equipment should list everything, get the list stamped by U.S. Customs before leaving the U.S., and carry an assignment letter and copies of receipts with them, along with plenty of traveler's checks. Canadian law requires a bond, and payment of a temporary import tax at the port of entry. Cash or traveler's checks only are accepted. The rate is 7.5% bond, plus 7.5% tax, on equipment's used value. This is refundable on leaving.

Professionals should avoid all this by getting a "Carnet" and an insurance bond before leaving home. A business visa may be needed to do assignments in Canada. Consult Canadian consulates, provincial tourist offices and/or customs for more.

Quebec

Montreal is what I wish our American cities could be; beautifully clean, safe, fun and sophisticated. Although some people don't speak English, virtually everyone understands it. Montrealers (and Quebeçois in general) are much more appreciative of foreigners' efforts at French than many French people are. Place Ville Marie is the heart of downtown Montreal; explore little side streets nearby. There are very fine views from Mount Royal Park. See the Expo site too. If you can, also visit the photogenic, almost totally French-speaking Gaspé Peninsula. Quebec City is eastern Canada's premier tourist attraction. It's steeped in history (the decisive battle for Canada between Britain and France was fought there). The site of the city is superb; there are great hotels, great food, great ambiance and it's small enough to grasp in a few days. I have not been to the ice carnival held each February, but would like to.

Ontario

I regret that I have not yet been to Toronto. I know that the skyline is famous, there is a fine subway, and amazing shopping malls, and that the city is very cosmopolitan. I have discussed Niagara Falls, Ontario under New York State (my apologies to Canadian readers). Ottawa, Ontario is the dignified Federal capital of Canada, it is situated on the historic Rideau Canal, and it too has a famous ice festival in February.

One of the two "icons" of Canada is, of course, a redcoated Royal Canadian Mounted Policeman ("mountie") on horseback. Most RCMP's today wear blue uniforms or plainclothes, drive cars and keep a very low profile. However, you can see them parade in full splendor in various provinces from May to September. Consult provincial tourist offices or the Ceremonies Department at RCMP headquarters in Ottawa. Phone (613) 933-3751. If you call in early May, you can get exact dates and places of performances for the whole season. The RCMP spokesperson recommends especially the last week of June in Ottawa each year, because the band, the Musical Ride, and equestrian events can all be seen then.

Western Canada

A friend says that Banff and Lake Louise in the Canadian Rockies are superb, but allow extra time for photography, the weather is often foggy or misty. The RCMP Academy is in Regina, Saskatchewan (Canada's breadbasket province) and red-uniformed "mounties" can be seen there too.

Booming Vancouver and Victoria, famed for flowers and both in British Columbia, are popular with Western U.S. visitors and foreign tourists. They are said to be rather English in atmosphere. There are now thriving Asian communities in both cities also. My English niece, Elizabeth Martin, who has been to both cities several times to visit relatives, says: "Go, they're great, but they don't look a bit like England!"

The other "icon"—of Western Canada anyway—is the elaborately carved, brightly painted totem pole; there are fine examples in Stanley Provincial Park, in Vancouver.

When you go to any region of Canada, you can preview the highspots and wild places by looking at the picture books on different provinces by the fine Canadian landscape and travel photographer, Sherman Hines. I own his book, *The North*, and would love to go to the Yukon, though I think I'll avoid winter!

Overseas Travel

In the chapters which follow all of my recommendations are made for photographic and visual reasons; they do not take political considerations into account. In these times when the world order is rearranging itself, check current conditions before you travel in many regions. On the other hand, don't necessarily be put off traveling just by a negative story you see on TV. New York City, for instance, which seems to generate only bad news nationwide, is still a wonderful tourist destination if you take the sensible precautions I recommend any traveler take almost everywhere. (See below and Chapter Fifteen.)

Background and Up-to-the-Minute Information for Foreign Countries

The United States State Department puts out background papers on over 140 countries, for a very small fee each. Order them individually by calling the Citizens' Advisory Center (listed in Chapter Fifteen, Planning) or through any branch of the United States Government Printing Office. (All of these background papers are summarized in *The Location Photographer's Handbook*, see Chapter Fourteen).

Canadians can get travel publications from the Canadian Government Publishing Center, Supply and Services, Canada, Ottawa, ON K1A059; phone (819) 956-4802. Provincial branches of this office will also have material.

Safety Tips for Traveling Photographers

- Always carry money and documents in a very safe place, but most especially if using crowded public transport. (Lots of New Yorkers use zippered waist pouches.)

- Remember that thieves watch airports worldwide. When in transit carry your own camera and film bags.

- Count the total number of pieces of luggage you have, and keep all luggage close to you at all times.

- Never flaunt cash, especially large bills outdoors; be very cautious when leaving banks or exchange offices, or when using street cash machines.

- Do not travel with very expensive clothes, or much jewelry at all.

- Dress to blend as much as possible with the locals; in very nondescript fashion in big-city streets and poorer areas.

- Carry all photographic equipment, including tripods, in inconspicuous bags, (I sometimes wrap my tripod in a black garbage bag) and don't work alone outdoors at night. I even put black tape over the Nikon nameplate of my cameras to make them less expensive-looking.

- Never, ever leave any luggage of any kind, especially camera equipment, unattended, even locked in the trunk of a car. (Cars with out-of-town, or state, or province, or region, or rental or foreign license plates are prime targets for professional thieves in all countries.)

- Don't photograph police, soldiers, or military installations in most countries, or slums in many countries. Very poor people everywhere almost always deeply resent being photographed, and could react angrily if you attempt to sneak pictures of them. I do not blame them. Slums, sad, poor people and the like are not true travel photography subjects anyway. (See also Chapters Fifteen and Sixteen.)

Where to Get Travel Information

Most countries today have National Tourist Offices in New York and/or Los Angeles, Chicago or San Francisco, as well as in Toronto or Montreal. They send free information for tourists. Some countries are also represented in Atlanta, Boston, Dallas, Denver, Miami, New Orleans, Seattle and Vancouver. If you cannot locate a National Tourist Office (some are called something slightly different) call the country's Embassy in Washington or Ottawa, or the Permanent Mission to the United Nations in New York, or consulates in major cities.

Travel Advisories

The following chapters of this book deal with some places that have current United States State Department Travel Advisories (warnings) on record. (For more details on how to receive these see Chapter Fifteen.) While caution is obviously advisable everywhere, you should be aware that problems often affect only parts of countries or regions under advisory, and that there are sometimes problems in countries where no advisory has been issued. Get up-to-the-minute information by phone from local contacts or United States or Canadian Consulates overseas if in any doubt about the safety of a region.

Where Professionals Can Get Travel Information

If you are a professional photographer on a definite assignment, always mention this when you call. Ask for the Press Office; some are very helpful with advice. You will always be asked to show a written letter of assignment before any material help is offered.

Enquire about regulations for importing professional equipment, and if you need a "Carnet"(see Chapter Fourteen.) Find out whether you will need a visa for any visit, a visa only for a long visit, or a business visa.

For the names of recommended guide books, see Chapter Fifteen, Planning.

The Caribbean

Almost everywhere in this beautiful part of the world is highly photogenic, and weather and cloud effects are often truly spectacular. My only cautions are to avoid photographing in harsh noon light, and always ask permission before taking people pictures.

Bermuda

Strictly speaking, Bermuda is in the Atlantic, not the Caribbean, but to me it has a Caribbean "feel." The island is one of my all-time favorite places. Rent a motor scooter and ride anywhere for pictures of pastel painted houses with stepped white roofs designed to catch rain water, fabulous pink beaches and turquoise seas with real surf (my favorite is Coral Beach—snorkel from the reefs by the caves at the far end; take your underwater camera, the fish are fabulous.) Bermudians as a rule are charming friendly people (but always ask permission for people pictures). There are pretty and historic towns, especially St. George; great boating; and plenty of good places to stay for all budgets. Bobbies (cops) wear British type helmets and Bermuda shorts. They are much photographed. Get overall views from Gibbs Hill Lighthouse, and the frequent ferries from Hamilton. Bermuda is getting a bit built-up, but is not yet spoiled. Avoid Easter week (packed with college students). September is mild, green after August storms, my favorite month.

Puerto Rico

My advice to photographers going to Puerto Rico is to see the old Spanish colonial quarter of San Juan first (it's currently being spruced up). Then, visit the ramparts of El Morro Castle commanding San Juan harbor, and just outside the city, Luquillo Beach—a splendid crescent enclosed by huge coconut palm trees; you can buy split coconuts and roast pork from little roadside stands. The "must" tourist expedition is to the rain forest of El Yunque; this is not Amazon-sized but you can get some jungly pictures there. I recommend then leaving the capital and driving around the island for the best pictures. Look for resorts with great palm-fringed golf courses and fine white beaches. I like the little ports on the north coast which have bright-painted houses and boats.

The United States Virgin Islands

Both St. Thomas and St. Croix have superb white beaches; I suggest getting a car and driving around on both islands. Hitch (or pay for) a ride on a Hobi-Cat for pictures of the islands from the glorious turquoise water. To live a recreated Winslow Homer scene, take an islander's sailboat from Christianstead, St. Croix to the Virgin Islands National Underwater Park. (I once had a skipper who steered his bright yellow painted craft with a rope tied to his big toe and to the rudder.) The park is fabulous for snorkeling—and I'm told, scuba diving. Of course take an underwater camera, or at least take a glass-bottom boat ride.

I am told that reconstruction from the severe hurricane damage of a few years ago is almost complete.

I have never been to the British Virgin Islands, which are small, rather quiet, and have a couple of very exclusive resorts.

Underwater Photography Advice from a Non-Expert

Rules one, two and three for underwater photography are to get close to your subject. But, a caution for all non-scuba divers: Underwater pictures taken just below the surface are blurry if very high shutter speeds are not used. Because of big waves pushing me around, I took a disappointingly high percentage of blurred pictures in the Virgin Islands reefs, and suggest you do better by shooting Kodachrome 200 at shutter speeds of at least 1/500 of a second. Refraction changes one's perception of size underwater (things look about 25% bigger than they are in reality) and the light is very, very blue even a few feet below the surface; it gets deeper blue as you go down.

Professional underwater photographers use flash, and work extremely close up. The flash brings color back to marine life and vegetation and stops motion. A 28mm lens is recommended.

Even underwater duffers like me can take good fish pictures just below the surface, if water is calm, not too deep and if you wait and let the fish come close. (Carry fish food to encourage this!) I have made good underwater shots from the shallow reefs off Coral Beach in Bermuda. It's also fun to shoot underwater in swimming pools, clear lakes and streams.

Nikon's Nikonos professional underwater cameras are famous. Konica and Minolta make neat little "point and shoot" cameras for beach use and (shallow depth) underwater pictures. Kodak and Fuji make disposable (shallow depth) underwater cameras. (See also Chapter Three.)

Underwater Photography, by Charles Seaborn, gives an expert's advice.

If you are very serious, and want to take an underwater photography course, the Nikon School of Underwater Photography is very well thought of. I'm told that a course is included in the price of a Nikonos camera. (Contact Nikon, and see Photography Courses, in Chapter One).

The Bahamas

The tourist "must" in Nassau is the straw market, and I like the horse-drawn carriages, the old British Colonial Hotel, (now a Best Western) and the waterfront area where small inter-island boats unload. The handsome police wear white uniforms with pith helmets. It's okay to photograph them. Freeport permits gambling (cameras are allowed inside only by special permission; if you get it you must bring your own models during the rare times the casinos are closed to the public). Exterior casino architecture is great fun if you like kitsch. Bahama out-island beaches are some of the most gorgeous in the world; the clear turquoise water is the temperature of a tepid bath, to sail around on a Hobi-cat or Sunfish is divine. Take an underwater camera.

Always ask permission before taking "people pictures" in the Bahamas and everywhere else in the Caribbean.

Cuba

My photographer neighbor Sigrid Estrada, who is a much-traveled German citizen, went there recently. She said it is clean, neat and picturesque, though very poor as expected; the people are friendly. A travel agent friend says she believes that the official United States government policy of discouraging travel there by American citizens will soon end. I hope so.

Haiti

Tourism to Haiti is practically nonexistent at present. I am told that if you go you should not venture far from your hotel without a guide. I mention Haiti at this even more than usually troubled period in its history only because it is my very favorite place to photograph in the Caribbean—a beautiful place of artists, craftsmen and terrible poverty. The old Hotel Olofsson has the wonderful ornate wooden gingerbread architecture that can also be seen throughout Port au Prince. The cathedral, decorated with murals, and the huge, central covered market which sells superb paintings and handicrafts (as well as everything else) are fabulous.

There are lovely clean white beaches an hour from Port au Prince, and in the interior, villages that look like some I saw in Africa. When things improve, and you do go to Haiti, fly or drive (if it is safe) to the citadel of Sans Souci (it takes a day by Jeep, the roads are truly awful but the scenery is verdant, mountainous and worth some jolting). Toussaint L'Ouverture's fortress is a romantic ruin, and the cemetery in the nearby town is full of pastel tombs, flowers, and boys leading goats. I bought a painting by the roadside for $5 in U.S. dollars. The artist was very pleased to make the sale. If you speak French you will do fine in Haiti, the educated people all speak it.

The Dominican Republic

This country, which shares the island of Hispaniola with Haiti, is poor also. It is popular with New Yorkers and other East coast vacationers, and is said to have some very pleasant, not too expensive resorts. I have never been there.

Jamaica

I once spent two weeks being driven all over Jamaica, both by a tourist board representative, and by British friends who lived in Kingston. It is a very beautiful island indeed; I'm told by a Jamaican friend that it has largely recovered from the terrible hurricane of a few years ago. Highlights: The Land of the Maroons, in the remotest part of the Blue Mountains. Dunn's River Falls and nearby Ocho Rios. A visit to a ruined sugar mill. White Brahma cattle, with egrets sitting on their shoulders. River rafting on the Rio Grande. Small country villages on Sunday, with children dressed in their best for church. The great fruit and vegetable market at Montego Bay.

You should be aware that there is some antitourist feeling in Jamaica, a very poor country where a few visitors have been less than courteous to the locals. Always ask permission before taking people pictures. If you can travel with a Jamaican friend or guide, you are likely to get better ones. Don't even think of photographing the slum areas of Kingston.

Martinique

This is a very green, mountainous island and politically is a department of France. Mont Pelée, which erupted in the early 1900's killing many thousands of people, is in the north. The formerly most important city of Martinique, Saint Pierre, was almost destroyed at that time but is still quite photogenic, and has a memorial to the volcano victims. The island capital, Fort de France, did not excite me much but it does have very good French/Caribbean food. The big tourist attraction of Martinique is the museum commemorating Napoleon's beloved Empress Josephine, who was born in La Pagerie. My favorite things to photograph on the island were the wonderful plants and trees. It rained a lot when I was in Martinique. I haven't been to the other big French island, Guadaloupe.

Trinidad

Carnival here is less well-known than the one in Rio, but is one of the great shows of the world; preparations start immediately after the last one ends and heat up around Christmas. If you get to Port of Spain a week or so before Shrove Tuesday, you will see massed steel bands, small parades and festivities, and, for the three days before Ash Wednesday, huge parades of brilliantly costumed people everywhere. Apart from Carnival, the island has sugar cane plantations, asphalt pits and some industry. Remarks above about Jamaican peoples' attitude to tourists, also apply here to some degree.

The Antilles

The island of Sint Marten/St. Martin is half Dutch and half French. It has splendid beaches, but is now quite busy, and the Dutch capital Phillipsburg is rather built up with a busy night-life; the French side of the island is quieter and the more exclusive hotels are there.

The nearby island of St. Barts is French, a charming, green, hilly dot in the ocean, and very exclusive and very expensive. It is a favorite vacation spot for wealthy French families.

I haven't been to most other islands in the Caribbean, but I have not heard anything bad that should put you off going anywhere.

Central America

If you love colorful ceremonies and Indian culture, gorgeous handicrafts, fine beaches, and places which are not too touristic, much of Central America will appeal to you. It is also a current travel bargain. Obviously, check travel advisories before you go.

El Salvador

When things improve, go. It is one of the physically loveliest places I have ever been. I spent a week photographing dormant volcanoes, ancient ruins in the jungle, roads lined with brilliant-yellow flowering trees, almost deserted white and black sand beaches, colorful fishing ports, and the pleasant (at least in the part I stayed) city of San Salvador. The people I met were nice too.

Panama

Tourism in Panama is presently dead, but things do change. If you go, the Panama canal is the "must"; the Gattun Locks are a very good picture point; great railroad engines called "mules" tow ships into and out of the immense lock chambers. I went to the San Blas Islands from a cruise ship. The islanders are famous for making "bolas"—cloth panels intricately cut out and appliquéd and beautifully designed and sewn in brilliant colors—once they were used for blouses and shirts, now they are produced as art for tourists. Antique bolas are much prized. (I bought two and made I some nice pictures of the seller also.)

Costa Rica

A travel agent friend recently came back from this small Pacific country. She says it is like coastal Mexico 30 years ago, with uncrowded beaches, and pleasant, not enormous hotels. My friend says Costa Rica is a "hot" place to go.

Mexico

I may be the only person who likes the border towns between Mexico and the United States (but not everything there of course). I've been to Ciudad Juarez, Nogales and Tijuana. Of course they aren't the real Mexico, nor do they show our neighbor at its best, but there are wonderful markets, craft shops, delicious food, amusing things to photograph and nice people. The less attractive things can be avoided fairly easily. I have also been to Cancun and Cozumel via a cruise ship; these resorts aren't authentic Mexico either, but I enjoyed them too. My ambition is to go to Oaxaca which, I have been told by several people who know Mexico well, is extremely beautiful, and is absolutely the "real" Mexico, with great Indian culture and magnificent archaeological sites close by.

Guatemala

I have only been here briefly, while on a cruise. Well-traveled Central America hands say the place is gorgeous. Currently, political conditions are troubled.

South America

My first big travel assignment was to South America, and I still rate it as one of the best trips I ever made. I worked on an audio/visual for an airline, and I spent six weeks in Chile, Argentina, Brazil and Peru. I have been again since, on separate trips to Brazil and to Venezuela. Here are my impressions:

Argentina

This enormous country is physically varied and has not been too much visited in recent years. Happily, the political situation has improved, and judging by recent newspaper and magazine articles, Argentina seems to be coming back onto the tourist map. Buenos Aires (often called BA) is a huge and very sophisticated city; it looks quite a lot like Paris in places. It is definitely under-photographed because my stock pictures of it still sell after twenty years. I best remember attending the ballet at the famous Teatro Colon (and riding in the elevator of the elegant Plaza Hotel, with Dame Margot Fonteyn and Rudolph Nureyev on several occasions).

I love cemeteries; the elaborate La Recoleta is the biggest and most ornate I have ever seen; it is in the north of the city, and is shown off as a tourist attraction. The bright-painted corrugated-iron houses and funky restaurants of La Boca, an Italian workingman's district are made for photographers. (I attended a "futbol" match in the big stadium in La Boca, and was one of about ten women in a crowd of some 100,000 passionate male fans; Argentina is a many times over soccer World Cup winner). There are big outdoor restaurants on the outskirts of Buenos Aires where parrijade—sides of beef and many smaller unnameable (and some to my palate uneatable) cuts of meat—are grilled over open pits. Mar del Plata is a very crowded seaside resort near BA.

Bariloche is an Alpine-inspired resort in foothills at the southern end of the Andes, at the edge of Patagonia. There are very good hotels; it's an exclusive ski resort in winter, and a center for walkers in spring and fall. The nearby forests are lovely— they are said to be the model for the forest drawings in Walt Disney's classic "Bambi." Close to Bariloche is a chain of lakes leading to nearby Chile. The biggest Argentine lake is called Nahuel Huapi, and it's surrounded by Andean peaks and pine forests. I took boats and busses from Chile to Argentina. The two-day trip includes this lake, and can be done in reverse (from Bariloche to Osorno, Chile). I highly recommend it, if you don't mind a night at a plain hotel in Peulla Chile (reservations are advised). The lakes are absolutely gorgeous and I would do the trip again at the drop of a hat. I checked and it's all still possible. You can also take a one day trip in summer, or cross the border quite quickly by car or bus. I drove across a little bit of Patagonia, from Bariloche to the small city of Trelew, founded by Welsh settlers (the Welsh seem to be assimilated and Spanish is the only language I heard on the streets). The part of Patagonia I saw was basically rather gray, flat and desolate.

I'm told there are still some horse fairs, where gauchos (cowboys) perform great feats of horsemanship, but all I saw of the great Argentine cattle industry were a few gauchos driving small herds of cows or sheep.

One thing I regret is not having visited English cousins who have an estancia near Tucuman, in the northern Argentine province of Salta, near the Bolivian border. (Believe it or not, the British consulate in Buenos Aires refused to give me the address.) The widow, children and grand-children of the founder run the place now; I hope to visit them all one day; my cousin who has been there says the area is remote and beautiful, and that it's almost desert in some parts of the province.

Iguassu Falls, on the Argentine/Brazilian border, is South America's greatest natural attraction. I didn't get there either; you can also see it from Brazil.

Brazil

Sadly, reports now indicate that street crime in downtown Rio de Janeiro has reached epidemic proportions. Check conditions before visiting the city, and be extremely careful if you go. The less intrepid should visit the countryside, or wait till things improve. Then, go by all means, because Rio is truly one of the world's most beautifully situated cities, surrounded by a chain of tall round-topped mountains, the famous Sugar Loaf is in front. There are also girls from Ipanema, good hotels and a relaxed ambiance too. I met artists and writers there on my two visits, had delicious food, and stayed in excellent hotels on Copacabana, one of the world's great beaches. Photograph from boat cruises around the harbor, and take the funicular to the classic vantage point up to a mountain topped by a great concrete statue of Christ, who looks down onto a fabulous view of Rio. (Do this shot at sunset through "blue time" if possible.)

Whether from Ipanema, Copacabana or other beaches the girls of Rio are famous for their beauty and tiny bathing suits; the men aren't too bad either! Kite flying on the beach is a big sport; hawkers sell the big cloth bird kites, which make great inexpensive props and souvenirs.

Ouro Preto, in the state of Minas Gerais, is Brazil's most perfectly preserved Portuguese colonial town; with pastel-colored baroque churches and houses dating from the 17th and 18th century. There are also a lot of nice young mining students; one of them, who spoke good English, guided me in the town, which should be a must for all visitors to Brazil. Do not miss the church of Bom Jesus do Matozinho at nearby Congonhas. It has wonderful carvings of the twelve apostles outside. They were sculpted in the 18th century by a master called Aleijadino, which means "little cripple" in Portuguese.

Recife (formerly Pernambuco) has nice beaches and a colonial quarter but is now mostly modern. It disappointed me; it was not as nice as the memory of my mother's pictures. Alas, I did not go to Salvador (formerly Bahia) because of a glitch in planning. That place, famous as being the "soul" of Brazil, is poor, and it too is said currently to be crime-plagued.

The views of the great Iguassu Falls from the Brazilian side are said by a Brazilian acquaintance to be terrific, better than those from Argentina.

Chile

Chile is still a country for travelers, not tourists. If you can speak a bit of Spanish, I especially recommend southern Chile, one of the most beautiful places I have ever been. It is a great combination with travel in Argentina's lake district (see above). I have heard that Chile is considered a very safe country for travelers.

I was there on my first travel assignment, more than twenty years ago, doing an audio/visual for the national airline, Lan Chile. I plan to return one day. The flight down, over the cordillera of the Andes and the 22,000-plus foot high Mount Aconcagua, is magnificent.

The beauty of Chile is not in its capital, Santiago, although you should see the main sights around the Plaza de Armas and vicinity, and possibly visit the big vineyards an hour or so south of Santiago. For me, the reason to go to Chile is down south. Flying from Santiago to Puerto Montt takes about two hours, you still follow the great chain of Andes peaks and, eventually, see four perfectly cone-shaped, snow-capped volcanoes (each alone looks as beautiful as Mount Fuji). The biggest, most famous peak is Osorno; and once in a while it smokes. I stayed a couple of nights in the fair-sized town of Puerto Montt, a working port; I'm told you can still photograph bright-painted warehouses and fishing boats and sea birds in abundance. Small boats still go to neighboring islands, and big ones down to Punta Arenas, the southernmost city of Chile. Busses and taxis connect with Puerto Varas and Ralun, where there is a nice hotel where I stayed a couple of days.

The air in southern Chile is very clear (there is a major observatory in the region). The countryside is pastoral, with well-tended wheatfields and vineyards owned largely by the descendents of German settlers. Occasional horsemen go by. I'm told this scene has changed little since 1968.

Steamers still ply the lakes, called Lago Llanquihe, Lago de Todos Santos, and Lago de Esmeralda; they probably still at depart at unpredictable hours. (I missed one lake steamer because it left early, a not uncommon occurrence with local transport in Latin America.) Stay overnight in Peulla, Chile and connect with steamers over the border on Argentina's Lake Nahuel Huapi, and buses to the fine Argentine town of Bariloche, center of a popular ski resort area (see Argentina, above). All the Chilean lakes are surrounded by blue, jagged mountains—part of the Andes chain. Lake Esmeralda lives up to its name, and really is bright green. When I was there, the weather was perfect. I mostly wore a turtleneck and a safari jacket in fall (our spring) though I'm told late April is often cloudy or rainy. If you go a bit farther south in Chile from Puerto Montt (I didn't) you will reach the Paine, or Torres de Paine National Park; I am told by travel writer Carla Hunt that the Torres are four spectacular jagged pink mountains, and very photogenic. The area is popular with naturalists, trekkers and climbers from Chile's cities and other countries who want solitude, beautiful scenery, and the opportunity to view wildlife, and who don't mind roughing it a bit, or cold weather. It seems that colonies of guanacos, which look a lot like llamas, live in this national park and there are penguins further down, and whales off the coast. Boats leave for the numbing, stormy reaches of Cape Horn, Tierra del Fuego and Antarctica from Punta Arenas in the extreme south of Chile.

Valparaiso, an hour or so north of Santiago, is another matter. The climate is mild. This busy port was founded by British settlers. I remember best the ancient funicular cable cars climbing past wooden streets clinging to the surrounding mountain and the English street names. At one time there was a large British colony in Valparaiso (my mother's touring English theater company went there in the 1920's) but the English are now pretty much assimilated. I stayed in the pleasant resort of Viña del Mar across the bay and photographed fine parks and mansions and ate (and photographed) delicious "ceviche"— fresh seafood marinated in lime—served at a flowery terrace restaurant overlooking the water.

Lan Chile, the national airline, is the place to get travel information.

Ecuador

I haven't been to this small Andean country; these tips are from Carla Hunt, a well-traveled writer friend who specializes in Latin America. The handicrafts in general, and especially at the Saturday market in Otavalo, are magnificent. The most Indian town is Rio Bamba; the "Avenue of Volcanoes" between Guyaquil and Quito is well worth photographing. The Gálapagos Islands in the Pacific belong to Ecuador. The extraordinary wildlife there was of course made famous by Charles Darwin, and was the basis for his theory of evolution.

Peru

Lima was the capital of Spain's great empire in all of the Americas, so it is well worth lingering to see the fantastically decorated Lima cathedral. The glass coffin and rather gruesome, mummified, purported remains of the conquistador Francisco Pizarro are among the cathedral's many attractions. The Gold Museum with surviving Inca masterpieces is a must. There are many other ornate buildings around the huge central Plaza de Armas where everyone strolls on summer nights. This plaza is a good place to get pictures of people. It almost never rains in Lima, so the city is rather dusty, but the center is quite well kept.

From Lima, take a plane to Cuzco, a busy city with great Indian markets, colonial churches and a good art museum. Always ask permission for people pictures here; you may sometimes be refused; but of course the Inca descendents' religious beliefs should be respected.

The highlight of any trip to Peru, and a world highlight, is of course the ancient Incan stronghold or temple of Macchu Picchu. The train ride from Cuzco to Macchu Picchu is great, with many twists and turns as it labors past occasional little villages where Indians spread out goods to sell by the tracks and lead strings of little llamas with fluttering eyelashes (like pretty young girls)— you can almost touch them from the big open windows of the train as it labors up especially steep sections of track. Alarming gorges which I didn't care for much can also be seen en route. I had only one day at the ruins, a stupid piece of planning I wasn't responsible for. You should stay over at least one night, two or three if possible. Walk around the temples, and climb to shoot down on the complex and the higher conical peak of Huayna Picchu behind it. I am sure sunset and sunrise there would be wonderful. My stock pictures of Macchu

Picchu have been steady sellers ever since.

Italian friends made a nature movie in the Iquitos region of the Amazon jungle, and said it was marvellous. It's another place I want to visit some day.

At the time of this writing, the U.S. Government has an advisory (warning) on travel to Peru, (because of terrorist activities by the Shining Path guerilla movement). Check for the latest information before you plan a trip there.

Venezuela

Caracas is a busy, extremely modern city with broad boulevards and tall skyscrapers. It must have a colonial past, but to me this is very well hidden. Like all the Latin American cities I have visited, it does have some terrific nightlife. Venezuela's Caribbean coast and Margarita Island are popular with New York area tourists (I made only a brief stop at Margarita from a cruise ship; it was pleasant but the beaches were quite crowded).

The considerable money in Venezuela comes from oil; I photographed the refinery in the desert at Punto Fijo and oil derricks in Lake Maracaibo. Further into Lake Maracaibo are fishing villages on stilts, where the Indian people travel by dugout canoe. I photographed from one with an outboard.

Friends recommended very highly that I go to the Caracas residents' favorite resort area of Merida in the the Venezuelan Highlands, said to be the most beautiful (and cool) part of the country. Unfortunately at the time I had another commitment and couldn't make it.

Angel Falls, Venezuela's other great tourist attraction, is the world's highest; it is in the southern, hot and jungly part of the country. People go trekking in the general area.

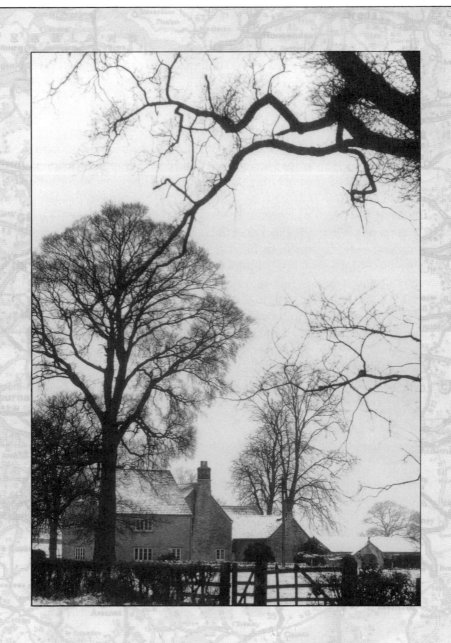

Chapter 18

Travel Highlights: Europe, the Mid-East & Africa

Well, you probably know where I'm going to start...

The United Kingdom

The weather in the British Isles can be bloody awful or absolutely fantastic for photography. A sparkling clear spring, summer or fall day with a breeze and big multi-colored clouds (yes, there can be) sailing by is fantastic, as good as weather can get. Maximize you chances of good photographs by going to western and northern regions in late April, May and June, and in September and early October. It is statistically proven that these months are drier. They are also relatively uncrowded.

London

London is wonderful to photograph at any time of the year. Besides growing up there (my recollections may be tinted by rose-colored spectacles) I have returned almost annually for the last 25 years, and sometimes gone there several times in one year. I have shot spring, summer, fall and Christmas assignments, and visited in February and November too, so it's not just fond memory that makes me say this. In winter, you are much warmer outdoors in London than you are in New York. Always take a raincoat (but buy your woolly sweater on arrival, they are a genuine bargain.)

Take some "bright" film like Fuji Velvia, or Ektachrome Plus 100 for grey days. I take super fine-grain Kodachrome 25 Professional for warm early and late light for fine days, especially when I go to London and Southeast England, which truthfully has only about half the annual rainfall of New York. (But they have more gray days.)

London is still primarily a Victorian city (we thought it very ugly in the '50's when I was a teenager in art school) with lots of Georgian enclaves and some ancient buildings. There is plenty of modern architecture too, the best of which incorporates a feeling for the stone, cream-painted stucco and ornate red-brick tradition. London is very large and sprawling, with most of the important sights north of the Thames River.

The Bayswater, Queensway and Lancaster Gate districts (where I spent my teens) flank the great Kensington Gardens on its north side, and are on two main Underground (subway) lines, about a fifteen-minute ride from Piccadilly Circus at the center of London. The number 88 bus runs along the main Bayswater Road to Marble Arch, Oxford and Regent Streets, and then to the center of London. The Bayswater/Queensway area has a good range of moderate/medium priced hotels (I like the Coburg) and Lancaster Gate has the first-class Royal Lancaster, where I have often stayed. The staff is very nice and the hotel is comfortable and convenient though not particularly pretty outside.

Marble Arch is on the Central Underground line, close to busy Oxford Street, which is lined with shops; it is very convenient but most hotels in that area are expensive. The "smartest" part of London today is mostly south of Kensington Gardens/Hyde Park, roughly including Belgravia, Knightsbridge, Sloane Square, and parts of Kensington, with ridiculously high hotel prices.

To orient yourself on a first visit, take a two hour London Transport tour on a double-decker red bus; they leave from near the Piccadilly, Marble Arch and Victoria Underground Stations; on fine days the busses are open-topped. The tour will show you the Houses of Parliament and Big Ben, the Tower of London and Tower Bridge, the Bank of England, St. Paul's Cathedral, Buckingham Palace, and the major shopping thoroughfares of Piccadilly, Park Lane, Oxford Street, Regent Street and the Strand. After that, you can take city buses. If your budget is tight, catch the number 88 bus anywhere along its route and ride it to the Tate Gallery and back instead of taking the tour; this bus passes most of the famous sights listed above. (The Tate is the British and modern art gallery, and has a fabulous Turner collection.)

Underground trains are much quicker than busses. (Get a combined bus/ Underground pass at any station the first day; you will save a lot of money but you need a picture.) Subways are considered very safe, except for rowdies leaving pubs late at night—the system shuts down by about 12.30 a.m. Some busses run all night. Taxis (expensive) or minicabs (slightly less expensive and ordered by phone) are alternatives.

If you are on assignment, and need the use of a car, a driver who knows London is almost essential—the modern one-way system in the many narrow twisty old streets was deliberately designed to discourage even Londoners from driving (they weren't discouraged). Rush hours on the main arteries in and out of central London make New York's Long Island Expressway or the LA freeways look underused. Parking in London is metered and hard to find. There is also a nasty device called a "boot" which meter maids and men in blue clamp on your wheel for overtime street parking.

In London I gravitate to the street markets, especially the Portobello Road, Camden Lock, Camden Passage and Caledonian/Petticoat Lane markets. The Goldhawk market, near where I went to art school, now has many of London's Arab residents as customers—many women are fully veiled. See Londoners of all social classes, colors and religions, ditto for tourists, and earnest British provincials picking and haggling over vegetables and fruits, curtains and towels, tee shirts, furniture, silver, family relics, ghastly souvenirs, antique and just plain cracked china, old junk, auto parts, secondhand books, new cassettes, ethnic jewelry, and good, bad and indifferent antiques.

I love pageantry, and there's something going on just about every week in summer as well as the normal Changing the Guard ceremony outside Buckingham Palace and Changing the Horseguards at Whitehall each weekday. Get to these two hours ahead for good positions to photograph. Best vantage points are in front of the statue of Queen Victoria opposite the Palace's main gate, and to the left inside the courtyard at Whitehall.

On a fine day go to a band concert in one of the Royal Parks for another chance to get pictures of military uniforms. You'll also get Londoners sitting on striped deck chairs enjoying the music while they picnic, drink tea or wine, or just lie on the grass sunbathing with minimal clothing. The British are far from prudish. On warm days in the park you can sometimes see outlines of people making love under a blanket. No one around them takes any notice.

To get symbolic pictures of London theater (I've sold a lot of these for stock) start at Piccadilly Circus,then walk up Shaftesbury Avenue as far as Cambridge Circus; then retrace your steps and walk down to the Haymarket; after that continue past Trafalgar Square to the beginning of the Strand. These three streets comprise most of London's famous West End theater district.

Trafalgar Square is where Admiral Lord Nelson surveys huge bronze lions, pigeon-feeders and tourists from atop his tall monument, and where the elegant St. Martin's-in-the-Fields church (a model for many classic American churches) stands near the National Gallery, home of one of the world's great art collections. There is an oddly half-sized statue of George Washington in front of it. At Christmas, a great tree from Norway stands in Trafalgar Square.

A river trip on a launch from Westminster Pier, under Big Ben, is another favorite of mine; you will get fine views of old, new and recycled London from the water. Get off at Tower Pier, see the Tower and the Crown Jewels (which may not be photographed) and the famous Beefeaters (who wear scarlet and gold only on two days a year; normally they are in dark blue and crimson).

Tower Bridge is another London icon; go to the top for fine London views of the Tower, the City (historic and financial London) and of the modern towers rising south of the Thames in the new Docklands development area.

To visit the Docklands, take the new elevated Docklands Light Railway from the Tower terminus for the fifteen minute ride to Canary Wharf—there are good views from the little trains. Get off and photograph what is billed as "the city of the 21st-century"—the largest office and apartment development scheme in Europe—being built on land and over water once used for now obsolete docks. I like it especially because I don't want to see England become just a museum. Continue on the same train to Island Gardens and walk through a foot tunnel under the Thames to Greenwich to see Sir Christopher Wren's masterpieces—the Royal Naval Hospital, and the Royal Observatory. There you will see the marker for the 0° longitude line where Greenwich Mean Time is measured. Visit the naval museum and nearby, outdoors, the tea clipper ship Cutty Sark. Take a launch back to Westminster or walk to the newly redeveloped Tobacco Wharf shopping and restaurant complex, which is a bit manicured but has some nice shops and pubs.

After you have covered London's high spots, wander on your own safely almost anywhere (though I don't recommend the vicinity of the big railway stations late at night, or parks after dark). You will find your personal favorite interesting vistas, neighborhoods, pubs and people to complete your unique photographic coverage.

England

In the far northwest, I love the mountainous Lake District (most of it is a National Park) with lots of sheep, narrow roads with thick stone walls and ancient slate-roofed farmhouses. Visit the lakes in April or May (when blossoms and spring lambs make it look positively idyllic on fine days) or September or October. It is too crowded in summer—it's a very favorite place for British vacationers, especially walkers and climbers. Grasmere is a good center for the lakes. I stayed in a great guest house there a couple of years ago; it's called Banerigg, and faces Rydal Water, a small lake beloved by Wordsworth.

Go to a Lakeland Games if you can, the one at Wastwater in early October is as traditional as they come, with sheepherding demonstrations, wrestling, fell races and displays of crafts. Drive to the Langdale Valley, and to Buttermere. Beatrix Potter's house at New Sawrey is a great attraction, but often crowded.

In northeast England, visit the great Roman Wall, built to keep out savage Scottish tribes, and the castles of now quiet, beautiful Northumbria, once ravaged by Vikings. Literary pilgrims can go to the wuthering Yorkshire moors which boast Haworth Parsonage, home of Emily Brönte and her siblings, but fans of James Herriott say he is now Yorkshire's most famous author and prefer the gentler dales. At local cattle markets and shows you can easily conjure up stand-ins for his three veterinarians among the booted, green-waterproof clad, tweed-capped farmers and gentry. In the peaceful North York Moors National Park, Bylands Abbey is the romantic ruin of a great monastery destroyed by the forces of King Henry VIII. It's surrounded by manicured green lawns. There's a good pub/restaurant opposite.

I spent many childhood vacations with relatives in the mountainous (for England) Peak District, near Buxton; it is another big chunk of northern England that is a national park.

In East Anglia, Cambridge is a jewel. Parts of the University, colleges dating from the 13th-century, are world-class architectural treasures. Students and visitors from all over the world keep the place lively but don't overpower it. Go in spring and fall when students are in residence. Walk along "the Backs"—the college gardens by the River Cam. From Cambridge, go further east in spring to see endless flower fields in bloom (it's flat and quite like Holland, just across the North Sea). There are great churches dating from East Anglia's prosperous 16th-century heyday as a center of the wool trade, and Boston in Lincolnshire has one of the biggest. (Boston is where the Pilgrim Fathers started on their long journey to America, via Holland.)

Norwich is a historic city with a cathedral, and not too far away is Flatford Mill along with other recognizable Norfolk scenes painted by the great landscapist John Constable.

Sussex, the south coast county where I spent other holidays as a kid, is prosperous commuter country but still has lovely, empty, grassy "downs" (uplands) and other unspoiled places, and Bodiam Castle is splendid. The next county of Kent is just south of London and has the great house of Knole with a deer-filled park; nearby is Sissinghurst Castle with gardens created by the writer V. Sackville-West. The White Garden is one of the most famous in England. Kent has many other "stately" places too.

Wiltshire is a big county in the center of southern England. It has mysterious Stonehenge (which alas now has to be protected by fences) and Salisbury, the tallest cathedral spire in England. Boys play cricket in its shadow in summer. There are also several ancient white horses cut into rolling chalk "downs" and a number of stately homes, the most famous (and busy) is Longleat, the seat of the Marquess of Bath who breeds and exhibits live lions. Don't miss Lacock Abbey where Fox Talbot made his pioneering photographic discoveries, a museum there commemorates his achievements. Bowood House and gardens are very lovely. Wiltshire boasts some nice English villages with plenty of charm but nothing especially unusual about them. I stay with friends in Aldebourne, which has a fine old church, a historic nonconformist chapel, a pub on the village green, a general store and some thatched cottages.

Cornwall and Devon are famous for their mild climate and many beauty spots, but they are way too crowded in summer. When you go, see Mousehole (pronounced Mauzel) my favorite Cornish fishing village. Somerset is scenic, but Bath sometimes gets very crowded indeed. Photograph the renowned Roman baths, Georgian terraces and visit the fine Royal Photographic Society museum in spring or fall if you possibly can. Wells has my favorite English cathedral—swans swim beside it.

The Cotswolds in Gloucestershire and Warwickshire are considered the quintessential English landscape—but take back roads in summer. All the above busy places can be enjoyed in spring, fall or even winter. I have shot Christmas in England in the Cotswolds twice, it snows regularly (especially near Snowshill). There are foxhunts led by men in pink coats (of course I root for the fox, but the hunt is beautiful just the same). There are very good hotels that "do" a traditional Christmas package (four or five days of caroling, parties, entertainment and good food)—they are very popular with well-to-do English city dwellers, so book well in advance if you fancy this idea yourself.

Scotland

Edinburgh, the capital, is handsome, with a looming medieval castle on a great rock, and fine Georgian squares and crescents in the New Town. There is a huge university and a famous medical school, which keeps the place young. The famous Edinburgh Festival in late August and early September attracts world-class talent and large crowds and keeps the city international, which it has been since Mary Queen of Scots returned from France.

Glasgow, once called the second city of the British Empire, has always had a vigorous cultural life and fine Victorian architecture, but was once known for bad slums too. Most of these are gone today. The center of the city, spruced up, is very definitely on the tourist map.

Edinburgh and Glasgow are an hour apart, and just a day's drive from some of my favorite scenery in the world: the western highlands and especially the rugged islands off the west coast of Scotland. I think these places will be refuges for people who appreciate beauty and relative solitude long after sunnier places are wall-to-wall condos.

Go to the charming port of Oban for ferries to Mull. Stay in Tobermory; then drive around to see the island and take small boats to the tiny Isle of Iona, where there is a resident monastic community, and the strange eight-sided black basaltic rock formations of Staffa, the setting for Mendelsohn's Fingal's Cave overture. Then take a ferry to Barra, one of the haunting Outer Hebrides. This beautiful isle is the original of the classic British movie "Tight Little Island." (A whole shipload of Scotch was wrecked there the 1940's.) From Barra, take ferries to Harris and Lewis, returning via the rugged Isle of Skye. (Hotel and ferry reservations are needed in midsummer.) Or return to the mainland via Ullapool.

Wales

I have been only to the Welsh borders, but my mother loved the coast and vacationed (and took pictures) at Tenby. My niece, who attended the University of Aberystwyth, recommends the whole west coast as very scenic. Barry Hicks, the late chief photographer for the British Tourist Authority, once told me that Caernarvon Castle was the finest in Britain. Snowdonia in north Wales is a national park, beloved by British climbers. Portmeiron, the "folly" of a famous Welsh architect, Sir Clough Williams Ellis, is an Italianate group of buildings that was featured in "The Prisoner," a classic television series. It has just been refurbished and opened as a very exclusive resort hotel. South Wales is somewhat industrial. On the border of England and Wales, Ross on Wye and the Wye river valley are gateways to the Brecknock Beacons National Park.

Northern Ireland

Troubled Northern Ireland is beautiful and worth photographing. One day, many visitors will come back. Don't even think of being an investigative photojournalist here! If you stick to scenery you will be fine. Take the winding Antrim coast road north from Belfast (not a pretty city) past splendid

Carrickfergus Castle and the little fishing villages of Cushendun and Cushendall to the strange basalt rock formation called the Giant's Causeway (and a golf course where I once caught a perfect rainbow on film). Come back inland via Lough Neagh, Ballymena, Antrim, Newry and the Mountains of Mourne.

The Republic of Ireland

I've been many times to the Irish Republic. The people are friendly, funny and kind. The most scenic part to my eye is Connemara in the far west. Ashford Castle at Cong is a great country hotel; well-to-do French and Belgians go there for the salmon fishing, and perhaps also because the food is very good!

I once spent a day photographing a lovely lady in County Donegal, who knitted sweaters to augment her small pension. Her cottage had a peat fire with a perpetually brewing pot of tea on the hob, family portraits of kin in England, America and Australia, and a world-class collection of china souvenir ornaments.

Weather permitting, take a boat from the fine small city of Galway to the remote isles of Aran. You will alight by coracle—boats made of tarred canvas stretched over woven frames—Robert Flaherty would still be quite at home.

The famed Lakes of Killarney, Ring of Kerry and the "Gaeltacht"—the Irish-speaking area on and around the sea-girt Dingle peninsula—are in the far southwest. I once attended the Ballinasloe Pony Fair, held each September, and got some of my all-time favorite "people pictures" of Ireland.

Alas, there are few thatched cottages left anywhere in Ireland, though there are plenty of fine Georgian houses, many of which are now hotels.

Ireland's capital, Dublin, is full of photographic interest; the often ornate pubs, Georgian Parliament buildings, the Trinity College (university) area, Merriam Square and its surrounding streets are my favorites (and many other visitors' too). The General Post Office, where the Irish rose against many centuries of British rule on Easter Sunday, 1916, is the great shrine of modern Ireland.

I am sometimes asked for pictures relating to Ireland's great literary heritage. I should have pictures of Swift, Yeats, Wilde, Shaw, Joyce, O'Casey and Behan's birthplaces, residences and more, but do not. This might be an interesting project for a travel feature or for a stock photographer.

France

Americans either love France or they hate it. So do the British. I truly love France (my French is not too bad, which helps). The French feeling about Anglophones is somewhat similar, but French people are getting a bit more tolerant of foreigners with bad pronunciation. Today, many young French people and those who deal with tourists speak good English.

Paris

In Paris, I often stay in Saint Germain (which has plenty of budget, moderate and medium-priced hotels—I like the d'Angleterre) or with friends in Passy (an expensive but convenient neighborhood). When working, I often stay next door to the city-centre Paris Opera, in the belle-epoque Grand Hotel. It is extremely convenient, handsome in a rather plush manner, and the phones work perfectly. It has very good room service, and the best French breakfast I know. The hotel is always busy (the Café de la Paix is on the ground floor) and not cheap.

For a first visit to Paris take a Cityrama double-decker sightseeing bus tour. They leave from the rue de Rivoli near the Place des Pyramides, which is adorned with a huge gold-covered statue of Joan of Arc. You wear earphones for the taped commentary as you see the Place de la Concorde (where the aristocrats were guillotined in the French Revolution), the Tuileries Gardens (where French boys in long flapping shorts sail model boats), the Church of the Madeleine, the Invalides historic military hospital and Napoleon's tomb, the Place de la Bastille, the Palais du Louvre, the Musée D'Orsay (it's very light and easy to photograph inside), Nôtre Dame (always packed with people), la Sainte Chapelle (go back and visit this gorgeous chapel on your own), the Seine and its many bridges (especially the ornate Pont Alexandre III, a favorite of fashion photographers), and of course the Eiffel Tower and Champs Elysées. Then you will have central Paris straight in your mind, and can travel by bus or Metro or taxi to get about on your own.

It's not totally impossible to drive yourself in Paris, but you must be used to very busy city traffic; as usual parking is difficult, and there are those "boots" again.

Take the open bateaux mouches (sightseeing boats) for photographs from the Seine; walk along the quais of the left bank past Nôtre Dame for pictures of young lovers, dog walkers, booksellers and barges (you will need wide-angle as well as zoom lenses). The best view of the Eiffel Tower is looking over sculptures, pools and powerful Trocadero fountains across the Seine (get off at the Alma Metro station, cross the wide plaza and walk down some steps). For another fine view of the tower and all Paris, go to the very high Montparnasse tower (Tour Montparnasse) observation deck. (This view is especially good at dusk.)

Paris is now in many ways a very modern city. You'll be prepared for this modernity if you land at Charles de Gaulle Airport at Roissy, where you whizz on escalators through plastic tubes between floors. There are more of these at the Centre Pompidou (popularly called the Beaubourg), the modern art museum in eastern Paris. The surrounding shopping/entertainment area is great for people photography. The new Opera House is on the Place de la Bastille. The new science museum complex at La Villette on the eastern outskirts of Paris is also very modern and well worth a visit. When I was there last, a famous avant garde theater group was performing outside an old warehouse complex now reserved for the arts. The show, featuring a huge pink papier-maché volcano which erupted periodically, was in its third straight day.

I'm sure you have seen pictures of I.M. Pei's glass pyramid in front of the Louvre. Parisiens don't like it, but they didn't like the Eiffel Tower at first either. Take a bus from the Gare du Nord vicinity to get to the totally touristy, but quite fun, Place du Tertre, in the former artist's quarter of Montmartre. Today, sidewalk artists sketch portraits, and much mass-produced art is purveyed to the citizens of Manchester, Munich, Matsuyama and Minneapolis. Walk down to see relatively unspoiled old Montmartre, it still looks like a Utrillo painting. Stop at the cemetery if you like such places.

Very upper-class-French and very pleasant is Passy, where, as I mentioned, I am lucky enough to stay sometimes. The traditional Marché de Passy is held on the low, narrow, pedestrians-only, rue de l'Annonciation. Smart Parisians, working people from the old district, and foreign diplomats' wives and servants shop there for fresh produce, kitchen utensils, overalls and the like three times a week. On the same street are a tiny hotel, a gourmet food store, bakeries, antique shops, a bookstore, and expensive clothes shops. Nearby is a big Inno, a wonderful popular-priced French chain store that sells everything. (Take the Metro to Passy or Muette stations and walk a few blocks to this area.)

The suburb La Defense is the most modern quarter of Paris. Take one of the network of fast R.E.R. trains for a twenty minute ride if you want to photograph there.

In April, 1992, Euro Disneyland will open at Marne-la-Valleé, east of Paris. The R.E.R. network will take you there from the center of the city in 40 mimutes.

French Provinces

I've been almost all over France, and love just about everywhere except the overbuilt, jam-packed Riviera and the slightly dreary northeast near Belgium (but things are looking up in that area with the Channel Tunnel construction). You are almost guaranteed to make good pictures in Alsace, which has timbered villages and houses with window boxes full of flowers; a charming mountainous "wine route"; the historic cities of Strasbourg and Colmar (both of which have superb ancient centers); and, of course, great food and drink. I photographed a master baker in Colmar, his forebears have worked in the same building since 1776!

Burgundy is the richest province of rich France; it has distinctive architecture with steep multicolored tiled roofs, some of the most famous vineyards in the world, friendly people and food and drink to die for. Don't miss the 14th-century Hospice de Beaune, or the photography museum at Châlons-sur-Sâone, birthplace of Nicéphore Niépce, who is only now getting his rightful due as the man who first captured a photographic image. Burgundy is surprisingly uncrowded even in the French vacation month of August.

Brittany is a one of my favorite regions of France, but is a special taste because the weather is often damp. The southern coast is more sheltered than the north (which is famous for especially fierce winter storms). Take a raincoat and "bright" Velvia or EPP film to photograph Brittany's Celtic carvings, large and small stone fishing villages, lighthouses, cliffs, seabirds and wide, empty (except in mid-summer) beaches. Take a ferry from the naval port of Brest or from le Conquet, a pretty fishing village and resort, to the still remote island of Ouessant, with great rocks lashed by surf, a lighthouse museum, colonies of seabirds, and old ladies (a few still wear island costume) who lead sheep around on rope halters. I have been there three times; it is a truly magic place. Get hotel reservations six months ahead for midsummer; the island has few rooms, and some French families return year after year. You can stay in a bird-watching hostel too, the place is a paradise for ornithologists in spring and fall.

Very much on the beaten track is the magnificent Mont St. Michel, on an islet at the border of Brittany and Normandy; photograph it from across the marshes at sunset; if you go into the citadel on a summer day you will be almost overpowered with visitors; but if you stay overnight, you will have the place almost to yourself at dawn.

For a completely different feeling, see the equally historic and almost desolate World War II Normandy invasion beaches, hunks of rusted tanks and trucks are still embedded in the sand on Omaha beach; the Pointe du Hoc is where Texas rangers stormed an impossible clifftop fortification. The endless cemeteries above all the invasion beaches are deeply affecting; there are usually a few legionnaire-capped American or Canadian or British veterans looking around. I was there for the 40th anniversary in 1984, when the locals (and France in general) gave the returning vets and their wives a fantastic welcome.

For still another Normandy mood, go to Monet's house and especially garden at Giverny. These are as lovely as the paintings but, yet again, get there very early in the day in summer. Professionals can get permission to photograph when the gardens are closed to the public.

In the Loire valley all but the most famous châteaux are reasonably uncrowded even in August. Several have "*Son et Lumière*" programs (the French invented the sound and light show) and elegant buildings bathed in different colored lights make fine photographs.

In the extreme southwestern Langedoc region of France is Carcassonne, probably the most superb example of a medieval fortified city in the world— part of the recent movie "Robin Hood Prince of Thieves" was shot there. If possible, plan to stay overnight in early fall. Visit the nearby Minérvois wine country, then enter the walled city in late afternoon. Photograph the floodlit inner citadel, and the outer ramparts, at "blue time", when you can feel the mood of the place. Not too far away is Minérve, a red-roofed fortified village in a deep gorge which was a stronghold for heretics in the 13th century.

The only part of Provence to go in summer is well north of the coast (but the Negresco hotel in Nice and the Grand Hotel in Cannes are still great). Drive in Haut Provence to find fortified stone villages; two charming recent French films, "My Father's Glory" and "My Mother's Castle," based on Marcel Pagnol's childhood, show the region to perfection. Drive and find you own favorite villages and, if you have a chance, drive further north, to the Dordogne region.

Chamonix-Mont Blanc is the skiing mecca of the French Alps; the succession of cable car rides past the Aiguille du Midi is thrilling (the highest in the world) the peaks are snow-capped even in midsummer, but as usual at their best in winter.

Fly to Corsica or take a boat from Nice. It's a beautiful, rather rugged island; the birthplace of Napoleon. Amusingly (for a Britisher anyway) his fine monument in Ajaccio lists all the battles except one—Waterloo.

I plan to keep going back to France until I am 95, God willing.

Monaco

The principality is well worth a visit to see the pink Palace where in summer white-clad sentries in peppermint-candy-striped boxes stand guard against hordes of tourists. Photograph the palatial yachts in the harbor from the cliffs nearby; the botanical gardens are nice too. Monaco as a whole is a bit too crowded and built-up for my taste. Photography is never permitted there, but go into the great old casino for fun and to look at the gamblers anyway.

The Netherlands (Holland)

One of my favorite countries. You don't have to have a car to photograph in Holland; trains and busses are excellent. Of course you can bike too in that world center of cyclists. Holland at first sight may disappoint you; it seems a mass of highways and electric pylons. Take back roads in the countryside to find its charm. Amsterdam is a very handsome city, but jammed with cars, bikes and tourists, it's difficult to get good pictures from canal boats because they are low and mostly glassed in. Take a boat with an open front or back. You can get "instant Amsterdam" pictures from the bridges around Rembrandt's handsome red-shuttered house near the Spui, and, in the late afternoon, from the cruise boat pier in front and to the left of the central station. The flower market near the ancient gold-topped mint tower is a pretty morning shot. Denizens of the red light quarter around the Zeedyke and their customers do not appreciate photographers at any time of day. Photography without flash is okay in the Rijksmuseum and Van Gogh museum.

The winding, flower-banked River Vecht is lined with small gabled houses and fine mansions, and crossed with white drawbridges straight out of a Van Gogh painting. It's a popular weekend resort area for well-to-do Amsterdammers.

Marken and Volendam are picturesque, touristic, and the places to find locals in Dutch costumes (they usually charge for photographs).

Zaanse Schans, near Zaandam with three active windmills, and traditional green painted houses, is one of the best museum villages in Europe.

Go to to unspoiled Haarlem for pretty street and canalscapes, a great cathedral and Frans Hal's fine house with a museum of his work. Haarlem is close to the tulip fields. Photograph them, and the Keukenhof Gardens at Lisse, in full bloom in April and early May.

Near Rotterdam visit Madurodam, a huge photogenic miniature Holland built as a memorial to Peter Maduro, a young man who died in World War II. Near Rotterdam also is a famous row of windmills at Kinderdjke. There is a very nice and rather unknown group of windmills set in pastoral country at Aarlandervein, near Arnhem. Willemstad, a gem of a small fortified town surrounded by water, is a Dutch national monument.

If you can attend the annual *Stichting Stamboek van Rond und Plat Bodem Jachten* (I hope I got that right) in July, you will get some wonderful pictures. This "Reunion of Round and Flat-Bottom Yachts" attracts sailing-barge enthusiasts, including Dutch royalty, for a week of racing, showing off their beautiful boats and socializing. It is held at a different port around the Ijsel Meer each year.

The city of Maastricht, which has a great farmer's market, and the south of Holland in general is underphotographed and very seldom on tourist itineraries, which is a pity. Carnival in Maastricht is a big event.

Belgium

The ancient convent—the Béguinage—by the river in Bruges is reason enough to go to Belgium. Nuns still stroll in the gardens wearing the old garb of long black robes with starched white "butterfly" coifs. Ornate 17th-century merchants' houses line the canals of Bruges and also of Ghent—where you should not miss the ultra-formal and elegant Grand Café. The waiters wear classic black uniforms with white aprons down to the ground, and the price of a cup of coffee is what you might expect. The Grand Place in Brussels is enclosed by the finest merchants' houses of all, best photographed floodlit, and there are charming little old streets behind the huge Place. The Atomium and other attractions at the former Brussels World's Fair site outside the city are worth a look, as is Tournai, a historic city with a festival where papier-maché giants are paraded each June. The biggest photography problem in Belgium is the weather—it has usually rained a lot when I have been there.

Denmark

Copenhagen's Victorian-style Tivoli Gardens is open late spring to early fall. The Moorish, Chinese and other amusement pavilions are lit with millions of colored bulbs, there are lots of Danes among visitors from all over the world, and the Boy's Guard in black bearskin hats and red coats parade several times a day. Blue dusk is the magic time at Tivoli.

Blue-clad royal guards stand in red sentry boxes at Copenhagen's Royal Palace; on holidays only, they wear red uniforms. There is a nice pedestrians-only street leading from the main Radhus square; it passes some splendid churches with tall green copper spires. (The most famous spire in the city is in the shape of intertwined dragons' tails.) A good open-boat harbor cruise (where of course you can spot the Little Mermaid) starts from the Nyhaven canal. Nyhaven is flanked by very handsome, brightly painted brick buildings; most house sailors' bars, tattoo and other parlors. But it's very clean and quite safe, in the daytime anyway. Aunt Minnie might get a kick out of it.

Rural Denmark is rather flat, mostly agricultural, green and pleasant with some yellow mustard fields and old farms and castles here and there. There are good beaches in Jutland. The Island of Funen is a favorite summer resort area too. Hans Christian Andersen's hometown of Odense is picturesque; there is a pleasant folk village not far away. Hamlet's castle of Elsinore (Helsingfors) is huge but was to me a bit disappointing (no Hamlet movies have been made there). It's close to where you can take a ferry to Malmö, Sweden.

Sweden

Stockholm has a fine situation, straddling several islands in the Baltic. The city is mostly rather modern with busy roads, but has an old quarter with narrow streets and tall churches around the royal palace. There is a huge open-air produce and flower market in downtown Stockholm, where I take my favorite people pictures, and a fine walking street, lined with cafés. Don't miss the Carl Milles sculpture garden with hundreds of his graceful copper figures cavorting amid fountains. It is about an hour outside the city proper. The 18th-century royal palace at Drottningholm, and especially the superb small opera house in the grounds, should be seen, and if you can get opera tickets you'll enjoy the experience. (You'll have to sneak opera photographs during the applause.) Evening cruises from Stockholm to nearby Baltic islands are pleasant in summer.

I haven't explored the rest of Sweden, but a travel-writer/photographer friend told me that the big island of Gottland (scene of Ingmar Bergman movies) is well worth the trip, with Viking and Hanseatic relics and lovely beaches; but book ahead, hotels in the capital, Visby, are crowded in midsummer.

Norway

This to me is the most photogenic of the Scandinavian countries. Oslo has an impressive modern town hall overlooking the harbor, and a huge beer garden full of handsome youth in the middle of its small equivalent of Central Park. Opposite this park, the dark but atmospheric Grand Café in the hotel of the same name, once played host to Ibsen and Strindberg; many of the customers are still very formally dressed older Norwegians. The "must see" just outside the center of Oslo is the Vigeland sculpture park, with thousands of monumental nude figures illustrating life from birth to death. If you drive from Oslo to Bergen, a scenic trip I recommend, go via the Hardanger Plateau. You will see deer and occasional traditional-style sod-roofed cabins. It often snows even in summer.

A wonderful, rather new, wood-paneled resort hotel, the Hovdestoylen, is at Hovden. I was there once when a group of Norwegian pensioners was visiting. Everyone congregated in the dance hall after dinner (dances are big throughout Scandinavia) and this was the only time in my life when 80-year-old ladies came up and asked me to dance. We had a riotous time!

The west coast of Norway is often rather rainy, so allow extra time to get good pictures. The historic port of Bergen is surrounded by hills, has a busy harbor where tall ships sometimes visit, and a huge daily fish and flower market. The row of Hanseatic warehouses has been designated a world cultural monument by UNESCO; there is a well-restored old-town outdoor museum complex and a funicular with spectacular views. Drive from Bergen via pretty Voss to Sogndal where big local ferries (which run frequently in summer) go up different fjords. (You must reserve months ahead for long mailboat cruises from Bergen to Lapland, the Arctic Circle and reindeer country.)

If you can visit Geirangerfjord or Sognefjord or Hardangerfjord in late May when the apple blossoms are out you will see Norway at its loveliest. Seven hundred year old wooden churches, tiny fjord-side villages and waterfalls of all shapes and sizes can all be photographed, and the people proudly wear national dress for holidays. "Unsettled" weather in the west is the only real problem for photographers.

Finland

Helsinki is another agreeable Scandinavian capital with a harbor location and a marvelous open-air market. The sturdy white-blonde-haired market ladies wear brilliant yellow, orange and red cotton Marimekko overalls and hats, perhaps to ward off the blues of the long, dark Finnish winters. You can buy the usual fruit, vegetables and flowers, plus woodenware, baskets, Lapp souvenirs and reindeerskin mittens. The Seuraasari folk village nearby is well done. Around Helsinki you can photograph and visit some of the buildings designed by the great Finnish architects Aalvar Alto and Eero Saarinen. Finland's second city, Turku, has a castle and is where overnight ferries to Stockholm, Sweden, leave.

Most of the rest of Finland is empty of people; bright and dark green in summer, with shimmering birches and millions of pine trees. Towns are connected by arrow-straight roads; you pass a lot of blue lakes. Around the coast there are thousands and thousands of tiny islets, most big enough for just a few pine trees. If you know any Finns, you might get invited to sail out for a stay in a summer cabin, or a picnic and a sauna.

Iceland

I haven't spent long on this somewhat remote Scandinavian island, considered the Western outpost of Europe, but I liked the brightly painted little capital of Reykjavik. The handsome blonde Icelandic people are very friendly. I saw bubbling geysers, and sheep and wild ponies on moorlands near Reykjavik. I'm told the rest of the countryside is also moorlands and well worth exploring by car in midsummer, when the late evening light is sometimes extraordinary. An active volcano on an offshore islet is Iceland's biggest tourist attraction.

Germany

The first time I went to Germany, in 1963, was with distinct apprehension. My father was in the British Army in two world wars. But Germany is lovely in many places. Germans as a people are among the most intrepid travelers in the world, and they appreciate and travel a lot in their own country, too. The tourism facilities are unsurpassed. Young Germans (and many older ones) are very friendly and open, and concerned about things that matter, like the environment. Accommodations range from world-class hotels to *"zimmer mit fleisswasser"* (rooms with running water) in private homes—all are the best possible of their own kind. Many of the world's top hotel managers today are German. I have made in all about twenty visits to the country. My favorite places for photographs are, from north to south: the city of Cologne (photograph the cathedral with a long lens from across the Rhine); the most scenic stretch of the Rhine from around St. Goarshausen to Boppard; and the quiet scenery along the Mosel/Moselle river from Koblentz to Trier.

Then see the best-preserved medieval walled towns of Germany, Rothenburg (very crowded in summer) and Dinkelsbuhl.

I've described another favorite region of Germany, Bavaria, in Chapter Fifteen. While in Bavaria go to Baden-Baden, an extremely elegant spa and casino city. It is a place to see very formal, wealthy Germans relaxing, and some very high-powered gambling indeed (no cameras are allowed in the casino).

Berlin

It's easy to use subways and buses to get around Berlin, which I feel I hardly need to describe in detail to you because it's been on TV so much since the wall came down. There are modern, broad busy streets, a lively youth scene, lots of bars, cafés and discos, and the Tiergarten, an enormous park with a zoo. The symbolic shot of West Berlin until now has been the brown broken spire of the Kaiser Wilhelm church, preserved as a memorial next to a very modern church seemingly built entirely of stained glass. I imagine that with re-unification, the former East Berlin is changing every day; but the Communists lovingly restored many historic buildings on the broad Unter Den Linden making it an impressive (if somewhat heavy) sight when I saw it about fifteen years ago. Obviously, as Berlin becomes Germany's capital again, there will soon be much construction. On a clear day, there is a fantastic view over the city from the observation deck of eastern Berlin's TV tower. I hope the Germans don't dismantle the great Russian war memorial in the east of the city; it is black granite or marble; very powerful and moving.

Munich

Munich is a busy, mostly modern city, but has an ornate medieval mechanical clock with dancing figures on the Rathaus (city hall). You can stand in the big square and photograph them every hour. The lively arts quarter, called Schwabing, has some great restaurants and a youth culture that looks almost indistinguishable from American or British.

Not too far from Munich, the Black Forest around Triberg can be dark and spooky in bad weather. I got lost on back roads there once in a fog and was quite scared; in the more open parts there are timbered and thatched farmhouses and huge barns to be seen at frequent intervals.

My neighbor Sigrid Estrada, a photographer who grew up near Hamburg, made her first long trip through the eastern part of Germany (the former DDR) last fall. She recommends taking the road from Hamburg along the Baltic and seeing the old towns of Vismar, Schwerin and the Hanseatic port of Rostock. Another German travel photographer I know suggests touring the eastern Hartz Mountains region.

Switzerland

You can manage without a car in Switzerland if you must, the trains and Post Buses are superb. My favorite places: the car-free resort of Zermatt where you can photograph that ultimate Alp, the Matterhorn; if you can go in winter when horse-drawn sleds are the transport and cosmopolitan crowds of skiers fill the place, you will see Zermatt at its best. The Engadine, around St. Moritz, is a region of tiny villages and spring meadows full of brilliant yellow and blue Alpine flowers. Surprisingly, it is uncrowded three seasons of the year.

Not too far from St. Moritz is the still-remote Romansch-speaking area of Switzerland. Go to Tarasp-Scuols and drive (or take the Post Bus) up a long winding road to Ftan, or Fetan, once recommended to me by a Swiss tourism official as the most beautiful village in the country. I agree. Houses with painted designs on the thick stone walls cluster around a church with a spire that has an onion dome on top. Dark-brown goats wander in the narrow streets and there are log barns and meadows full of pinkish-gray cows with long silky eyelashes eating cowparsley. The sharp teeth of the Dolomites stand high behind the village. I have been to Ftan in winter, spring and summer and it is always lovely, always empty.

I also love the Ticino canton which borders Italy. There are ancient stone farms with thick slate roofs (your car may be blocked by cows being herded along the roads), and cherry orchards. The pretty lakeside resort of Lugano seems to be the only place in the region with significant numbers of tourists.

Lichtenstein

I feel this tiny country is designed mainly for people who collect rubber stamps in their passports. A fine castle and some vineyards; but the capital of Vaduz is mostly given over to souvenirs, post cards and duty-free cigarette selling.

Austria

If you drive to Austria from Switzerland, you can take the Arlberg pass if you have steel nerves and don't mind heights; but you can't stop for pictures because enormous trucks, tour buses, timid flatlanders like the British and Dutch in low-powered campers and cars, and motor bikes all clog the narrow winding road, which has terrifying drop-offs. I took the tunnel the second time. The Tyrol is the most mountainous part of Austria and has many ski resorts. All are decked with flower boxes in summer, but to me they look their very best in winter.

I love Salzburg, a city that lives up to its reputation. It still looks like "The Sound of Music"; all the scenes were shot in and around the town and are recognizable. Salzburg ladies of all ages wear pretty dirndls, men sport green knickers with red check shirts on all possible occasions, and there is a good open-air market. Though packed with visitors, especially at festival time, Salzburg still smiles at all of them. You are almost guaranteed to get good pictures if you take the funicular up to the Winkler Casino terrace in the late afternoon, and aim your 200mm lens over red umbrellas and the spires of old Salzburg to the castle which dominates the city. All this is floodlit starting at dusk, which is unbelievably considerate to photographers. The narrow Getriedegasse is a medieval pedestrian street lined with wrought iron and stained glass shop signs (and just a few small flags that say Eis Kreme, Kodak and Fujifilm too). A 43-80mm zoom works well here. The Salzkammergut is a busy and picturesque lake resort region outside Salzburg on the way to Vienna.

Vienna is harder to get a visual handle on than Salzburg; the floodlit twin towers of St. Stephen's Cathedral, the baroque stone buildings along the "ring" roads and some "konditorei" interiors are all a good bet for Vienna pictures. Viennese ladies of a certain age in hats, and men in jackets and ties, sit for hours reading newspapers, sipping and nibbling in these coffee and pastry shops. There are open-air waltz demonstrations in summer, and you can try too, if you wish. I took one of my all-time favorite "grab" pictures in Vienna's Prater park; it was of an old gent blissfully reading a nudie newspaper. The amusement park there has the big ferris wheel where Harry Lime and Holly Martens rode around at night in "The Third Man," looking down at the ant-like people below. The old eastern end of Vienna is very untouristy; it is full of dusty textile shops and has a famous Jugendstihl (or art-nouveau) post office, built around 1910, that still looks modern. Viennese and tourists alike go to the wine village of Grinzing outside the city to drink new wine and sing in summer and fall.

Southern Europe

If you like tradition and guaranteed warm weather, this part of Europe is for you. The only problems for photographers are that many places are crowded in midsummer, and there is some overbuilding in popular coastal areas.

Spain

I've already written that Spain is booming, with the fastest-growing economy in Europe. For many years the sunny Costa Brava has been a favorite of my native countrymen, who have not improved it. I would avoid at any cost the concrete jungle of cheap high-rise hotels at Torremolinos, Benidorm and nearby resorts. But you can escape the masses by going that extra mile. For instance, an English friend has a house on the beautiful, very popular island of Majorca—up in the hills in pretty Fornelutz, set amid olive groves and windmills. The next hill town of Dera was home to the scholar and poet Robert Graves. My friend swims at Soller. In these places you are light years from the hordes that pack the discos and bars of the port of Palma.

The Costa del Sol around Malaga is busy but better. Marbella is a chic resort. Andalusia is old Moorish Spain. Seville is very crowded at Easter, largely with Spanish pilgrims. I spent a week there photographing one Holy Week. The penitents' robes date from the Spanish Inquisition and were the inspiration for the costumes of the Ku Klux Klan. They are still very scary, especially at night, when the parades are lit by candles and torches. Ronda is a pretty town. My stock pictures of Granada and Cordoba have sold consistently; these places may still be underphotographed. In very busy Toledo, of course see El Greco's paintings and house and the oldest synagogue in Europe; then drive around the Ebro outside the town for good views over the city and looping river from a tourist restaurant's terrace. Madrid and Barcelona (where the "must" is Gaudi's Sagrada Familia cathedral) are both big, busy cities; I've visited them only in midsummer, when they are grillingly hot, so haven't enjoyed them as much as I doubtless should. Apart from covering the "musts," my preference in Spain is to drive in the interior of the country, and see smaller castles and traditional villages, vineyards and olive groves, leaving the busiest places to others. In Spain, you may or may not want to photograph bullfights. If you do go, be sure and get good front seats on the shady *(sombra)* side, and save some film until late in the afternoon for good light and long shadows.

Keep equipment close to you in Spain; street crime exists in the big cities.

Portugal

Underphotographed. Apart from the beautiful southern Algarve coast, largely colonized today by the British, Portugal is probably the least tourist-developed country in Western Europe. Lisbon is a pretty city, though a part of the oldest quarter burned a few years ago. The busy coast road from Lisbon to exclusive Estoril and attractive Cascais has sandy beaches, colorfully painted fishing fleets and a pleasant Portuguese family holiday atmosphere.

North of Lisbon, the Atlantic coast facing the New World is exposed to pounding winter storms. Nazaré is a famous formerly-isolated fishing port surrounded by high cliffs; now it has many visitors. Only the old people still wear the traditional plaid costumes, but the boats are as colorfully painted as ever. Have a wonderful fish stew at one of dozens of plain restaurants along the beach. Portugal's second city, Porto, has had long ties with Britain because of the port-wine trade. You can visit and photograph the wineries. The city is jammed with cars. In the center of Portugal there are fields of cork and olive trees; the three E's—the towns of Elvas, Estremoz and Evora—are especially worth photographing.

Italy

Italy was the first country where large numbers of "tourists"—British aristocrats finishing their education—traveled. It has been the number one tourist country ever since, and has so much to offer that I can only scratch the surface here. If you can visit the great sites out of season, you will enjoy them more because they will be less crowded. I like the cooler spring, fall and even winter weather in Italy too.

Venice

As I've said elsewhere, Venice is wonderful, but overphotographed. Take local vaporetti (water busses) to photograph along the canals; they are less jammed than express ones. The Accademia bridge is the place to stand for Grand Canal views. Fleets of gondolas pass under it at dusk. The Arsenale is very fine—and a bit less crowded than other major Venetian sites.

Florence

The best overall view is from the high Piazza Michaelangelo across the Arno.

The covered straw market is fun. The only hope you have of getting a snapshot or two of the original of Michaelangelo's David is by getting to the Accademia museum half an hour before it opens, to be early in line. (The sculpture in the Piazza del Duomo is a copy.)

Rome

This is a big city, but you don't need to start with an overall guided tour—the things you want to see are very close together. Start at my favorite spot, the circular Piazza Campidoglio, an architectural gem (however the statue of Marcus Aurelius designed by Michaelangelo is absent for restoration at present). But there is another huge sculpture, a relief of a reclining man, in the piazza; nearby is a famous small bronze of Romulus and Remus being suckled by a wolf—it is the emblem of Rome. There are monumental fragments of Roman works, including a hand taller than a man, in the courtyard of the Capitoline museum, and many more Roman relics inside. Strangely enough, not every visitor to the city goes to this marvellous place. Just below the piazza is the best view I know of in Rome, straight over the ancient Forum. Nearby is a bus terminus (next to the huge Vittorio Emmanual monument) that lets you easily reach anywhere in the city. A short walk away is the Colosseum and the entrance to the Forum.

The view up the Spanish Steps over the turtle fountain, from the Piazza de Spagna, is especially nice in spring when huge tubs of azaleas decorate the steps. The house where the English romantic poet Keats lived is to the right.

Overall views of St. Peter's Square are marred by crowd control barriers installed since the attempt on the life of the Pope. Photograph St. Peter's from across the Tiber, the view from the vicinity of the Castel san'Angelo is a classic.

The Trevi Fountain has just been restored. Go very, very early if you need a shot of it without thousand of tourists tossing three coins in the fountain.

Don't take a car to downtown Rome. Roman drivers are descended from gladiators, and taxis are cheap.

Drive or take a bus to Hadrian's Villa and the water gardens at Tivoli, outside the city. Both make splendid pictures, but oh, the crowds! (The Tivoli souvenir stands are so enormous and varied they are actually interesting as subjects in their own right.)

The Rest of Italy

Be sure to save film for some of these scenic Italian towns and regions: Cortina D'Ampezzo, the center of a famed winter resort area (the surrounding Dolomite peaks are strangely shaped and dramatic). Sermione, with a beautiful castle and moat. The tiny workingmen's islands of Burano and Chioggia, near Venice, which have colorful painted houses. Porto Ercolo, now a charming, very exclusive seaside resort. Lucca, with a fine market. The Renaissance hill towns of Assisi and Ravenna and Siena, which have some of the greatest art and architecture ever created, and of course draw a lot of visitors but not nearly as many as Florence or Venice.

The best way of all to photograph in Italy's countryside is to drive, stay off the autostradas and find your own favorite small towns and villages. I recommend Route 222 from Siena, which takes you through the Chianti wine country.

In June, on back roads from Florence to Rome, you will pass fields of red poppies shaded by olive trees, with occasional white oxen or black cows grazing in them. The hilly area near Rome called the Abruzzi has quite a few pretty old towns, each perched on a separate hill. I like Norcia.

Caution: Be very, very careful of your equipment and money in the old Trastevere quarter of Rome, indeed in all of the city and farther south. I had my pocket picked while photographing an opera performance at the Baths of Caracalla. But a nice policeman gave me a ride to my hotel in his squad car. (And, of course the vast majority of Italians are honest. I once left a camera in a Venice trattoria after a rather vinous lunch. It was returned to me when I found the place again two hours later, by anxiously waiting waiters.)

Obviously though, you can't rely on such honesty anywhere in the world.

South of Naples park overnight only in guarded places. I have known tour bus drivers who could only find street parking to sleep on the bus to prevent the tires from being stolen!

I have driven from Brindisi in the toe of Italy to Naples and Rome, and don't especially recommend the long drive (except for seeing Pompeii, which can be done from Rome). The south of Italy is mostly flat, the towns a bit drab. Naples itself is like an old grand duchess a bit down on her luck. Capri is beautiful of course, but much, much too crowded in summer for my taste; the Blue Grotto can feel like Coney Island sometimes. If you go to Capri, go off-season, and see the Swedish writer Axel Munthe's villa.

A friend who knows Sicily well has told me that it is beautiful, with Roman temples and arenas and splendid churches, and some unspoiled offshore islands.

Greece

A country I would go to at the drop of a hat, with or without a camera. One of the truly great vacation places of the world. The only problem is that in midsummer, practically every northern European agrees with me.

Athens

I'm not a person who needs every comfort, but my advice is to invest in an airconditioned hotel room in smoggy Athens in summer. I have stayed in the best (the elegant Hotel Grande Bretagne) and one of the worst hotels in Athens (the latter will be nameless, a humid, mildewy, none-too-clean sweatbox on Omonia Square).

The Grande Bretagne is on Syntagma Square, where you can lounge on overstuffed swing chairs under white umbrellas and eat (and photograph) sinful ice creams. Across the square, the six-foot-plus burly Evzones (elite guards) stomping up and down in front of the pink Presidential Palace don't look in the least like ballet dancers in their white uniforms with frilly skirts, cute red pillboxes, thick white wool stockings and heavy black clogs.

After you have "done" the Acropolis with a wide-angle lens (get there early or just before closing time) and photographed it at "blue time" with a telephoto from the Pnyx hill (stay until dark if there is a sound and light performance, these start around 9 p.m.). Then you can sup, and photograph under narrow streets roofed with grapevines in the ancient Plaka district.

When you have seen the National Archaeological Museum, where photography is allowed but requires a fee even for amateurs (this is true here and in most Greek museums), see the fabulous Monastiraki flea market. Then you've done the best of Athens and can take a ferry from Pireaus to just about any Greek island. These, to me, are the real reasons to go, and to photograph, in Greece.

The Greek Islands

Near Athens, Hydra has a superb harbor, Poros nice beaches. The more distant Cyclades are the most beautiful of all the Greek islands. "Musts" to see and photograph, crowded in July and August, are Mykonos (and nearby sacred Delos) and high Santorini and its neighboring volcanic islet which still smoulders slightly. Amorgos (where I once spent a very enjoyable week); Astipalea, Folegandros and Naxos are my suggestions for more "off the beaten track" islands. Most small island hotels are clean but basic; as an alternative you may find a nice room with a family. Patmos in the Dodecanese is a cruise ship stop. It has a famous monastery with only a few ancient monks remaining; Greek friends vacation there.

Corfu, off the Albanian coast, is green and lovely but for my taste too full of English-owned villas with names like Bide-a-Wee and Dunroamin. It boasts a perfectly beautiful little monastery on an islet that is much photographed but unfortunately right under the approach to the Corfu airport. I've stayed in the big thatched-hut Club Med on the island which is nice and quite cheap.

The ruins of Knossos on Crete, the Greek island closest to the African continent, are a "must" see, the beaches are good but crowded in summer.

Rhodes is to me the most beautiful of the big Greek islands. In summer here too though, the beaches and major sites are crowded.

Delphi , on the mainland again, is Greece's most sacred site, with the Temple of Diana my favorite vantage point. The light is best very early in the morning.

Eastern Europe

Mostly troubled in this time of great change, Eastern Europe has much to offer photographers because the years of Communism have preserved a very traditional way of life. You might not want to live where horse carts are still used for transportation for instance, but there is no denying they are very photogenic.

Yugoslavia

Current news is dismaying, but when it improves, go. Croatia has a marvelous Adriatic coastline, though summer beaches are normally crowded (especially with German and Austrian visitors)—there are some quieter islands off the coast. Dubrovnik, is in Dalmatia, and was a former outpost of the Venetian Republic. It is one of the most beautiful and complete walled cities in Europe. Photograph down onto it from nearby hills.

Inland, Mostar, once a part of the Turkish Ottoman Empire, is still picturesque and rather Eastern-looking, with mosques, a fine market, and an ancient bridge over a gorge (from which you can get "instant Mostar" pictures). Belgrade, the capital of Serbia, is to me a large gray, rather dull city, except that it has a fine ancient fortress and a pleasant, small, artist/entertainment quarter called Skardarlia. The southern province of Macedonia, close to Greece and Albania, is poor, makes for rough driving, but is beautiful in many places.

Hungary

Budapest is reclaiming its reputation as the Paris of the east. If nothing goes wrong the country will be soon one of Europe's top travel destinations. Like Vienna, it has historic coffee shops. The Café New York is a riot of art nouveau lamps and a hangout for the local intelligentsia. Be sure to see it when you get to the city. Overall views down onto the Danube bridges, the enormous Hungarian parliament buildings and huge paddle steamers on the (brown, not blue) Danube are best taken at "blue time" from near the Hilton hotel (which rather tastefully incorporates a ruined monastery) and the Fisherman's Bastion on the high Buda side of the city.

Outside Budapest, around Lake Balaton, there are lake resorts beloved by Hungarian and Austrian and German city dwellers. Farther east is much less trampled; there are three interesting K's, the cities of Kecskemet, Kiscunfelegyhaza and the plains national park of Kiskunsag with lots of sheep (there are a lot of other K's in that area where I haven't been).

Czechoslovakia

Prague is beautiful, but to me rather sad, I can't exactly say why. I have been there twice (not since liberation); the second time I felt that the beautifully preserved city tends to be too much like a museum (perhaps it needs some modern architecture like London and Paris). You may not agree, and neither do people who make period movies—"Amadeus" was filmed there. The views up from the sculpture-adorned Charles Bridge to Hradcany Castle and down from the astronomical clock tower onto the Old Town Square are especially fine.

The Old Synagogue dates from the 13th century, and has a packed graveyard though almost no living Jews remain. There I once took a photograph that sums up my feelings about Prague: in a spring drizzle, an American Jewish acquaintance walked, hunched over with pain, looking for the names of great-grandparents. His other relatives had died in a concentration camp.

The places I like best in Czechoslovakia are the tiny villages of Bohemia, with cottages that now are often weekend retreats for well-connected families from Prague. They are usually painted a cheery yellow and white, with dark red tile roofs. There is often a village green with a pond, and once in while, some honking flocks of fat geese being driven by a buxom farm woman wearing an apron and a kerchief.

Romania

I went there only once, in the mid-1970's. I stayed two weeks, and was driven around a lot by a chauffeur in a huge black Soviet limousine. He had Stalinist ideas about starting time, coffee breaks, lunch breaks, tea breaks and quitting time. Since then, I have been selling stock pictures of Romanian dancers, Dracula's castle at Bran, the very nice folk village outside Bucharest (to paraphrase Will Rogers, second prize is two weeks in Bucharest) and the green hills of Transylvania. Perhaps, until recently, I was the only photographer ever to have visited the countryside of Romania! I am told that some of the pretty farm villages I photographed were probably bulldozed in Ceaucescu's insane redevelopment schemes. After the sad scenes we have all seen in the last couple of years on TV, it looks as though Romania will be off the tourist maps for years to come.

Poland

I went to Poland one snowy March on an Orbis tourist office sponsored trip for magazine editors, writers and photographers. We had red-carpet treatment, but that is not the only reason I loved Poland. Men in crisp uniforms with high boots, or rumpled suits and shapeless shoes, bent at the waist to kiss the hands of ladies of all ages. People in the streets carried single tulips decorated with ribbon—the Poles seem to adore flowers.

Warsaw

In this city I saw and heard the single most fantastic opera performance I have ever attended, in the biggest opera house I have ever seen. (It was Alban Berg's *"Wozzeck,"* with an ultra-modern set, at the Teatr Wielki.) While Prague's preservation was to me slightly depressing, I felt that the old center of Warsaw was a monument to courage and ability to surmount disaster. Having been levelled during the Warsaw Uprising at the very end of World War II to stumps of rubble like a very old man's teeth, it had to be totally rebuilt. (There is a museum in the Old Town Market Square that has photographs documenting all this.) I was told that this square, and other important buildings, were painstakingly recreated according to paintings of the city by Canaletto, who painted Warsaw almost as lovingly as he did Venice.

Also in Warsaw are the remains of a Gestapo prison, now a museum. Outside is a huge old tree, with shields painted with people's names nailed to it. They were covered with fresh tulips. While I was photographing, an old couple came up, and talked to me in French. I photographed them outside the prison where he had spent three years, she one, and lived. Less than ten percent of the people who went in there ever came out again.

Warsaw has some very nice cozy coffee shops with thick oriental rugs, and a lively disco scene. Despite the men's deplorable suits, the young women have a sense of fashion. In Warsaw I met a lovely artist, in her 80's, a sort of Polish Grandma Moses, who painted from memory scenes of her girlhood in what is now Byelo-Russia. I now regret not having felt free to spend the $250 in dollars she asked for a large painting.

Near Lodz (pronounced something like "wooch") I photographed in a village where old ladies make dolls with Polish costumes, and cut and paste traditional pictures from bright tissue paper. I did buy one of these, for $5. Cracow has a beautiful ancient market square which survived the war. The flower market was doing a booming business when I was there, perhaps because Polish winters are long, gloomy and starved of color. I photographed the famous 14th-century arcaded Cloth Hall with flower stalls in front of it, from a low angle to avoid the clumps of coal-smoke-blackened snow that lay on the ground.

Pope John Paul II served as a cardinal in Cracow before his elevation. In the market square is the red-brick cathedral where he often celebrated Mass. His birthplace, a yellow stucco house in a very small town not far from Cracow, has a shop on the ground floor.

I persuaded my hosts to let me skip a lunch party with local tourism bigwigs, and a guide took me for a drive in the countryside. Horses and carts and horse-drawn sleds shared the road with a few cars and trucks. At a village market, all the farm vehicles were horse-drawn. (For me, not for them, this was lovely.) Country cottages were painted bright colors, often blue, and were half-timbered and thatched; very pretty but, my guide told me, very primitive. Polish girls don't want to live in them and are moving to the cities in ever increasing numbers. Boys follow them, and there is now a big shortage of farmers in primitive agrarian Poland.

The Former USSR

What can I write that won't be out-of-date by the time this is printed? Not much probably. If political conditions permit, it is certainly well worth seeing and photographing what is after all one of the great regions of the world, with a rich cultural history, more and more of which is being reclaimed daily.

Russia

I have been to Russia twice, in 1963 and 1983. Though there were great changes in that twenty years, Perestroika and Glasnost had not yet appeared, no coups or restorations had occurred and there was no thought that Communism would disappear and the Soviet Union become a commonwealth of independent states. Let us fervently hope that Russia and the other republics solve their economic problems and continue to progress towards democracy.

St. Petersburg (formerly Leningrad)

A magnificent city, built of course by Peter the Great. St.Petersburg/Leningrad is not a bit depressing though faithfully restored and somewhat museum-like in the center. Of course you will go to the Hermitage Museum in the Winter

Palace. It's painted pale green outside, white and gold inside, and is mostly daylit, so photography is no problem. Stroll along the banks of the River Neva, see statues and cathedrals and the elegant admiralty building. I photographed Russian sailors guarding the historic battleship Potemkin. Take a hydrofoil to Petrodvorets, the tsars' summer palace outside the city. There are gilded fountains, the imperial Russian eagle decorates gates and domes, the whole thing is superbly kept up by the government. In the surrounding park, there are lots of youth groups on vacation. The monument to the 1941-42 siege outside the city is very moving. Russian newlyweds put their wedding bouquets on the mass graves, and bemedalled war veterans are proud to be photographed. In midsummer, daylight lasts till 11 p.m.

Moscow

Red Square and St. Basil's Cathedral, and the Kremlin complex with red marble walls and golden-domed churches, are of course the photographic "musts" in Moscow. You can photograph all of them from one spot in the middle of Red Square if you are lazy. After that, wander or take the subway to as much of the city as your spirit of exploration (and of course current political realities) permit. See the University district, and of course the popular Gorky Park. The Tretiakov art gallery has superb icons dating from the 12th century. Russian circuses are the world's best; if you get a chance to go, do so. Photography is no problem.

I have not been to the rest of the former Soviet Union, I want one day to visit Tashkent and Samarkand. Another ambition is to take the Trans-Siberian Express to Vladivostock. A member of my family, a great-aunt who performed in a dance act across Europe, made this trip in 1911! I know people who have done it more recently; they highly recommend it for atmosphere if not luxury.

The Middle-East

This crucial part of the world is obviously to be approached with some caution at the present time. It is also pretty inacessible to women photographers, but the places I mention are easy to visit, and I have enjoyed my stays there. Of course, check government travel advisories before you go.

Turkey

When I was alone in Instanbul on my first visit twenty years ago (and considered not unattractive) I did not feel as harassed as I have occasionally in other predominantly Moslem countries. (Church and state are separated in Turkey.) Istanbul is a fabulous, frenzied, teeming city, reminding me in a curious way of New York. You can shoot the great pointed spires of Saint Sophia and the minarets of many mosques as well as the Golden Horn (the backlit water really gleams just about every sunset) from the pierced iron Galata Bridge. The big smoky ferry and tug boats dashing to various spots along the Bosphorus and beyond are also dramatic. To photograph in the warrens of the covered Grand Bazaar use fast film or flash. The Topkapi Museum (scene of the '60's caper "Topkapi" featuring Peter Ustinov as an inept emerald thief) and its garden are musts. There are some wonderful, just slightly seedy, wooden hotels outside the city that somebody surely ought to use in a movie one day.

I flew from Istanbul to Izmir, on Turkey's south coast, but friends who visit family there recommend the overnight ferry (advance reservations are necessary). I took a car and driver down the coast as far as the small resort of Bodrum (mostly prosperous families from Istanbul and German visitors vacation there) and returned on the same road, seeing storks nesting on Roman columns, ancient painted houses, millions of olive trees, and vineyards, wheatfields and peasants riding camels en route. On another visit to Turkey, this time from a Greek cruise ship, I went to Ephesus, a great ruined Roman city famous for its eight-seater marble communal toilet among other attractions. The nearby modern town of Kuçadasi has a good bazaar.

One of my German photographer friends, Margot Granitsas, recommends Cappodocia in Anatolia, famed for strange rock formations. Turkey is very popular with German, French and British travelers.

(For specific information on photographing in Moslem countries, see under Pakistan, in Chapter Nineteen.)

Egypt

One of the world's great travel experiences. Cairo is huge and chaotic, I don't recommend wandering around without a guide. The "musts" are several beautiful mosques (where I as a woman was not permitted to penetrate beyond outer courts) and the Egyptian Museum, where photography of the treasures is permitted (without a tripod or flash). Guides prefer groups of tourists, for obvious reasons, but you can probably find an English-speaking taxi driver who will show you the city and take you out to the Pyramids and Sphinx for not too much money. (Make it clear to him that you will give him a good tip at the end if he does what you want and does not insist on visiting tourist shops.)

You will share the road to the Pyramids and Sphinx at Giza with camels, donkeys, water trucks, motor coaches, kamikaze taxi cabs, very old and very young pedestrians, huge trucks belching fumes, Mercedes Benzes and big modern busses. Giza village is very touristy. I hired a camel and driver in advance to pose for me in the empty desert next day at dawn. About half a mile west of Giza, with the Pyramids backlit by the sunrise, is a good early vantage point, well away from the shops on the main road. You must book well in advance for a room at the famous Mena Palace Hotel at Giza; I could not get in.

There is an evening sound and light show at the Pyramids and Sphinx that makes for very good pictures (get there very early for a front seat on the bleachers).

To get to Luxor and the Valley of the Kings, you can fly or take a train. I flew for time reasons. The train is said to be air-conditioned and very good, and I am sure would be an interesting ride. There are plenty of freelance guides at the ruins in Luxor; mine showed me a well-thumbed letter of recommendation from Elliott Erwitt! Allow at least two or three days here, to get the most from the Valley of the Kings. I was in Luxor in July (the low season for visitors) and photographed the ruins in grilling heat with respectful thoughts about the stamina of Maxime Du Camp and Francis Frith, who did not have comfortable air-conditioned rooms to return to after work. Luxor itself is quite a nice town, with horse carriages pulling tourists on palm-shaded avenues. There are traditional mud-brick houses surrounded by palms on the outskirts. I hired a dhow for a cooling, late afternoon sail, and got nice views of agricultural pursuits along the Nile's banks which have been pretty much unchanged for thousands of years. I did not plan my stay in Egypt well, and could not get space on a flight to Abu Simbel, so I want to return there one day.

There are many agreeable and rather expensive boat tours along the Nile. See under Pakistan, in Chapter Nineteen, for information on photographing in Moslem countries.

Israel

I went to Israel to photograph for the very large Christian pilgrimage trade, about fifteen years ago when things were temporarily rather peaceful. Obviously caution must be exercised today—do not attempt to be a crusading reporter! Jerusalem is of course the "must" in Israel, sacred as it is to Christians, Jews and Moslems, and worth several days; the classic overall view of the city and the golden Dome of the Rock is from the beautifully planted Mount of Olives. I spent most of a day at the Western (or Wailing) Wall. Non-Jews (and women) cannot get too close; a medium telephoto lens is needed. (Dress conservatively and carry a head covering for visiting all religious shrines.) The place believed to be Jesus's birthplace in Bethlehem was to me a disappointment; it's marked by a small church smothered with ornate 19th-century silver ornaments; but the country around was positively Biblical, with shepherds in robes tending flocks of goats. I'm told it's unchanged today.

The Holy Land pilgrimage trade in Israel is organized by Lebanese-descended Christians. I wanted to meet some Jewish Israelis so I arranged a stay in a kibbutz called Nof Ginosir on the Sea of Galilee, where oranges are grown; it was easily done on the spot and cost about the same as a moderate hotel. This was the thing that I personally enjoyed the most in Israel. When I inquired if the place could still be visited, the Kibbutz hotel representative in New York said yes, but advance booking is now advised. He also told me that a 2,000 year-old boat was discovered there, close to the shore, about five years ago. It had been preserved almost perfectly in sand and silt, and is now in a small museum at the kibbutz. It was certainly a fishing boat.

An English friend who skin-dives has told me that the Red Sea near Eilat is a fabulous dive location. If you go there, you should visit St. Catherine's monastery in the Sinai desert where Jesus fasted for 40 days and nights.

Morocco

A wonderful country for photography. Tangier is a cubistic white harbor city, with very good hotels. Caution: I hated all the professional local guides I met there on my three different visits; they seemed to think of me only as a walking cash machine, to be steered into tourist shops (where of course they hoped to earn a commission on my purchases). If you know of, or can find any willing locals like young photographers, or students, to show you around, avoid guides in Tangier.

I must say, though, that the professional guides in Marrakesh are more considerate and very proud of their city. The good hotels of Marrakesh are like lovely oases with big swimming pools (which I much enjoy in the great heat, though I don't usually swim when working). Alas, my client wouldn't go for the luxurious Hotel Mamounia, where Winston Churchill often stayed. The great square of Djemaa El F'na is one of the most fabulous "people photography" places in the world, with storytellers, snake charmers, dervish dancers, water carriers hung with brass cups and jugs, all purveying their talents and wares to sightseers in from the countryside. Take a guide there, smile a lot, and hand out small tips for all pictures. Since some people take pictures in the square for a living; I would be very cautious about handing out free Polaroids here. You will not only be resented, but you will be undercutting their livelihood. (Since competition from people who will work for almost nothing is a factor in the travel photography business, I say this with deep feeling!) The entire Street of Wool Dyers is hung with skeins of brilliant saffron, purple, red and blue, drying in the sun.

In June each year there is a festival outside the city walls, where horsemen perform at a gallop and shoot off rifles into the air. Needless to say, one June when I found out that the festival was starting two days after I had planned to leave, I extended my stay. Best of all in Morocco is to hire a car with a driver and go into the countryside. Once I came upon a horse and camel trading fair and had no problems taking pictures. (Two photographer couples I know have driven unescorted, but I confess I am chicken about driving alone in back country Morocco. I am advised it is not at all a good idea for Westerners.) One day, I want to look up Ingrid and Humphrey and Claude in "Casablanca" (which was actually shot on a Hollywood back lot).

I have not been to Algeria or Tunisia, both popular holiday places for Europeans; my sister in England has been to Tunisia which she says sadly is very poor.

All these countries are of course Moslem; again, see photographing in Moslem countries in the section on Pakistan, in Chapter Nineteen.

East Africa

Go, go, go to see, experience and photograph the annual migration of wildlife. Not only will you get great pictures, but your mere presence will help just a little to preserve the animals and the game parks since tourists bring much-needed hard currency to East Africa.

Kenya and Tanzania

My month in Kenya and Tanzania was the most marvelous assignment I have had to date; and I'm looking forward to returning there in the summer of 1992. My stock pictures from East Africa have been steady sellers for years.

To photograph wildlife long lenses (from about 200 to 500-600mm) and a good tripod are musts. The Land Rover I rented from the United Touring Company of Nairobi was specially adapted for photography/filming, and had a sturdy shooting-platform and a sliding roof. (A window clamp is useful for photographing from inside some tourist minibusses, or from hired cars without sunroofs. Experienced Africa hands Ann and Carl Purcell recommend beanbags.)

Almost all wildlife pictures are taken from vehicles; get one with four wheel drive and a roof opening, if you are on assignment. The animals ignore Land Rovers and minibusses, seeming to think them part of the landscape. Take wide-angle as well as telephoto lenses (I use from 20 to 500mm lenses) to show animals both in close-up and in herds in their environment.

If you can avoid entering Kenya or Tanzania as a professional photographer, do so. There are quite stiff commercial photography fees to pay. I'm told too that you run the risk of the odd customs official seeking a "consideration" to pass your equipment. As many tourists carry several 35mm cameras and lots of film, posing as a tourist is not usually any problem. If in doubt query Kenyan and Tanzanian consulates before you leave. (See also Customs, Chapter Fifteen.)

Always ask permission to photograph people in Africa; some, like the Masai in Kenya, routinely expect payment. I don't totally blame them, and always tip well if the subject is cooperative. After all, I am making money off him or her. An alternative is to buy a craft object at the many places they are sold, and then, with the help of your guide, ask permission for photographs. I have two charming paintings bought in East Africa, and photographed the artists besides.

For safety, it is recommended today that you always travel in East Africa with a local guide, and that you stay relatively on the beaten path of established game lodges. Check travel advisories before making plans. Lawyer Frank Montgomery, a dedicated amateur photographer and a former student of mine, and his wife Lois took a private tent-safari by Land Rover in Kenya in April 1991; they had a fine time and no problems. They loved the Norfolk Hotel in Nairobi, where Teddy Roosevelt stayed. Their nice Kikuyu guide spoke perfect English and several local languages including Swahili. The Montgomerys visited Northern Kenya, where I have not been yet. Island Camp was their favorite spot. Their trip was organized by the Ker and Downey company of Nairobi.

Many people who go to game parks want to see as many different animals as possible. When they spot a certain species, they check it off on a list, take a snap or two and then quickly move on to add others to their "collection." (You can believe this or not, but I know it from experience!) So, the only group safaris I can wholeheartedly recommend to serious photographers are photography tours; inquire of travel agents and consult the guides to photography schools, tours and workshops mentioned in Chapter One.

Tips for Wildlife Photography

I don't take specialized equipment to Africa, and personally feel that normally good photographic skills plus patience and an awareness of light are what are needed to get good animal photographs. If in doubt about your skills, I highly recommend practising by spending time at a good zoo where the animals are uncaged behind moats, as the lions are in the African Plains area of the Bronx Zoo here in New York. (If it weren't for the different vegetation you could almost imagine yourself in the Serengeti!) The San Diego Zoo is especially fine and spacious, and the National Zoo in Washington, DC is good too. Bird sanctuaries and wildlife parks and refuges everywhere are also good places to practice. Use slow to medium speed film, and the highest possible camera shutter speeds. Don't forget to take wide-angle views that show the landscape as well as telephoto close-ups. You could also take a nature photography course. (Guides to photo workshops and photo tours are listed in Chapter One).

When on safari, patience is one necessity. The other is to get up before dawn (around 5 a.m.) and shoot till about 8 or 9 a.m. then rest at midday and photograph animals again from late afternoon through sunset (around 7 p.m.)—these are the animals' feeding times.

I work with 20mm, 28mm, 43-80mm, 80-200mm and 500mm lenses and use all of them. My pictures of lions and elephants especially have sold very well indeed as stock.

Zimbabwe

This country (formerly Rhodesia) has game parks, but the "must" is the famous and fabulous Victoria Falls, guaranteed to produce a rainbow in the late afternoon. Drive around the rim for best vantage points. Fly over the falls in a light plane, too. There are hotels nearby; and a model African village where masks and crafts are made for tourists, and evening dance performances are offered. The capital of Harare is where you change planes for the falls; there are some unusual rock formations just outside the city that are worth photographing.

Republic of South Africa

Now that apartheid is weakening, one can go to South Africa with a clearer conscience. There is no doubt that the country is very beautiful, and most hotels very good. Ask permission for people pictures everywhere. Johannesburg is a modern city of skyscrapers. Almost every weekend, just outside the city, you can photograph very athletic displays by gold miners who dance for tourism and competition, and to forget their hard lonely lives for a while. I personally hated the tourist-trap Zulu "villages" near Johannesburg where bare-breasted women are exhibited, but at Middelburg, about two hours northeast of Johannesburg, there is a living museum village of N'debele people. They wear dignified robes and headdresses and are famed for their artistry. The village is called Botshabelo. It has splendid decorated houses, with yellow, brown and blue geometric designs on a white ground, looking like early 20th-century avant-garde art. The women do the painting, and some can be persuaded to pose in their best striped wool blankets. Buy some of the intricate beadwork they make, which is very decorative. If you give out Polaroid prints the ladies are thrilled.

My father, who acted there in his youth, told me Cape Town was a beautifully situated city and he was right. (But he never took any pictures of it.) Cape Town faces the Indian Ocean at the southern tip of Africa, and was originally a coaling and repair depot for British Navy ships when they guarded the interests of the Empire around the world. There is a scenic cable car ride up to the famous flat-topped Table Mountain behind the city. (Table Mountain is quite often covered by a white "tablecloth"—a thin layer of clouds.) There are still many South Africans of British descent; many of whom live in and around Cape Town, and the surrounding, and very beautiful, Cape Province. This southernmost province is considered to be a hotbed of liberalism in South Africa. Its most famous resident is Archbishop Desmond Tutu.

I do not know where the famous South African novelist Nadine Gordimer lives, but of course she was recently awarded the Nobel Prize for Literature.

My favorite place to photograph in all of South Africa is the "wine route" near Paarl, north of Cape Town, where you can visit and photograph many wineries, and taste the excellent wines too. Some wineries are in two-hundred-year-old step-gabled Dutch Colonial (Boer) mansions painted bright colors. The area is full of gardens and vineyards and backed by distant blue mountain peaks. I also drove down to see the Cape of Good Hope, which has a small lighthouse and a shingle beach covered in enormous tendrils of seaweed as thick as my arm, but is otherwise a disappointment. Near Port Elizabeth, the so-called garden route is also very pleasant.

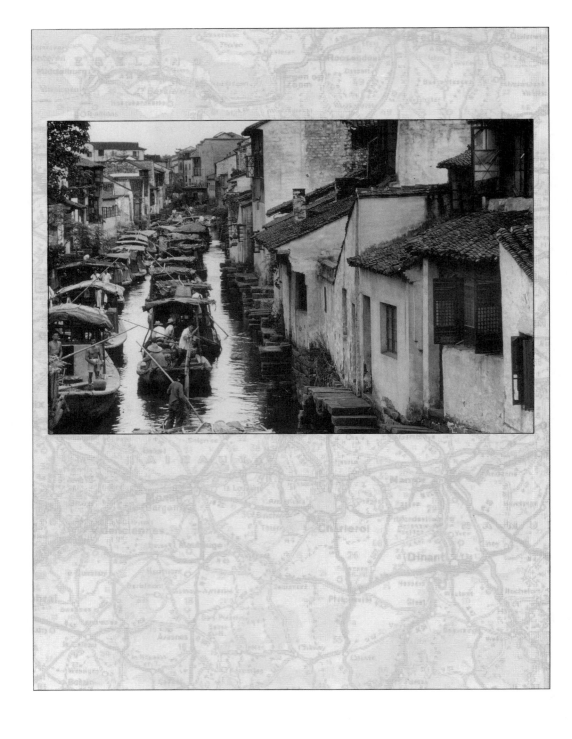

Chapter 19

Travel Highlights: Asia and the Pacific

Asia, the world's largest continent, is currently one of its most popular and photographed travel destinations. Asia is very varied, the people are friendly and the tourism facilities among the best in the world. Any photographic trip here is almost guaranteed to produce interesting images, but concentrate on people, industry, and aspects of culture if you want to make stock sales.

Japan

I am an out-and-out Japanophile. I have made four long visits there and mostly traveled alone. Not only do the Japanese make superb cameras, their country is superb to travel in. If you love cities, as I do, you will rejoice in being able to walk almost anywhere in Tokyo or Kyoto at 3 a.m. and risk nothing worse than a few giggles from tipsy teenagers. Japan has some of the best hotels I have ever stayed in, period, and Japan is often fun. I am lucky enough to have a great stock agent in Tokyo, Bob Kirschenbaum, founder of Pacific Press Service, who speaks, I am told, wonderful Japanese (he is a goldmine of helpful information to visiting photographers). I once spent an evening with him and noted American travel photographer Mike Yamashita, whose Japanese, he says, is serviceable. With these guys, I toured the small bars of Tokyo. In one, the Francophile host wore a beret and looked a lot like the late great movie actor Charles Boyer. With our (somewhat) mutual French, and my two translators, I sipped Suntorys, chatted till late into the night., and felt like a resident.

Tokyo

Stay in Shinjuku, a super-modern and fun entertainment district. It is extremely safe. (Don't miss the Yodobashi camera store. It's billed as the world's largest.

Now if only the yen would drop!) They have things in the immense store you can't get even in New York, like my favorite Minolta soft-leather shoulder bags.

Japan is a very, very formal country. People bow, shake hands all the time and constantly exchange business cards. (Get a bilingual one printed overnight at any good Japanese hotel.) The daily opening of the Keio department store in Shinjuku is a ritual almost as elaborate as Changing the Guard in London. To see it, be outside the Keio's main entrance at 9:30 a.m.

The Tokyo subway is modern, clean, fast, cheap, safe, goes everywhere, connects with mainline trains and has station signs in English. Be warned, the morning and evening rush hours are jam-packed.

Taxis are not too expensive (that is relatively speaking; everything in Japan is expensive for Americans and Canadians at present); taxi drivers wear white gloves. Sometimes in the evenings on the Ginza, taxis won't stop for mere tourists, they are off on mysterious errands having to do with regular patrons, like bar hostesses. Very near the main Ginza subway entrance is a second floor restaurant with huge windows; get a cup of coffee and a pastry and sit by the window at "blue time" for a superb view of the dazzling neon-lit street. (Take a tripod.)

The Akasusa Kannon temple has a great red gate with a huge red paper lantern hanging from it. It's one of the icons of Tokyo. The crowds of pious people burning sticks of incense around a bronze cauldron at the entrance are good to photograph. Surrounding the temple is a popular shopping area with hundreds of stalls selling everything from wind-up toys and kimonos to kitchenware and electronics. Tokyo's Ueno Park is another great "people photography" place and also has the national art museum. On no account miss the huge classic screens painted with gold and delicate flowers, or the photography section. The city's enormous Tsukiji fish market is great in the early morning; one of the chase scenes in the thriller "Black Rain" was filmed here.

The Imperial Palace is surrounded by a wall and a moat in tranquil, green Hibiya Park, you can get nice pictures of it from around the Nijubashi Bridge; there is a subway stop of the same name. I like photographing the bleachers in front of this spot (and in front of all important monuments in Japan) where hard-working local photographers record endless groups from the provinces; the tourists are often kids in bright caps or severe dark-blue high-school uniforms.

The Meiji shrine is the last "must" place in Tokyo, peaceful and beautiful with red-and-white robed priests, crowded with worshipers only on festival days.

The Rest of Japan

Outside Tokyo, take the train anywhere, and don't even think of driving unless you are in the capable hands of a Japanese or international corporation; rental cars and chauffeured cars cost a fortune, many roads are poor and with signs only in Japanese. Among tourist attractions about an hour from Tokyo by train is the great Buddha of Kamakura (groups of kids line up for pictures in front of it all day long) and the Fuji-Hakone National Park, where lake steamers are an agreeable way to see and photograph the region. Alas, the sacred Mount Fuji is often smogged in. If you stay a night or two at the ornate wooden Furama Hotel nearby you will have a better chance of seeing it than you will on a one-day trip.

When traveling alone in Japan (you should, it's fun and totally safe) have your destination and hotel name written down. If you get lost (and you will) nice people from all over will come and rescue you; some will insist on going far out of their way to get you where you want to go. The price is letting them practice their English, which is often fairly incomprehensible, but everyone enjoys the whole exchange.

Nikko is a huge shrine much beloved by the Japanese; it is always jam-packed, but the crowds are agreeable. You can "do" it in a day from Tokyo by train and bus. I took a favorite picture there, of white-clad pilgrims in a drizzle, carrying brilliant yellow umbrellas each with one large red spot. The Nikko temple complex is an absolute riot of carved, painted decoration that includes the three wise monkeys, dragons and other beasts. There are also forests of stone lanterns and a pretty, real forest around it.

Take the "shinkansen" or bullet train from Tokyo to Kyoto; it passes Mount Fuji, which as I said is not often visible because of smog. (Get a seat on the right, reservation required, and get to the station early for pictures of the trains themselves; they leave very frequently). Be prepared to leap on (or off) your bullet train, the doors stay open for about one minute.

The jewels of Kyoto are increasingly hidden among the buildings of the modern city, and include the Ryoan Zen garden, the Golden Pavilion and the Silver Pavilion, and the garden of the Heian Shrine which has a splendid scarlet torii gate. Japanese families, with women wearing kimonos, often go to this pretty place to celebrate birthdays, christenings and other festive days, and have their pictures taken. They don't mind if you photograph them too. My stock pictures of all this have been very good sellers.

As all the popular shrines in Kyoto (as elsewhere in Japan) are crowded, especially in spring and fall, you will have to be patient and wait for gaps in the streams of people when you want to evoke mood. I was once in Kyoto for the lantern festival, which is pretty at night; alas, the participants wore eyeglasses, wristwatches, and sneakers with their ornate costumes, which spoiled the mood of the daytime parades a bit for me.

I have never seen a geisha outdoors in the Gion district of Kyoto where they work, but have managed to grab a few quick shots of young apprentice geishas, called "maikos," hurrying somewhere. If you want a private appointment to photograph one or the other, it can be arranged by your hotel concierge, but at a very high price. Even to arrange a private tea ceremony in a Japanese home is very expensive. An easy way to get pictures of maikos and geishas, a tea ceremony, puppeteers, traditional actors and musicians, is to attend the Gion Corner show for tourists, which is good, and quite inexpensive.

I actually prefer Nara to Kyoto. Its tourist spots are a bit quieter. There is a huge 13th-to-18th century wooden Buddhist temple set in a park where fuzzy horned deer eat bread out of your hands, and a Shinto temple too. Near Nara and Kyoto is Japan's second city, and major port, Osaka, where I once set sail for a cruise down the coast of China. Osaka Castle is impressive but is a copy of the antique original. You might want to visit the Tennoji botanic garden.

I have not been to Hiroshima or southern Japan or to the northern island of

Hokkaido and hope to do both one day. They have both been highly recommended to me, for different reasons of course.

Korea

If you watched the Seoul Olympics on television you know that Korea doesn't look like the reruns of TV's "M.A.S.H." anymore. It has one of the fastest growing economies in the world, and Pusan, where I spent two days on my way to China, is a great place to buy sneakers and much other merchandise. There are some lovely old sites remaining nearby. The Sokkuram is an ancient man-made grotto which contains a famous three-times life-size marble Buddha sitting in a quiet cave in a hillside near Kyjongju. Pulguk-sa is a collection of small temple halls painted brilliant colors. The very extensive temple complex at T'ongdo-sa has many gray-clad Buddhist monks, fierce-carved temple guardians and brilliantly painted and decorated ceilings.

The government built a resort at Bomun; it is popular with locals as well as foreigners. I took some pictures of a bride and groom there as they posed for official wedding pictures on an ornamental stone bridge. She was in a traditional long pink dress, he in a dignified gray robe. In Korea I liked best the lively markets and the very friendly and outgoing Korean teenagers, many of whom speak quite good English. Despite my fears, I thought that the national dish of kimchi (aged, fiery cabbage) was delicious.

Taiwan, Republic of China

Another of those super-growth Pacific economies, with horrendous traffic in the capital, Taipei (a subway is under construction), and much modern building everywhere. But there is the great National Palace Museum with exquisite art—don't miss it. (Photography without flash is permitted; take an FLD or 30M filter for the fluorescent lighting.) The Grand Hotel gets my vote for the most spectacular design of any hotel I've ever seen (it's a huge, red-pillared palace decorated with painted dragons and with a curved gold-tiled roof set in very nice large grounds). Taipei also has the huge Lung Shan Temple and other, very colorful temples which are all fine for people watching and respectful photography.

I was taken by a Taipei tourism official to the Fu-Shing Dramatic Arts Academy. There, students from the age of ten spend eight years learning the characters and elaborate make-up required for the traditional Chinese Opera. The seniors are very accomplished. It is a splendid place to take photographs. I am told you can have your Taipei hotel call 790-9127 or 793-4028 to arrange a visit. The same tourist official also took me to an enormous place curiously named the Hoover Theater Restaurant, which has a rather good, well-lit revue with pretty girls, singers, acrobats and dancers. Taking pictures of the acts with a telephoto lens was no problem; the audience was fun too. (Some of the other entertainment places in Taipei are definitely not for Aunt Minnie.) Finally, the movie posters and advertising signs in Taipei are spectacular and

Taiwanese food is absolutely superb; there are many fine restaurants.

A very popular tourist excursion from Taipei is the day flight to the marble Taroko gorge; to me the misty gray-and-green place is nice but no Grand Canyon; there are a couple of very pretty pagoda-shaped temples in the vicinity and a village where costumed aboriginal people perform dances for tourists.

There is a bamboo forest near Sun Moon Lake, a favorite resort for Taipei's citizens. The Wen Wu Temple there is a photographic must. This is usually a two-day excursion from Taipei. If you drive (or much better, are driven, local drivers are ferocious) in the countryside of Taiwan you will still see peasants in conical hats tending rice fields, little boys leading water buffaloes, fishing boats on lakes and quiet traditional villages.

Hong Kong

One of the world's great travel destinations, pulsing with life. The fabulous harbor is surrounded by mountains and packed with skyscrapers; and you can often see ancient junks under full sail among modern shipping of all nations. Great views for photographers are inexpensively reached via the funicular tram to Victoria Peak, the sturdy Star Ferries that crisscross the harbor, and the top decks of the brightly painted but ancient British tramcars of Hong Kong Island. Double-deck busses ply Nathan Road, which is festooned with huge neon signs; it is the busiest and widest shopping street in the tourist and hotel area of Kowloon. There are observation lounges with great views in most good high-rise hotels. Street markets are good places to photograph people. The so-called Poor Man's Night Club, a night market near the pier where ferries leave for China, is especially lively.

On the other side of Hong Kong Island from the central business district is Aberdeen, with fantastically painted and neon-decorated floating barge restaurants (which serve surprisingly indifferent food). The Typhoon Shelter at Aberdeen is where you can see thousands of people who live permanently on their junks. Hire a small boat to photograph them up close if you wish.

I was lucky enough to be in Hong Kong once for the Fishermans' Festival in June, when junks decorated with huge multicolored silk banners parade along the harbor; there are also dragon dances, fireworks and street decorations in the densely packed residential sections near the water in western Hong Kong Island. (The Dragon Boat festival is in September.) Wander on your own in this area to find pictures, you won't have far to walk. If you can take a Chinese-speaking friend, acquaintance or guide, you will do better with street photography of people than if you go alone. Unlike mainland Chinese, or the Taiwanese or Koreans, Hong Kong residents who do not work in big business or banking or the tourist industry are not particularly friendly to Westerners. Not unfriendly, but they tend to turn away.

Visit, if you wish, the big camera shops at the beginning of Nathan Road in Kowloon. There is a good one on the ground floor outside the Hyatt Hotel. (Be sure and check New York prices first though!) A real problem for photographers in Hong Kong is the summer weather. It's warm and humid, often misty or rainy, and sometimes the place is truly fogged in. Avoid July and August if you possibly can. Fall is clear and I think it's the best time to go.

I do not believe for a minute that wonderful Hong Kong is going to turn drab and totally Communist when the British leave in mid-1997.

China

Despite political considerations, China is absolutely one of the world's greatest travel photography destinations. The regime's achievements are impressive if you don't like traveling among desperately poor people, which I do not. Children are healthy (with a lower infant mortality rate than our own!), streets swept clean, and the ordinary people friendly (though I am told now much more reserved than they were before the terrible events of Tienanmen Square). There are plenty of comfortable enough hotels in China today, and the landscape, cultural monuments, art and people are such that I am told by a travel agent friend that China will soon be a "hot" travel destination again.

I have been to China twice, the first time in 1977 (thinly disguised as a housewife) on a tour from Hong Kong along with a great many other American and European journalists and photographers calling themselves executives, teachers, planners and other innocuous occupations. This was just before the United States and China resumed diplomatic relations. We went to Guangzhou (formerly Canton) and surrounding farms, factories and villages. Guangzhou was then just what I expected, men and women all in uniform blue, seeming millions of bicycles, and there were red banners with slogans, red flags and pictures of Chairman Mao everywhere. Because it is so near Hong Kong, I am told that Guangzhou is now the most prosperous and "fashionable" city in mainland China.

In 1983 I cruised down the China coast on a luxury liner. We called at Dalien (formerly Port Arthur), Quingdao, and Tianjin (formerly Tientsin) where we took a train for Beijing. There I was lucky enough to have a private car and a very charming, courteous guide, Mr. Liu, who spoke perfect English. (He was sent to help me because I had helped entertain the first group of Chinese photographers to visit New York.) Of course, he showed me first the Imperial City (use wide, wide-angle lenses to show the whole scene). We went to the Forbidden City, the Summer Palace, the Marble Boat, and the nearby Sun Moon Lake and the Temple of Heaven. (If you want a very good preview of all this, rent the video of Bertolucci's "The Last Emperor," large parts of which were actually filmed in the Imperial City.) We also walked around the small streets of Beijing. At that particular moment the watermelon harvest was at its peak; there were mounds of melons on almost every corner, and melon-eaters everywhere, even on bicycles. Next day we drove via the Ming Tombs, guarded by fierce, oversized stone warriors, to the Great Wall, passing misty and very Chinese-looking mountains en route.

The Chinese are enthusiastic tourists in their own country, but rather than sit on benches for group portraits as the Japanese do, they rent Seagull cameras (similar to Rolleiflexes) at the site, buy a roll of black-and-white film and take their own pictures. Entrepreneurs develop negatives in little booths on the spot. There were plenty of these guys at the Great Wall; presumably the prints are made by other entrepreneurs when the tourists arrive home.

The Great Wall is jammed with visitors (mostly Chinese) on the side to the right of the main entrance, where you walk up a steep section of the wall to a fortress. To the left of the entrance though, if you climb a more gentle few hundred yards, you will have the wall almost to yourself. It snakes for miles over sharp green mountains before disappearing from view. Once in a while a solitary walker, or a couple of solders in white peaked caps, or a few giggling girls in flowered cotton dresses, may go by.

If you saw Steven Spielberg's "The Empire of the Sun," you will recognize Shanghai; the waterfront, it seems, has hardly changed since the 1940's setting of the film. Shanghai's streets are jammed but not depressing, I did not see any beggars. People sit on string chairs and play cards or chat; there are outdoor shoemenders and barbers and vendors of just about everything. As always, the seemingly plentiful food markets and busy movie theaters, which have huge hand-painted posters, are good places to photograph people. So is the waterfront park near the Bund, where in the early morning large groups of fitness enthusiasts perform Tai Ching exercises.

You are normally not alone in China for a second. Apart from political considerations, I just don't think that in crowded China they understand the concept. But in Dalien, I managed to slip away from my fellow cruise members. Dalien is a naval port, a seaside resort for Shanghai dwellers and an interesting place. I walked on the beach and photographed a football team with a red banner, sailors in caps with pompoms, and very well-muscled young Chinese men in briefs doing acrobatics. My guide reproached me when I found him, and said he could get into bad trouble if I did that again. (I apologized by buying him a book later.) In Dalien we were taken to a factory that makes shell pictures; I think their main market must be all the Chinese restaurants of the world. In another rather nice seaside city, Quingdao, more vacationers from Shanghai gathered small edible shellfish into pails; these looked a lot like the winkles beloved by the working-class English at the seaside, which are eaten with a pin. As Quingdao also has a long pier with a pagoda on top, the place felt to me quite a lot like Brighton, England. Quingdao was briefly a German concession port, the Germans left behind the art of brewing delicious beer.

My favorite place in all China is Souzhou. A part of the thousand-year-old Grand Canal runs through the city which some travelers have called the "Venice of China." There are ancient gray houses with brown-tiled roofs lining the narrow canals; a steady stream of straw-roofed barges are pushed along the canals by boatmen with bamboo poles, it all looks like a Chinese painting. Outside Souzhou, the barges sail in narrow channels through lush green rice fields.

In Souzhou is one of the single most wonderful places I have ever seen, the mansion and lovely water-garden of the Humble Administrator. This 17th-century court official was sent from Beijing to root out corruption in the provinces. He was so thorough in exposing tax evaders that the bribes that had to be paid him to look the other way were much higher than the bribes had ever been before. The stunning mansion is the result. It has a dark-brown tiled roof with upswept corners meant to ward off evil spirits; they are supported on great pillars of polished dark-brown wood as smooth as silk. Inside, many of the rooms are sparsely dotted with elegant, simple furniture. Many others are just roofed terraces that look out onto streams, bridges and artfully-placed rocks set among ponds filled with water lilies and huge lotus plants. Patience is needed to get pictures without too many visitors (the place is quite quiet at lunch time). Get a preview by visiting the Chinese court in the Metropolitan Museum of Art in New York.

My photographer friend Michal Heron has been to Inner Mongolia and the famous mountain and lake region of Kweilin. My ex-husband (a former photographer) has been to Xian, where the life-size antique warriors are on display, and to Tibet. These places are highly recommended by them for scenery and atmosphere if not always comfort.

Singapore

A very successful, now ultramodern, city-state governed and peopled mostly by Singaporeans of Chinese extraction. There are many Malay, some Indian, and a few European Singaporeans too. Another famous harbor (take a boat tour for views of the massed shipping and downtown skyscrapers). This city's surroundings are flat; though there is a cable car that gives good views from the top of a hill called Mount Faber to a nearby small island.

There are more great hotels, and much great shopping in Singapore. Most workers live in huge, clean, high-rise apartment blocks. Kids still wear British-type school uniforms. One of my two favorite places in Singapore is the Tiger Balm Gardens, a piece of world-class kitsch: a riotous jungle of life-sized and over-life-sized concrete figures of men and beasts illustrating Chinese folklore, and painted in brilliant colors. (There is a smaller version in Hong Kong too.) My other favorite place is the bar of the original, two-story colonial Raffles Hotel dating from British days, and celebrated in the short stories of Somerset Maugham. This bar is just about the only remnant though, of the old, romantic Singapore of tiny Chinese shops and river boats, some of which still existed on my first visit in the 1960's. (Most current residents don't miss the old city at all I'm sure.) Sit in the Raffles' courtyard-garden under fan-shaped palm trees, and sip the Singapore gin slings served there. They are powerful, photogenic (pink with small white paper umbrellas) and will restore you after a hard day of checking camera prices!

Stalls selling Chinese fast food cooked over steaming woks near the riverfront are good to photograph, the food is good too. There is a well-done tourist show where you can photograph pretty Chinese and Malay ladies in costume, and a day excursion to a Malaysian mainland fishing village where naked boys dive from boats for coins.

Malaysia

I have only been there only once and only briefly. The mostly modern city of Kuala Lumpur has some nice mosques, good hotels, and a splendid railway station with minarets. I took a trip from the city to photograph a nearby rubber plantation, which was totally new and interesting to me.

Absolutely every guide book I have read highly recommends the interior of Malaysia, and it's a "hot" destination for the with-it young, especially from England, Germany, Sweden and Australia, so I'm mentioning it here even though I don't personally know it. A former student of mine (a scuba diver) went to the island of Tiamin in 1990 and says it was uncrowded, inexpensive and unspoiled, though accommodations are not luxurious. Diving equipment and even underwater cameras can be rented locally. My photographer friends the Fishers stayed in Penang in the sixties, and want to return. Penang is famous to the British, and I'm told it's still a relatively undiscovered place with hospitable people and gorgeous beaches. The Fishers also recommend the Cameron Highlands, and say they are cool and reminiscent of England. Sabah and Sarawak on Borneo are still considered pretty exotic, but are increasingly being visited by travelers who want to find "unspoiled" Asia. I would very much like to get to know Malaysia one day. I guess all these places are underphotographed. Malaysia is a Moslem country. (See notes on this under Pakistan, later in this chapter.) Caution: I am told that journalists in Malaysia are more restricted today than they were as recently as five years ago.

Thailand

The city of Bangkok is a mixture of the awful and the wonderful. Among the former are terrible traffic and crowding, a humid climate and pollution in summer, bad smells in several places, and a lot of ugly buildings. Among the latter are very good hotels, including the Oriental (which often makes "world's best" lists in travel magazines), immense and gorgeous temples, lovely friendly people, great food, and lots of shopping bargains. Do not let the first put you off the second. Best temples are Wat Phra Keo (the Temple of the Emerald Buddha) which is elaborately decorated with gold-leaf covered stupas, and gray-and-white stone Wat Po, where a huge reclining Buddha lies decorated with flowers. You could spend days in either temple and not take all the possible pictures. There are usually groups of smiling and unselfconscious purple or saffron-robed monks walking around under orange umbrellas in both places. It's fun to walk around Bangkok's side streets and see all the little shops; machinery repair shops of all kinds are especially busy in the city, often spilling onto the sidewalk—sometimes I've seen whole cars in the process of being dissected.

There is a pleasant evening river cruise, and a special outdoor show for photographers sponsored by Agfa where you can shoot pretty Thai dancers in towering gold headdresses and fierce young kick-boxers having a real go at each other.

Bangkok's once-famous canals have mostly been filled in; to see a floating market you must now go about 40 miles outside the city. Damnern Saduak still has a good floating market. Hire a private guide with a boat, and glide along klongs where pretty ladies wearing blue pajamas and wide raffia sunhats sell vegetables and fruits arranged with artistry on narrow pointed boats that look a bit like gondolas. My stock pictures from this place have sold very well.

My photographer friends the Fishers, who lived in Thailand for two years, recommend a day trip from Bangkok to the Bridge on the River Kwai and say that Chiang Mai, Thailand's other great tourist attraction, is much cooler than Bankok. It's a great handicraft center, and a fine jumping off point for excursions to remote mountain villages. Elliot Hester, a student of mine, recommends Phuket Island, which has beautiful beaches. Check current travel advisories though, before you go to Thailand.

The Philippines

I certainly recommend the Philippines visually. Manila has broad boulevards, good hotels, colorfully painted "jeepneys" to get around in, and very pleasant people, but street crime is a big problem, even in politically stable times. When conditions improve, by all means visit. The ancient Spanish-built Fort Santiago has great thick walls you can walk around; nearby is Manila Cathedral. Once, I was in Manila on Palm Sunday and photographed thousands of devout celebrants wearing their best clothes and carrying palm fronds and crosses in the vicinity of the Cathedral. It was a lovely sight. There are very beautiful handicraft shops in Manila, and a good craft village near the airport.

Popular day excursions from Manila are a drive to Taal Lake and a ferry trip to see fortified Corregidor Island. I liked best the rides themselves, once outside the city; passing low-lying fields, abundant roadside fruit stands, small farms and villages. A short flight from Manila goes to Bagiuo, a resort with pleasant gardens that is an escape from city heat. The surrounding scenery is of piney mountains. There are lots of other beautiful places to photograph in the Philippines, but by all means check current political conditions before planning your trip.

Indonesia

Indonesia is a lovely country, and currently "in" with travelers who want to enjoy unspoiled Southeast Asia. But the charm of Indonesia is most definitely not in its capital, Jakarta, where in 1969, I stayed three sweaty, mosquito-bitten nights in the worst hotel I've ever been stuck in in my life. (The electricity was out, so therefore was the ceiling fan; the shower barely worked; the mildewed, broken-tiled toilet had no seat and dripped continually; and the desk clerk offered to come and take my mind off my troubles.) The city was packed for an international conference, so I was bumped out of my comfortable room at the Hilton by a high-rank military delegation. Jakarta now has more hotels, and I am sure they don't do things like that to visitors, but the experience soured me on the city, which I'm told is still hot, crowded and, in places, smelly.

Java

Jakarta is on the island of Java, which, like most of Indonesia, is Moslem (see later in this chapter for tips on photographing in Moslem countries).

The interior of Java has a great tourist attraction, the splendid temples of Borobudur, which are still not on everyone's Indonesian itinerary.

A former student of mine, and an enthusiastic underwater photographer, Walter Koch, took a big ferry from Djakarta to Kelymutu Island, and another ferry to Lompok. There are tourists in all these places, but not too many. There are also dive shops. Walter also recommends Flores, another Indonesian island, which has a volcano with three lakes on top, each a different color. I've seen his shots of the black, blue and aquamarine craters and they are beautiful. Walter says if you follow the Lonely Planet guidebook to Southeast Asia (see Chapter Twenty), you can't go wrong in the region; the book is very accurate.

Bali

The charms of tiny, Hindu Bali are legendary. I have been there twice, stayed on the wide Sanur beach, and spent a total of three weeks being driven around every nook and cranny of this beautiful island. I went back eight years after my first visit, when Bali was more crowded but still very peaceful almost everywhere. I am told that the southern coastal strip has recently become rather developed, and that Kuta Beach in particular is for what is sometimes called "the Four-S set" (sun, sea, sand and sex). It has bars and discos and is popular especially with young people from the Antipodes, and divers like a former student who dived nearby to photograph a wreck of an American ship sunk by Japanese gunfire in World War II. (For more on underwater photography see the section on the U.S. Virgin Islands, in Chapter Seventeen.)

Bali is still lovely and unspoiled in the interior, although some roads are crowded, and some locals now ask for tips if you want to take their picture. You can hire a car with a driver for not too much money, circling the island in one day if you must; or you can drive yourself, though I wouldn't care to. There are Hindu temple festivals to see somewhere almost everyday, women carry towering gold-paper-decorated flower-and-fruit offerings on their heads. Most villages stage different traditional dances regularly for festivals; these are not tourist offerings, although tourists are welcome. The Legong, Barong and Kechak dances are highly stylized, very different from each other, and should all be seen. At Batubalan, dance performances for tourists are given daily; these are very well done and highly photogenic. Dances are also staged at the big Sanur Beach hotels. I have stayed twice at the oldest, the Bali Beach. It is an ugly concrete tower, but is very nice inside. The terraced front rooms look out over broad sands; the sea is dotted with outrigger canoes.

Quieter, and more authentic, are the central villages of Celuk, Mas and Ubud; these are arts and crafts centers, and have some very pleasant, quiet hotels.

If you ask your guide, he will take you to see good artists and craftsmen at work. In Bali, often several people at one time work on the same painting, which makes for amusing photographs.

My favorite big Balinese temples are at Tanah Lot, Goa Lawah and Purah Besakih, but there are plenty of tiny ones too, whose names are known only very locally. If you get a chance to see a Hindu funeral, take it, and your camera. If you are respectful, photography is no problem. The funerals are beautiful and not at all sad. Once you have done the highlights in Bali, as usual the best thing of all to do is just to drive until you see a scene that you like, and then get out and walk around to photograph. Young Balinese women no longer go bare-breasted outdoors—too many photographers perhaps?

Bali is verdant, with no real seasons. Within a few miles of each other on the same day I have photographed steep rice terraces in first growth; a man with a brace of pink oxen plowing wet paddy fields; people in plaited sun hats planting rice; and others tending young shoots. A few miles farther on, the population of a whole village was communally threshing rice. When you get out of the touristy beach areas, you may find a tiny village market, a funeral procession, a priest and followers walking through rice fields under fringed white umbrellas, or a man driving geese or oxen. A lovely thing to do in Bali is to hire your own outrigger canoe at just about any beach and glide out (with 20mm lens on one of your cameras) to photograph your boatman, the shore and mountains—and just to feel Balinese for a while. Don't rush through Bali, give it time to reveal itself.

I should add here, after all this enthusiasm, that many photographers have been to Bali before you—my stock sales of this island have not been great although I have lovely pictures—because Bali is definitely overphotographed.

Cambodia

Things change, and maybe ordinary travelers will be able, or wish, to visit this beautiful, tragic land again in the not-too-distant future. My 1969 visit was a high point of my travels; the city of Phnom Penh charming, filled with monks wearing bright orange, each carrying an orange or lemon-colored umbrella (and I'm still selling stock pictures from that visit). Pnomh Penh also had lovely handicraft shops; beaten silver table decorative items were a local specialty. The real reason for a travel photographer to go to Cambodia though, is to see the temples of Angkor Wat and nearby Angkor Thom, truly among the great works of man.

I know that the monks may well now be murdered, and the temples are partly overgrown by jungle again, but, I still say if you get a chance to visit Cambodia and see Angkor Wat, go.

India

India is a wonderful country, the world's most populous democracy, but it is definitely not for the timid. Despite its terrible political and religious and population problems, and despite the fact that to travel in India means you cannot ignore poverty, beggars and sometimes despair, it is a great place for photographers, and the Indian people are almost all friendly to Westerners. Among the great things I have photographed are the Jain Temple in teeming Calcutta, the bazaar in Srinagar, floating flower sellers and houseboats on nearby Dal Lake, and the mighty Himalayas near Gulmarg. These last three are all in Kashmir, which, sadly, currently is closed to foreigners because of an undeclared war between the Moslem majority seeking independence and the Indian government. One can only hope this beautiful place will soon be peaceful again.

Beggars

As hard as it seems, do not give money to beggars or even candy to children in Calcutta, or anywhere in India; many people are professional beggars, and even if they are not, you will almost instantly be inundated with hundreds of people pressing close, a very uncomfortable feeling indeed. When you travel in India, you must accept that you cannot solve its problems.

Moghul masterpieces I have photographed in India include the world-famous inlaid marble Taj Mahal in Agra (it's every bit as beautiful as it is supposed to be; go early or late for good light and to avoid crowds); the great outdoor observatory and pink palaces of the city of Jaipur in Rajasthan; and the Red Fort in India's capital, New Delhi, which also has a fine modern government area.

The most sacred place in India, and my favorite place there for photography, is the city of Varanasi (formerly called Benares). To photograph the thousands of Hindu pilgrims who daily immerse themselves from the ghats (stone steps) along the river Ganges, hire a private boat with guide and glide past the many riverside temples. Each day, starting at first light, thousands of colorfully, fully-clothed people climb down the steps leading to the wide Ganges, immersing themselves in the holy river, and washing vigorously with soap. Dawn light is from behind you, and flat onto the crowds, making for great zoom-telephoto lens shots. From time to time, ornate funeral barges full of mourners scattering the ashes of someone cremated, and throwing wreaths of lotus flowers, float past in the middle of the river. Tiny lanterns are floated too. On the eastern bank of the river, vultures wait. Occasionally, corpses are not incinerated for specific religious reasons; for instance, members of the Parsee sect are left exposed in Towers of Silence. I did not see this, but I did see the tiny arm of a baby in the river. In the city, which is not very large, there are hundreds of temples and many houses decorated with paintings of gods and traditional designs. Because of the huge pilgrim trade, there are busy sidewalk markets where cheap holy pictures, brassware, painted toys, silk and cotton fabrics and brilliantly colored piles of powdered make-up and spices are sold.

In the afternoon, hire a car and drive a few miles in any direction outside Varanasi to find farm country that looks positively biblical, with white oxen pulling unpainted wooden carts and turning water-wheels, men in long white tunics and girls in white saris, and occasional small villages made of pale mud-bricks. Everywhere, and always, there are people stooping in the fields.

Additional suggestions from my amateur photographer friend Pat Collyns who recently spent three weeks touring and photographing in Rajasthan: She says do not miss the Ranthambhore Tiger Reserve. She also loved the costumes worn throughout the whole region; and says that the Lake Palace Hotel in Udaipur is one of the most fabulous places she has ever been, with the highest Indian standards of beauty and design and the highest Western standards of comfort.

I strongly suggest you deal with a good travel agent or tour company and have confirmed reservations before you go to India, unless you are very young, strong, patient and adventurous. Comments on getting and changing reservations and coping with officialdom in the Pakistan section (see later in this chapter), apply to a very considerable extent in India also. (See Raghubir Singh's book, *Rajasthan, India's Enchanted Land,* for a preview of this most beautiful part of India.)

Nepal

The fabled Hindu kingdom is a place I am going to visit in the not too distant future, God willing. I hope to catch a fleeting glimpse of the world's highest mountain, Everest, and to photograph wildlife. From my amateur photographer friend Pat Collyns, I know that Kathmandu has superb temples. She recommends Pokhara, as a starting-point for a Himalayan trekking expedition (these can be arranged on the spot) and liked the Fish Tail lodge (hotel) there— it is on a lake. She also enjoyed the Tiger Tops lodge in the Royal Chitwan National Park, where she photographed from the back of an elephant. Advance airline and Western-style hotel reservations for Nepal are a must for all but the most intrepid. Treks are arranged on the spot for individual travelers.

Pakistan

The North West Frontier Province of Pakistan is the most exotic, romantic and remote place I have ever been, with endless photographic opportunities. The bazaar in the provincial capital of Peshawar is packed with thousands of jewelry and carpet sellers, arms dealers, sidewalk dentists (their shops are decorated with ferocious pictures of false teeth!), sweet and tea shops, spice dealers, portrait photographer's studios, and much more. The men are often turbaned, robed and bearded, the few women you see are all partly or completely veiled. Brilliantly painted trucks, motorized rickshaw taxis, busses, horse carts and bikes thread their way through narrow streets. People are friendly, I was never refused permission for a photograph in the two and a half days I spent in the bazaar.

Photographing in Moslem countries

Both men and women should dress very conservatively at all times, and show as little skin as possible. Long pants are a must for both sexes. Women photographers should wear tops with high necklines and cover their arms at least to the elbow. Wearing a loose coat (I have a long baggy Gap jacket), or tunic to the knee over pants, will make women less conspicuous and better able to photograph in crowded markets, bazaars, etc.

To photograph inside mosques, first inquire if this is allowed. It is in Pakistan. (In more conservative Moslem countries this may not be permitted.) Certain areas of mosques are restricted to women, so I had to watch where I put my tripod. Everyone must remove shoes at the entrance to any mosque. Women must cover the head, shoulders and arms.

Always ask for permission before taking pictures of men. In Pakistan, they are often extremely handsome and (in my experience) quite willing to pose. Men should never try to photograph women, veiled or unveiled, in the street, because this may cause local men to become angry. Women can photograph some women, with permission, if they first have established some personal contact with them. Ask parents' permission before photographing children. In certain remote corners of Pakistan's North West Frontier Province, such as the beautiful Hunza valley, the women do not cover even part of their faces, are not quite so shy, and may be photographed, with their permission.

As I have mentioned elsewhere, to me a camera is sort of like a mask at a masked ball. It protects me and gives me anonymity. I am therefore not uncomfortable photographing alone in, say, the bazaars of Peshawar. However, a well-traveled woman writer I know says she prefers not to go to such places unaccompanied, even when very conservatively dressed, because she feels she doesn't belong.

The outing to the fabled Khyber Pass from Peshawar to the Afghanistan border is a great photographic journey. You leave Pakistan proper and pass into Pathan tribal areas, where robed, turbaned men routinely wear bandoliers of enormous bullets and carry either beautiful old rifles or high-powered automatic weapons, which is a bit unnerving. The start of the pass is marked by an arch shaped like a fortress, soon after come several forts and military barracks left by the British (in the 1890's) who were able to occupy this remotest corner of the Empire for only four years. The border is now guarded by the Pathan tribesmen, and also by the crack Pakistani Khyber Rifles regiment, which surprisingly retains many British traditions. They even have a bagpipe band which plays on special occasions! I was lucky enough to visit their mess, which is decorated with portraits of noted guests, including Presidents Bush and Carter and their wives, General Douglas MacArthur, and Queen Elizabeth and Prince Phillip.

It would be marvelous if Pakistan had more responsive tourist representation in North America. In lieu of this, take multiple copies of a letter of assignment and apply immediately on arrival to see all this, because permission to visit the Tribal Areas and Khyber Pass must be obtained from the Pakistan Tourist Development Corporation. This body has a branch in Dean's, a government-run hotel in Peshawar. Allow at least two days for permission to materialize. (I stayed in Dean's, which is shabby but clean and adequate, with pleasant service.) My advice is to take a Peshawar taxi to the Khyber pass, choosing a driver who speaks some English (many do). This will cost about $60.

From Peshawar, fly or take a hired car to Pakistan's capital, Islamabad, which has a fine modern mosque, and stay overnight (the Shalimar hotel in the twin city of Rawalpindi is convenient for the airport and will store luggage) for the early morning flight to Gilgit, the biggest town in the mountainous far north of Pakistan. The flight only operates in clear weather and is breathtaking; you fly eyeball to eyeball among great peaks (there are said to be 87 that are over 23,000 feet high) that are perennially snow covered; the highest one I glimpsed was Nanga Parbat (26,660 feet); on some days they say K-2, at 28,251 feet the second highest mountain in the world, is visible.

In Gilgit, stay at the Serena Lodge, which has comfortable rooms with terraces overlooking the Hindu Kush range, and a nice restaurant with views of 25,550 foot-high Mount Rakaposhi. In Gilgit, you can hang out in the small, colorful bazaar, take day trips by jeep, or arrange to go on a trekking expedition. Northern Pakistan, which is one of the great trekking areas of the world, has several private companies that arrange overland excursions.

I used the services of Walji's Adventure Pakistan, a private tour operator with a representative in Stamford, Connecticut. The cost of a new bright blue jeep, a driver and an excellent guide, Amjad Ayub (who turned out to have assisted *National Geographic* photographer Jonathan Blair when he was in the region for three months), was about $65 for a six hour trip. Amjad (whose English was fluent and idiomatic) recommended a drive as far as his village of Karimambad for a day-long look at the area. We drove along the new Karakoram Highway which joins Pakistan with China. The highway clings to the mountains and looks down onto the scenic and fertile Hunza Valley. Early in November, 1991, when I was there, poplar and fruit trees were gold and bronze; just past their best; mid October is peak time for fall foliage. April is the time for spring-green fields and white and pink fruit blossoms.

Longer tours by jeep, along the Karakoram highway into Western China as far as Kashgar, can be made by prior arrangement; but remember a visa for western China takes about six weeks so come prepared. Starting from Gilgit, these tours cost from about $100 per person per day. The Karakoram Highway, a world-class design and construction feat by Pakistani and Chinese engineers and laborers, follows the fabled "silk route" first taken by Marco Polo. Open to tourists only since 1986, it is increasingly popular with European and Japanese touring companies; and a few U.S. operators are also offering travel along this route.

Skardu is another northern town where treks and also serious mountaineering expeditions originate. As always, they should be arranged in advance. You can fly to Skardu from Islamabad, or go by jeep from Gilgit. I was not able to get there, but met a tour operator who offers a program for trekkers to sleep in luxurious Mongolian-type yurts (tents), which sounds interesting. Don't ask me about photographing on mountaineering expeditions—I am afraid of heights. Read Galen Rowell's *Mountain Light* for expert advice.

While you are in this corner of Pakistan, fly at dawn from Peshawar to Lahore, a pleasant city with some of the greatest Mogul architecture of the subcontinent. Primary viewing is the enormous red stone Badashi Mosque. It has three onion domes and four great minarets, was built by the Emperor Aurangzheb in 1674, and is one of the most splendid buildings I have ever seen, almost as beautiful as the Taj Mahal. Right opposite is the Lahore Fort, and nearby the marble Wazir Khan mosque, which alas I did not have time to see. I had a plane to catch (see later in this chapter). I know that Lahore is worth a stay of several days and plan to return someday, preferably in early March, when the National Agricultural Show, a week of animal exhibits, polo matches and displays of horsemanship and military pageantry takes place.

Sociologically, Pakistan is not as depressing as India; I saw few beggars in Lahore, none in Peshawar. The traffic is very heavy on major roads between big cities, rush hour in downtown Lahore has to be experienced to be believed.

I have not been to southern Pakistan. Dr. Kamran (Kim) Shaukat, a serious amateur travel photographer (and former student of mine), who grew up in Lahore, recommends the historic Indus valley province of Sind, south of Karachi, for its very colorful costumes. He also says not to miss Moenjodaro, the ruins of a 4,000 year-old Indus Valley civilization city—a must for archeology buffs.

I am enthusiastic about Pakistan; it is one of the most interesting places I have ever been, is definitely underphotographed, and seems to me to provide a different view on the Moslem world. English is widely spoken, there are English language signs almost everywhere, and some newspapers in English too. There are hotels in the deluxe, first-class and moderate price ranges, and the food is great if you like mild-to-hot curries, shish kebabs, interesting variations on rice, and yoghurt and dried fruits and nuts. Most Pakistanis I met were very pleasant, they like to talk and to know what Westerners think about their country. I would have enjoyed meeting some professional women, who exist in quite large numbers especially in Karachi, a huge, sophisticated and crowded city, apparently sort of the New York of Pakistan. (Go there in winter, summers are very hot.)

Pakistan International Airlines (PIA) is the only source of tourism information on the country, with offices in the USA and Canada. Do not count on them for the precise information you get from, say, the British Tourist Authority. PIA does a good job in the air. They give you a free hotel room between their many flights connecting small Pakistani cities with international gateways such as Islamabad, Lahore and Karachi, a reason to fly PIA the whole way. However, their ground service leaves something to be desired.

In my file-drawer of places to go, Pakistan is a top off-the-beaten-track destination for seasoned travelers, not casual visitors. Visually and culturally it is well worth the effort. If you can, go.

A Cautionary Note About Third World Travel

You will need a sense of humor and adventure when traveling. Do not expect Western standards of efficiency in Pakistan, a poor country. Communications are bad. While the private sector works reasonably well, dealing with public officialdom on all levels can be boring, time-consuming and frustrating. The large bureaucracy is slow and rigid at best; incompetent and infuriating at worst. I recommend making all your major travel arrangements before you arrive in the country, and sticking to them. Airports in particular can be a hassle—trying to get or even change a plane reservation is a major operation that can often take hours (the reason I could not see more of Lahore). Immigration and check-in at airports are unregulated madnesses that can rival the New York subway at rush hour. Security is a stringent, time-consuming process.

I took three cameras, several lenses and 50 rolls of film into Pakistan, and was never queried about this. Hand luggage may be X-rayed and examined over and over again. Always put all your film in Simac lead bags (use the double thickness ones) and into your checked luggage, which is X-rayed once. Remove all batteries from cameras, flash units, even alarm clocks and flashlights, and put the batteries in checked luggage also, or they may be seized from hand baggage. Be prepared to open everything, and to be personally patted down very thoroughly indeed.

The Pacific

The biggest gap in my travelling life is that I have not been to Australia and New Zealand. (I hope to rectify that soon, now that my daughter is growing up long-distance travel is becoming possible again.) As Down Under is today such a popular travel/tourism destination, I have researched it extensively, with the help most especially of the Collyns family, and most of all of Harry Collyns, who lives in Sydney.

New Zealand

Everything I now know about it is detailed in Chapter Fifteen, Planning.

Australia

Here is a summary of what I have learned about it:

Sydney is lively, livable and fun. The original Sydney settlement of The Rocks is now preserved. Ferry boats leave from downtown Circular Quay, close to the Sydney Opera House, crisscross the famous harbor and give fine photographic views of those twin icons, the opera house and Sydney Harbor Bridge. (Go to any performance at the opera house if you can; it encompasses several venues besides the principal opera/concert hall.)

A monorail which runs from downtown Sydney to Darling Harbor gives fine views too. It's a shopping/entertainment area on the site of old docks, a bit similar in feeling to the South Street Seaport area in New York, Pier 39 in San Francisco, or Tobacco Wharf in London.

Paddington is a"trendy" quarter with painted Victorian row houses with cast-iron balconies; in photographs they seem like parts of London and New Orleans mixed together. Best British-type pub in downtown Sydney is the Royal. Best Australian-style pub (with outdoor barbecues) is the Oaks Hotel on Military Road in the suburb of Neutral Bay. A fine and pretty fish restaurant is Doyle's, in the suburb of Doyle's Bay.

Best high view over all of Sydney is from the Sydney Tower. Don't miss going to a Test Match (world-class cricket) if you are in Sydney (or Melbourne) when one is being played.

See lifesaving demonstrations at Bondi and Manley Beaches close to downtown Sydney. Many Sydneyites celebrate Christmas with a picnic on these beaches. Respect all signs about sharks!

Kosciusco National Park, about four hours by car from Sydney, is in the Snowy Mountains. The scenic park has a ski-resort area with good hotels, most only open in winter.

Melbourne is conservative, but lively, cosmopolitan, and somewhat industrial. Nearby Phillip Island is a penguin reserve. I'm told the trip there is crowded.

Perth is the very modern capital of Western Australia, famous as a yachting center, where the America's Cup resided for a while.

Adelaide in South Australia is considered conservative, rather English, and is surrounded by wine country.

Canberra, Australia's federal capital, is a modern, garden city.

Brisbane is big and bustling, the main gateway to Australia's number-one tourist attraction, the Great Barrier Reef. You can also get there from Cairns or Townsville (also busy cities). Most of the reef is within the Great Barrier Reef Marine National Park. The Whitsunday Islands at the southern end of the park are the most developed, with many hotels and sailing centers. There you can hire your own boat or even helicopter to get to the reefs. You can skin-dive (and take a diving course; a former student got his Advanced Underwater certification at Airlie Island, and says dive-shops are everywhere along the coast). Snorkelling and photographing coral and fish from a glass-bottomed boat are other options, depending on your aquatic abilities, taste and pocket book. Heron Island has a resort hotel, and guided walks on part of the nearby reef at low tide are possible. Lizard Island near quiet Cookstown is further north, and recommended for those who prefer being closer to nature than to their fellow man; there is an exclusive resort there, as well as camping facilities. Close by, Hinchinbrook Island is even quieter, for campers only.

Note: Swimming is inadvisable in far North Australian waters because of jelly fish. (For underwater photography suggestions, see the section on the Virgin Islands in Chapter Seventeen.)

Alice Springs is the heart of the "red center"—the desert of the great Australian Outback; nearby Ayer's Rock is especially holy to Australia's Aboriginal people. Close by are the Olgas, a group of 28 great round red rocks, also holy. The whole area is preserved as the Uluru National Park, and administered by

Aboriginal people. You can learn about the "Dreamtime"—the heart of Aboriginal belief—and see art in the park region. (*The Songlines*, by the late Bruce Chatwin, is an absolutely fascinating book about these first Australians, and their spiritual ties to just about every living creature, hill, rock formation and watering place in the country.)

A fine-art photographer friend, Barbara Adelman, who spent three weeks in the Alice Springs area a couple of years ago, says the red rocks are magnificent, but cautions that the area is extremely popular with Australian and foreign tourists and that to get permits for professional photography is difficult. She also says that in the high season, the resorts around Alice are fully-booked, and plane flights, balloon flights, and groups of hundreds of rock climbers at sunrise and sunset mean that the great Ayer's Rock is not as peaceful as one might wish. Barbara advises photographers to keep a low profile, and to avoid Alice in June and July (Australia's midwinter, the coolest time in the Outback). She also suggests going to White Gum Park for kangaroo pictures, and to Kings Canyon, another very holy place only partly open to visitors, for marvelous scenery. She also photographed the annual Aboriginal Dance Festival. That year, it was held at Cape York in Northern Queensland—near Laura, a tiny Aboriginal settlement. Barbara also enjoyed quiet Green Island, in the Great Barrier Reef National Park, which has a crocodile reserve.

The Katunga National Park in the Northern Territory is Australia's largest. It is tropical, mostly wilderness, with plenty of wildlife (the scenic parts of the movie "Crocodile Dundee" were shot there). The Wet (season) is from November to March; the Dry, the rest of the year. Fly to Katunga in a small plane, or drive from Darwin in about four hours to the heart of it; there are hotels (including one in the shape of a crocodile) and campgrounds. Recommended in high-season is to go hiking or camping with a four wheel drive vehicle, well away from the day-tourist reception area.

The Aboriginal Lands in Arnhem Land in the Northern Territory can be entered only by permit, which must be applied for a couple of months in advance. Professional photography is not encouraged, although short tours with guides, where some photography may be possible, can be booked on the spot. I would take a tour featuring art and artists.

Note: It is absolutely essential to ask all Aboriginal people for permission before taking their photographs. If you do not, you will almost certainly be unwittingly offending someone's religious belief. There are also fines in Australia for desecrating sacred Aboriginal sites, and this may occasionally be taken to include photographing them. So, again, ask permission.

To photograph Australia's animals, best bet is to go to game reserves; the Sydney zoo has fine specimens of kangaroos, koalas and other indigenous species too if your time is limited. Apparently, koalas are not quite the cuddly little beasts of the television commercials; they bite and have to be handled by professionals. There are parks where you can see (and pet) them near both Sydney and Melbourne.

Cloncurry is in the heartland of the Australian sheep country. If you want to photograph a sheep station, this area would be a good bet.

The Pacific Islands

Long trans-Pacific flights, even from the West Coast, to Asia or the South Pacific are grueling unless you go first class, which is sometimes possible if a client is paying. From the East Coast, exhausting nonstop flights are to be avoided altogether unless you absolutely have no choice. It would certainly be no hardship to break any journey at Hawaii, Tahiti, Fiji or the Cook Islands, which are the choices. (You can also break a journey to Japan in Alaska, and to Southeast Asia in Guam, both of which I have done. Even a few hours break to stretch my legs makes a huge difference to the way I feel at the end of a long plane journey.)

Don't go to any South Pacific island expecting the locals to be wearing grass skirts and loincloths, which they do nowadays only at tourist shows. Tourism is, in fact, the main industry in almost all the islands. You must, in most cases, leave the main towns and most highly developed islands to get the relaxed feeling you came to find.

Hawaii

I have stopped only briefly on Oahu; the famous view of and from Diamond Head is fine at dusk. A drive around the lush interior of Oahu is enjoyable, you pass some lovely houses. Downtown Honolulu is congested. I stayed in a quite unpretentious hotel right on Waikiki Beach, which I liked. Almost everything in Honolulu except the hula-hula shows seem to celebrate Polynesian cultures from further across in the Pacific, which is amusing. The Arizona Monument to the victims of Pearl Harbor and the Cemetery of the Pacific in the great green bowl above Pearl Harbor had the effect on me that all war memorials do, they made me want to cry.

On my future-planned great Pacific trip I will (I hope) visit the other Hawaiian islands.

Tahiti and Other French Dependencies

The capital of the dependencies of France in the Pacific is Papeete, on the island of Tahiti. I am told it is very busy. The islands of Bora Bora and especially Moore still, it seems, look somewhat like the scenes painted by Gaugin in the late 19th-century, but even they have had considerable recent hotel development.

To get really off the beaten track in the South Seas, all these well-known archipelagos have smaller islands reachable by local plane or steamer or small boat; consult the relevant tourist offices.

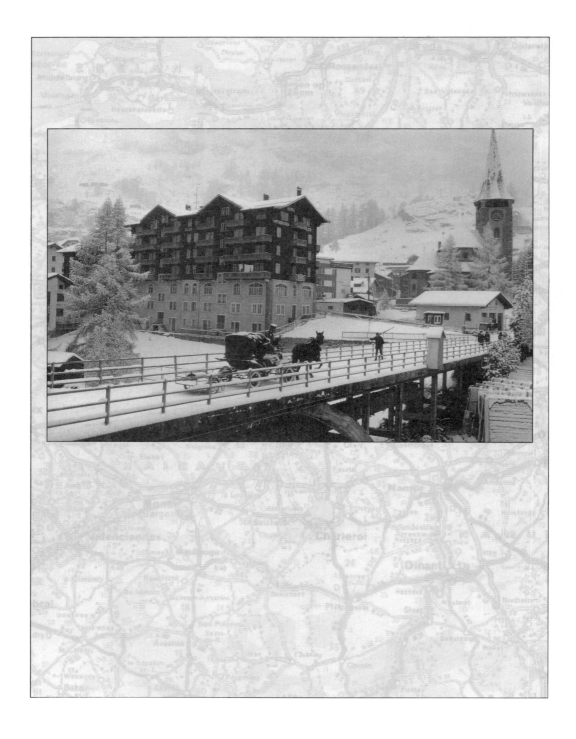

Chapter 20

Model Releases and Resources

Model Releases

All of these model releases may be copied or adapted for your own use. I suggest reproducing them three to a page; keep two copies, and give the model one. Add your name and address and phone number if you wish. It reassures models and I have never had any problems from doing this.

Short Form Model Release, and Translations

ENGLISH

MODEL RELEASE

Date:_____   Place:_____

I _____
(please print clearly)

hereby grant _____

permission to use, copyright and publish the photographs taken of me today for purposes of advertising and trade in all lawful media.

Signed _____

FRENCH

AUTORISATION

Date:_____   ˙Lieu:_____

Je, soussigné(e) _____
(veuillez écrire en lettres d'imprimerie)

autorise _____

l'utilisation, l'enregistrement du copyright et la publication des photos prises de ma personne
ce jour à des fins publicitaires et commerciales dans toutes les médias legaux.

Signé _____

SPANISH

AUTORIZACION DE MODELO

Fecha:_____   Lugar:_____

Yo _____
(por favor, escriba en letra de imprenta)

por la presente autorizo a _____

a utilizar, registar como propiedad intelectual y publicar con fines publicitarios o comerciales,
en todos los medios de difusión legímos, las fotografías que entrego en la fecha.

Firmado: _____

PORTUGUESE

AUTORIZAÇÃO DO (A) MODELO

Data:_____   Lugar:_____

Eu _____
(favor escrever claramente)

por meio desta, concedo a _____

a permissão de obter a reserva dos direitos autorais e de utilizar e publicar as fotografias tiradas
da minha pessoa hoje, para fins publicitários e de comércio em todos os meios de comunicação
legais.

Assinado: _____

ITALIAN

AUTORISAZZIONE DI MODELLO

Dato:_____   Luogo:_____

Io _____
(scrivere in modo chiaro)

con la presente garantisco a _____

il permesso di adoperare, esercitare i diritti e pubblicare le fotografie fatte a me oggi per scopo pubblicitario e per la vendita ai giornali.

Firmato _____

GERMAN

ZUSTIMMUNG ZUR VERÖFFENTLICHUNG

Datum:_____   Ort:_____

Ich _____
(bitte deutlich drucken)

gebe hiermit _____

Erlaubnis, die Fotografien, die heute von mir aufgenommen wurden, in allen legalen Medien der Werbung und des Gewerbes zu benützen, hinsichtlich urheberrecht gesetzlich zu schützen und zu veröffentlichen.

Unterschrift _____

DUTCH

TOESTEMMING VAN MODEL

Datum:_____   Plaats:_____

Ik, _____
(gelieve in drukletters te schrijven)

geef hier aan _____

toestemming om de foto's die vandaag van mij zijn gemaakt te gebruiken, het kopijrecht te behouden en de foto's te publiceren in advertenties of te gebruiken voor alle wettige media.

Ondertekend _____

DANISH

ERKLÆRING

Dato:_____ Sted:_____

Jeg _____
(Venligst Skriv med blokbogstaver)

giver hermed _____

tilladelse til at benytte copyright og offentliggøre de billeder jeg har taget I dag med henblik på annoncering og salg i alle offentlige tilgængelige media.

Underskrift _____

FINNISH

VALTUUTUS

Päivämäärä:_____ Paikka:_____

Minä _____
(painokirjaimin)

annan täten luvan _____

käyttää ja julkaista kaikin oikeuksin minusta tänään otettuja valokuvia mainos-ja mynninedistämistarkoituksissa kaikissa laillisissa julkaisuissa.

Allekirjoitus _____

NORWEGIAN

FULLMAKT

Dato:_____ Sted:_____

Jeg _____
(vennligst skriv tydelig)

gir herved _____

retten til å bruke og distribuere fotos hvor i jeg figurerer, inkludert opphavsrett; i media, annonser og alle legale publikasjoner.

Signatur _____

SWEDISH

FULLMAKT

Datum:_____ Ort:_____

Jag _____
(vänligen texta tydligt)

beviljar fotografen _____

tillstånd att använda och publicera bilder fotograferade av mig i reklamsyfte i alla lagliga publikationer.

Signeras _____

ICELANDIC

LEYFI

Dagur:_____

Staður:_____

Ég_____ (skrifið með prentstöfum)

veiti hér með _____

ótakmarkað leyfi til útgáfu ljósmynda sem teknar voru af mér í dag í tilgangi auglýsinga og kynninga í öllum löglegum fjölmidlum.

Undirskrift_____

CZECH

Souhlas se zveřejněním.

Datum: _____

Místo: _____

Já _____ (uveďte jméno čitelně hůlkovým písmem)

tímto uděluji _____

souhlas s používaním autorských práv a zveřejňovaním mých fotografií pořízených dnes pro reklamní a obchodní účely ve všech zákonných sdělovacích prostředcích.

Podpis: _____

HUNGARIAN

MODELL ENGÉDELY

Dátum:_____ Helység:_____

Én _____
(kérjük nyomtatott betükkel)

engedélyt adok _____ (fényképész neve)

hogy a rólam ma készült fényképeket felhasználja bármilyen hirdetésben vagy egyéb szakmai célra, ujságban, folyóiratban vagy bármi más hirközló szeryben.

Aláirás:_____

POLISH

POZWOLENIE NA PUBLIKACJE

Data: _____

Miejscowość: _____

Ja _____ (proszę drukować)
podpisuję ten dokument że pozwalam aby mię fotografować. Takźe pozwalam aby kopje mojej fotograffi, zrobionej obziś, uźywano w reklamach handlowych i w środkach masowego przekazu.

Podpismo: _____

RUSSIAN

РАСПИСКА
в передаче прав

Дата: _____ Место _____

Я _____(просьба писать разборчиво)

настоящим разрешаю _____

использовать, обеспечивать авторское право и публиковать свои фотографии, сделанные сегодня, для целей рекламы и торговли во всех законно зарегистрированных средствах массовой информации.

Подпись _____

GREEK

ΠΡΟΤΥΠΟ ΑΝΑΚΟΙΝΩΣΗΣ.

ΗΜΕΡΟΜΗΝΙΑ _____

ΤΟΠΟΣ _____

ΕΓΩ _____

δια του παρόντος δίδω την άδεια να χρησιμοποιήσετε κόπυραιτ (Δικαίωμα πνευματικής εργασίας) για να δημοσιεύσετε τις φωτογραφίες που μ έχετε βγάλει σήμερα για διαφημιστικούς και εμπορικούς σκοπούς σ' όλα τα νόμιμα μέσα ενημερώσεως.

Ο, η υπογεγραμμένος(η) _____

TURKISH

FERAGATNAME ÖRNEĞİ

Tarih:_____

Yer:_____

Ben, _____

her türlü kanuni reklam ve medys ticaretinde kullanilmak gayeleri ile bugün çekilen fotoğraflarımın,

telif ve yayımlanma iznini bu vesileyle _____ ' (a) / (e)

veririm.

İmza_____

ARABIC

تصريح

التاريخ: ــــــــــــــ

المكان: ــــــــــــــ

انا، ــــــــــــــ الرجاء كتابة الاسم بوضوح .

اعطي بهذا التصريح الاذن باستعمال وبتسجيل الحقوق ونشر السور المأخوذة لي

اليوم لاغراض الدعاية والتجارة في جميع الاوساط الاعلامية القانونية.

التوقيع ــــــــــــــ

HEBREW

שחרור הדוגמן

תאריך: _____

מקום: _____

הנני: _____ (אנא כתוב ברור)

ממציא בזה היתר לשמוש, לזכויות יוצרים, והדפסה של התמונות בהם אני צולמתי היום, למטרות פרסום מסחרי בעיתונות הפועלת עפ־י החק.

על החתום: _____

CHINESE

弃权书

时间:_____

地点:_____

我,_____ 谨同意 _____ 得以在一切合法传播媒介中,

为广告和贸易的目的,使用、取得版权及出版其今日为我所拍之照片。

签字:_____

JAPANESE

肖像使用承諾書

日時: _____

場所: _____

私 _____（はっきりと書いて下さい）は、
_____ に対して、
本日私を撮影した写真を、すべての合法的な媒体における広告及び商業目的の
ために使用し、著作権を設定し、公表することを、この書面を以て許可します。

署名: _____

KOREAN

사진 권리 위임장

날자 : _____

장소 : _____

나 (본인) _____ 는 〈 성명은 한글로 깨끗하게 〉

아래 열거한 권리를 _____ 에게
위임 한다.

i. 내가 오늘 모델로 출연한 모든 사진에 관한 권리.

/ 내가 오늘 모델로 출연한 모든 사진을 합법적인
미디아 매체에 상연 광고 목적으로 전부 또는
부분 적으로 복사 또는 출판할 권리.

서명 : _____

INDONESIAN

PENGELUARAN MODEL

Tanggal:_____ Tempat:_____

Saya _____
(tulis dengan jelis)

dengan ini memberikan _____

izin untuk meggunakan, hak cipta dan penerbitan foto-foto gambar saya yang diambil ini hari
untuk.keperluan periklanan dan diperdagangkan diseluruh hukum media.

Tertanda_____

TAGALOG/PHILLIPINO

PAHAYÅG NG MODELO

Petsa: _____

Pook: _____

Ang nakalagda _____ (pakilimbag nang malinaw)

ay nag bibigay - pahintulot kay _____ o sa _____
na gamitin at ilathalà ang mga larawang nauukol sa akin sa araw na ito sa hangaring ipabatid sa
madla at ibaliwas sa lahat ng legàl na lathalà at himpilang pang-telebision.

Lagda: _____

THAI

วันที่ _____

ใบยินยอม

ณ _____

ข้าพเจ้า _____ (โปรด เขียนตัวบรรจง)

ยินยอมให้ _____

นำไปใช้ตลอดจน เป็น เจ้าของลิขสิทธิ์และการตีพิมพ์ซึ่งรูปถ่ายของข้าพ เจ้าในวันนี้

เพื่อวัตถุประสงค์ในการโฆษณาและการค้าตามวิธีของสื่อมวลชนที่ถูกกฎหมายโดยทั่วไป

ลงนาม _____

MALAY

PENGELUARAN MODEL

Tanggal _____   Tempat _____

Saya _____
(tolong tuliskan secara terang)

dengan ini, memberikan izin kepada _____

untok megunakan, ka cipta dan menerbitkan semua gambar-gambar saya yang diambil pada
hari ini untok.dipergunakan pada adpertensi dan perdagangan berdasakan hukum yang berlaku.

Tandatanggan _____

PUNJABI

یکھیوار کی تے رضا منت دراسطے اجازت نامہ

دع پارہ _____

جا _____

میں اجازت دیندیاں آں اے جہڑیاں

تصویراں آنے میریاں بیاں گیاں ان

اوناں دی رضا مندت نے چھیوار کی

فرید اری وراسطے کتن جا کدی کارا

دستخط _____

URDU

اجازت نامہ برائے اشاعت

تاریخ _____

مگہ _____

میں سمی _____

اس امر کی اجازت دیتی ہوں کہ جو میری تصویرین کی

گئی ہیں وہ میرا کستیرو تجارت استعمال میں لائی

جا سکتی ہیں ۔

دستخط _____

HINDI

नमूना प्राज्ञा-पत्र

तिथि _____

स्थान _____

मैं _____

अनुमती देती हूँ _____

कि उन सभी अपनी तस्वीरों

को जो आपने आज ली हैं,

सभी अधिकृत प्रकाशन सामग्री

में विज्ञापन हेतु प्रयोग करने का

आप को पूर्ण अधिकार प्रदान

करती हूँ ।

हस्ताक्षर _____

SWAHILI

MFANO

Tarehe: _____   Mji: _____

Mimi _____
(maandishi makubwa tafadhali)

natoa kibali kwa _____

kutumia picha zangu zilizopigwa leo na kuzichapisha kwa matangazo ya biashara inavyohitajika kwa nija zote halali za mawasiliano.

Sahini _____

STANDARD MODEL RELEASE

Date_____ Location_____

For good and valuable consideration, receipt of which is acknowledged,

I,_____

(please print name)

hereby and irrevocably consent to the use, copyright and publication of the

photographs taken of me today by _____

(photographer)

and those whom he/she may designate, including _____

for purposes of advertising and trade, in all lawful media.

Signed _____Phone #_____

Address _____

Witness:_____Date _____

STANDARD MODEL RELEASE FOR MINORS

I, _____ the parent/legal guardian of

(print name)

_____ a minor, age _____ hereby

(print child's name)

give permission to _____

(photographer)

and _____

(client)

to use, copyright and publish the pictures taken of my child today, in all lawful media.

Signed_____ Date _____

Address_____

The pictures are described as follows:_____

_____

LIMITED MODEL RELEASE
(For models who do not wish to sign a blanket release.)

Location_____ Country_____

Group Name/Number_____
(Or, name of cruise ship, hotel, etc.)

Tour Director_____
(Or name of cruise director/host etc.)

I, the undersigned hereby give _____
(photographer)

and _____
(corporation)

permission to use, copyright and publish the photographs taken of me today, alone or in company with others, in their tour/cruise/hotel/resort brochures.

My name may/may not be used.

Name:_____ Date: _____
(please print)

Address and telephone number_____

Signature_____

If the subject is a minor, please also complete portion below:

I am the legal parent/guardian of _____,

age _____, years and I hereby give permission for the use of his/her picture in your

brochures. His/her name may/may not be used.

Signed_____

Relationship_____

Note: A model release is required for all recognizable pictures of people in any form of tourist promotion, including travel catalogs. This type of limited release can be used for "models" who are clients of your tourism client.

Some may be prominent professional people and all have probably paid a lot of money for the trip/cruise/hotel, etc. Such "models" are frequently willing to pose—even enjoy it—but are unwilling to sign an unlimited model release. Also, your client may not wish you to ask their clients to sign an unlimited release, not wishing to exploit them.

Client "models" can also write out a letter of permission by hand; some with legal training may prefer to do this. Of course, with any type of limited release, it would be very unwise to use these pictures later on for general stock purposes.

PROPERTY/ANIMAL RELEASE

I, _____ the owner of the property/animal
          (print name)

located at/described as _____

_____

hereby give _____ the right to
                     (photographer)

use, copyright and publish the pictures taken of my property/animal for purposes of advertising and trade in all lawful media.

Signed _____ Date _____

Address_____ Phone #_____

For the translations, my sincere thanks to:

Mahmut G. Aygen; CEDOK; Andrew Chang; P. K. Chockwe; Government of India Tourist Board; Olivia Grayson; Grazia Neri, Milan; Mora Henskens; Mubarak Hussain; Maria Javier; Eleni Koumas and Lucy Marouletti; Sabina Lida; Hella Koln Mills; Pacific Press Service, Tokyo; Adang Sanusi; the Scandinavian Tourist Boards; Singapore Tourist Promotion Board; Stock Photos, São Paulo; Tourism Authority of Thailand; and the United Nations Camera Club. For assistance in obtaining translations, thanks also to Suzanne Goldstein, Audrey Gottlieb and Nadeem Nazar.

Resources

Space limitations mean I only have room to list the head U.S.A. offices of photographic corporations, which are often in the New York metropolitan area. Many companies also have offices in Los Angeles or San Francisco, and Toronto or Montreal. I apologise to West Coast and Canadian readers especially for these omissions. Readers who live in or near Atlanta, Chicago, Dallas, Miami or other big cities may also find local offices for many of the firms listed below.

Note: All addresses, phone numbers and most especially toll-free (800) numbers and fax numbers change quite frequently. Remember the invaluable services provided (free) by telephone directories and (not free) by information operators. The directory of toll-free numbers that can be called from your area is reached at (800) 555-1212. This applies also to Canadian listings. (Not all toll-free numbers, however, are published/listed, and not all those listed below work from all states/provinces.)

Photographic Equipment Manufacturers

35mm and Medium Format Camera Systems

Bronica
GMI Photographic Inc.
1776 New Highway
P.O. Drawer U
Farmingdale, NY 11735
(516) 752-0066, Fax (516) 752-0053

Canon USA
1 Canon Plaza
Lake Success, NY 11042
(516) 488-6700, Fax (516) 354-9007

Contax
Yashica Inc.
100 Randolph Road, CN 8062
Somerset, NJ 08875
(908) 560-0060

Fuji
(See under film)

Hasselblad
10 Madison Road
Fairfield, NJ 07004
(800) 338-6477
or (201) 227-7320, Fax (201) 227-3249

Leica
156 Ludlow Street
Northvale, NJ 07647
(800) 222-0118
or (908) 767-7500, Fax (908) 767-8666

Mamiya America Corp.
8 Westchester Plaza
Elmsford, NY 10523
(914) 347-3300, Fax (800) 321-2205

Minolta Corp.
101 Williams Drive
Ramsey, NJ 07446
(201) 825-4000, Fax (201) 327-1475

Nikon Inc.
1300 Walt Whitman Road
Melville, NY 11747
(516) 547-4200, Fax (617) 494-0249

Olympus Corp.
Crossways Park
Woodbury, NY 11797
(800) 221-3000, Fax (516) 349-2471

Pentax Corp.
35 Inverness Drive East
Englewood CO 80112
(303) 799-8000

View and Specialized Cameras

Fuji
(See under film)

Horseman
(See Minicam/Ampac under strobes)

Linhof
HP Marketing Corp.
16 Chapin Road
Pine Brook, NJ 07058
(201) 808-9010

SinarBron Inc.
17 Progress Street
Edison, NJ 08820
(908) 754-5800

Toyo Cameras
(See Mamiya America Corp.)

Wisner Classic Mfg.
732 Mill Street
P.O. Box 21
Marion, MA 02738
(508) 748 0975

Zone VI Inc.
P.O. Box 219
Newfane, VT 05345
(802) 257-5161

Lenses

Schneider
Schneider Corp. of America
400 Crossways Park Drive
Woodbury, NY 11797
(516) 496-8500

Sigma Corp. of America
15 Fleetwood Court
Ronkomkoma, NY 11779
(516) 585-1144

Tokina Optical Corp.
1512 Kona Drive
Compton, CA 90220
(213) 537-9380
(800) 421-1141, Fax (516) 496-8524

Film

Eastman Kodak Co.
343 State Street
Rochester, NY 14650
(800) 242-2424
or (716) 724-4000, Fax (716) 724-0663

Fuji USA Inc.
555 Taxter Road
Elmsford, NY 10523
(800) 755-3854
or (914) 789-8100, Fax (914) 482-4955

Polaroid Corp.
575 Technology Square
Cambridge, MA 02139
(800) 343-5000 or (617) 577-2000

Lead-Foil Film Protector Bags

Sima Products
8707 North Skokie Blvd
Skokie, IL 60077
(708) 679-7462

Filters & Gels

Cokin Filters
(See Minolta under cameras)

Hoya Filters
Uniphot Corp.
Woodside, NY, 11377
(718) 779-5700

Kodak Filters
(See Eastman Kodak under film)

Rosco Laboratories
38 Bush Avenue
Port Chester, NY 10573
(914) 937-1300

Schneider/BW Filters
(See under lenses)

Tiffen Corp.
90 Oser Avenue
Hauppage, NY 11788
Phone (516) 273-2500

Singh Ray Filters
(See Saunders Group/Domke under accessories)

Flash and Strobe Manufacturers

Balcar
  Tekno Inc.
  38 Greene Street
  New York, NY 10013
  (212) 219-3501

Broncolor Inc.
  (See Sinar Bron, under view cameras)

Comet World Corp.
  311-319 Long Avenue
  Hillside, NJ 07205
  (908) 688-3210

Dyna-Lite Corp.
  (Same address as Comet World)
  (908) 687-8800

Elinchrom Inc.
  Elinca SA
  Renens
  Switzerland
  or c/o Ken Hansen Lighting
  920 Broadway
  New York, NY 10010
  (212) 673-7530

Lumedyne Inc.
  6010 Wall Street
  Port Richey, FL 34668
  (813) 847-2777

Metz Inc.
  (See Bogen, under flash/strobe accessories)

Minicam
  Ampac Inc.
  910 Sahara Drive, NW
  Cleveland, TN 37312
  (615) 478-1405

Norman Enterprises Inc.
  2601 Empire Avenue
  Burbank, CA 94063
  (818) 843-6811

Profoto/Sweden
  Atelier Systems Ltd
  146 Barton Avenue
  Evanston, IL 60202
  (708) 866-7960

Speedotron Corp.
  310 South Racine Avenue
  Chicago, IL 60607
  (312) 421-4050

Sunpak Inc.
  ToCAD America
  401 Hackensack Avenue
  Hackensack, NJ 07601
  (201) 342-2400

Vivitar Corp.
  9350 De Soto Avenue
  Chatsworth, CA 91313
  Phone (800) 700-9862
  Fax (818) 700-2890

Flash/Strobe Lighting and Accessories

Armato's Photo Service
  67-16 Myrtle Avenue
  Glendale, NY 11385
  (718) 628-6800
  (Vivitar modifications, batteries and more)

Bogen Photo Corp.
  565 East Crescent Avenue
  Ramsey, NJ 07446
  (908) 862-7999
  (Lightstands, tripods, meters and more)

Chimera Inc.
  1812 Valtec Lane
  Boulder, CO 80301
  Phone (800) 424-4075
  or (303) 444-8000
  (Portable fabric light boxes)

Cougar Design
  220 East 23rd Street
  New York, NY 10010
  (212) 989-7670
  (Vivitar accessories, lightstands, more)

Domke Inc.
  The Saunders Group
  21 Jet Drive
  Rochester, NY 14624
  (716) 328-7800
  (Vivitar accessories, Domke bags, lightstands, etc.)

Quantum Instruments
1075 Stewart Avenue
Garden City, NY 11530
(516) 222-0611
(Rechargeable batteries; slaves, triggers)

Wein Products Inc.
115 West 25th Street
Los Angeles, CA 90007
(213) 749-6049
(Slaves and triggers)

Hot Lights and Equipment

Lowel Light Manufacturing Corp.
140-58th Street
Brooklyn, NY 11220
(718) 921-0600

Matthews Studio Equipment Inc.
2405 Empire Avenue
Burbank, CA 91504
(818) 843-6715

Smith Victor Corp.
301 North Colfax
Griffith, IN 46319
(219) 924-6136

Equipment and Accessories, Misc.

Calzone Case Co
225 Black Rock Avenue
Bridgeport, CT 06605
(800) 243-5752
(Hard shipping cases)

Gitzo Tripods
Karl Heitz Inc.
34-11 62nd Street, Box 427
Woodside, NY 11377
(718) 565-0004

Gossen Meters
(See Bogen under flash/strobe accessories)

Lightware Inc.
1541 Platte Street
Denver, CO 80202
(303) 455-4556, Fax: (303) 477-1235
(Equipment cases)

Linhof Tripods
(see under cameras)

LowePro USA
2194 Northpoint Parkway
Santa Rosa, CA 95407
(707) 575-4363
(Camera bags and backpacks)

Minolta Meters
(See under cameras)

PermaPak Rechargeable Batteries
(See Mamiya, under cameras)

Pic Light Stands
American Photo Instruments
12 Lincoln Boulevard
Emerson, NJ 07620
(201) 261-2160

Sekonic Meters
RTS Inc.
40-11 Burt Drive
Deer Park, NY 11729
(516) 242-6801

Slik Tripods
Slik America Inc.
3 Westchester Plaza
Elmsford, NY 10523
Phone (914) 347-2223, Fax (914) 347-5617

Tenba Quality Cases Ltd.
503 Broadway
New York, NY 10012
(212) 966-1013
(Camera bags and cases)

Tiltall Tripods
(See Hoya/Uniphot, under filters)

The specialized items listed below are rented or purchased from professional photograpic dealers. The head offices will be able to refer you to nearest dealers.

110-220/240v Portable Transformers

Signal Transformers
500 Bayview Ave
Inwood, NY 11696
Phone (516) 239-5777, Fax (516) 239-7208

Stancor Products
131 Godfrey St
Logansport, IN 49647
(219) 722-2244

Generators

Homelite
Division of Textron Inc.
1441 Carrowinds Boulevard
Charlotte, NC 28241
(800) 242-4672

Honda Motors America Inc.
Power Equipment Div.
4475 River Green Parkway
Duluth, GA 30136
(404) 497-6400

A.C./D.C. Power Inverters

LTM Inc.
11646 Pendleton Street
Sun Valley, CA 91352
(800) 762-4291 or (818) 767-1313

Trace Engineering Co. Inc.
5917 195th N.E.
Arlington, WA 98223
(206) 435-8826, Fax (206) 435-2229

Vanner Inc.
4282 Reynolds Drive
Hilliard, OH 43026
(614) 771-2718, Fax (614) 771-4904

Gyro Stabilizers

Kenyon Gyro Stabilizers
Ken Lab Inc.
P.O. Box 128
Old Lyme, CT 06371
(203) 434-1619

Recommended Repair Services:

Professional Camera Repair Service
37 West 47th Street
New York, NY 10036
(212) 382-0550
Custom work; they are experienced in dealing
with rush repairs from all over the world.
Ask for Rick Rankin or Herb Zimmerman.

Flash Clinic
9 East 19th Street
New York, NY 10003
(212) 673-4030
Sales and service; custom work; on professional
flash/strobe equipment. Ask for Larry Farrell.

Professional Associations:

Advertising Photographers of America (APA)
Room 601, 27 West 20th Street
New York, NY 10011
(212) 807-0399
(Chapters in major cities.)

American Institute of Graphic Arts (AIGA)
1059 Third Avenue
New York, NY 10021
(212) 752-0813
(Many members are graphic designers.)

**American Society of Magazine
Photographers (ASMP)**
Head Office: 419 Park Avenue South
New York, NY 10016
(212) 889-9144. Fax (212) 779-9446
*(33 Chapters nationwide; general, associate,
student, overseas and sustaining members.)*

**American Society of Picture
Professionals (ASPP)**

Townsend P. Dickenson,
current ASPP President
c/o Macmillan Publishing Corp.
866 Third Avenue
New York, NY 10022
(212)-702-3836
or home phone (203) 853 4834.
*(Members are professional picture researchers;
some photographers also.)*

**Canadian Association of Photographers and
Illustrators in Communications**
400 Eastern Avenue, # 250
Toronto, ON M4M 1B9
(804) 751-0471

Picture Agency Council of America (PACA)
currently c/o
Marty Lokan,
President,
Allstock Agency
222 Dexter Avenue
North Seattle, WA 98109
(206) 282-8116
Fax (206) 286-5082
*(Information is also available from any member
stock picture agency.)*

**National Press Photographers
Association (NPPS)**
3200 Croasdaile Drive
Durham, NC 27705
(919) 383-7246
(Most members are news photographers.)

Professional Photographers of America (PP of A)
1090 Executive Way
Des Plaines, IL 60018
(800) 786-6277
(Many members are commercial photo studio owners.)

Society of American Travel Writers (SATW)
1100 17th Street, Suite 1000
Washington, DC 20036
(202) 429-6639
*(Some photographers or writer/photographers are
members.)*

**Society of Photographers' and Artists'
Representatives (SPAR)**
1123 Broadway
New York, NY 10010
(212) 924-6023

Professional Publications for Photographers

Bacon's Publicity Checker
Bacon's Media Directories
332 South Michigan Avenue
Chicago, IL 60604
(800) 621-0561
or (312) 922-2400, Fax (312) 922-3127
*(Directory of consumer and trade magazines
classified by subject, with circulation figures;
aimed at public relations professionals.)*

**Guide to Photography Workshops and
Schools (annual)**
Shaw Associates Educational Publishers
Coral Gables, FL 33133
(305) 446-8888

Photo District News
P.O. Box 1983
Marion, OH 43305
(800) 669-1002
*(Indispensible monthly trade paper for
professional photographers.)*

Photographers' Market (annual)
Writers' Digest Books
F & W Publications
1507 Dana Avenue
Cincinnati, OH 45207
(513) 531-2222

**Photography and Travel Workshop Directory
(annual)**
Serbin Communications
511 Olive Street
Santa Barbara, CA 93101
(805) 963-0439

Professional Photo Source
Professional Photo Source Inc.
568 Broadway, Suite 605A
New York, NY 10012
(212) 219-0993

Standard Rate and Data Guides
Standard Rate and Data Services
3004 Glenview Road
Wilmette, IL 60091
(800) 323-4588, or (708) 256-6067
*(Directories of magazines and advertisers,
classified by subject with circulation figures and
annual billing. Annuals. Special Canadian
directory.)*

Travel Industry Personnel Directory
Fairchild Books
7 East 12th Street
New York, NY 10003
(800) 247-6622
Fax (212) 887-1865

Traveler's Guide to Museum Exhibitions
Museum Guide Publications Inc.
P.O. Box 2539, 1619 31st Street, NW
Washington, DC 20007
(202) 338-1500

Creative Directories

(Individual photographers and stock agencies advertise in these top directories, which are distributed free to qualified art directors and picture buyers.)

American Showcase and
Corporate Showcase
915 Broadway
New York, NY 10010
(212) 673-6600

Black Book Stock and
The Creative Black Book
115 Fifth Avewnue
New York, NY 10003
(212) 254-1330

Direct Stock
10 East 21st Street
New York, NY 10010
(212) 979-6560, Fax (212) 254-1204
(Individual photographers advertise here.)

Stock Workbook
Scott & Daughters
940 North Highland Avenue
Los Angeles, CA 90038
(800) 447-2688, or (213) 856-0008
(Mostly stock agencies advertise here)

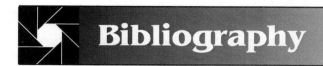

Bibliography

Recommended Books of Beautiful Travel-Related Photographs:
(Obviously these reflect my personal taste; they are not all "pretty" pictures.)

Allard, William Albert.
The Photographic Essay.
Boston MA: New York Graphic Society/
Bullfinch Press,Little Brown Co., 1989.

Avedon, Richard.
In The American West.
New York: Harry N. Abrams, 1986.
(Also anything else by Avedon.)

Brandt, Bill.
Literary Britain.
New York: Aperture, 1986.
(See also **Portraits**. Austin, TX: University of
Texas Press, 1982, and anything else by Brandt.)

Bull, Clarence Sinclair.
The Man Who Shot Garbo.
Hollywood Portraits.
New York: Simon and Schuster, 1989.

Edgeworth, Anthony.
The Marines.
New York: Doubleday and Company, 1988.

Fabian, Rainer and Adam, Hans-Christian.
Masters of Early Travel Photography.
New York: Vendome Press/Viking Press, 1983.

Haas, Ernst.
The Creation.
New York: Penguin Books, 1988.
(See anything else by Haas also.)

Hines, Sherman.
The North.
Halifax, NS: Nimbus Books, 1984.
(Also see any of his other books on Canada.)

Kaplan, Peter B.
High On New York.
New York: Harry N. Abrams, 1986.

Lanker, Brian.
**I Dream A World: Portraits of Black Women
Who Changed America.**
New York: Stewart, Tabori & Chang, 1989.

Lawliss, Chuck.
The Great Resorts of America.
New York: Holt, Rinehart and Winston, 1983.

Maisel, Jay.
On Assignment.
Washington DC: Smithsonian Institution Press, 1990.

Mark, Mary Ellen.
The Photo Essay.
Washington DC: Smithsonian Institution Press, 1990.

Meyrowitz, Joel.
A Summer's Day.
New York: Times Books: 1985.
(Also see other books by Meyrowitz.)

Newman, Arnold.
One Mind's Eye.
Boston, MA: New York Graphic Society/Little
Brown, 1974.

Rajs, Jake.
America.
New York: Rizzoli, 1990.
(See also his book **Manhattan**,
New York: Rizzoli 1985.)

Rowell, Galen.
**Mountain Light. In Search of the
Dynamic Landscape.**
San Francisco: Sierra Club Books 1986.
(Note: This is also a "how to" book.)

Rosenblum, Naomi.
A World History of Photography.
New York: Abbeville Press, 1984.

Singh, Raghubir.
Rajashtahan, India's Enchanted Land.
New York: Thames & Hudson, 1989.

Recommended Business, How To and Specialist Photography Books:

Published by Allworth Press, New York:

Crawford, Tad. **Business and Legal Forms For Photographers,** 1991.
Gordon, Elliott and Barbara. **How to Sell Your Photographs and Illustrations,** 1991.
Heron, Michal. **How To Shoot Stock Photos That Sell,** 1990.
Heron, Michal. **Stock Photo Forms,** 1991.

Published by The American Society of Magazine Photographers, New York:

Assignment Photography. (Monograph), 1991.
Forms. (Monograph), 1990.
Stock Photography Handbook, 1990.

Published by Amphoto, New York:

Brackman, Henrietta. **The Perfect Portfolio,** 1984.
Freeman, Michael. **Light,** 1988. (See his other books also.)
Guilfoyle, Ann, Ed. **Wildlife Photography, The Art and Technique of Ten Masters,** 1982.
Lloyd, Harvey. **Aerial Photography,** 1990.
Marx, Kathryn. **Photography For The Art Market,** 1988.
McGrath, Norman. **Photographing Buildings Inside and Out,** 1987.
Meehan, Joseph. **Panoramic Photography,** 1990.
Neubart, Jack. **Industrial Photography,** 1989.
Pertweiler, Gary. **Secrets of Studio Still Life Photography,** 1990.
Purcell, Ann and Carl. **The Traveling Photographer,** 1988.
Rosen, Frederick W. **Promoting Yourself As a Photographer,** 1987.
Seaborne, Charles. **Underwater Photography,** 1988.
Schaub, George. **Shooting for Stock,** 1987.
Taylor, Adrian. **Photographing Assignments on Location,** 1987. (Interviews with, and pictures by, eleven fine travel photographers, including John Lewis Stage and Pete Turner.)

Published by Eastman Kodak Company, Rochester, NY:

Kodak Professional Photoguide, 1989.
Kodak Workshop Series:
   Electronic Flash, 1987.
   Existing Light Photography, 1987.
   Using Filters, 1987.

Published by Simon & Schuster, New York:

Hedgecoe, John. **The Art of Color Photography,** 1989.

Kodak Pocket Guides (Series) 1985:
   Nature Photography.
   Sports Photography.
   Travel Photography.
   35mm Photography.